E-learning Tools and Technologies

A consumer's guide for trainers, teachers, educators, and instructional designers

By

William Horton
and Katherine Horton

Wiley Publishing, Inc.

Publisher: Joe Wikert

Editor: Robert M Elliott

Editorial Manager: Kathryn Malm

Managing Editor: Vincent Kunkemueller

Copy Editors: Karen Eddleman and Jane Aronovitch

Media Development: William Horton Consulting, Inc.

Text Design and Composition: William Horton Consulting, Inc.

This text is printed on acid-free paper.

Library of Congress Cataloging-in-Publication Data:
0-471-44458-8
1. Employees--Training of--Computer-assisted instruction. 2. World Wide Web. I. Title.

HF5549.5.T7 H635 2000
658.3'42404--dc21   99-088038

Printed in the United States of America

10   9   8   7   6   5   4   3   2

FAQ about this book

Decisions about technology and tools for e-learning are being made by managers and instructors who know little about technology, or by information technologists without the participation or benefit of educators. *E-learning Tools and Technologies* will give teachers, trainers, instructors, educators, administrators, and instructional designers the knowledge they need to pick tools and technologies that support their e-learning efforts. It will also help information technologists understand the e-learning tools they may be asked to help select, combine, and maintain.

This book represents the needs and viewpoints of consumers of these technologies. It will help consumers plan, select, and combine the tools they need for their individual projects. Readers will learn to identify the range of hardware, software, and services needed for e-learning projects, understand major categories of tools, see what each category produces, learn the major vendors in each category, and develop criteria for picking specific products. In addition, the book contains chapters to help readers combine separate tools into effective systems, ensure a rational purchasing process, and pick and implement e-learning standards.

The book is supported with a Web site containing evaluation checklists, design forms, tips and tricks, and an extensive list of e-learning tools.

WHO IS THIS BOOK FOR?

More and more technology is being purchased and used by people with little technical training or knowledge. The phase of techno-maniacal early adopters is passed. The people who are tasked with buying technology and getting it all working are not just information technologists but instructional designers, training department managers, school administrators, teachers, instructors, and trainers.

At the same time the complexity has increased. Those wishing to deploy e-learning must choose from hundreds of tools in many separate categories, including learning management systems, learning content management systems, authoring tools, and collaboration environments, all of which are evolving at a bewildering rate.

People who are not technology experts need a systematic way to identify the types of tools they need, find vendors, evaluate their products, and combine them into useful systems. This book fills that need.

It is essential to get purchasing decisions right the first time. These products are expensive and you must justify your decision. It is hard to switch once a product has been implemented and integrated into your operations. There will be less money available after your first purchase proves inadequate. And you may lack credibility the second time around.

Who should buy and read this book? Anyone involved in e-learning, that's who. Here are some specific groups and what we hope each will get out of this book.

Group	How they need and will use the book
Teachers, instructors, and trainers	To understand the technologies they are now required to use to deliver their courses over networks.
Instructional designers and course authors	To select tools and technologies to carry out their plans and designs for e-learning.
Managers, supervisors, and team leaders of training groups	To plan the mix of tools they need to create original e-learning or to convert their existing classroom training to e-learning.
University students in programs in education, instructional technology, related fields	As a textbook for a course in e-learning technology or as independent study of technologies that underlie their chosen field.
University and school-district administrators	To understand the technology they must purchase and install. Be able to communicate with their information technology specialists.
Executives, directors, and chief learning officers	To set policies and strategies for the technical infrastructure needed to support their e-learning, performance support, and knowledge management initiatives.

Group	How they need and will use the book
Information technologists	To broaden their understanding of tools and technologies so they can support their organization's e-learning, online information, and knowledge-management efforts.
Vendors of e-learning technology	To understand how their specific products fit into the overall scheme, to be able to discuss technology with buyers, and to better suggest solutions to buyers.
Subject matter experts who want to create a course	To help them figure out where to start and what tools and services they will need.

IS THIS JUST MORE HYPE?

This is a consumer's guide to technology—not a collection of press releases from vendors and researchers. No company has paid to have its products included in this book (Darn!). The mention of a product is not an endorsement and absence of a product is not a condemnation. All products have merit and all can be improved.

You'll find no science fiction here. All the tools and technologies mentioned here are commercially available products—except for those in the last chapter which unashamedly speculates on trends. Universities and research labs are working on neat ideas that someday might turn into reliable, easy-to-use products—but you won't find these ideas here.

This book will help you decide if you really need a tool and then arm you with facts and criteria to pick the best product.

WHAT'S SPECIAL ABOUT THIS BOOK?

In addition to its basic content, this book contains some extra goodies to enhance the reading experience.

▶ **Lists of potential vendors**. For each category of tools discussed, the book lists the major vendors and provide contact information.

▶ **Questions to make vendors squirm.** For each category of tools, the book lists questions potential buyers should get answered before signing on the dotted line.

► **Rants and opinions**. A cartoon curmudgeon pops up now and then to colorfully point out the limitations of current categories of products and to add a dose of appropriate skepticism.

► **Tips and tricks**. Although this is not a how-to book, it does include tips on using the major categories of tools. The authors offer their advice on how to get the most from a tool and how to avoid the most common mistakes new users make.

WHAT ABOUT A WEB SITE?

This book has its own Web site at horton.com/tools. There you will find the following items.

► **Lists of tools and vendors**. These lists are periodically updated so the material in the book remains current.

► **Design forms for picking and configuring tools**. These include forms for listing users' current tools and technologies; for cataloging the required hardware, software, and network connections; for combining software tools to create a complete system.

► **Spreadsheets** for evaluating tools, calculating amortized costs, computing return on investment, estimating download speeds, predicting needed storage space and connection speeds, and other common computations.

► **List of file formats** including the names, nicknames, extensions, and other interesting information about the file formats widely used in e-learning.

► **Updates** and new information to round out the material in the printed book.

Contents

Contents

Contents

Tools and technologies for e-learning

You're on a mission—to make skills and knowledge available to anyone, anytime, anywhere. You will need a generous budget and people to help you spend it. And, you will need technology. You'll need technology to create e-learning, educational Web sites, online tutorials, and knowledge management solutions. Where do you begin?

You first must understand the technologies that underlie such efforts. You have to be able to combine separate tools to create, offer, and deliver content. Such knowledge can be complex and highly technical. And few projects can be done with just a single tool or technology. To complicate matters, tools and technologies change at a frightening rate. Technologies evolve and mature and new tools are continually being developed. Companies form, merge, and go out of business in the span of a few years—or less.

How do you, then, get the complete, objective, and current information you need to plan projects and carry them out? Fortunately, the very technologies you need to learn about provide you with solutions.

 Hi. I'm William Horton. You can call me "Bill." I pop up like this to offer my private suggestions and opinions.

Most of the detailed, factual information you need is available on the Web, but finding that information and understanding it requires higher level knowledge. This book will provide you with some of that knowledge.

 I'm Katherine Horton, or "Kit" for short. Like Bill, I pop up occasionally to add my observations and comments.

Here you will learn how to analyze the need for technology, the major categories of tools and technologies, the flagship products in each category, the key issues in picking particular tools, and procedures for combining separate tools and technologies into a systematic solution.

This section will prepare you to leap into the following sections that deal with specific categories of tools and with the process for acquiring them. We'll start in chapter 1 with the people involved in e-learning and what their roles imply about the need for tools and technology. In chapter 2, we'll

 I'm the guest commentator. My name is Thorndon Killabit. My nickname is "Thorny." I pop up to say the things Bill and Kit are too polite to say.

look at different types of e-learning to see how each is built from different mixes of tools. Then, in chapter 3, we'll lay out a scheme for making sense of the many different categories of tools needed.

1 People first

Technology doesn't make e-learning. People do. The right starting point for any exploration of technology is the people for whom the technology is needed.

In this chapter, we introduce the cast of characters, help you find your role, and consider what each role requires. We then help you tailor your designs and strategies to the technologies learners already have. And when you're feeling completely overwhelmed, we point out groups of people who can help you.

PARTICIPANTS AND PROCESSES

To make sense of the tools and technologies needed for even a simple project, you need a framework or checklist of the major categories of technologies needed. Let's take a look at a simple way of classifying the technologies.

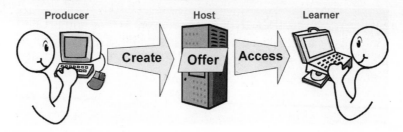

Start by looking at the groups of people involved and the technology they need for the activities they individually perform: the producers of e-learning, those who offer the course or Web site, and the learners themselves. The process of building e-learning is commonly referred to as *creating*, and it is performed by the producer. The next process is *offering*, performed by the host. The process of taking e-learning is commonly referred to as *accessing* and is performed by the learner.

Let's look at each of these participants and processes in more detail.

Producers include the designers, authors, writers, illustrators, photographers, animators, videographers, and other creative souls who collectively bring e-learning products into being.

Learners go by many names. They are typically called students. If the e-learning is designed as an online document or knowledge-management system, they are referred to as readers or users.

The **host** is the organization that makes e-learning widely available over a network, so the learning product is accessible by learners and those who must administer, maintain, and support it.

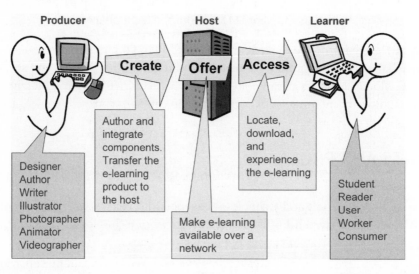

The process of *creating* covers the activities of producers as they author and integrate components into an e-learning product and transfer that it to the host, which *offers* the e-learning. Likewise, *accessing* refers to activities performed by the learner who locates, logs into, and experiences the e-learning.

To recap:

▶ Producers create e-learning.

▶ Hosts offer e-learning.

▶ Learners access e-learning.

WHAT DO THEY NEED?

Each of the participants—producer, host, and learner—requires three forms of technology: hardware, a network connection, and software. The learner probably requires a personal computer to access the learning product and a network connection of at least moderate speed. In addition to the basic operating system of the personal computer, the learner requires add-ons such as a Web browser and media players.

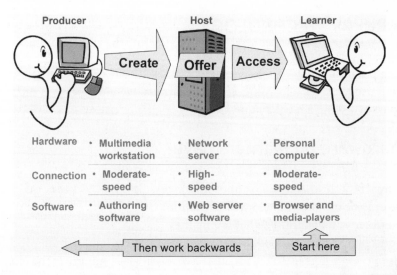

	Producer	Host	Learner
Hardware	• Multimedia workstation	• Network server	• Personal computer
Connection	• Moderate-speed	• High-speed	• Moderate-speed
Software	• Authoring software	• Web server software	• Browser and media-players

⟸ Then work backwards   Start here ⟹

The host requires a network server. You can think of it as an ultra-powerful personal computer optimized for delivering information over a network. The host also needs a high-speed network connection so it can deliver information to many simultaneous learners. And the host requires Web-server software, perhaps including special collaboration tools and media servers.

The producer uses multimedia workstations for preparing the graphics, animations, icons, video clips, sounds, and other media needed. The producer also needs a moderate speed network connection. In fact, it may be best if the producer's connection is no faster than that of the learner's so the producer experiences the learning product at the same speed as the learner. The producer also needs specialized software to create and edit the various media needed.

Typically, a workstation for creating e-learning costs twice as much as the personal computer needed to access the e-learning.

In putting together your technology plan, be sure to start at the right side of this diagram. Always start with the technology used by the learner, and then work backwards. On some projects you may have no control over the learners' choices for technology. And, even if you can choose technology for learners, there will be far more learners than hosts and producers. So the costs of technology for learners may dominate the budget. Let's take a closer look at how learners' technology influences your technology plan.

TARGET LEARNERS' TECHNOLOGY

The starting point for any technology plan is a quick survey of the technology that learners will use to access e-learning. It is the learners' technologies you must target. You can start by asking a few key questions.

What hardware do learners have?

Learners must be able to access a computer to take advantage of your offerings. The exact capabilities of that computer will determine what media they can view and play. Knowing these capabilities, you can design learning products that work with the computers learners already have; or, at least, minimize the extent of upgrades they need. Let's consider some of the components of the learner's computer system, see some typical configurations, and think about how these components will affect your e-learning design.

 Confused by bits, bytes, Ks and other measures of digital data? See appendix A.

Accessing	
Processor:	Pentium III 400 MHz
Memory:	64 MB
Display size:	800 x 600 pixels
Colors:	16-bit
Hard disk:	2 Gigabytes available
CD or DVD:	6X speed CD-ROM
Audio:	16-bit, 44 KHz stereo
Video input:	(not required)

Here you see a portion of a technology specification from a recent project showing learners' current computer hardware.

If you would like to see a form for such specifications, it is available at the Web site for this book (horton.com/tools).

The computer's *processor* determines the speed with which it can perform common operations. You may, for example, discover that your learners' computers have Pentium III processors running at a speed of 400 megahertz. E-learning that uses lots of sound, animation, and especially video, requires a very fast, late-generation processor.

The amount of *memory* in the computer, say 64 megabytes (MB), determines how many programs and how much data the computer can effectively manipulate at once. If your e-learning uses large graphics or multimedia, or requires loading several programs at once, a generous helping of memory is necessary.

The *display* determines how much the learner can see at once. For display, you should be concerned with the size of the display, measured in pixels, and in the color depth, which determines the number of colors that can be displayed at once. Screen size restricts how large your pages and other displays can be. It also determines how many tasks learners can attend to without having to scroll or flip back and forth among several windows. Color depth affects color fidelity and the smoothness of gradations. A color depth of 8 bits is sufficient to display 256 colors. This may be enough for graphics with large areas of the same color. However, if the graphic contains gradations of color, learners will see large distracting bands of solid colors rather than the subtle, continuous tones you intended. A depth of 16 bits is enough to display thousands of colors and smooth gradations of color.

If your e-learning requires installing software or storing data on the learner's computer, you need to be concerned with available space on the learner's hard disk. Even though computers today come with disks considered enormous by yesterday's standards, these disks are soon filled with scanned pictures, downloaded music, and what not. Make sure that your e-learning does not require more space than the learner has available or is willing to part with.

Many computers come with a CD-ROM (Compact Disc, Read-Only-Memory) or DVD (Digital Versatile Disc) drive. You could deliver complete learning products or just their multimedia components using such drives. However, you need to know the type (CD or DVD), the speed (e.g., 6X normal speed), and whether the drive can write as well as read these discs. Such drives provide an alternative to network connections for transferring programs and content to and from the learner.

The entertainment world spells it disc while the computer world spells it disk. Since CD-ROMs and DVDs evolved from audio CDs, the disc spelling stuck.

Today, most personal computers come with circuitry built in to play and even record sound. The quality of the sound circuitry determines how well you can use sound. You may also need to consider whether learners have headphones so they can listen to voice, music, and other sounds without disturbing those around them.

Video input is yet another capability to consider. The ability of learners to record video into their computers makes it possible for them to participate in video conferencing as well as to submit recordings of themselves performing required activities.

How do learners connect to the network?

To access remote information over a network, the learner must have a connection to the network. This connection consists of circuitry in, or attached to, the learner's machine as well as cabling and other hardware joining that computer to the network proper. The details are complicated. Fortunately you need to know only a few characteristics about that connection.

Accessing	
To: ☐ Intranet ☒ Internet	
Type: ☐ LAN ☒ Dial-up ☐ Wireless	
Speed: ___56K___ bits per second	
Cost: _0 USD_ per _minute_	

This portion of the technology specification shows information about learners' network connections.

First you need to know whether the learner is connected to the organization's intranet (that is the organization's local area network), to the Internet, or to both. Most office computers are connected to an intranet; most home computers are connected to the Internet directly. The nature of this connection determines what the learner can access, the need for security, and where you should host your e-learning.

A second consideration is the type of connection. The connection may be through a local area network, a dial-up modem connection, a broadband connection, or a wireless connection. If this network terminology is a bit hard to follow, come back to this segment after reading chapter 5.

Each of these possibilities can add wrinkles to your plan. If learners have to dial in to establish a connection, their usage will be less spontaneous than that of learners whose connection is always active. Typically, learners connected to a local area network have more reliable service than those dialing in from home or from laptop computers on the road.

A third concern is the speed of the connection, for example, 56 kilobits per second (Kbps). Keep in mind that rated speeds are seldom achieved in practice. For planning purposes, you may want to use a speed of half the rated speed of the connection.

A fourth concern is the cost of the connection. That is, does the learner have to pay for the time they are connected? Flat-rate charges are common in the United States but not everywhere. If learners pay a high fee for each minute of connection, your design should minimize the time they are connected.

What software do learners have?

The learner's hardware is important, but so is the software that runs on that hardware. Let's look at some of the main categories of software that you should be concerned with.

Accessing	
Op sys:	Windows XP, 2000, or 98
Browser:	IE 6 for Windows, Netscape 6 for Macintosh
Media players:	PowerPoint Animation Player
	Macromedia Shockwave Flash
	Windows Media Player or RealOne Player
	Acrobat Reader
Java VM:	Sun or Microsoft JVM 1.1

This portion of the technology specification shows what software learners currently have installed on their computers.

The first is the operating system. It might be a version of Microsoft Windows or a Macintosh operating system. The operating system determines what other software can run on that machine. So, knowing the operating system is crucial for designers. Not all tools are available for all operating systems.

The next important software component is the Web browser, typically Internet Explorer or Netscape Navigator. (Browsers are covered in detail in chapter 6.) The browser not only displays Web pages but other media as well. Some media and file formats are displayed right in the browser and are referred to as *browser-native* file formats. Other content may require a variety of media players, browser plug-ins, controls, and other components. Some of these components play a single proprietary file format, while others can play a range of media. (Media players are covered in chapter 7.)

A final software component is a bit obscure but equally important. That is the Java virtual machine. This is the component that enables the computer to run programs written in the Java programming language. The idea is that Your Information Technology department may be able to help gather this information. Use this as an excuse to begin talking about your e-learning plan.

programmers write the program once and it can then be played on any computer with a Java virtual machine installed, regardless of the operating system. Sounds simple, but both Sun and Microsoft offer Java virtual machines, and they frequently update them to fix bugs and add capabilities. Therefore, some Java applications and applets require a specific version of Java virtual machine.

WHAT CAN YOU LET OTHERS DO?

✳Developing learning products is a complex and expensive business. Keep in mind that you and your immediate organization need not deal with all these issues. You can choose to farm out some of the work. The same tools and technologies are needed, but someone else may provide or operate them as a service. You will still need to understand the basic technical capabilities required but you will not have to purchase, install, maintain, and operate the tools.

Some organizations choose to do it all themselves. They analyze, design, build, and evaluate their e-learning. Many other organizations, especially smaller companies and departments, find they can be more effective by hiring others to do parts of the development. Although all development could be outsourced, some phases are more commonly outsourced than other phases. These decisions profoundly affect your technology plan.

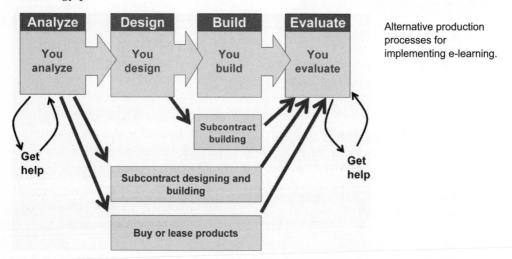

Alternative production processes for implementing e-learning.

Whichever approach you take—doing it yourself or subcontracting some or all development tasks—you will almost certainly need to be involved in the analysis phase, which sets the objectives for your project, and the evaluation phase, which determines whether those objectives were met. These two phases concern the intimate needs of your organization and are not efficiently performed by outsiders. You may want to get assistance for these phases from your IT (Information Technology) department or from external consultants.

Subcontract production

One common option is to subcontract the building of the course to a firm specializing in e-learning, multimedia, or Web-site construction. This relieves you of having to maintain a staff of technical specialists and the associated hardware and software producers require. It also lets you pick the firm whose capabilities match precisely the design you have created.

Even so, you will most likely have to *specify* which technologies and file formats the subcontractors should use. For instance, you may tell them that they cannot use Macromedia Flash to create animations because your Information Technology department does not allow Flash files through the firewall.

Subcontract design and production

Another common approach is to subcontract both the design and build phases. In this approach, you turn to a systems integrator or consultant to deliver a complete solution. By subcontracting both these phases, you save maintaining a production staff and the associated technology, thereby keeping your focus entirely on results and away from the details of how those results are to be achieved. This approach, however, comes at a cost: a loss of control over the details of the result.

Buy or lease e-learning

Instead of subcontracting the design and build phases, you may choose to buy or lease existing courses or other learning products from an application service provider (ASP) or a portal. This approach works well when your training needs can be met by courses with generic content.

Essentially, the ASP maintains an e-learning library on its server. With this approach, almost all of the producer and hosting technology is handled for you. You merely rent access on behalf of the learners. The ASP maintains, supports, and updates tools as needed. Your only concern is that learners have the technology required to access the e-learning.

NOW WHAT?

Remember, people come first. Identify the people involved in your project and let them guide you in selecting tools and technologies. Here are some steps you can take to get started.

① **List all participants in you e-learning project**. Don't stop with those directly involved—include all stakeholders, such as those whose support is required and those whose cooperation you will need.

② **Identify what each participant contributes and what each requires**. Some contribute labor to create media while others may just approve progress reports.

③ **Catalog the tools and technologies possessed by intended learners**. While you are at it, investigate their technology skills and attitudes toward using technology to learn.

④ **Think about what you want to do in-house and what to outsource**. Consider your mission, your schedule, budget, and management style. Make some provisional decisions.

2 Types of e-learning and the technologies required

E-learning can be defined broadly as any use of Web and Internet technologies to create learning experiences. Such an inspirationally open-ended definition, though, does little to help you narrow in on the specific tools needed for an individual project. To narrow in, you need to think about the specific type of e-learning you want to create. Different types of e-learning require different tools and technologies.

Your view of e-learning may be highly influenced by what you have personally experienced. So, take a look at several ways e-learning is used today. You may be familiar with some of them, but a few may be new to you. This chapter covers:

 These types represent broad categories. Within each, there is a spectrum of possibilities.

- ▶ Learner-led e-learning
- ▶ Facilitated e-learning
- ▶ Instructor-led e-learning
- ▶ Embedded e-learning
- ▶ Telementoring and e-coaching

For each type of e-learning, this chapter examines its structure, suggests where to use it, and discusses the technology needs for each approach.

LEARNER-LED E-LEARNING

Learner-led e-learning aims to deliver highly effective learning experiences to independent learners. It is sometimes called standalone or self-directed e-learning. Content may consist of Web pages, multimedia presentations, and other interactive learning experiences housed and maintained on a Web server. The content is accessed through a Web browser.

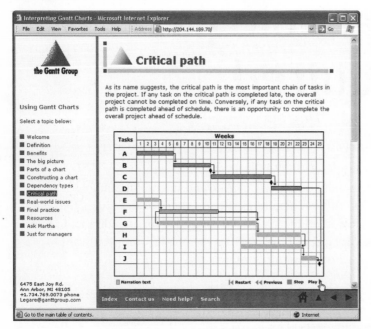

Take a look at this example of learner-led e-learning from the Gantt Group (horton.com/tools).

The experience of taking learner-led e-learning is not unlike that of taking a computer-based training (CBT) course from CD-ROM. (Note: CBT happens on the learner's computer. Learners do not have to be connected to a network or the Internet.) Where learner-led e-learning goes beyond CBT is in the potential to track learners' actions in a central database and to include Internet resources.

In learner-led e-learning, all the instruction must be provided through the

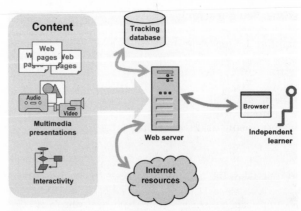

Here's a diagram of the components of learner-led e-learning.

course materials. There is neither an instructor nor a facilitator to help learners over the rough spots. There is no mechanism to allow concurrent students to communicate and share ideas. Nor are there any restrictions of when and how much the learner studies. The learner is truly independent.

Here is a list of the technology this type of e-learning might need, grouped by the type of people involved.

Technology needed for learner-led e-learning		
Producer	**Host**	**Learner**
▶ Video and audio capture equipment (chapter 4) ▶ Multimedia workstations for creating and editing video, audio, graphics, and animations (chapter 4) ▶ Moderate speed network (chapter 5) ▶ Web-site authoring tools, for creating individual Web pages, organizing Web sites, and maintaining links (chapter 15) ▶ Course authoring tools (chapter 14) ▶ Multimedia tools, for editing video, audio, photographs, etc. (chapter 17)	▶ Server hardware ▶ Server operating system ▶ Fast Internet connection (chapter 5) ▶ Modems for remote users if the content is hosted behind a firewall (chapter 5) ▶ Web server software (chapter 8) ▶ Streaming media server software (chapter 13) ▶ Learning management system (LMS) for enrolling and tracking learners (chapter 9) ▶ Learning content management system (LCMS) for reusing content modules (chapter 10)	▶ Multimedia-capable computer (chapter 4) ▶ Internet connection (chapter 5) ▶ Web browser (chapter 6) ▶ Media players for playing media types not handled by the Web browser (chapter 7)

This list is inclusive. In other words, if you exclude video from your e-learning, you can eliminate tools such as video editing software, video capture devices, streaming media server software, and a Web-browser plug-in for playing video.

 It amazes me how many people still use disk-oriented CBT tools. Maybe they don't know that Web-oriented tools can create e-learning that runs fine from a CD-ROM or local hard disk. Or perhaps they enjoy redoing their project when they later have to move it to the Web.

The example course you viewed before (horton.com/tools) requires all the types of tools listed under Producer in the list. Hosting the course requires a server, its operating system, Web-server software, and a fast connection to the Internet. Because learners are not tracked, there is no need for a tracking database like a learning management system. Learners need the technology listed under Learner and a moderately fast connection to the Internet due to the large amounts of audio used in the course. The specific media players for this course are the Macromedia Flash animation plug-in and an MPEG video plug-in.

⚡FACILITATED E-LEARNING

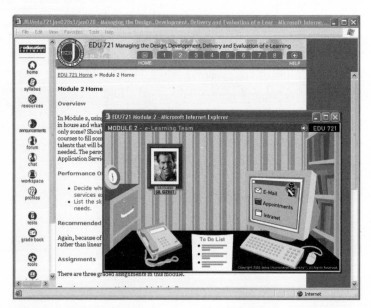

Facilitated e-learning combines the reliance on Web content found in learner-led e-learning with the collaborative facilities found in *instructor-led e-learning* (discussed later). It works well for learners who cannot conform to the rigid schedule of classroom training but who want to augment learning through discussion with other learners as well as with a facilitator. Assignments are typically made by posting them to a class discussion forum, where learners can also "hand in" their completed homework.

Unlike an instructor, the facilitator does not actually teach. The facilitator does not directly conduct learning

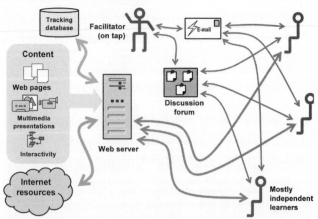

Here's a diagram of the components and information flow commonly found in facilitated e-learning.

events or try to wrest control from the learners. The facilitator is on tap. The facilitator answers questions from learners and helps solve problems. The facilitator may also grade and evaluate assignments.

The following table lists technology commonly needed for facilitated e-learning.

Technology needed for facilitated e-learning		
Producer	**Host**	**Learner**
▶ Video and audio capture equipment (chapter 4)	▶ Server hardware	▶ Multimedia-capable computer (chapter 4)
▶ Multimedia workstations for creating and editing video, audio, graphics, and animations (chapter 4)	▶ Fast Internet connection (chapter 5)	▶ Internet connection (chapter 5)
	▶ Server operating system	▶ Web browser (chapter 6)
	▶ Modems for remote users if the content is hosted behind a firewall (chapter 5)	▶ Media players for playing media types not handled by the Web browser (chapter 7)
▶ Moderate speed network (chapter 5)	▶ Web server software (chapter 8)	▶ E-mail program like Outlook or Eudora (chapter 11)
▶ Web-site authoring tools, for creating individual Web pages, organizing Web sites, and maintaining links (chapter 15)	▶ Streaming media server software (chapter 13)	**Note**: Access to a discussion forum is usually through a browser and, hence, does not require special software.
	▶ Learning management system (LMS) for enrolling and tracking learners (chapter 9)	
▶ Course authoring tools (chapter 14)	▶ Learning content management system (LCMS) for reusing content modules (chapter 10)	
▶ Multimedia tools, for editing video, audio, photographs, etc. (chapter 17)	▶ Discussion forum software (chapter 11)	
	▶ E-mail server software (chapter 11)	

INSTRUCTOR-LED E-LEARNING

Instructor-led e-learning uses Web technology to conduct conventional classes with distant learners. These classes use a variety of real-time technologies, such as video and audio conferencing, chat, screen-sharing, polling, whiteboards, and the plain old telephone.

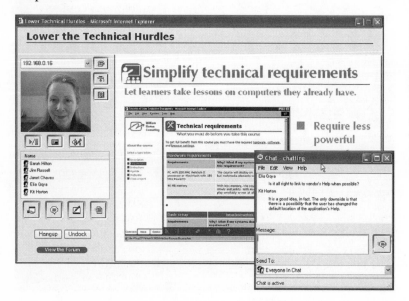

Here is an online course in progress. Kit is the instructor. Using Microsoft NetMeeting, she is chatting with a student while showing PowerPoint slides.

The instructor typically shows slides and conducts demonstrations. These presentations are transmitted by a streaming media server along with the instructor's voice and possibly a video image of the instructor. Learners may use a media player for the presentation and they can ask questions by typing their questions into a chat window or sending them by e-mail. If all learners have fast connections, this back channel may use audio conferencing. Like facilitated e-learning, assignments are

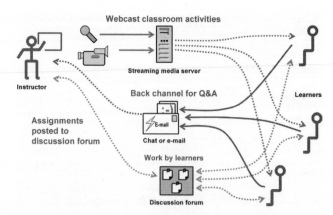

Here is a diagram showing the flow of information typically found in instructor-led e-learning. The dotted lines represent information pulled or requested by participants. Solid lines represent information sent by participants.

posted to a class discussion board, where learners can also hand in their completed homework.

Instructor-led e-learning will seem familiar to learners. It has the same structure and expectations as the type of training they have experienced most of their lives. It requires the least effort to convert materials. Just hold them up in front of the video camera or scan them in. Unfortunately these similarities are deceptively seductive. Much material does not work when filtered through the medium of Internet video, and few instructors yet know how to teach remotely.

Take a look at the technology needed for instructor-led e-learning.

Technology needed for instructor-led e-learning		
Producer	**Host**	**Learner**
▶ Multimedia computer capable of viewing audio and video input (chapter 4) ▶ Microphone and perhaps a video camera (chapter 4) ▶ Presenter's version of the online meeting client component (chapter 11) ▶ Presentation software (e.g., PowerPoint) for preparing display (chapter 11) ▶ Other software to be demonstrated ▶ Other authoring tools, such as Adobe Acrobat, for producing content learners can download (chapter 18)	▶ Server hardware (may require separate machine for streaming media) ▶ Server operating system ▶ Fast Internet connection (chapter 5) ▶ Web server software (chapter 8) ▶ Online meeting, virtual-school, or collaboration system providing slide presentations, audio conferencing, video conferencing, chat, application-sharing, whiteboard, and discussion forums (chapters 11 and 12)	▶ Multimedia-capable computer (chapter 4) ▶ Web browser (chapter 6) ▶ Client for online meetings, virtual-school, or collaboration systems (chapter 11) ▶ Connection to the Internet (chapter 5)

Bandwidth (how much data can travel over a connection per second), is the limiting factor in determining the mix of media learners will receive. Video, which requires a great deal of bandwidth, is used infrequently for Internet-based classes because learners will not all have fast Internet connections. On the other hand, if a class is being offered over a LAN, video may be a viable choice—if the internal network is fast and not overloaded with other traffic.

Take a look at an instructor-led class. Here are some Web addresses to try. They go to various vendor sites where live, promotional classes are taught on a regular basis. Keep in mind that these demos are sales talks, not e-learning classes.

▶ www.centra.com/events/index.asp

▶ interwise.com/na/live/index.asp

▶ webex.com/home/services_training.html

▶ placeware.com

EMBEDDED E-LEARNING

Embedded e-learning provides just-in-time training. It is usually embedded in computer programs, Help files, Web pages, or network applications. It may even be a component of an Electronic Performance Support System (EPSS).

Here is an example of e-learning that is embedded in a Help file about defining a System Data Source Name, or DSN (horton.com/tools).

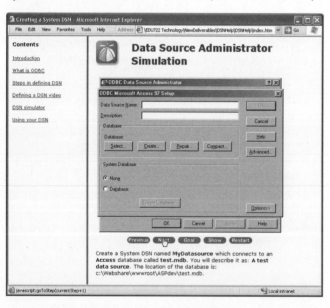

The first page is a simple Help topic listing the steps necessary to create a System DSN. If users still have difficulties creating a System DSN, they are invited to use a simulator to practice the procedure.

Click on *Steps in defining a DSN* to see a Help topic on the procedure. Click on *DSN simulator*, to practice the procedure.)

Embedded e-learning caters to the solitary learner who has a problem that needs to be solved immediately. It is often located on the learner's computer and is installed along with the program with which it is associated. Embedded e-learning can also be entirely Web-based. For instance, a user may have problems with a printer. From the

Help menu, the user accesses a Web-based troubleshooting procedure. Once the problem is identified, the user may be offered an opportunity to take a short tutorial to help them understand the concepts and avoid the problem in the future.

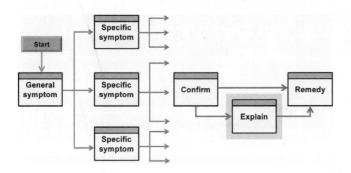

In this troubleshooting procedure, the user starts with a general problem then methodically steps down to a specific symptom. After confirming that the selected symptom indeed indicates the source of the problem, the user chooses whether to go directly to the remedy or to a tutorial explaining the problem. This tutorial is an example of embedded e-learning.

The following table lists the technologies needed for embedded e-learning.

Technology needed for embedded e-learning		
Producer	**Host**	**Learner**
► Multimedia workstations for creating and editing video, audio, graphics, and animations (chapter 4)	► Server hardware*	► Multimedia-capable computer (chapter 4)
► Moderate speed network (chapter 5)*	► Server operating system*	► Internet connection (chapter 5)*
► Web-site authoring tools for creating individual Web pages, organizing Web sites, and maintaining links (chapter 15)*	► Fast Internet connection (chapter 5)*	► Web browser (chapter 6)*
	► Modems for remote users if the content is hosted behind a firewall (chapter 5)*	► Help viewer
► Course authoring tools (chapter 14)	► Web server software (chapter 8)*	
► Multimedia tools, for editing video, audio, photographs, etc. (chapter 17)		* If e-learning is located on a server for Web access.
► Help authoring tools (chapter 14)		

The main technological issue in the success of embedded e-learning is file size. If the e-learning is to reside on the user's computer, the user may decide not to install the tutorial files if they significantly add to the amount of disk space needed by the application. If the user must access the tutorial material from the Web, file size is also a major consideration. Because there is no way to be sure how the user will connect to the Web, the tutorial files need to be small enough to download quickly at speeds as low as 56 Kbps.

TELEMENTORING AND E-COACHING

Telementoring and *e-coaching* use the latest technologies for one of the oldest forms of learning. They use video conferencing, instant messaging, Internet telephones, and other collaboration tools to help mentors guide the development of protégés.

Mentoring relationships tend to be long-term and focus on career development. Mentors offer learners a more knowledgeable and perhaps more mature partner from whom they can learn things not written in books or taught in classes.

The term *mentor* harkens back to Homer's *Odyssey*, where the character Mentor was charged with the education of Odysseus's son Telemachus. Athena, the goddess of wisdom, always took the guise of Mentor when advising the young boy.

Online coaching has a more short-term, project-specific goal. In online coaching, the contact between adviser and learner is more precisely defined. It is usually limited to a specific subject, such as the solution of a particular problem or completion of a specific project. The online coach serves as a technical or business consultant rather than an adviser or confidante on personal matters and overall career growth.

Many large and medium-sized companies recognize the value of telementoring in capturing and communicating higher-level knowledge and wisdom. It plays a big part in knowledge management initiatives.

From a technology viewpoint, telementoring may require nothing more than a telephone and e-mail. More sophisticated telementoring and e-coaching requires more technology, as listed in the following table.

Technology needed for telementoring		
Producer (mentor)	**Host**	**Learner (protégé)**
▶ Personal computer (chapter 4) ▶ Microphone for audio conferencing (chapter 4) ▶ Video camera for video conferencing (chapter 4) ▶ Moderate speed network for audio, but high-speed network for video (chapter 5) ▶ Client software for online meeting system (chapter 11)	▶ Server hardware ▶ Server operating system ▶ Fast Internet connection, especially if using audio and video (chapter 5) ▶ Web server software (chapter 8) ▶ Online meeting or collaboration server (chapter 11) ▶ E-commerce components to compensate mentors	▶ Personal computer (chapter 4) ▶ Microphone for audio conferencing (chapter 4) ▶ Video camera for video conferencing (chapter 4) ▶ Moderate speed network for audio, but high-speed network for video (chapter 5) ▶ Client software for online meeting system (chapter 11)

WHAT NOW?

In this chapter you had an opportunity to examine five common types of e-learning and the technology they require. Remember, these five types represent just a few of the many types and hundreds of hybrid forms of e-learning possible.

To apply the ideas in this chapter to narrow the list of tools and technologies, you will need to:

1 Clearly define the business, performance, and learning goals of your project. Write them down and get a consensus.

2 Decide what type of e-learning will best accomplish your goals. Use the types mentioned in this chapter as a start and consider other types and hybrids as well.

3 List the hardware, network connection, and software learners already possess.

4 Separately list the additional hardware, network connection, and software required by producers, hosts, and learners. Use a 3 x 3 matrix to organize your data.

	Producer	Host	Learner
Hardware			
Network			
Software			

Make this matrix big—like an easel pad.

5 Don't worry if your choices are tentative and sketchy. The rest of this book will help you refine your decisions.

In the next chapter, you will have a chance to consider the categories of software tools needed for an ambitious e-learning project. By understanding these categories, you can more quickly identify individual tools you want to consider.

3 Categories of tools

The most painful question we get as consultants is "What tool should I use for e-learning?" What is painful about the question is that it shows the questioner has been misled to believe there is one single tool that does everything everybody needs to do to create, host, and access e-learning. Successful e-learning projects may require dozens of software products chosen from hundreds of candidates sprawling across several categories.

This chapter outlines the several categories of software you may need to consider for your e-learning project. These categories will help you understand which products you need.

These categories are not based on permanent fixtures with clear, well-defined boundaries. Categories are continually being created, merged, and subdivided. As products add more and more capabilities, they may span several categories. Still, understanding these categories will help you articulate what you need and what products to consider.

 Where does this naïve, one-tool-does-it-all view come from? I blame:

1. Unscrupulous vendors
2. Consultants who've never create any e-learning
3. Writers of over-simplified magazine articles
4. Contractors specializing in one tool only
5. Wishful thinking of buyers

LEVELS AND TASKS

E-learning is produced in various units of scale and scope ranging from collections of multiple products to individual, low-level components. It is important to understand these units because they influence the design techniques and tools used to create them.

Levels of granularity

Units of learning span a range from complete curricula down to individual media components. In e-learning, the size of each of these units of learning is referred to as its *level of granularity*.

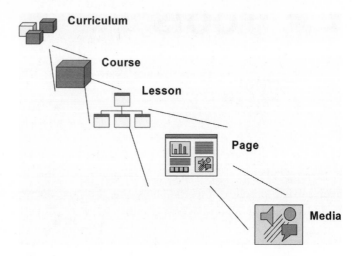

At the top is the *curriculum*. The curriculum is a collection of learning products, for example, an academic program including related courses in a subject area, or a library of books on a certain subject. A curriculum is composed of individual courses, books, and other e-learning products.

Courses are typically composed of clusters of smaller *lessons*, each organized to accomplish one of the major objectives of the course as a whole.

At a lower level are the individual *pages*, each designed to accomplish a single low-level objective that answers a single question. Such units may also be called *screens* in multimedia presentations or topics in online Help.

So what are *learning objects*? The term learning object generally refers to a reusable component at the page, lesson, or, perhaps, course level. Items at the media level are sometimes called *content objects*, but seldom learning objects.

At the bottom level are *media* components. These are the individual pictures, blocks of text, animation sequences, and video passages that contribute to the page.

Tools for every level and task

Let's look at a framework for classifying the categories of software tools needed for the various levels of learning products and required tasks. This tools framework uses a rectangular grid.

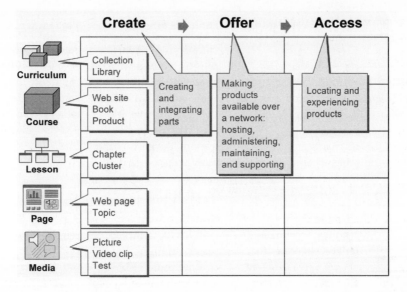

The levels of learning products are arranged vertically in rows. The processes are arranged horizontally in columns.

Everyone in e-learning needs tools—the producer creating the content, the host hosting it, and the learner accessing it. In addition, tools are required for each level of learning product. Here are the capabilities needed at each level for each process.

Level	For producers creating	For hosts offering	For learners accessing
Curriculum	Creating curricula consists of locating and integrating separate courses into a coherent sequence or other structure.	Hosting curricula and setting up online schools requires presenting these collections of courses to learners in ways that show relationships among the individual products and perhaps tracks which the learner has accessed or completed.	Accessing collections requires tools to find them where offered and to enroll or subscribe to them.

Level	For producers creating	For hosts offering	For learners accessing
Course	Creating courses requires integrating separate clusters and pages of content as well as providing overall navigational mechanisms such as a table of contents or index.	Offering individual courses requires ways of making them available to learners as a coherent whole. It may also require tracking the parts of the individual course they have accessed and completed.	Accessing individual courses requires the capability to open the course for display, choose from its lessons, and navigate among them.
Lesson	Creating lessons requires selecting and linking pages or other objects into a coherent navigational structure.	Offering lessons requires the ability to present multiple pages or other components as a coherent whole.	Accessing lessons requires the ability to select among its individual pages.
Page	Creating pages requires entering text and integrating it with graphics and other media. It may also include inserting cross-reference hypertext links.	Offering individual pages requires dispatching them to learners as requested.	Accessing pages requires a way to request them and to display them when they arrive.
Media	Creating media components requires creating the individual pictures, animations, sounds, music, video sequences, and other digital media.	Offering media components requires supplying them as requested. It may also require storing them economically and streaming them efficiently.	Accessing media components requires the ability to play or display the individual media.

A complete e-learning solution will require software to supply each of these capabilities. Let's see how groups of capabilities are provided by categories of software tools.

CATEGORIES OF SOFTWARE TOOLS

Using the framework of levels and tasks as a backdrop, let's look at how various categories of tools might contribute to an e-learning project. We'll build one step at a time to make it easier to follow.

We start with core tools that are likely to be part of any project. The learner will likely use a Web browser (chapter 6) to access content offered on a Web server (chapter 8). A big part of that content may have come from a Web site authoring tool (chapter 15).

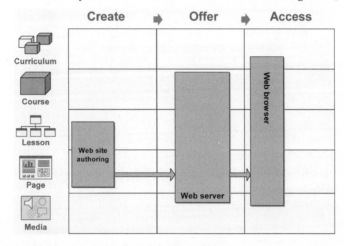

Content may also come from tools for creating e-learning (chapter 14), either as CBT or Web-based training (WBT). These tools may be supplemented by tools for creating and offering tests and assessments (chapter 16).

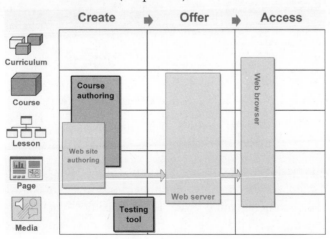

Projects involving collaboration among distant learners may rely on collaboration tools (chapter 11). Collaboration tools usually consist of a server component that routes messages among learners and a collaboration client that runs on the computer of the individual learner. Some collaboration servers can work directly through the browser, but most require some client tool. Collaboration tools include popular online meeting products and services.

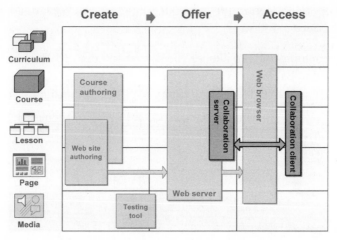

Sound, animation, video, and other media may require specific authoring and editing tools (chapter 17). Video and sound may also require special media servers (chapter 13) to ensure that they play efficiently over the network. Some media may require media players (chapter 7), especially for displaying media in proprietary formats.

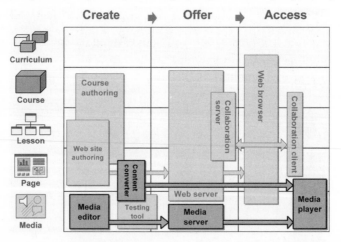

Many e-learning projects reuse existing documents, spreadsheets, and slide presentations. Content converters (chapter 18) help producers make existing documents and other content available online. Some content converters convert content to a proprietary format and require an equivalent viewer or player (chapter 7) for learners to see or play the converted content.

For large-scale projects involving dozens or hundreds of courses, organizations may invest in large, server-based systems to manage the whole development and administration of learning. A common solution is a learning management system or LMS (chapter 9), which simplifies the administration of many learners taking many courses. Another option is a learning content management system or LCMS (chapter 10), which manages the development of complex courses, especially ones that customize their content to the needs of individual learners by assembling reusable units of education called learning objects.

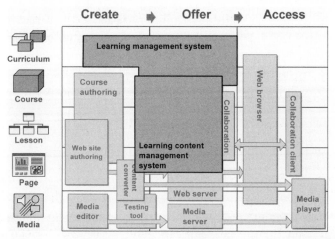

Extending the classroom structure to the Web is the job of the virtual-school system (chapter 12). Such systems combine learning management capabilities with collaboration features to provide online analogs for common classroom learning events, such as lectures, discussions, and grade books. They also go by the name course management system.

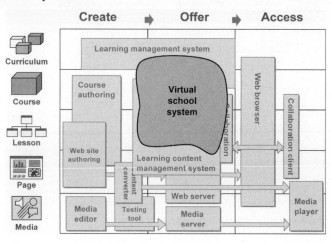

Although the categories may seem overwhelming at first, they will become familiar as you study them further. Anyway, few projects require more than a handful of these categories.

WHAT NOW?

In this chapter you saw how learning products range in size and scope from the smallest media element to an entire curriculum. At each level or unit, there are technologies to create, offer, and access e-learning. These units and processes form a framework that we will use throughout this book to organize the vast array of tools and technologies. This framework will enable us to talk about them in a logical and organized way. We'll come back to these categories in chapters 6 through 18.

To put this scheme of classifying software products to work for you:

❶ On the tools framework, identify your organization's area of responsibility. For example, do you buy courses, organize them into curricula, and offer them to learners?

❷ Fit tools you are familiar with into their slots in the tools framework. Some tools may fill multiple slots.

❸ List as many tools as you can for each of the categories identified in this chapter.

As you read subsequent chapters and as you refine your technology plans, update this framework.

Before diving into these software categories, we are going to talk about the hardware needed to create and access e-learning—and the networks that carry it.

Hardware and networks

Computer hardware and networks are the foundation of e-learning. They provide the infrastructure on which software and content depend.

Hardware and networks are the most difficult aspects of technology to change once they are in place. They may be under the control of learners or your own Information Technology (IT) department. Yet it is important for you to understand the potential and limitations of hardware and networks. You must speak the vocabulary to deal with those who control these technologies and to understand their concerns about e-learning.

Sometimes you have no choice over what hardware and network you or your learners use for e-learning. If you are selling e-learning packages to a wide market, you may have no choice but to design the packages to run on the hardware and networks learners already have—or limit your market to those who have hardware and networks meeting your requirements. There are, however, some cases where you can influence the hardware and networks used to access or create e-learning.

▶ **Outfitting a computer learning lab**. Suppose you want to set up an environment where learners can take e-learning on machines especially configured for that task. You may set up such learning labs so students eager to learn have a quiet place, free of interruptions. In such labs, learners can focus on taking e-learning and have access to technical support should they need it. In outfitting learning labs, you want to purchase computers and configure networks ideally suited for e-learning.

▶ **Influencing IT standards**. Many organizations rely on their IT department to specify standard computers for use by employees and to maintain the organization's networks and Internet connections. Standardizing enables purchasing in quantity, lessens support costs, and ensures equity. Because one important use of the organization's computers and network is for taking e-learning, you will want to ensure that all computers purchased by the organization are capable of playing e-learning content. Therefore, make sure your voice is heard when your organization decides to upgrade and solicits input from various departments.

▶ **Provisioning a development team**. Creating e-learning content may require more powerful computers than those required for mainstream tasks, especially if e-learning relies on sound, animation, video, and other advanced media. Developing e-learning may require additional devices, such as a digital video camera, microphone, and scanner. You may need to specify these specialized workstations in detail. Developing e-learning may also require connection to servers that host e-learning content.

Even if you cannot control what computers and networks learners use to take e-learning, this section will help you understand the capabilities of the technology learners already have. First we'll discuss the hardware needed for creating and accessing e-learning (chapter 4). Then we'll discuss the networks need to transport e-learning (chapter 5).

4 Hardware for e-learning

Creating, hosting, and accessing e-learning requires vast amounts of software. That software runs on hardware. This chapter will help you pick the necessary computer hardware for your e-learning project and understand how to design for it.

WHAT TO LOOK FOR IN HARDWARE

Computers are just boxes full of chips, circuits, disks, wires, and other components that provide the capabilities needed by computer users. Let's take a tour of the major components needed by those who create and take e-learning. We'll take a black-box view. That is, we won't worry about the guts inside the box so much as the capabilities provided by those guts. For example, we won't be concerned whether the video circuitry is on the main circuit board or is provided by a separate circuit board. Instead, we'll concentrate on the specifications to use when you start shopping.

This approach is fine for people who are going to be buying already assembled computers. If, however, you are going to build your own computers from components purchased separately, you may want to consult a site, such as basichardware.com, that provides more detailed discussions of each hardware component.

 As you read this chapter, periodically pause to examine your computer. See if you can find the features mentioned here.

Computers have evolved over the decades to offer a common set of features. Open a computer catalog and you will see similar features mentioned for most comparable models. Though the exact numbers and specifications of each may vary, they are all variations on the same theme.

Here is a typical computer for designing and developing e-learning, with callouts labeling the main features.

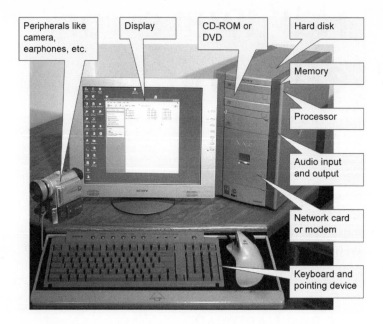

Let's look at these features, what each contributes and what to specify for computers used in e-learning.

Processor

The *processor* is the thinking part of the computer. Often called the CPU (central processing unit), it is a small unit of highly sophisticated circuitry that carries out billions of operations per second. It resides on the motherboard, the location for the main circuitry of the computer. The longer term, central processing unit, is actually more accurate as most modern computers contain several auxiliary processors to handle video, sound, and other tasks. But we'll use the term *processor* as an abbreviation.

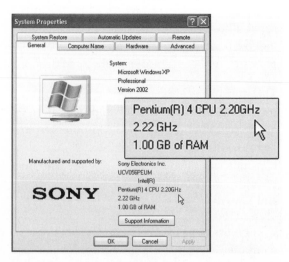

On computers running Windows, you can see your processor model and speed in the System Properties window.

The processor is the most important component of the computer. Every instruction given, either by an application or the operating system, is processed by the processor.

Speed

The most important criterion in a processor is its speed, measured in megahertz (MHz) or gigahertz (GHz). A 2.2 GHz processor, for example, performs 2.2 billion operations per second.

Within a processor family (Intel and AMD, for instance) faster is better. However, it can be misleading to compare processor speeds of one family of processors against another. A PowerPC G4 processor may run slower than an Intel Pentium processor of equivalent processing power.

 If you are a little unclear about the different ways of measuring digital data, take a look in the appendix A before you continue reading this chapter.

Processor speed is especially important in tasks that involve intricate calculations. Recalculating enormous spreadsheets, editing large scanned graphics, or transforming digital video sequences are all tasks that tax even fast processors. However, unless e-learners are viewing lots of animation and video or navigating virtual-reality worlds, processor speed is seldom the crucial factor. More often, performance is limited by network speed. Multimedia developers, however, may need a very fast processor for creating and editing multimedia, especially digital video.

Although faster is better, faster is also much more expensive. A top-speed processor may cost 10 times as much as a processor of half that speed. While you do not want your computer to become obsolete too soon, you also do not want to pay too much for it.

Brand

Users of Windows, Linux, or Windows PCs can choose processors from Intel or AMD. Although Intel spends a lot of money promoting its brand and users get a nifty "Intel inside" logo, most experts feel processors from AMD are reliable and capable.

For Macintosh computers, the processor is typically a PowerPC G4 processor. No other brands of processors are available.

Generation and model

Processor designs evolve through generations, for instance, Intel's 8086, 80186, 80286, 80386, 80486, Pentium, Pentium II, Pentium III, and Pentium 4. Within generations are specific models, such as low-power variants for use in laptop computers.

In general, later generations have more specialized features, such as specific instructions for handling multimedia data more efficiently. A later-generation processor may benefit multimedia authors, but those taking e-learning will probably see little difference between adjacent generations of a processor model.

The variants are too many and too subtle to guide purchasing decisions. It may be better to consider outward effects, such as overall battery life, rather than whether a processor has power-saving modes.

Internal cache

Most modern processors contain special quick access memory right on the chip. This internal cache is used to store recent commands and data so the processor can find them if it needs them again soon. The internal cache increases the effective speed of the processor. Caches are specified in terms of the amount of memory they contain, for example, 256 KB (kilobytes). More is better.

The boost in speed benefits all operations but is probably not critical for e-learning.

Recommendations

Those taking e-learning seldom need the latest model processor. You can safely choose a second-most recent generation processor at about 60% of the top available speed. If learners will be viewing lots of rich media, such as video or three-dimensional, virtual-reality worlds, you need to consider the latest-generation processor at about 80% of the top available speed.

Authors of e-learning need more powerful workstations, especially if they create multimedia or editing video. As a rule, get the latest-generation model that is 80% of the top available speed. Also, check the required processor speed for the operating system and all the authoring programs producers will be using. Make sure the processor is at least twice the minimum required speed.

Memory

The computer's memory is like human short-term or working memory. It is where the computer stores instructions and data needed for current tasks.

 For the curious, this is what common computer memory looks like. But don't go yanking memory out of your computer to have a look. Memory chips are a tad delicate, and static electricity can zap them into permanent amnesia.

4

Hardware for e-learning

Computer memory is usually referred to as RAM, or Random Access Memory. When you boot up the computer, the operating system loads its instructions into RAM. In addition, every application you start loads its set of instructions into RAM. On top of that, data that you are currently working on is loaded into RAM.

When you quit a program, the memory it used is freed up for other purposes. If you fail to save your data before quitting the program or turning off your computer, that data is gone, lost, bye bye, adios, tough luck.

On Windows-based computers you can see how much memory is installed by looking at the System Properties window.

Capacity

The more memory the computer has, the more processes it can run at the same time— and the faster it can run them. The operating system takes up a healthy chunk of memory, as does a Web browser and any media players or viewers required to display content. If the learner wants to take notes or do some calculations on what the browser displays, other programs may be required.

Memory also makes the computer run faster, as the processor can read data and instructions from memory faster than from the hard disk.

So, how much memory is enough? Memory sizes are specified in megabytes (MB) or gigabytes (GB). A megabyte is about a million bytes of storage and a gigabyte is about a billion bytes. You will need enough memory to hold all the programs and data you need to run at the same time, including the operating system.

When buying a computer, you will probably see two memory capacities listed: the standard memory and the expansion capacity. The standard capacity is how much memory is on the system as priced. The expansion capacity is the total memory the system can hold.

Speed and type

Other aspects of memory are pretty much determined by the computer you buy. You must buy memory that is compatible with your computer.

Memory speed refers to how quickly the computer reads data from memory and writes to it. Because most meaningful operations by the processor involve reading and writing data from memory, the speed of memory can affect overall speed.

A wide number of types of memory chips and boards are available: parity and non-parity, DIMMS, SIMMs, RIMMS, RDRAM, SDRAM, buffered, and unbuffered. Unless you are an engineer designing a system, you have few choices here. The computer manufacturer will install compatible memory in the unit you buy. If you upgrade or replace that memory, you must make sure the memory you buy is compatible with your computer. When you order, look for your brand and model listed by the memory vendor. And get a money-back guarantee on any memory you add.

Recommendations

For those taking e-learning, a good rule is to double the recommended memory requirements of the operating system. For example, Windows XP Professional recommends 128 MB of memory. Double that and you have 256 MB of memory, which should be enough for most e-learning activities.

For those authoring e-learning, consider the memory requirements of the authoring tools you will most likely use at the same time. To calculate the amount of memory needed, add up the minimum recommendations for tools likely to be used at the same time. Then, double the total. Or, just quadruple the operating system requirements.

If your learners have limited memory in their computers, design your e-learning to play in browsers and restrict the number of separate media players required. Limit the use of large graphics and see if you can get along without that video of your latest lecture series.

Hard disk drive

The *hard disk drive* in a computer is like your long-term memory. It remembers even while you sleep. It is where your programs and local data reside. You can see the disks installed on your computer when you display its hardware list.

Capacity

The most important factor for a hard disk drive is its capacity. *Capacity* measures how many gigabytes the disk can store. More is better.

You will need enough disk space for all the programs and data you need to have readily available, as well as data temporarily downloaded from the Internet. Start by adding up the disk space required for the operating system, all major application programs, utilities, and personal work files. The biggest use of disk space in many cases, however, is not for business programs and data, but for downloaded digital music files. Okay, maybe you're studying the vocal styling of pop divas, but it adds up.

E-learning itself does not usually add too much to the disk size learners require. They need space for the browser and all the media players and viewers necessary to experience e-learning content. If they are taking courses from multiple sources, the e-learning may have to store a couple of different browsers and a generous number of players and viewers.

Keep in mind that Web pages and their content are cached. That is, temporary copies are written on the learner's hard disk Large graphics can take up considerable space in the cache, as can video and sound, unless they are received in a streaming format (chapter 13). Also consider whether courses will require learners to download large files to their hard drive.

Authoring e-learning definitely requires a large disk. Authoring e-learning typically requires several complex (large!) programs that can range in size from 40 MB to over 100 MB. Work-in-progress also requires storage for multiple versions, often in their uncompressed formats.

Speed

Nothing can be done with data until it is read from the disk into memory. If the disk is too slow, the processor wastes time waiting for the disk to read or write data. There are several indicators of disk speed.

▶ **Rotation speed**. The faster the disk rotates, the sooner the read-write heads can get to the piece of data needed. A disk that rotates at 10,000 revolutions per minute (rpm) is faster than one spinning at 5,400 rpm—and make a higher pitched whine.

▶ **Access speed**. The time required to read a piece of data from the disk is referred to as the disk's access speed. Shorter times are better. A 5-ms (millisecond) time is twice as fast as one of 10 ms. A millisecond is 1/1,000 of a second.

▶ **Cache**. Many disks contain onboard high-speed memory to hold the most recently accessed data, just in case the processor needs it again soon. Cache is measured in kilobytes (KB) or megabytes (MB). More is better.

For those taking e-learning, most disks are adequately fast. For those authoring large media files, speed can be an important factor because it reduces the time spent waiting for the file to be read from the disk or written to it.

Interface

For a hard disk, the term *interface* refers to the circuitry used to control disk operations and connect it to the rest of the system. Two interfaces are common: IDE and SCSI. Don't worry what these stand for; almost nobody remembers.

 I know what they stand for. IDE is Integrated Drive Electronics, and SCSI is Small Computer Systems Interface.

Today, both are adequate for most purposes. SCSI is generally preferred for high-performance applications, such as editing video, but the Ultra-DMA and Ultra-ATA variants of IDE drives seem to work as well.

Recommendations

For those taking e-learning, make sure there is enough disk space for all their programs and data—beyond the space required for the operating system and other purposes. Do the math. Add up the disk-space requirements of all the programs that will be installed on the computer. Reserve space for work files and personal data the learner will store on the system. Then, include the browsers, viewers, and players needed to view e-learning. Finally, add some extra disk space to cache the last 100 pages the learner viewed with their browser.

For authors creating large media files like audio and video, specify the biggest, fastest disk you can. If you don't want to be on the cutting edge of technology, select a disk drive that is about 80% of the largest capacity available.

For authors working on smaller, less bandwidth-intensive files, do the math as you did for the learner. Remember all the work files, authoring tools, and utilities producers need. And don't forget the players and viewers that authors need to test and preview their creations.

Video card

The video display is determined by two components, the video card inside the box and the monitor connected to it. By *video card* we mean the circuitry that generates the electrical signals sent down a cable to the monitor.

This view of the back of a computer shows the back plate of the video card, which is in a slot inside the computer. The area that is boxed is the video connector. A cable goes from this connector to the monitor.

Choosing the right video display is crucial, because it determines the legibility and aesthetics of text, graphics, animation, and video.

There are several factors that determine the quality of video display, and there are tradeoffs among these factors. To experience the features of your video card, you must select a monitor that can display what the video card can send it.

Resolution

Video cards generate displays a certain number of pixels wide by a certain number of pixels high, for example, 1,024 x 768 pixels. More is better. The higher the resolution, the more data there is on the screen and the smoother the lines and edges.

A pixel is one grain of light on the screen. The term is a contraction of "picture element." I guess "picel" looked funny.

Effective e-learning is possible at resolutions of 800 x 600 pixels. However, more space allows learners to easily compare related areas of the display, take notes, and run computer programs.

For authoring e-learning, a big display is necessary to compare source and results, to manipulate multiple programs at once, and to keep good notes. Make sure your chosen resolution exceeds the minimum requirements of all the authoring tools you plan to use.

No author should be allowed a screen larger than the learner's screen.

Color depth

Color depth is a technical terms referring to the number of bits used to represent each pixel on the screen. The more bits per pixel, the more different colors can be used at once. Black and white screens have a color depth of 1 pixel, which can be black or white. An 8-bit color depth allows for 256 distinct colors. Most systems today have 16-bit color, which allows thousands of colors or 24-bit which supports millions of colors—far more than any human being can distinguish. Even greater color depths are available, not for more colors, but for special effects like transparency.

For those taking e-learning, 8-bit color is barely adequate, as the display may have bands of solid color rather than smooth transitions. With 8-bit color, learners may experience color variations across computer platforms or browser brands. With 16-bit and higher bit depth, colors are accurate, and transitions are smooth and consistent across platforms and browsers.

For those authoring e-learning, especially graphics and video, 24-bit color depth is necessary. Fortunately, most video cards today support 24-bit or higher color depth.

Refresh rate

Refresh rate determines how frequently the video card redraws the image on the screen. If the rate is too slow, the screen flickers. What is annoying for a few minutes becomes a migraine after a few hours. A refresh rate of 60 Hz is too low. Aim for 75 Hz or higher for a cathode-ray tube (CRT) monitor. Note: refresh rate is not critical for a liquid-crystal display (LCD) monitor. LCD monitors are found in laptops and flat-panel displays.

Video memory

Most video cards have on-board memory to speed up operations. A system for typical office activities might have 4 MB of on-board memory, but a system used for gaming or 3-D modeling would require 32 MB or more.

Video memory is also important because it determines tradeoffs necessary among resolution, color depth, and refresh rate. A video card may have high ratings for all of these items, but without adequate video memory, a learner may not be able to have high resolution, high color depth, and a high refresh rate at the same time.

Acceleration

Graphics cards boost the speed of display operations. This acceleration benefits complex video display operations such as rendering 3-D models or computing visibility of overlapping, translucent objects. (Yes, we mean games.) Most e-learning gets by just fine without acceleration. If you use a lot of complex animation, virtual-reality worlds, or other simulation programs, however, acceleration improves the smoothness of the visual display.

Multimedia authors who create and edit multilayered graphics or three-dimensional models will greatly benefit from an accelerated video card because they will have to wait less time while their monitor display redraws. (For some applications, this can be quite time-consuming.)

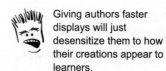 Giving authors faster displays will just desensitize them to how their creations appear to learners.

Multiple monitor support

From its third model on, Macintosh computers allowed users to connect multiple monitors. Windows has recently added this capability. Now, users who need more screen space can just attach more monitors—provided they add extra display cards or their display card supports multiple monitors. Though not necessary for e-learners, multiple monitors can be a boon for developers who use one monitor to edit their creations and another to view them the way learners will.

Recommendations

For e-learners, you need to take three factors into consideration: resolution, color depth, and refresh rate. To view e-learning and conduct other day-to-day activities, a resolution of 1,024 x 768 is a safe choice. Specify a color-depth of at least 16 bits. This ensures that color graphics appear as intended, with little or no color banding. Finally, make sure that the video card can display the specified resolution and color depth and still achieve a refresh rate of 75 Hz for a CRT monitor or 60 Hz for a LCD monitor. To achieve all these requirements at once requires adequate video memory.

Authors of e-learning require a minimum resolution of 1,280 x 1,024. Many of the authoring tools used today display many windows simultaneously—all of which the author may need to see to be productive. Specify a color depth of at least 16 bits to ensure adequate color fidelity. If the producer will be editing photographs, then specify a color depth of at least 24 bits. Specify a refresh rate of 75 Hz for a CRT monitor. And, you will need graphics acceleration if authors will be editing large, multilayered graphics, animations with transparencies, or three-dimensional models. A 4X rate of acceleration should be adequate.

Video monitor

A well-chosen monitor can make e-learning pleasant. A poorly chosen monitor can make it painful and frustrating.

The video monitor displays what the video card sends it. The characteristics of the monitor parallel those for the video card. You obviously need a monitor that is matched to the capabilities of the video card and vice-versa; otherwise you are wasting money on capabilities nobody will ever see.

 Display can make or break e-learning. Do not expect people to sit in front of a blurry, jittery, grainy display as eyestrain gives way to a migraine.

Physical size

The size of the monitor determines the area of the display in inches or centimeters. Size is usually measured from corner to corner diagonally across the display area. For office work, a 17-inch (approx. 43 cm) monitor is typical. For multimedia authoring, a 21-inch (approx. 53 cm) monitor is common.

Keep in mind that the physical size does not itself determine how many pixels are displayed. It only determines the amount of space available to display pixels. The number of pixels displayed in that space (the resolution of the video card) depends on the relationship between the dot pitch of the monitor and its physical size.

Dot pitch

Dot pitch refers to the spacing of dots on the monitor. Dot pitch is usually stated in fractions of a millimeter. For example, a dot pitch of .25 mm displays 4 dots per millimeter. The higher the number, the more widely spaced the dots.

A lower number (more closely spaced dots) displays smoother edges and lines. It also crowds more information into a smaller area. If the dot pitch is too low, text may not be legible and objects may appear too small to be recognized. Thus, the dot pitch must be small enough to fit the resolution output by the video card onto the physical size of the monitor, yet large enough to be legible.

For those taking e-learning, a moderate dot pitch of 0.27 mm is usually adequate. Those authoring e-learning may need a denser display and want a dot pitch of 0.24 mm.

Type of display

There are two main types of monitor display units: CRTs and LCDs. CRT stands for cathode-ray tube and represents the big heavy boxes with television-like displays. LCD stands for liquid-crystal display and is found on laptops and the thin desktop monitors.

Currently CRT displays (See the example shown at the left.) are less expensive, especially for larger screen sizes. And, the overall image quality may be a bit better and colors more accurate.

LCD monitors are smaller, lighter, and generally brighter. Laptop computers would not be possible without them. They have a couple of other advantages: They do not flicker and their display does not get fuzzy over time. For desktop systems, LCD monitors are dropping in price and gaining favor, largely because they take up only about 10% as much desk space as an equivalent CRT monitor.

 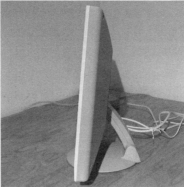

A front view and a side view of an LCD monitor.

For e-learning, either works fine, though cost may be an issue, especially if you need a large display area.

Refresh rate

The *refresh rate* of the monitor is the frequency at which it redraws the screen. This rate should be as fast as or faster than the refresh rate of the video card. In a CRT display, a refresh rate lower than 75 Hz leads to noticeable flicker. If possible, get a monitor with a refresh rate of 85 Hz or higher.

Remember that e-learners and authors of e-learning spend hours staring at a computer screen. Make this time comfortable and productive.

Recommendations

Pick your monitor and video card as a matched set. For those taking e-learning, a medium sized display of 16 inches (approx. 41 cm) with a moderate dot pitch of 0.27 mm should be adequate. Just make sure the monitor can support the resolution and refresh rate you specify for the video card.

For those authoring e-learning, get as large a monitor as you can afford—at least 17 inches (approx. 43 cm) with a dot pitch of 0.24 mm. Again, make sure the monitor supports the resolution and refresh rate specified for the video card. If desk space is limited, opt for an LCD model.

Optical drive: CD-ROM or DVD

Most computers today come with a drive for reading, and perhaps writing, optical discs, such as CD-ROMs and DVDs. The physical size of these discs is standardized, but a large number of different types of discs exist, so it is important to ensure your computer can read and write the ones needed for your purposes.

 CD-ROM stands for Compact Disc-Read Only Memory. DVD stands for Digital Video Disc or Digital Versatile Disc, depending on whom you ask. And CD-RW stands for Compact Disc-Rewriteable.

Since most programs come packaged on CD-ROMs, the ability to read the basic CD-ROM format is almost a requirement today. Much e-learning delivered over a network, however, does not require a CD-ROM. But a CD-ROM is handy for delivering content to those who are not always on a network or for making more media available than can be downloaded conveniently.

Disc formats

Here is a list of optical disc formats and how they might be used in e-learning.

Format	Specifications	Use in taking e-learning	Use in authoring e-learning
CD-ROM	Read-only 650 MB	For media that would take too long to download For e-learning while not connected to the network	Loading authoring programs

Format	Specifications	Use in taking e-learning	Use in authoring e-learning
CD-A (Audio)	Read-only 72 minutes	For music samples in courses about music	Reading in music for use in multimedia
CD-R	Write once and read 700 MB	For submitting assignments too large to transmit by the network	Backing up work files Exchanging files with other developers who are not on the network
CD-RW	Read, write, and rewrite 700 MB	For submitting assignments too large to transmit by the network	Backing up work files Exchanging files with other developers who are not on the network
DVD-ROM	Read-only 4.2 GB	For media that would take too long to download For studying video, film, and music	
DVD-RW (used by most home DVD players)	Read, write, and rewrite 4.2 GB	For submitting assignments with video and other rich media	Backing up work files Exchanging files with other developers not on the network
DVD+RW (allows multi-session recording)	Read, write, and rewrite 4.2 GB	For submitting assignments with video and other rich media	Backing up work files Exchanging files with other developers not on the network

Each drive may support multiple formats. Make sure you know which it can read and write. Also consider the cost of blank recordable and rewriteable discs.

Speed

Burning a disc means recording on it, not throwing it in the fireplace, though that might be the fate it deserves.

CD-ROM drives often specify speed as 24X, 32X, or something else X. These represent multiples of the basic speed at which a CD-audio disc is read; however, the numbers provide only an approximate indicator of actual performance reading data from the disc. For e-learning, any rating over about 12X should suffice.

For those writing (burning) discs, the speed ratings can make a difference in how long it takes to record an entire disc of data. Obviously recording at 12X will take less time than at 8X. For those authoring e-learning, you may want to invest in a disc that writes at a fast speed, so you don't waste hours waiting to back up your day's work or send test files to a client. Obviously if you work in video, the need for speed is even greater.

Recommendations

For those taking e-learning, get a CD-ROM drive. Period. For the near future, a CD-ROM drive is essential equipment. The speed of standard CD-ROM drives is more than adequate for anything learners might do, including accessing audio and video.

For those authoring e-learning, specify a drive that also supports writeable discs (CD-R or CD-RW). If video is a big part of your efforts, splurge on a DVD+RW drive. Pay attention to the speeds at which these drives write, rewrite, and read data. For a CD-R or CD-RW, a write speed of 24X, a rewrite speed of 10X, and a read speed of 40X are adequate.

DVD-RW and DVD+RW drives often read, write, and rewrite CD-R and CD-RW discs. Until DVD formats become more common and standardized, make sure others can read the discs you create.

Audio

Although text and graphics are sufficient for some forms of e-learning, more and more e-learning incorporates elements of sound, music, and voice.

The quality of sound heard by learners is a product of the internal circuitry that converts digital data to analog sound signals and the external speakers that play that sound.

Here is a view from the back of a computer. The boxed area shows the sound-out port for headphones and speakers, the line-in port for powered microphones, and the port for unpowered microphones.

For simple uses of audio, the standard audio capabilities built into even low-cost computers are sufficient for most e-learning. All that is needed are inexpensive speakers. Advanced uses of audio, such as for language or music instruction, may require advanced sound capabilities and sophisticated speakers. Let's look at some of the factors to consider.

Number of speakers

Sound systems produce three-dimensional images of sound by playing slightly different sounds through speakers at different locations near the listener. The first breakthrough in three-dimensional sound occurred as two-channel stereophonic music became popular in the 1960s. Most computer systems today play stereo sound, but other configurations are possible.

▶ **2.1 Channels** – combines a subwoofer with the standard left and right speakers. The subwoofer plays very low frequencies. Because human hearing cannot easily detect the direction of low-frequency sounds, the placement of the subwoofer is not critical.

▶ **4 Channels** – surrounds the listener with left and right speakers in front and left and right speakers behind.

▶ **4.1 Channels** – adds a subwoofer to the four surrounding channels.

▶ **5.1 Channels** – adds a subwoofer and a front-center channel to the standard 4-channel setup.

These configurations are more common for home entertainment and gaming systems than for e-learning. In general, the standard two-channel stereo sound setup is adequate for e-learning.

Some exceptions may occur. For teaching music or for sound effects, a 2.1 channel setup may give higher fidelity reproduction. If the subject matter is film, a 5.1 channel setup may be useful to duplicate the theater sound experience. Immersive, real-time simulations can also benefit from one of the 4+ channel setups that surround the listener.

Power

Most computer sound systems output a signal just powerful enough to play through headphones. For freestanding speakers, the sound must be amplified. That's why most computer speaker sets include an amplifier. The power of the amplifier is customarily rated in watts. These ratings are notoriously unreliable and frequently exaggerated by disreputable vendors. Quality speakers that claim a 20-watt power rating may sound better than lesser speakers that claim a 50-watt rating.

Unless you are teaching rock guitar (which needs to be loud) or classical violin (which needs minimal distortion), a modest power rating should be sufficient.

Headphones

Most people taking e-learning prefer to do so privately. They don't want to share the experience with the whole office. Their cubicle neighbors likewise appreciate the experience not being shared. If sound is part of e-learning, consider providing learners with headphones on which to listen. Consider two types of headphones: high-quality and lightweight.

▶ **High-quality headphones** (pictured) typically feature full ear-muffs that surround the ears. They are more comfortable and block surrounding noise better; however, they are more expensive than lightweight headphones, ranging from $50 to $150 USD.

▶ **Lightweight headphones**, such as those popularized by the Sony Walkman, provide excellent sound quality and fit easily in a briefcase with a laptop. They are quite inexpensive, about $25 USD.

Unless your subject is sound or music, lightweight headphones are adequate for taking e-learning. For creating and editing voice, music, and sound effects, splurge on a good set of high-quality earphones.

 Some corporate e-learners object to wearing headphones, fearing that managers and co-workers will think they are just listening to music. To solve this problem, one training department distributed headphones with a banner that draped across the back of the head, saying "Don't bother me. I'm e-learning."

Microphones

To capture voice and other sounds, you need a good quality microphone. This should be a simple decision, but often it is complicated by the different kinds of audio-in plugs found on computers.

Type plug	Type microphone required
Line-in	Powered microphone
Microphone	Unpowered microphone
USB	USB microphone

A second decision concerns the physical form of the microphone. Common forms of microphones used in e-learning include:

Form of microphone	Use
Hand-held	For high quality recording, especially when fixed to a stand rather than held in the hand.
Headset	Where both headphones and microphone are needed in one package. Especially convenient when the speaker moves about and uses hands. Also good for reducing ambient noise by keeping the microphone positioned close to the mouth.
Lavaliere (pictured below)	For unobtrusively recording the voice of a presenter or interviewee.

Line-in, powered, lavaliere microphone

For those taking e-learning, the standard sound capabilities of standard computers are adequate. Just provide inexpensive, lightweight headphones. There are several exceptions. If the subject is music, film, video, sound, or another subject where the quality of sound is crucial, upgrade the audio system to match that required for the subject. Microphones are not usually needed unless learners are studying a foreign language where they need to record phrases for playback and comparison.

For those authoring e-learning, the audio system should be as good as that required by students. In addition, be sure to provide high-quality headphones.

USB headphone/microphone combo and attached digitizing unit

If authors will be recording small segments of narration, a USB headphone/microphone combination is a good choice. These combos have a digitizing unit at the end of the USB cable where the audio from the microphone is processed directly before being captured by the computer. Because the USB unit processes the sound input, the quality of the sound is not dependent on the computer's own audio circuitry.

Network interface

Computers hooked to a local area network need circuitry to communicate with the network. Such circuitry is called a network interface card (NIC). As a network connection is crucial for e-learning, this is a must-have component for computers not connecting via a modem.

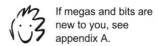 If megas and bits are new to you, see appendix A.

Most enterprise local area networks are Ethernet-based, where users connect by one of these NICs:

▶ **10Base-T** – communicates at 10 megabits per second

▶ **100Base-T** – communicates at 100 megabits per second (Fast Ethernet)

▶ **10/100Base-T** – communicates at 10 or 100 megabits per second depending on the speed of the network

▶ **Gigabit Ethernet** – communicates at 1000 megabits per second

If a NIC is not included with a computer, you can add an inexpensive 10/100Base-T card.

The boxed area shows an RJ45 network connector on the back of a computer. The RJ45 plug is the most common type of Ethernet network connector.

Another local area network technology is Token Ring. It requires a special Token Ring NIC.

On laptops, the NIC may be built into the computer. Otherwise, the most common NIC for laptops is contained in a PCMCIA card (those business card-sized units) which fits into the laptop's PCMCIA slot.

4

Hardware for e-learning

PCMCIA network card for a laptop computer.

PCMCIA = Personal Computer Memory Card International Association. If you call it a "PC card" you'll sound like an IT pro.

For it to work, it must be inserted into the thin slot on the side of the computer.

Modem (Dial-up)

A modem connects a computer to a telephone and thence to e-learning. Dial-up modems convert the digital signals of computers to and from the analog sounds that can be transmitted over phone lines.

The term modem is a contraction of the phrase "modulator/demodulator."

Those squawks, buzzes, and hums when you log onto AOL are the analogous sounds of digital data.

The boxed area on the back of this computer shows the RJ11 port on the modem where the incoming telephone line is connected. You can connect a telephone to the other port.

A modem may be needed for e-learners who take e-learning from computers at home or from laptop computers while traveling.

Protocol

Protocol is just a book of rules about how two devices can communicate over a line. For modems, the protocol determines the effective speed. It specifies such things as who goes first, who listens for whom to finish, how data is compressed, and how errors are recognized and corrected.

Two common protocols are 56K and K56Flex. K56Flex is reportedly a bit better over noisy phone lines. In addition to one of these protocols, your modem should comply with the V.90 standard for transmitting data downstream to modems at 56 Kbps.

 Don't forget to look where they put connectors. If the connectors you frequently change are at the back of your computer and your CD-ROM at the front, you better put the computer on a lazy Susan so you can twirl it back and forth.

Other types of modems

Besides modems for plain old telephone service (POTS), modems are available for connecting to Digital Subscriber Line (DSL) telephone service and to cable TV lines. Modems for these services are typically provided as part of the service.

Recommendations

Remote learners—those taking e-learning from home or while traveling—will likely connect to the Internet or your organization using a modem. If DSL or cable-modem service is available for these remote learners, they will need a network adapter to connect to the DSL or cable-modem unit.

If DSL or cable-modem is not practical, a dial-up modem is needed. For a dial-up modem, select one that uses the 56K or K56Flex protocol and follows the V.90 standard.

Case or form factor

The term *form factor* refers to the size of the box in which the computer is packaged. Common form factors include: full-tower, mid-tower, mini-tower, desktop, and laptop. Some issues to consider in picking a form factor:

▶ **Portability**. Obviously laptop computers are more easily transported than desktop and tower models.

▶ **Footprint**. Tower units take up less surface area than a desktop unit. In addition, mid- and full-tower units can sit on the floor.

▶ **Room for expansion**. Laptops offer little room for adding disk drives and other components. Full-tower units usually have a few slots available for additional cards or bays available for additional disks.

▶ **Cooling**. Larger cases let more air circulate around components. Hence, components run cooler and may last longer.

Keyboard

The standard keyboard that comes with most systems is adequate for authoring and taking e-learning.

If e-learning requires extensive typing, you may want to invest in an ergonomic keyboard, such as Microsoft's Natural Keyboard. In any case, you want a keyboard with a responsive, comfortable feel and spring to the keys. Be careful with some ultra-small laptops with nonstandard keyboard layouts.

The Sony Vaio Z505 (pictured at left), for example, has a half-sized Shift key on the right side of the keyboard. The lack of a regular sized Shift key frustrates touch typists.

 I'd rather type on the heads of rattlesnakes.

 I love my teensy, tiny computer.

Mouse or other pointing device

For most e-learning, the basic mouse that comes with most systems is adequate. The same is true for the touchpad or finger-stick used on laptop models. If you want to upgrade, though, consider an optical mouse—no mouse balls to clean! Some people prefer a trackball, feeling it reduces fatigue and strain on the wrist.

For those authoring graphics, you may want a stylus-tablet that makes drawing more like using a pencil.

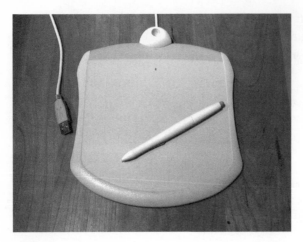

A stylus-tablet that connects to a computer's USB port.

 A stylus-tablet is great for drawing on slides and whiteboards in collaboration tools.

Video camera

Video cameras capture video that can be used directly for video conferencing or edited to produce video presentations. In choosing a video camera, you need to consider how you will use the video and how the computer imports video.

Type camera

Two main types of cameras should be considered.

- ▶ **Video conferencing camera**. A small video camera that sits atop the user's monitor to capture their face in video conferencing sessions.

- ▶ **Camcorder**. A contraction of camera and recorder, the camcorder both captures and records video. A camcorder can also feed live or recorded video into the computer.

The video conferencing camera records a small video image adequate for use in presentations and video conferencing sessions. Such cameras are relatively inexpensive.

A video conferencing camera connected to a computer's USB port.

Camcorders record higher quality video than video conferencing cameras. They are common and vary widely in price and quality.

A camcorder connected to a computer's IEEE 1394 port.

4

Hardware for e-learning

Type of connection

There are several ports, or types of connections, through which video can be sent to the computer.

Type of connection	Works for
IEEE 1394 (Firewire, iLink)	Importing digital video and controlling video recorders, such as those from Sony, that have an IEEE 1394 connector.
USB	Importing video from USB video conferencing cameras.
TV-In	Capturing analog video from analog video cameras, televisions, and VCRs. Capturing analog video requires a special video-capture card.

Recommendations

For capturing talking-head videos of presenters or learners in video conferencing activities, get an inexpensive USB video conferencing camera.

For serious video production, get a digital camcorder equipped with an IEEE 1394 interface. Note: Sony calls this interface iLink; Apple Computer calls it Firewire.

Ports

Ports are the plugs on the front, back, and sometimes sides of the computer through which the computer connects to accessories, networks, and other devices.

As an example, here are the locations of the various ports on the back of a Sony PCV-RX600N computer.

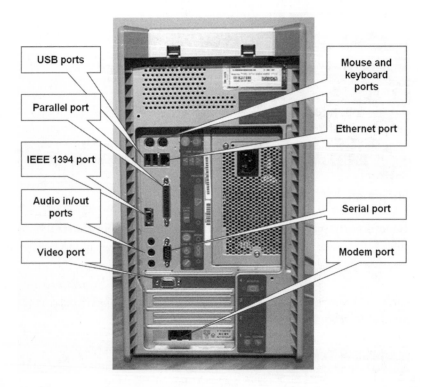

Some ports have been covered already, but there are others you should know about.

	General use	Use in e-learning
USB	Connecting Universal Serial Bus (USB) keyboards, microphones, scanners, cameras, and other devices	Connecting cameras and microphones for conferencing activities Capturing media for authoring
TV-Out	Displaying video on a large-screen television	Editing conventional video

Infrared	Communicating with laptop computers and other mobile devices, typically to synchronize data on the two devices	Loading lessons onto a mobile device
Serial	Connecting to older devices that do not have a USB connection	Loading lessons onto an older device
Parallel	Connecting a printer or scanner	Printing out lessons for reading offline

OTHER FACTORS IN PICKING HARDWARE

When specifying computer hardware, you need to consider factors beyond technical capabilities. These factors include warranty, support, service, and upgradeability.

Warranty

Warranties vary widely in what they cover and for how long they run. When purchasing a computer, be sure to read the warranty information carefully. The warranty may cover all parts, labor, and shipping; just parts and labor; or just certain parts. The warranty usually does not cover components installed after the computer was manufactured. The warranty period may be as little as 90 days to as long as 3 years. Individual components or add-ons you purchase have their own warranty coverage. Manufacturers also vary in the speed and cheerfulness with which they honor warranties.

Support

After the warranty, look at your support options. Where can you get help when something goes wrong?

The first place to look is the hardware manufacturer's Web site—not the online retailer from whom you may have purchased the unit. Find the customer support page and look for support options such as:

▶ **Telephone number** where you can obtain 24x7 support. Note whether the number is toll-free or not. Telephone access charges can add up while you wait for your turn with a support specialist. Also, notice whether the telephone support is free. If so, for how long? If you plan to buy large numbers of the vendor's products, you should investigate the costs of unlimited phone support. Many vendors have some kind of subscription service for their corporate clients.

▶ **Support Web site** where you can find a list of Frequently Asked Questions and can search the vendor's online database for the problem you are experiencing. You may want to test the quality of the support site. For instance, look for the answer to a common question like "What kind of memory does my computer have?" What initially looks like a great support site may be a little thin in detailed information. Look for upgrades and patches for factory-installed components. Customer-centered vendors are continually posting upgrades and enhancements as they discover problems.

▶ **Discussion forum** moderated by the vendor's technical support department, where customers can ask questions and get advice. You can learn a lot about a product just by reading postings in such a discussion forum.

Service

Another big issue to resolve is where you must go to get service. For laptops, it is customary for the vendor to send an empty, preaddressed air-freight box in which you can return the laptop for repair. How can you handle larger units? Do you have to transport or ship them somewhere or will a service technician come to your location? Do you have to ship it to the manufacturer in the original box? You can usually locate this information on the vendor's support Web site.

Another service issue is whether parts are available for past models, especially for things people damage or lose. This is a common need for laptop owners because laptops frequently come with peripherals like a floppy disk drive or CD-ROM drive. And laptops often have special connectors for video out, video in, and network connections. These peripherals and connectors can be damaged or lost.

Upgradeability

Computers that may not be adequate for e-learning can often be tweaked, tuned up, and tricked out to work just fine for e-learning duties. Often an upgrade of key components can add a couple of years to the useful life of a faithful box. Upgradeable components may include memory, disk drives, ports, and processors.

Memory

Increasing the amount of memory is probably the most performance-enhancing upgrade you can perform. When you purchase a computer it comes with memory.

However, it may not come with all the memory it can accommodate. For example, you might purchase a computer with 512 MB of memory; however, the computer may be upgradeable to 1 GB of memory.

To upgrade memory, you need to know how much memory the computer currently has, the maximum amount it can accommodate, the number of banks or slots that are available, whether any banks are free, and the sizes of memory that each bank can hold. Suppose you have a computer that has 512 MB of memory provided by four banks all occupied with 128 MB chips. The computer is upgradeable to 1 GB. To upgrade, you would need to replace the existing 128 MB chips with 256 MB chips.

Upgrading memory requires opening the case of the computer and using nonmagnetic tools on an antistatic surface. Unless you love this sort of thing, a computer repair technician can handle the installation for you.

Additional disk drives

Adding more storage space to a computer can certainly extend its usefulness. Computers with larger cases usually have multiple bays where you can add an additional hard drive, optical drive, etc. To add a drive, you need to know the size of the bay (for instance, full- or half-sized), whether there is a connector power plug available inside the case, and the kind of interface the connector supports. Like installing memory, adding a disk drive requires opening the case and you may want to engage the services of a repair technician to do the installation.

USB and IEEE 1394 ports for peripherals

You can add Universal Serial Bus (USB) or IEEE 1394 ports to older computers that don't have them by installing the necessary cards. Such cards fit into slots on the computer's main circuit board and their ports come through the back of the computer so that you can easily add the new type USB or IEEE 1394 devices.

Before purchasing such cards, you need to know whether there are slots available, what kind of slots they are, and whether your operating system can support these devices. Again, find a good computer technician to help you determine your needs and capabilities.

Processor

If you're the kind of person who swells with pride when called a computer geek, upgrading the CPU may be an option. You can add a year or two of life to a favorite computer by upgrading its processor.

 You can call me "geek," "geekette," or "Her royal geekness."

However, it is not always a simple matter. You may find that other components are not compatible with the new and faster processor.

It is somewhat easier to add a processor to a multiprocessor workstation. Some high-end workstations like those used for rendering three-dimensional graphics, for example, can often have more than one processor. You may choose to spend less money initially by purchasing the workstation with only one processor. Later, when the processor price drops, you can install the second or even third to increase the workstation's efficiency and speed. As long as you add the specified kind of processor, you seldom have to be concerned about component compatibility.

SERVER HARDWARE

This chapter, however, does not expressly cover purchasing computers to run Web servers, database servers, collaboration servers, and other server systems. The needs of server machines to host e-learning are different from the needs of computers for authoring and accessing e-learning.

The purchase of server machines is a strategic decision best made with ample involvement by IT specialists. Use this book to decide what software the servers should run. Once you have made your software decisions, you can discuss hardware requirements with your organization's IT staff or hardware vendor. No doubt they will want to know the answers to the following questions, which can guide your discussions on what server hardware to purchase.

▶ **How much content must you host**? What is the number and sizes of files to reside on your server?

▶ **What file formats must you serve**? Are most of your files text and simple graphics? Or, do you need to deliver video and audio as well?

▶ **What will be the rate of access**? What load will e-learning impose on the server? At what rate will learners request files from the server?

▶ **How will your requirements grow**? What will be your needs next year and the one after that?

▶ **Will the server need to run programs**, such as Perl scripts, Active Server Pages, or JavaServer Pages?

▶ **Do you have special reliability concerns**? What would be the consequences if a server drops out in the middle of a final exam?

Chapter 8 on Web server software discusses the relationship between server hardware and software for offering e-learning.

WHAT NOW?

Until you have picked your software, you cannot make a final decision on hardware. You can get started, though, by cataloging the computer hardware in place. Using this chapter as a guide:

1 Identify the types of computers possessed by learners and authors of e-learning.

2 Group these computers by types of machines with similar capabilities. You may, for example, identify a few types of desktop computers and a few types of laptop computers.

3 Catalog the specific technical capabilities of each of these types of computers, using the criteria in this chapter.

4 As you identify software you need, compare its requirements to the capabilities possessed by existing hardware. Note the gaps.

5 Decide how to close those gaps. Consider whether to pick other software to match your hardware, whether to upgrade existing hardware, or whether to purchase new hardware.

Now that you have a good understanding of the hardware needed to create and access e-learning, it is time to move on and talk about networks. Networks provide the pathways along which your e-learning travels. Many design opportunities as well as design constraints are imposed by the speed and capacity of these pathways.

5 Networks for e-learning

Networks are the pathways along which e-learning travels. Without them you would not be able to read a file from a server, share documents with remote team members, send or receive e-mail, or experience the vast resources of the Internet.

This chapter won't make you a network engineer or qualify you to play one on TV, but it will help you talk to network engineers. It will introduce you to the terms, concepts, and issues necessary to understand the possibilities and limitations networks offer for your e-learning solutions.

IN THE BEGINNING WAS SNEAKERNET

Before there was a computer on every desk, most of us (who are old enough to remember) sent memos, distributed documents, and shared photocopied cartoons of a politically incorrect nature by putting them in a big, tan interoffice envelope with the recipient's name printed neatly (or otherwise) on the next available line. This distribution of information by hand has in hindsight been dubbed *SneakerNet*—ironic, huh?

Even though networked computers are now ubiquitous, many small organizations still use SneakerNet. In small organizations, workers may have a computer on their desk, but these computers may not be connected to each other. When the employees need to transfer computer files to one another, they copy them to floppy disk or writeable CD-ROM and "walk" them to their destination.

 Take this chapter in little bites. I'm an engineer, I've got a computer science degree, and I've been fooling with computers for over 30 years. Still, I move my lips when I read this chapter. This stuff is technical.

Let's go beyond SneakerNet and see how networking can benefit our e-learning endeavors. First, we'll talk about the various kinds of networks. Then we will look at how networks are built, going from the simplest workgroup network to a multinational enterprise connected to the Internet. We will also talk about mobile learners and the special issues they pose. Finally, we will turn to wireless networks to see how they fit.

TYPES OF NETWORKS

Networks come in three sizes: small, large, and literally global. Each scale of network uses somewhat different technologies. The three sizes are more properly called local area networks (LANs), wide area networks (WANs), and the Internet.

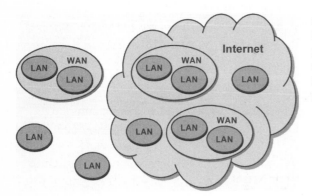

Some potential connections among LANs, WANs, and the Internet.

LANs may exist alone or as part of a wide area network. These WANs, likewise, may stand alone or may be part of the Internet.

Local area networks are the smallest units. LANs serve individual workgroups, departments, and small businesses. WANs serve sprawling corporations, universities, government agencies, and other organizations with widely scattered offices and facilities. There is only one Internet, hence the honorific "the" and the capital "I." As far as global networks go, the Internet is pretty much the only player, at least in the inner solar system.

Let's look at each of these types of network and what technologies they use. We'll start small.

Local area networks

A *local area network* typically consists of workstations, servers, printers, and other equipment that are joined together by a common communications link and that are shared by the members of a workgroup, a department, or a small office. For example, in our office we have eight workstations, two file servers for storing common data files, a separate print server with two printers attached, and a printer connected directly to the network.

And why, pray tell, does a two-person company need so much hardware?

The main LAN technologies are Ethernet and Token Ring. Token Ring and Ethernet require different cables, hubs, switches, and other equipment. A Token Ring LAN can be connected to an Ethernet LAN, but components of the two types cannot be mixed on a single LAN. Let's consider the merits and place of each.

Ethernet

Ethernet (also known as IEEE 802.3) is the most extensively used network technology. The most widely installed Ethernet systems are called 10BASE-T and provide transmission speeds up to 10 megabits per second. 100BASE-T is faster and provides transmission speeds up to 100 megabits per second. Even faster is Gigabit Ethernet which enables speeds up to 1000 megabits per second. And, yes, there is an even faster type of system called 10-Gigabit Ethernet with transmission speeds up to 10,000 megabits per second.

Token Ring

Token Ring, also known as IEEE 802.5, is the second-most widely used network technology. Elements on the network are joined together in a ring or star arrangement. (The technical term for the pattern of connections among computers is *topology*.) To send information to another computer on this network, the computer sending the information must first have the "token," or the right to send information. This token rotates among machines on the network. As soon as the sending computer receives notification that the information has been received, it passes the token to the next computer down the line.

Wide area networks

WANs typically connect separate offices and other remote locations within a university or company using T-1 and T-3 telecommunications lines or ISDN (Integrated Services Digital Network) carrier lines. These high-speed lines may be owned outright by the enterprise or leased from a telecommunications carrier (what we used to call a phone company). External learners may be connected to the WAN through a virtual private network, or VPN. We will talk later about T-1, T-3, ISDN, and VPN when we discuss connecting external users.

The Internet

The Internet is a social phenomenon, a global party, an obsession, the biggest time-waster ever, and an economic breakthrough. Yet at a less philosophical level, it is just cables and chips connecting hundreds of millions of computers. The name Internet can be thought of as a contraction for "inter-network network." That is, the Internet connects the separate LANs, WANS, and individual computers of universities, corporations, research institutes, government agencies, and private citizens into something approaching the scale of the global telephone network.

The network technology of the Internet is just a few steps larger and faster than that of a WAN. What makes the Internet work is not so much routers, switches, and a gadzillion kilometers of fiber-optic cables, but a bunch of bacterium-sized gnomes peering down the optical fibers and using semaphore flags to transmit and route our e-mail and Web pages.

These gnomes carry out a protocol called TCP/IP. That stands for Transmission Control Protocol/Internet Protocol. *Protocol* is a fancy word for rules of conduct. TCP/IP spells out how a Mac in Malaysia can send data to an ancient VAX in Venezuela or a UNIX server in Uganda, or to a Windows machine in Westphalia— and actually expect the data to thread its way across dozens of separate connections, detour around broken switches, and leap national boundaries to get there.

The next time you get an e-mail message from your sweetie or download a music clip, thank the Cold War. You see, TCP/IP evolved out of attempts by the U.S. Defense Advanced Research Projects Agency (DARPA) to invent a network that military commanders could use to send teletype messages to one another after nuclear war had turned most of the network into dust in the stratosphere. Such an expectation imposes some tough requirements for reliability and redundancy—just the thing if you want to build a global network that won't crash every time someone sends an e-mail with a typo or somebody trips over a power cord. TCP is so important, we'll tell you more about it later in this chapter.

PRIVATE NETWORKS

Now that you have mastered some basic concepts, let's look at what it takes to build networks of the types needed to create and offer e-learning. We will start with a simple network connecting two computers and a printer and work up through a multinational WAN.

A minimal network

The first network is simple. It connects two computers and a printer. Yet it lets you try out most of the concepts of networking.

Simple network connecting two computers (via a CAT-5 cable) and a printer (via a printer cable).

To connect two computers with network cards running the same operating system, all you generally need is a CAT-5 cross-over cable. CAT-5 is short for Category-5 unshielded twisted pair (UTP) cable and it is the basic cabling that connects most computers and other devices, at least within a single office. A cross-over cable differs from a straight-through cable in that the wires cross over one another from one end of the cable to the other. You can visually identify a cross-over cable by putting the RJ-45 connectors at each end side-by-side and comparing the sequence of colored wires. If the sequence is different, it is a cross-over cable.

To add a printer to this network, simply connect the printer to one of the computers using the printer port and designate it as a shared printer. Voila! You now have a peer-to-peer network, often abbreviated P2P. This simplicity is possible because each computer's operating system (Windows 98, Windows 2000, Windows XP, Mac OS X, etc.) has a networking component called a Network Operating System, or NOS, which controls the flow of data between the computers.

Though simple, this network has some practical uses in e-learning. You could use it to test e-learning. One computer could play the role of the server and the other, the role of the learner's machine. This network is also a good test bed for experimenting with networking concepts without endangering the whole Internet.

A network for e-learning developers

You probably need to connect more than two computers. Let's say you must set up a network for a small e-learning development group. This network will accommodate four developers with computers, a printer, and some kind of network storage device for project files and backups.

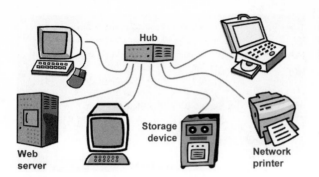

A simple network for developing e-learning. All devices are connected through a central hub.

Now that the network involves more than two devices, or nodes, you need a hub to connect each node or item on the network. A *hub* is like the hub of a wheel. It takes the data that comes into a port (a connection point on the hub) and sends it out to all the other ports on the hub. It doesn't perform any filtering or redirection of data at all.

As you can see, the printer is connected directly to the hub. This is because it is equipped with a network interface card. Like the previous example, this is also a peer-to-peer network because each computer shares its resources with others on its network.

Finally, you might add a Web server, that is, a computer running a Web hosting service like Microsoft's Internet Information Server. How does this change the network?

Computers on this network can still share resources among themselves. But, with the Web server available, developers are able to upload e-learning Web content to a test site on the server, and view it by typing the address of the Web site into the address box of a browser. Testing on a Web server is essential if the e-learning content uses any server-side scripting such as Active Server Pages (ASP) or JavaServer Pages (JSP).

Behind the scenes, this network exchanges data using TCP/IP, which is required by the Web server.

A computer lab

At some point, you may need to set up a computer lab where students can come and take e-learning courses. You don't want the individual computers on this network to share resources among themselves. Rather, you want them to draw resources from a central shared server. Now you need to go beyond a peer-to-peer approach and take a client-server approach.

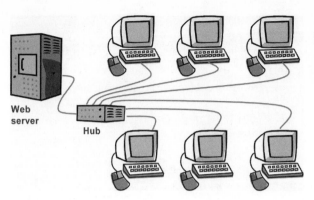

Network for a computer lab. Students' machines (clients) connect to a Web server through a hub. The e-learning content resides on the server, and the individual workstations have permission to access that content.

5

Networks for e-learning

With a client-server approach, common files, applications, and other resources are stored on a centrally located, high-speed server. The workstations, or clients, request resources and processing from the server. A client-server approach is very efficient, but it requires special software for the server as well as for the client machines. Typical network operating systems that support this approach are Windows NT and Novell NetWare. This approach also requires setting up the necessary permissions and shared directories.

If the e-learning consists of Web content, the server can run special Web-hosting software, and the individual workstations can access that content using installed browsers (clients).

Up to this point, we have been discussing very self-contained networks. Now we're going to see what it takes to connect these self-contained networks to each other and to the Internet.

A small-organization LAN

Putting together a local area network for a small business requires joining smaller network segments or clusters together.

This network consists of workstations, printers, and other network devices clustered around hubs, which connect to a central switch. A switch is more sophisticated than a hub. In larger organizations it is

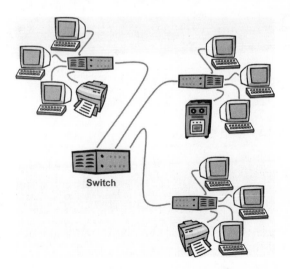

LAN for an organization with several departments. Separate network clusters are connected through a central switch.

commonly used in place of a hub as well as at the junction of two network segments. A switch differs from a hub in that each port can transmit data at the same rate as the entire network. If the network speed is 100 Mbps, then the transfer speed from the node to its port on the switch will be 100 Mbps (theoretically, that is). Switches are commonly used to connect all of the department-level hubs on the same network segment.

Large-organization WAN

Now we are going to go one step further in our survey of private networks and take a look at an organization that has a wide area network.

This diagram should look familiar. The part to the right, labeled "Home office" is the LAN discussed earlier. Each branch office uses the same hub-centered cluster. What's new are the connections among these separate LANs. At first it may seem a bit overwhelming, but don't shut down your neural network. We'll explain these new components gently.

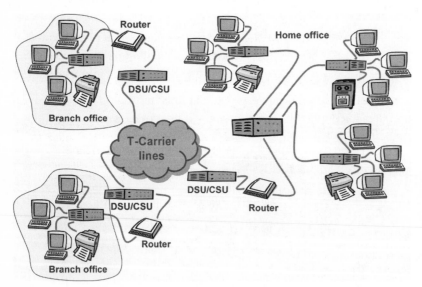

Here is a wide area network connecting home and branch offices through T-Carrier lines.

The DSU/CSU (Data Service Unit/Channel Service Unit) translates the digital data from the LAN into a format that the T-Carrier line can transmit—and vice versa. It is sometimes called a CSU/DSU.

Joining the LANs of these separate locations are T-Carrier lines. These telecommunications lines are leased or rented from a telephone company and are for the exclusive use of this organization.

A *router* is a device placed at the entrance to a network. For instance, in this example the router is placed between the T-Carrier's DSU/CSU and the start of the office's LAN, signified by the switch. Like all the other devices discussed in this section, routers ensure that data arrives at the correct location. Routers move packets between network segments.

Routers often include the features of a firewall—especially those used at the access point to the Internet—to protect the network from unauthorized access and dangerous content. They may examine the origin of a packet of data and determine if it is allowed to be routed onto certain LANs

So, if a workstation in a branch office wants to access a Web page stored on a home-office server, that request travels through the branch office's hub, out to its router and DSU/CSU, onto the T-Carrier lines, over rivers, through woods, under oceans, off a couple of satellites, onward to the DSU/CSU of the home office, through the home office's router and switch, which directs it to the hub connected to the Web server holding the page requested by the branch office (phew!). The page is delivered by retracing the route of the request. The e-world has come a long way from SneakerNet.

An intranet

An *intranet* is like an internal Internet within an organization. Web servers are connected to the LAN and serve Web pages in the same way as Web servers serve pages on the Internet. However, these Web pages are only available to computers on the LAN—unless special arrangements are made. We will discuss this in the section on connecting external users.

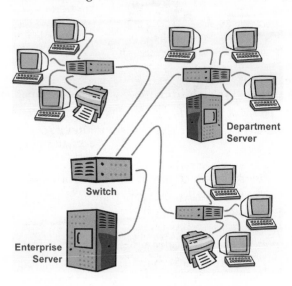

Department Server

Switch

Enterprise Server

Typical intranet. It contains a departmental Web server connected to a department's hub and an enterprise Web server connected to a switch serving the whole enterprise. Content on the department server is typically private to that department, while content on the enterprise server is available to all on the network.

Because intranets use the same protocols and file formats as the Internet, users on an intranet can make use of the rich collaborative environment made possible by Internet technology. If it is possible on the Internet, it is possible on an intranet. For instance, departments can have their own servers in addition to a server shared with the rest of the enterprise. Employees can collaborate using tools like NetMeeting, PlaceWare, and others. Enterprises can easily implement internal e-mail. Intranets enable training departments to offer Web-based e-learning to teach proprietary information because the content is kept safe within the organization's LAN.

An extranet

An *extranet* is a private network that an organization makes accessible to people outside the organization, for example, its customers, partners, vendors, or alumni. People with access to the extranet do not automatically gain access to the organization's intranet.

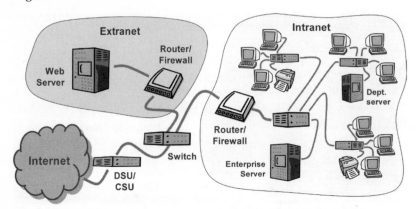

Typical extranet connected to the intranet and the Internet by a shared switch.

An extranet, like an intranet, uses Internet protocols. The difference is that an extranet is separate from an organization's LAN. Think of it as living just outside the drawbridge of the castle. It is clearly associated with the castle but not within its protective walls.

Extranets are commonly used by organizations to share information, like e-learning, with customers, vendors, and other partners. As such, extranets are protected with firewalls and require users to be authenticated.

Although authentication schemes vary, remote users typically access extranets using the virtual private network protocols discussed later in this chapter.

CONNECTING TO THE INTERNET

Up till now, we have been looking at networks isolated from the outside, public world. Such networks are adequate for e-learning within a community connected to that network. But what's the fun in that when there is a whole wide wonderful world outside?

Most networks are connected in some manner to the Internet. So too are most potential e-learners. In this section we are going to look at the various ways of connecting to the Internet and what each implies for people who want to create, offer, and access e-learning through these connections.

First you need an Internet service provider

In addition to the telecommunications conduits and equipment discussed earlier, you need an account with an Internet service provider (ISP) to access the Internet. An ISP acts as a tollgate between the Internet and individuals and organizations who want to connect to it. ISPs have the equipment and the telecommunication line access required to be a point-of-presence (POP), or access point, on the Internet for the geographic area they serve.

EarthLink is an ISP as well as AT&T Broadband, Juno, AOL, and MSN. In addition to these giants, there are many smaller, local companies that provide specific services to their geographic region.

Very large organizations—IBM, AT&T, MIT, and the like—are their own ISPs. That is, they connect their networks directly to the Internet. For people within these organizations, the IT department fills the role of an ISP.

So, how do you get from your computer or network to one of these ISPs? Read on!

Ways of connecting to the Internet

To reach your ISP and gain access to the content available on the Internet, you need a telecommunications connection. A connection can be as simple as a telephone line or as sophisticated as a microwave tower. These connections are crucial because they determine the speed, frequency, and ease with which learners can take e-learning. Let's consider some common types of connections from slow to fast.

Plain old telephone service

Worldwide, the majority of computers connect to the Internet through a telephone line using a dial-up modem. Though faster means of access are available in universities and corporate offices, the modem still rules for travelers and home users, especially those outside the U.S. and Canada. Many organizations with speedy networks have learned that their staff members frequently take e-learning remotely using dial-up modems—mostly from home computers and from laptops on the road.

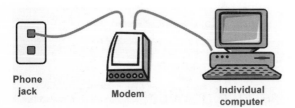

Individual computer connecting to the plain old telephone service (POTS) through a dial-up modem.

Phone jack   **Modem**   **Individual computer**

A dial-up modem converts the digitally encoded information from the computer into an analog form that can travel along the telephone lines and vice versa. Many modern computers have modems already installed inside their cases. Modems can also be standalone devices (like the one in the diagram below) that connect to a communications port on a computer (USB port, IEEE 1394 port, or serial port).

Modem speeds are measured in kilobits per second. The most common dial-up modem speed is 56.6 Kbps. We will talk more about the speed of modems when we discuss computing network transmission rates later in this chapter.

Integrated Services Digital Network

Another way to connect to the Internet is through an Integrated Services Digital Network (ISDN). ISDN transmits digital voice and data signals over the same kind of copper telephone wire as a regular modem, but at speeds up to 128 Kbps.

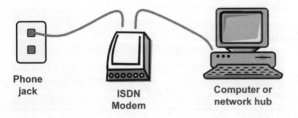

Computer or network connected to an ISP through an ISDN modem.

Phone jack   **ISDN Modem**   **Computer or network hub**

This setup requires an ISDN modem (more correctly called an *adapter*) to negotiate the connection between the computer or network and the ISDN line.

Although the diagram shows a single computer connecting by ISDN, the ISDN modem could be connected to a hub or switch to link an entire network to the Internet.

 You're asking, "If ISDN uses digital technology, why do I need a modem?" The term *modem* has become more generic and is used to describe just about any interface device that serves as a go-between for a single computer or an entire network and the Internet.

ISDN is a somewhat antiquated technology because most individuals prefer to take advantage of the superior transmission rates available from cable TV providers.

Cable television

Moving up the speed ladder, we have cable television, or CATV (community antenna television). A computer or computer network can be connected to the Internet via the same coaxial cable that carries the hundreds of TV channels. Making this connection requires a cable modem. The cable modem separates and manages the Internet data and converts incoming data to digital signals and outgoing data to radio frequency signals.

 E-learning? Yeah, right! The real reason for a cable modem is to watch sports and soap operas.

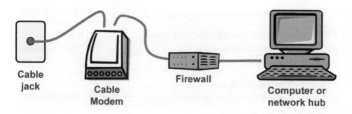

Cable jack

Cable Modem

Firewall

Computer or network hub

Computer or network connected to an ISP through a cable modem. The firewall protects the computer from evildoers on the Internet.

Unlike the previous access methods, cable access is always available, that is, the user does not dial up to their service provider each time they want to surf the Internet. Because they are always connected to the Internet, malicious users or hackers can gain access to their computer or entire computer network. To minimize this risk, many cable modem customers take some kind of protective measures. One of the most common of these measures is to use a firewall—named for the extra thick walls that separate townhouses and apartments to prevent the spread of fire. We will discuss firewalls in more detail a little later in this chapter.

Cable television connections offer potential download speeds from between 27 Mbps (highly optimistic) and 1.5 Mbps (most likely) and upload speeds between 2.5 Mbps (highly optimistic) and 256 Kbps (most likely). These speeds make cable modems an attractive option for many individuals and small businesses who already have cable television.

Cable access to the Internet does come with one important restriction: Most cable companies will not allow you to put an Internet server on their networks. Cable modems thus work well for accessing e-learning but not for offering e-learning.

Digital Subscriber Line

A Digital Subscriber Line, or DSL for short, is a high-speed connection that uses the same wires as a regular telephone line, like ISDN. Unlike ISDN it is always on.

As with the other access conduits we have discussed, a modem is needed between the phone line and the individual workstation or network to filter and manage the network traffic. Here's a diagram showing how a network might connect to the Internet using DSL.

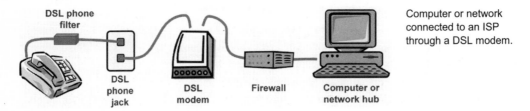

DSL phone filter

DSL phone jack

DSL modem

Firewall

Computer or network hub

Computer or network connected to an ISP through a DSL modem.

If the same DSL line is used for computer data and telephone calls, you need to place a DSL filter on the telephone line. Its purpose is to filter out the electronic noise caused by the digital data traveling along the same line.

Also notice that there is a firewall connected between the DSL router and the rest of the network. Like cable, DSL is always on. Therefore, it is important to take active measures to thwart hackers.

DSL comes in two main varieties: asynchronous and synchronous. These terms refer to whether data travels upstream (to the Internet) and downstream (to your computer or network) at the same transmission rate. Most individuals and small business will likely select asynchronous DSL (ADSL) because they can use the same line for Internet connection and for regular voice calls. Large organizations, on the other hand, are more likely to lease T-1 or T-3 lines discussed later.

How fast is DSL? Well, downstream rates are between 256 Kbps and 7.1 Mbps. Upstream rates are typically between 256 Kbps and 1.5 Mbps. However, DSL is distance-sensitive. That means that the shorter the distance between the DSL modem and the DSL service provider's DSL access multiplexer (DSLAM), the faster the transmission rates subscribers can potentially experience. For instance, our office is very close to a DSLAM; therefore, we have very fast ADSL service with download speeds of 1.2 Mbps and upload speeds of 1.1 Mbps.

DSL is superb for accessing e-learning and adequate for small organizations offering e-learning and performing other lightweight Internet access.

T-Carrier system

The T-Carrier system is an international digital telecommunications network. T-Carrier lines connect to the rest of the LAN through a DSU/CSU or Network Interface device.

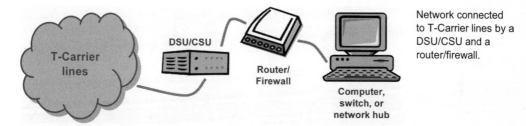

Network connected to T-Carrier lines by a DSU/CSU and a router/firewall.

Two common levels of the T-Carrier system are T-1 and T-3. A T-1 line has a maximum transmission rate of 1.5 Mbps. It is made up of 24 channels of 64 Kbps per channel. A T-3 line can transmit up to 44.7 Mbps using 672 channels of 64 Kbps each. T-Carrier lines are always on, are synchronous (or full-duplex), and speeds do not degrade over distance.

T-1 and T-3 lines are commonly used for connecting ISPs to the Internet. They are also leased by organizations with large bandwidth needs. For instance, an organization may host streaming video content from their own servers to a large number of simultaneous viewers. To ensure a positive experience for their viewers, they would need the kind of bandwidth available through a T-3 line.

What does bandwidth mean? Bandwidth originally referred to the width of the band of radio frequencies used to transmit a signal. The wider that band of frequencies, the more data got through. The term also triggers a telling visual analogy. Imagine a marching band. If it parades single-file past a certain point, it will take longer for the whole band to go by than if the band marches ten abreast. Marching ten abreast makes the band wider, hence it has greater bandwidth.

Smaller organizations with smaller bandwidth requirements can lease fractional T-1 or T-3 lines. That is, they can rent a fraction of the available channels. These fractional T-Carrier lines are sometimes called point-to-point lines because they connect the organization to a service provider or directly to the Internet if the organization serves as its own ISP.

Why might an organization choose a T-Carrier line over a DSL line with similar transmission rates? The main reason is that leased T-1 or T-3 lines are seldom shared with other customers. All the bandwidth you rent is yours to use, and it is not affected by distance from some particular location.

Still faster connections

Every month we could add to this list of connection methods. Gigabit Ethernet is coming online, large corporations are leasing Optical Carrier, and universities are tapping into the Internet2 backbone.

 At the end of this chapter is a list of theoretical network speeds for various connection types.

Since decisions on WAN and Internet connections are usually beyond the duties of most e-learning professionals, you just need to be familiar with the technologies and have an appreciation of their relative speeds.

Firewalls

Firewalls minimize the danger that hackers, viruses, worms, or other undesirables will gain unauthorized access to your network. This danger is greatest with "always-on" connections, like DSL, cable-television, and T-Carrier lines. Firewalls can be implemented in software or hardware.

Software firewalls

Software firewalls run as a program on individual computers and examine data coming through a network connection, allowing or disallowing the data depending on filters or parameters defined in the program. Software firewalls are most effective for individual computers connecting to the Internet rather than for networks. Firewall programs are part of some computer operating systems. They are also readily available from many third-party vendors.

Hardware firewalls

For networks with multiple computers and servers, hardware firewalls are commonly used. Like the software version, they filter data coming from the Internet and allow it to pass based on rules the network administrator sets in the firewall's programming. For instance, some network administrators may not allow Shockwave Flash files to be downloaded from a Web site. Or users may be forbidden to use the audio or video features of Microsoft Messenger when communicating with users outside their LAN.

Another feature of many firewalls is that they mask information about the networks they protect, that is, they act as a proxy or stand-in for all the computers on that network. For example, when computers behind a firewall make requests for Internet resources, those requests are sent to the firewall. The proxy services software of the firewall retrieves the requested data and then sends the data back to the requesting computer. To all, requests for data appear to be coming from only one Internet address—the address of the firewall.

Hardware firewalls exist as dedicated devices. But more commonly, features found in these dedicated devices are being incorporated into other devices such as routers.

Implications for e-learning

Firewalls can protect e-learners and e-learning content. They can also thwart effective teaching techniques and frustrate e-learners. To support e-learning, the firewall must be set up so it does not block media needed for e-learning. Firewalls may be set to block:

▶ Video, audio, and other "heavy" media whose bandwidth requirements could swamp a network.

▶ Programs learners must download, for example, simulations or trial versions of software.

▶ Media used in conferencing: video, audio, whiteboard, application sharing.

▶ File formats that contain embedded programs or macros, for example, Microsoft Word or PowerPoint.

▶ Files blocked for legal concerns. Some universities blocked MP3 files for fear students were violating copyright laws by downloading files through Napster and other file-swapping sites.

Keep in mind that firewalls may exist at the site offering e-learning and at the site taking e-learning. You may not be able to change both of them to suit your mix of media. We suggest you sit down with the firewall administrator for your organization and work out rules both of you can live with.

THE WONDER OF TCP/IP

TCP/IP, that unpronounceable jumble of characters, is the magic that makes the Internet possible. Also known as Transmission Control Protocol/Internet Protocol, TCP/IP is the communication language of the Internet as well as many LANs. This language is composed of two parts. The TCP portion specifies how data is disassembled into packets for transmission along the network and reassembled again at the correct destination. The IP portion specifies how each packet is addressed so that it arrives as the correct destination.

In this segment we will talk about IP addresses, domain names, and protocols—all the terms you need to be familiar with when you talk to your ISP or your IT department.

IP addresses

Every computer, server, or refrigerator on the Internet has a unique identifier called an IP address. Like a postal address or telephone number, an IP address is globally unique. If you want to contact us at William Horton Consulting, you could write us at 838 Spruce Street, Boulder, Colorado 80302 USA or ring us at +1.303.545.6964. Or you could contact us at 206.168.70.4, the equally unique IP address of our Web site.

IP addresses are written in dotted decimal notation, which is a shorthand way of expressing binary numbers. For instance, the IP address for one of our Web sites is 206.168.70.4. Without dotted decimal notation, the same IP address would look like this: 11001110101010000100011000000100. Try reading that to someone over the telephone.

So where do you go to get an IP address? If you are an individual or a small- to medium-sized organization, you get your IP address or block of addresses from your ISP. ISPs get their blocks of addresses (the ones they pass on to their customers) from their service providers. At the end of this chain is the nonprofit organization IANA, the Internet Assigned Numbers Authority.

Imagine that every time you wanted to access something on the Web, you had to type in a 32-digit binary number or even its dotted-decimal equivalent. Tiresome.

Today all you have to do is tell your browser to go to horton.com or some other Web address. How can typing names like horton.com take you to the correct Web site? Read on about domain names.

Domain names

A *domain name* is a text name that is associated with an IP address. Many organizations use their name or a product name as a domain name like ford.com, microsoft.com, or MIT.edu. So, a domain name is not just any name, but something closely related to a company's identity.

Various accredited registries like Verisign.com have the ability to register domain names and enter them into a distributed database called *whois*. In the whois database, each registered domain name is associated with some domain name server—usually one hosted by an ISP. It is on this server that a domain name is associated with an IP address that belongs to that server.

If you plan to offer courses publicly on the Internet, you probably want to register a domain name so that customers can easily associate your name or product with a Web address that will help them find your courses. If you are offering courses on your company's intranet, such a unique domain name is probably not necessary.

Internal network IP addresses

Many organizations use TCP/IP as the communications protocol for their internal networks. Each workstation, printer, server, network storage device—in short, each node or host—on the network must, therefore, have an IP address. Because the number of available IP addresses is limited, IANA set aside certain non-routable IP addresses for use within internal networks. Because these addresses are only used internally, they can be used over and over again by different organizations, thereby saving the other IP addresses for addresses that *are* nodes on the Internet. Internet routers are designed to ignore these non-routable addresses.

The IP addresses set aside for this purpose are:
- 10.0.0.0 through 10.255.255.255
- 172.16.0.0 through 172.31.255.255
- 192.168.0.0 through 192.168.255.255

Why are we mentioning this? Well, here is a situation where you may use internal IP addressing. If you plan to set up an e-learning development server or a server in a learning lab, you need to obtain IP addresses for each server. Your IT department will probably assign you one of these non-routable addresses.

Dynamic IP addressing versus static addressing

When you request an IP address for your test server or learning lab, you may be given a specific IP address (static addressing), or you may be told that the server will be automatically configured as soon as it is added to the LAN through dynamic addressing. Here's what dynamic addressing means.

Besides routing packets of data to the correct addresses, routers can have other features built in. One of those features is a Dynamic Host Configuration Protocol (DHCP) server. If this feature is enabled, the router will automatically assign an IP address taken from a pool of addresses to each node on its part of the network. When a device on the network is inactive for a specified period of time or is removed from the network, that device's IP address is put back into the pool and reassigned to the next active device on the network.

The advantage of dynamic addressing is that devices are automatically assigned an IP address with little or no input from the owner of the device. A downside is that since a device's IP address changes from day-to-day or hour-to-hour, communicating directly with that device may be difficult.

Static IP addresses are useful if you need to regularly communicate with another device on the network using a Web browser. Here are two common situations we deal with daily. We have a printer directly on our network and it has a Web-based administration interface. To check on its consumables like toner or change one of its settings, we simply open a browser and type the printer's IP address and we can then see the printer's administration page. The other device we need to communicate with daily is our test Web server. All our Web-based e-learning test sites reside on this server. To view these sites, we have to know the IP address of the server. To use static addresses, we disabled the DHCP server feature of our router and manually assigned IP addresses to each device on the network.

If you are a small organization, the question of dynamic versus static IP addresses may also come up when you sign up with an ISP. Because of the shortage of IP addresses, ISPs may not want to assign you your own IP address. Rather, they may prefer to assign you a temporary address from a pool as you make requests through them to the Internet. This scheme works fine unless you want to host a server from your location. In that case, you need to request several static IP addresses from your ISP. You need one for the modem/router between your Web server and the Internet. You need one for your Web server as well as one for each site you wish to host. You may also need one for an additional router or gateway between the Internet modem/router and the rest of your network.

Uniform Resource Locators

If you have ever typed in a Web address starting with "http://," you have used a uniform resource locator, or URL for short. URLs let you request a specific file out of the trillions of available files on the Web.

URL dissected

Here is an example of the full URL for a Web page. It is composed of several parts: the protocol, the domain name, the path to the file, and the name of the file. The protocol is "http" and stands for Hypertext Transfer Protocol. The domain name is "horton.com. " The file "templates.htm" is found in the "places"

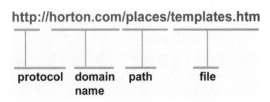

directory. That is, the file we want to view, "templates.htm," is located in the directory named "places" that is located at the top level of the Web site specified by "www.horton.com."

Common application protocols

Application protocols provide rules that allow client applications (like your browser, news reader, mail program, ftp program) to communicate with various applications that make up the Web services suite that run on a specially designed computer called a server. Here is a list of the common protocols you are likely to encounter in e-learning.

HTTP

Hypertext Transfer Protocol (HTTP) is the most common protocol. It allows the HTTP client in your Web browser to request and receive files (text, graphic images, sound, video, and other multimedia) from a server running a HTTP application. For example, http://www.horton.com uses the HTTP protocol.

HTTPS

Hypertext Transfer Protocol over Secure Socket Layer (HTTPS) is similar to HTTP. This protocol specifies how data sent to the server and received by the browser are encrypted and decrypted. This protocol is used by e-commerce sites and other sites where data security is important. Most of the up-to-date browsers support HTTPS. For example, https://www.regnow.com takes you to a secure server. You can tell this is true by looking at the bottom of your browser window where you will see either a locked padlock icon (Internet Explorer) or an unbroken key icon (Netscape).

FTP

File Transfer Protocol (FTP) provides a simple way to exchange files efficiently. FTP is not designed to display files, but to move them from machine to machine. FTP is used most often for uploading Web site files from a development computer to the server on which it will reside. It is also used where learners need to download large files that they will need to manipulate on their own computers. Users running an FTP client can download a file from a server hosting an FTP site, or upload a file to the FTP site.

Most operating systems have an FTP client installed. And, there are a number of third-party FTP client applications available. Both Internet Explorer and Netscape Navigator have an FTP client built in to allow users to download files using FTP. However, if you need to upload files, you will need to use your built in client or buy a third-party application. To visit an FTP site, go to ftp://ftp.microsoft.com.

MAILTO

The MAILTO protocol differs from the previous ones because it does not refer to a file that can be *requested* via the Internet but to an individual that can be *communicated with* via the Internet. For instance, typing "mailto:kit@horton.com" into your browser's address window will start whatever e-mail client you have configured as the default e-mail application on your computer, like Outlook or Eudora. Your e-mail client then communicates with the e-mail server on the Internet that handles communications for the individual identified by the mailto address.

NEWS

The Usenet News (NEWS) protocol makes it possible to reference Usenet newsgroups or specific Usenet articles. In e-learning you may use newsgroups as sources of additional information for learners. For instance, typing "news:microsoft.public.windowsnt.mail" into your browser's address window will open your news client and list the recent messages posted to this newsgroup.

The NEWS protocol does not specify how a client is to obtain the newsgroup referenced. A client must be properly configured to know what Network News Transfer Protocol (NNTP) server to access to obtain Usenet newsgroups and articles. Most ISPs have NNTP servers and will provide their clients with that information.

CONNECTING EXTERNAL USERS TO YOUR INTRANET

How can external users (distance learners, customers, vendors, remote offices, even the general public) gain access to e-learning that is made up of Web content and resides on an intranet or internal LAN?

You might ask, "Why not make it easy on ourselves and host the e-learning content on a server outside the intranet rather than from a server on an intranet?" Several issues factor into your decision. One issue is who makes up the bulk of your learners. Are a majority on the LAN or external to the LAN? Another issue is whether the e-learning content contains proprietary information that needs an extra layer of security. Yet another issue is the bandwidth of both the Internet connection as well as the LAN. Your decision on where to host content has to balance all these issues.

Let's assume that the e-learning content is on the LAN and you have to find a way to get your external learners connected without compromising the security of your LAN. Here are several ways organizations accommodate the needs of external users.

Modem banks

Until recently, the most common method for individuals to gain access to an internal network was through a dial-up connection from their modem to one of a number of modems connected to a server on the LAN. Once connected, these individuals would enter a password to gain access to the network. Once on the network, they might still need to log in to access other secured areas of the LAN.

Bandwidth and availability are the two biggest problems with dial-up modem access. First, the transmission speed of the connection is limited to 56 Kbps (on a good day with a tail wind). And there are only as many available connections as there are modems on the server.

Extending the WAN

Many large organizations have branch offices or campuses in multiple locations. To enable people at these remote locations to share and access resources at the home location (including e-learning), these organizations set up wide area networks using leased T-Carrier lines to connect these remote local area networks. To people at the remote location, accessing network resources is as easy as accessing resources on their own LANs.

For remote users in a fixed location like a branch office, WANs are a good solution but an expensive one for the organization to implement. And WANs do not solve the access difficulties faced by mobile users.

Virtual private networks

More commonly, organizations that need to connect external users to their intranets use a virtual private network (VPN). A VPN uses a public network like the Internet to connect just a specific group of people. What makes it "virtual" is that a VPN does not use a leased, physical telecommunications cable. Instead it employs a software protocol that creates a secure tunnel or pathway through the Internet to the LAN.

Remote learners connecting from hotels or from their homes using a 56Kbps modem or broadband connect to the LAN via the VPN, which works something like this: The laptop or home computer has a VPN client program. The learner's remote machine first establishes an Internet connection with an ISP and the VPN client goes in search of the organization's VPN server. Once the server is located, a dialog box appears for the user to enter a username and password. That done, data flows back and forth, protected by firewalls and sophisticated encryption.

There are other approaches to implementing a VPN as well. For security reasons, organizations often prefer to relegate shared resources to an extranet rather than allowing outsiders to connect directly to their intranet.

WIRELESS NETWORK CONNECTIONS

Wireless network connections use radio to transmit packets of data without the need for physical cables. More and more users access e-learning from mobile devices within their offices as well as from the outside, using mobile phones or wireless access cards. First we'll talk about wireless access within an organization. Then we will discuss access from cellular phones.

Wireless LANs

Wireless local area networks or WLANs are a common and useful addition to an organization's hardwired network. On our LAN, for instance, we have two wireless access points (like a wireless hub) physically attached to our existing LAN. These access points allow us to use our laptops untethered by a network cable on our LAN anywhere within our office or nearby.

There are three main wireless networking standards: Wi-Fi (802.11b), 802.11a, and Bluetooth. (Others, including, 802.11g, are coming.) These standards differ in transmission speed, transmission distance, and security protocols.

Wi-Fi (802.11b) networks

Wi-Fi, which is short for Wireless Fidelity, is the popular name for the IEEE standard 802.11b. It was the first and is the most widely used standard for wireless data networking. Wi-Fi devices are relatively inexpensive and can transmit up to 300 feet (from an access point) inside an office with walls or up to 1000 feet outside with no obstruction between the computer and the access point. Wi-Fi has a maximum transmission rate of 11 Mbps.

802.11a networks

802.11a is a new wireless standard for building wireless LANs. It can transmit data at rates up to 54 Mbps. However, its range is limited to 60 feet. Therefore, more access points are needed for their wireless networks. At the present time, 802.11a and 802.11b are not interoperable. They require separate access points and different network adapters, though some combination adapters are available.

Bluetooth networks

Bluetooth is used for moderate-bandwidth, short-range, low-power consumption data transfer between PDAs (Personal Digital Assistants), between computers and a printer, cell phones and other small devices. Some conference rooms are equipped with Bluetooth to enable laptops to communicate with each other as well as with the Internet. With a transmission rate of about 700 Kbps, Bluetooth is not good for transmitting high-bandwidth media but certainly is adequate for e-learning containing text, graphics, and simple animations.

 According to Bluetooth.com, this technology is named after Harald Bluetooth, a 10th-century Viking king renowned for building bridges throughout his realm.

Security issues

A word of caution about adding a wireless access point to your existing LAN: Let the IT department handle the installation. Wireless networks are somewhat harder to secure against unauthorized access. Unless you understand how wireless security schemes work, you may be laying bare your network to that funny looking guy with the laptop sitting at the picnic table in the park across the street.

Mobile telephony

Mobile users can access learning resources using public cell phone networks. They can connect through cell phone modems and through wireless access cards.

Cell-phone modems

A cell phone can be connected to a computer or PDA and thereby connect it to the Internet. In this setup, a cell phone is typically connected to a laptop's USB or serial port. The laptop then uses the cell phone as a modem to dial in to a modem on the company's LAN or to an ISP to connect directly to the Internet, an extranet, or a VPN. Maximum transmission speed is about 14.4 Kbps. Some wireless network providers have high-speed access in select geographic areas, with transmission rates between 40 and 60 Kbps.

Wireless access cards

Wireless access cards combine a cell phone and a modem into one unit. They are a little larger than a credit card, usually have a short antenna, and fit in the Type II PCMCIA slot of a laptop. Wireless access cards transmit data between 14.4 and 56 Kbps.

COMPUTING NETWORK SPEED

Networks never seem to be fast enough or files small enough. When designing a network or designing for it, you will frequently need to determine how quickly things download and calculate various factors of network speed.

Calculations

Here you will see how to calculate:

▶ Download time for a specific amount of content

▶ Maximum size of a piece of content that can download in a limited time

▶ Required network speed to support fast downloads

For an explanation of the units and abbreviations used in these calculations, see appendix A.

Calculating download time

How long will it take a Web page or other piece of content to download to the learner's system? Let's step through a simple formula for calculating the download time for a piece of content. Along the way we will see what factors influence this download time.

The formula for download time is simple, involving nothing more than simple multiplication and division. To compute the download time, we start with the size of the Web page or other unit of content. We divide this content size by the theoretical speed of the network connection multiplied by the efficiency of the network. The efficiency factor is necessary because few networks, modems, and interface connectors work at their theoretical speed all the time.

$$\text{Download time} = \frac{\text{Content size}}{\text{Theoretical speed} \times \text{Efficiency}}$$

$$= \frac{100\text{ K} \times 8\text{ bits/byte}}{56\text{ Kbps} \times 50\%}$$

$$= \frac{800\text{ K bits}}{28\text{ K bits per second}}$$

$$= 28\text{ seconds}$$

Consider this example. Let's say you have a Web page whose text, graphics, and other media total 100 K in size. (One K represents one kilobyte, roughly the equivalent of 180 words of text.) You need to multiply this figure by 8 to convert bytes to bits, so the units will be consistent. Then, you divide this product by the theoretical communications speed, say 56 Kbps (kilobits per second). If the modem and phone line worked perfectly, you would be done, but that is seldom the case; so you must multiply this theoretical speed by 50% to account for the effect of a noisy telephone line.

The result is 800 K bits per page divided by 28 K bits per second. Download time is thus 28 seconds.

Calculating file size

Often you must impose limits on the size of content to achieve a speedy download. A common approach is to set a goal that all content must download within a certain amount of time and then limit content to a size that will download within that amount of time.

The formula to calculate allowable content size is quite simple. It just requires multiplying three factors: the theoretical speed of the network connection, the efficiency of the network, and the acceptable download time.

$$\text{Content size} = \text{Theoretical speed} \times \text{Efficiency} \times \text{Acceptable download time}$$

$$= 56\ \text{Kbps} \times 50\% \times 10\ \text{seconds}$$

$$= 280\ \text{K bits}$$

$$= 35\ \text{K}$$

Let's look at an example. Suppose you are using a 56 Kbps modem. You already know that the phone connection is noisy and that this speed is rarely achieved. Therefore, you assume an efficiency of 50%. Your goal is to have each Web page download within 10 seconds.

Multiplying these three factors yields a size limit of 280 K bits. Because content sizes are not usually expressed in bits but bytes, divide 280 by 8 to get a content size limit of 35 K (kilobytes).

Calculating connection speed

How fast a connection speed is necessary for large units of content to download quickly? The calculation is not difficult but does involve several factors.

To calculate the theoretical speed, start with the maximum size of a unit of content. Then, divide this size by two factors: one is the allowable download time and the other is the efficiency of the network connection, that is, the fraction of the theoretical speed you can depend on.

$$\text{Theoretical speed} = \frac{\text{Content size}}{\text{Download time} \ \times \ \text{Efficiency}}$$

$$= \frac{100 \ K \ \times \ 8 \ \text{bits/byte}}{10 \ \text{seconds} \ \times \ 50\%}$$

$$= \frac{800 \ K \ \text{bits}}{5 \ \text{seconds}}$$

$$= 160 \ \text{Kbps}$$

Let's look at an example. Suppose that you want a 100 K Web page to download within 10 seconds over a connection that is 50% efficient. Start by multiplying the 100 K page size by 8 to convert bytes to bits. Then, divide by the target download time of 10 seconds multiplied by the efficiency of 50%.

Your network must, therefore, be fast enough to download 800 K bits in 5 seconds. That requires a theoretical speed of 160 Kbps.

For help doing the math

If you cringe at calculations and fumble at formulas, you can go to this book's Web site: horton.com/tools. There you will find a Microsoft Excel spreadsheet to perform various calculations, including the three discussed in this chapter.

Factors in network speed

The two main factors in network speed are the theoretical speed of the network technology and the efficiency with which that speed is realized.

Theoretical network speeds

This table lists common types of network connections and their theoretical (maximum) speeds.

Connection Technology	Theoretical speed
GSM mobile telephone	9.6 - 14.4 Kbps
Plain Old Telephone Service (POTS)	14.4 - 56.6 Kbps, depending on modem
ISDN, Integrated Services Data Network	64 Kbps - 128 Kbps
DSL, Digital Subscriber Line	512 Kbps to 8 Mbps
Cable modem	512 Kbps to 52 Mbps
EDGE, Enhanced Data GSM Environment	384 Kbps
Bluetooth wireless	700 Kbps
T1	1.5 Mbps
IBM Token Ring	4 Mbps
Ethernet 10BaseT	10 Mbps
Wi-Fi (802.11b) wireless	11 Mbps
802.11a wireless	54 Mbps
Fast Ethernet 100BaseT	100 Mbps
T3	44.7 Mbps
Gigabit Ethernet	1 Gbps
10-Gigabit Ethernet	10 Gbps

5

Networks for e-learning

Note:

▶ Kbps = kilobits per second (thousand bits per second)

▶ Mbps = megabits per second (million bits per second)

▶ Gbps = gigabits per second (billion bits per second)

Network efficiency

The term *network efficiency* refers to the fraction of the network's theoretical speed achieved in practice. This efficiency is a between 0% and 100%. You want us to be a bit more precise?

Network efficiency is difficult to pin down as it depends on many different factors and can vary from second to second. If precision is required, about the best you can do is measure network speed over a period of time and compute a statistical average.

The main factors in network efficiency falling below 100% include:

▶ Noise on the line, especially when communicating by modem over a public telephone line.

▶ Delays caused by intervening routers, bridges, firewalls, proxy servers, repeaters, and other devices along the network path from sender to receiver.

▶ Rerouting or repeating of messages required because of failure of some components on the network.

▶ Traffic levels that exceed network capacity.

▶ Collisions of packets of data. For instance, if two machines are sending packets of data simultaneously on a network, their packets will collide. The networking software on each computer receives notice of the collision. The software then times out for a random number of milliseconds and retries.

Efficiency tends to average between 50% and 90%. Slower than this, and the network needs maintenance. If you do not know what figure to use in calculations, use 50% to be conservative or 75% to be optimistic.

WHAT NOW?

Networks for e-learning may be complex and difficult to understand. They may demand generous budgets and ample technical assistance. But they are essential for effective e-learning.

While it may be tempting to just leave it to your IT or network service department, you may need to take an active role to ensure a match between e-learning designs and the networks they require. Here are some steps to get started.

1 **Inventory your current networks**. Using this chapter as a phrase book, talk to the IT department and ask them to help you sketch out a network. Put you-are-here markers on it to identify where learners will access e-learning, hosts will offer it, and producers will develop it

2 **Calculate the network speed required to deliver your e-learning content**. If this speed is higher than your network can provide, decide what limits you may have to put on the use of media in your e-learning.

3 **List the different environments from which your learners will need to access e-learning:** offices, home, hotel, seat 14B on United Airlines flight 472. For each location, plan how learners will connect to your e-learning content. Estimate the connection speed realistic from each location.

Tools for accessing e-learning

Unless learners can access your e-learning, they cannot learn from it. Learning requires tools to find, navigate, display, and play e-learning content. It requires tools that are reliable, simple to operate, and capable of displaying content precisely as intended.

Although tools for accessing e-learning are crucial, these are the components over which you may have the least control. So why study these tools? Only by understanding the capabilities and limitations of these tools can you:

	Create →	Offer →	Access
Curriculum			
Course			You are here
Lesson			
Page			
Media			

▶ Design e-learning that delivers the potential of its investment in technology

▶ Influence IT standards and purchasing policies that determine what tools learners in your organization can use

▶ Set up learning labs and other environments where learners can have the ideal learning experiences

Accessing e-learning requires several types of tools. Web browsers are the most basic and most important. They are covered in chapter 6. Also critical to the learning experience are media players and viewers to display media not handled directly by a browser. These are covered in chapter 7.

Client programs for communicating directly with server-based offering tools, such as online meeting servers, are covered in chapter 11.

6 Web browsers

A browser is a browser. Learners can pick any browser they want and your e-learning will look pretty much the same, right? Yeah, but only if your e-learning consists of nothing more than simple text.

Within the tools framework, browsers sit squarely in the Access column, spanning the Course, Lesson, Page, and Media rows.

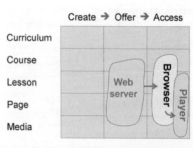

The choice of a browser is not independent of choosing other components, such as the Web server software used to host your courses. By pairing Web-hosting software with a compatible browser, you may be able to provide more value than each component alone could provide. For instance, interactivity can be provided by an appropriate mix of scripts running on the server and in the browser. In addition, security can be more easily implemented if the browser supports the security scheme implemented by the server. Knowing the capabilities of the server and browser allows you to assign duties appropriately.

Choosing a browser may also be based on what media players will be used—or not used—for the kind of content your e-learning will contain. To reduce or eliminate the need for media players, you may want a browser that plays most media without the need for additional software.

So, if you feel that e-learning should be more than TV pictures of paper pages, or if you are picky about how your pages appear, the differences, even subtle ones, among browsers need careful attention.

First, you'll be introduced to how browsers work, and find out why you need a browser to support your e-learning. Then you'll learn a bit about the most popular browsers (and a few of the less-well-known ones, too). Most important, though, we'll describe the browser features that are most relevant to e-learning and to you, as an e-learning developer.

WHAT IS A WEB BROWSER?

A Web browser provides the graphical user interface (GUI, pronounced "gooey") of the Internet. More to the point of this book, Web browsers are the core and starting point for most well designed e-learning. It is through browsers that most learners will experience it.

The wonder of Web browsers is that they provide a way to make information available to people around the globe. By reading files that are encoded in Hypertext Markup Language (HTML) and that include standard file formats, browsers from different vendors can provide the intended experience to learners using many different kinds of computers. A page displayed in Microsoft's Internet Explorer browser on a PC looks much the same as the same page displayed using Netscape's Navigator browser on a Macintosh. At least that is the theory.

HOW DOES A BROWSER WORK?

When we talked about networks, we spoke of a client-server model. The *client* was an individual computer or workstation on the network, that accessed applications and information from a central computer called a *server*. Just as there are client-server networks, there are client-server applications. You will encounter a number of them in this book. The World Wide Web is just such an application.

 In geekspeak, a Web browser is called a *user agent*. You will find it so listed in the log files of some Web servers.

A *browser* is a client application that runs on a local computer (client) and allows it to access and display Web content requested from a server running Web-hosting software. Both the browser and the server follow the Hypertext Transfer Protocol (HTTP), which defines rules for how files are to be requested and transmitted.

How do browsers get and display pages?

The seemingly simple act of requesting and displaying a Web page requires complex choreography involving the browser and the server.

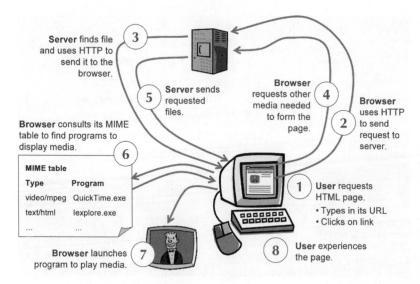

When a learner (1) clicks a link on a Web page, (2) the browser sends the request to the server specified in the link's URL (Uniform Resource Locator). The server (3) receives the request and determines the file and the file type being requested by consulting the server's MIME (Multipurpose Internet Mail Extension) table. Then it transmits the requested file along with the file type back to the browser. The browser (4) requests the other media needed to form the page, such as graphics, video, or audio. The server (5) sends along those files along with their file types back to the browser. The browser (6) interprets the MIME types to determine whether it can display the files by itself or whether the files (7) require either a plug-in or viewer in order to display properly. Finally, the user (8) sees the completed page.

Are MIMEs more than silent clowns?

File Types list from Windows XP where MIME-type information is stored.

I can almost hear you say, "But my browser doesn't need a server because it can open Web pages on my local computer!" That's right. This is an important feature of a browser: You can use it to access local Web content residing on your computer or somewhere on your LAN—content that does not reside on a Web server. This is because browsers include or have access to a local MIME-type list that specifies what applications to use for files with different extensions. Here is an example of such a list on a computer using Windows XP.

The moral of this story is that learners have a choice in determining what applications play what types of files. When someone installs a new application like a player or plug-in, they are usually asked what kinds of files they want the new application to open or edit. This information is stored either with the browser or in a master MIME-type list used by all applications on the computer.

Appendix B lists MIME types for file formats used in e-learning.

What else can browsers do?

If limited to requesting and displaying pages and their media, browsers would be adequate for entertainment and publishing—but mere footnotes in a book on e-learning tools. Additional capabilities make browsers a true foundation for e-learning. They can:

▶ **Display forms**. Browsers can display forms with blanks for learners to fill in, buttons for them to click, and lists for them to choose from. Learners' entries can be transmitted back to a server. Forms can be used to register learners for a class, ask their preferences, collect their homework, and conduct exams.

▶ **Run programs**. Browsers can contain and run programs written in a scripting language such as JavaScript or VBScript. These embedded programs can provide animation, self-scoring tests, puzzles, games, and other rich forms of interaction. In addition to running scripts, browsers can launch Java applets or Active X controls, which are programs in their own right.

▶ **Download files**. Browsers can use File Transfer Protocol (FTP) to copy a file from the server, for example, a textbook, case study materials, a computer program—or the latest computer virus. This feature is crucial for learners without a continuous connection to the network.

▶ **Upload files**. Browsers can send files from the learner's computer to the server. Typically this is done with a form field requesting the name of the file to upload. The learner clicks a Browse button, finds the file, and its name appears in the field. When the form is submitted, the file's data goes along for the ride. This feature lets learners submit complex homework assignments and examples of their work.

▶ **Support encryption**. Suppose you want to let students use credit cards to pay for their courses. How many would press the Submit button knowing their card number could be siphoned off anywhere along the route to the server? That's why browsers include security features, such as the ability to encrypt data sent from browsers to servers or servers to browsers.

Modern browsers are truly versatile tools that add capabilities with each version. Before you start building a needed capability into your content or require another add-on, consider whether you can (in the words of an oughta-be bumper sticker): Do it in a browser.

ALL BROWSERS ARE THE SAME, RIGHT?

All browsers display the text of Web pages in the same fashion. In that regard, they are all the same. However, the same Web page will likely not be displayed consistently from browser to browser, from operating system to operating system, or from browser version to browser version. For instance a Web page may look slightly different when displayed in Netscape 4.5 than it does when displayed in Netscape 6.2, or Internet Explorer 6, or in the same version of the browser running on a different operating system.

The following screen captures illustrate what we mean. We opened a Frequently Asked Question (FAQ) page containing dynamic HTML in various versions of Netscape and Internet Explorer using several computers running different versions of the Macintosh and Windows operating systems. The page should show a list of questions. Each question has an icon showing a "plus" sign (+) right before it. When a viewer clicks the "plus" sign beside a question, the next question is supposed to move down and the answer appears in the newly available space.

Here are the results we obtained in various browsers. (Note: The original Web page was targeted for Internet Explorer 4.7 and Netscape Navigator 4.7.)

Internet Explorer 4.7—Windows 98

The FAQ page displays as intended in Internet Explorer 4.7 running on Windows 98, First Edition. The dynamic HTML effects used to show and hide answers work as designed.

To make this page cross-browser compatible required adding a JavaScript to determine whether the browser is Internet Explorer or Netscape, and whether the version of Netscape is between 4.0 and 4.5 or higher than 4.5.

If the script determines that the browser is Netscape 4.5 or above, it uses a different procedure to create the expanding list

Netscape 4.7—Windows 98

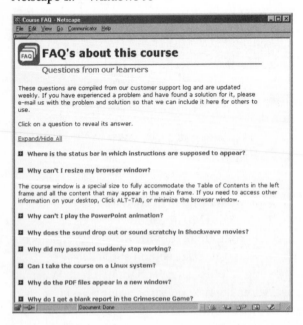

The page displays nicely in Netscape 4.7. The dynamic HTML effects used to show and hide answers work as designed.

Netscape 6.2—Windows XP

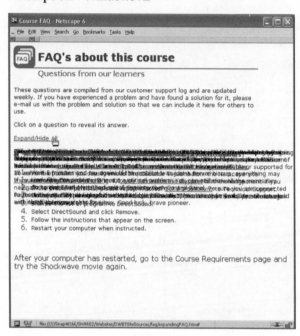

The page that worked fine in Netscape 4.7 appears garbled in Netscape 6.2. This version of Netscape does not support all the features previously supported in Netscape 4.7. Therefore, the dual coding used to ensure cross-browser compatibility does not work in this case. To make this page display correctly in Netscape 6.2 would require additional JavaScript programming.

Internet Explorer 6.0.2—Windows XP

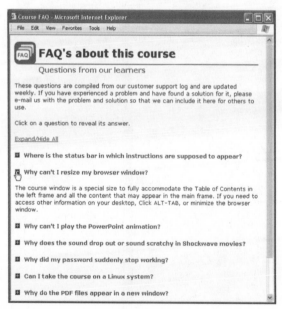

The FAQ page displays as intended in Internet Explorer 6.0.2 on Windows XP. The dynamic HTML effects used to show and hide answers work as designed.

Netscape 4.7—Macintosh, OS 9.2

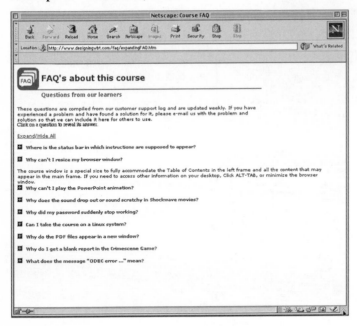

The original FAQ page displays fine in Netscape 4.7 for the Macintosh. The JavaScript correctly identifies the version. The expanding list works.

Internet Explorer 5.5—Macintosh, OS 9.2

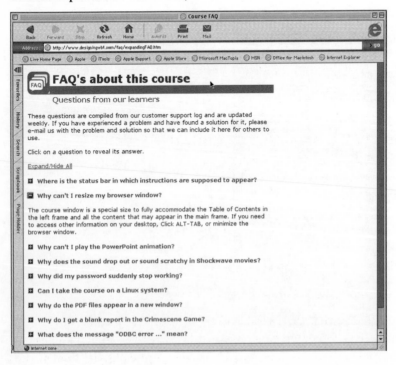

The same FAQ page displays OK in Internet Explorer 5.5 for the Macintosh, but the line under the page title is thicker than intended. The expanding list works.

Internet Explorer 5.5 — Macintosh, OS X

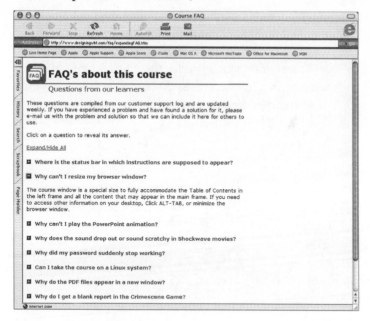

The FAQ page displays nicely in Internet Explorer 5.5 for the Macintosh. The expanding list works.

Netscape 6.2 — Macintosh, OS X

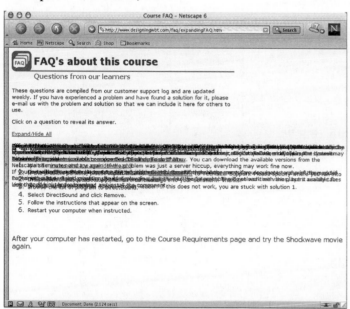

The FAQ page appears garbled in Netscape 6.2 for the Macintosh. The dual coding used to ensure cross-browser compatibility does not work in this case. To make this page display correctly would require additional JavaScript programming to accommodate Netscape 6 and higher browsers.

The moral of this demonstration is that browsers are pretty much the same, but differences—even between subsequent versions of a single brand—can make a hash of your careful designs. Making Web content "cross-browser" is often harder than most people think. And these examples are just from two brands.

POPULAR WEB BROWSERS

In the world of e-learning, the two big names in browsers are Netscape's Navigator and Microsoft's Internet Explorer. Together they account for the vast majority of corporate, educational, and home browsers. In addition to these giants, there are other specialty browsers and variants that are of interest to those designing and offering e-learning. Let's tour the showroom.

Internet Explorer

microsoft.com

Internet Explorer (IE for short) is very popular in businesses, especially ones that have standardized on Windows operating systems and/or Microsoft Office products. As of September 2002, all versions of Internet Explorer make up 88% to 90% of the browser usage on personal computers and workstations, according to thecounter.com. IE is currently available for the Macintosh operating system as well as for Windows.

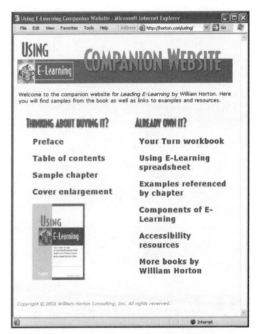

Page displayed in Internet Explorer 6

One of the pleasant side effects of Internet Explorer being tightly coupled with the Windows operating system is that it starts almost instantaneously. Internet Explorer is also well integrated with Microsoft's Office suite. If you link to Office documents like Excel spreadsheets or Word documents from within your e-learning, learners will be able to view these documents within the browser window—as long as the appropriate Office application is installed on their computer. This capability eliminates the need to open a new window and separately start up an Office application.

Moving into the geeky realm, IE supports Level 1 Cascading Style Sheets (CSS), Level 1 Document Object Model (DOM), Vector Markup Language (VML), and the proposed Synchronized Multimedia Integration Language (SMIL) 2.0 standards. It also supports client-side VBScript scripting in addition to JavaScript. Client-side scripts are little programs and routines that are

 This talk of DOMs, CSSs, and the like may seem like more detail than you need. However, as you design your e-learning, these capabilities will influence what features you can provide and how you will need to implement them.

included right in the HTML page and run in the browser. Internet Explorer can also display XML (Extensible Markup Language) files that reference either XSL (Extensible Stylesheet Language) style sheet or Cascading Style Sheets. This ability to parse and display XML files offloads work from the server to the learner's browser. That is, the server doesn't have to transform the XML file and the XSL style sheet into an HTML page each time the XML file is requested, the learner's browser does the work.

For businesses, Internet service providers, and other organization that may want a customized version of Internet Explorer, Microsoft provides an Internet Explorer Administration Kit that can be used to create a custom-configured installation package.

Netscape Navigator

netscape.com

Netscape was the first full-featured browser to make its way into homes, campuses, and businesses. It established the expectation that Web content could be displayed consistently from platform to platform. In fact, in 1995 Netscape had a market share of over 80%.

Netscape garnered its early popularity by adding its own extensions to the standard HTML tags supported by the World Wide Web consortium. The capabilities that resulted from these extensions were often flashier than what other browsers could produce. To attract Netscape users, Internet Explorer added its own special extensions to match and exceed Netscape's capabilities. As a result, Web sites that took

Page displayed in Netscape Navigator 6.2

advantage of a browser's special features were not easily displayed by the other browser without special scripting being added to the HTML pages. These incompatibilities still exist.

Today, Netscape is still found on home computers, on university campuses, and on operating systems other than Windows. According to thecounter.com, all versions of Netscape account for 10% of browser usage. The current version (7) is available for Macintosh, Linux, and Windows operating systems. If you need to support a variety of UNIX platforms, you will need to use either version 4.8 of Netscape Communicator or version 4.79 of Netscape Navigator.

Netscape supports CSS as well as Level 1 DOM and client-side JavaScript. Netscape can also display XML files with referenced CSS files—but not XML files that reference an XSL style sheet. There is a customization kit available that allows you to create a customized version of the Netscape browser. For instance you can add your logo and special bookmarks, eliminate features, pre-configure connection information, and build a special installation package.

Other browsers of interest

Almost all e-learning is designed for Netscape or IE browsers. So why consider other browsers? Because they are there? Or, because they may represent niche markets or be

important in testing emerging standards or meeting accessibility regulations. Here are some other browsers you may need to be aware of as you plan your e-learning project.

Mozilla

mozilla.org

Mozilla is an open-source browser available for Windows, Macintosh, Linux, and some versions of UNIX. According to the Mozilla Organization, this browser is designed for standards compliance, performance, and portability from platform to platform.

Mozilla is named for the original code-name of the product that came to be known as Netscape Navigator. Since 1998,

Page displayed in Mozilla

Netscape has built its browser on incremental releases of the Mozilla browser. However, the first public release of Mozilla 1.0 did not occur until June 5, 2002.

Along with the browser, the Mozilla installation also includes a news and mail reader, an Internet Relay Chat (IRC) client, and a minimal HTML editor. All in all, it is very similar in basic functionality to Netscape 6.2.

Since it is available as open-source, Mozilla can be customized, for example, to produce an ideal browser for your e-learning.

Amaya

w3c.org/Amaya

Amaya is the World Wide Web Consortium's test-bed browser. According to the W3C, Amaya was "specifically conceived to serve as a ... client to experiment and demonstrate new Web protocols and formats as well as new extensions to existing ones." Its features are limited. For instance, it does not support pop-up windows or frames. And its support for Cascading Style Sheets is still somewhat limited.

Amaya is unsuitable for general e-learning activities, especially if learners will be accessing third-party e-learning providers. Amaya does not support the level of interactivity needed for rich content. However, its support for the W3C Web Accessibility Initiative and

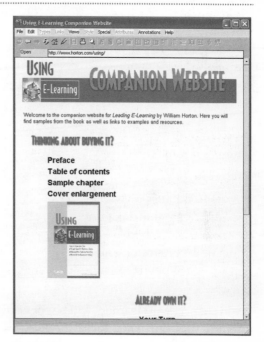

Page displayed in Amaya. Notice the misaligned columns.

specialized data formats, such as Math Markup Language (MathML) and Scaleable Vector Graphics (SVG), may carve out some niches for Amaya.

AOL

aol.com

AOL (America Online), the world's largest ISP, provides its users with a customized version of the Internet Explorer browser, which is surprising since AOL and Netscape are divisions of AOL Time Warner. However, there is a version of Netscape being tested that will probably be the default browser in upcoming versions of AOL.

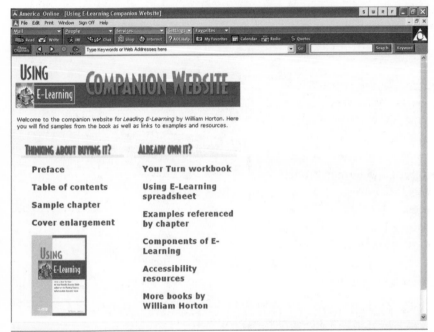

Page displayed in AOL, version 7. The page is well-formed, but notice the extra width due to the AOL-specific controls.

If you suspect your learners will be connecting to your e-learning using AOL, carefully test your content with the AOL browser—especially in situations where learners must log into a secure system. If there are difficulties, you may want to give your learners instructions on how to start either Netscape or Internet Explorer once they have connected to the Internet using AOL.

Opera

opera.com

The Opera browser prides itself on being small, fast, and standards-compliant. It is also noted for its ability to interface with accessibility aids for the visually impaired. Opera is available for a large variety of operating systems, as well as embedded systems like that found on the Nokia 9210i/9290 Communicator.

The most difficult issue developers will encounter will be in the ways Opera's Document Object Model differs from either IE or Netscape—especially when using dynamic layers. If your content is just static pages, these differences should pose no problems for you.

Page displayed in Opera

Lynx

lynx.browser.org

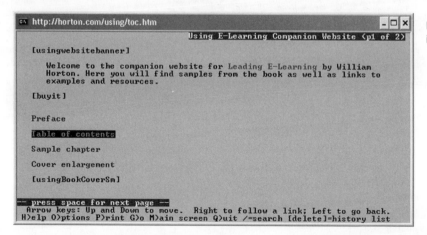

Page displayed in Lynx

Lynx is a well-established text-only browser used by people who do not need to see graphics or who do not want to wait for them to download and form. Lynx does not support frames, tables, or any visual media. It is included in this list for completeness; however, it is not an adequate platform for rich, interactive e-learning. Lynx may be helpful in debugging pages that thwart screen readers for the blind.

MSN TV

MSN TV is designed to let users navigate the Web and display pages on their television screens. We're not talking about high-definition television (HDTV) here. Oh no, we mean plain, ordinary, fuzzy TV that makes the screen of that antiquated computer in your basement seem as crisp and vast as the screen at your local Cineplex.

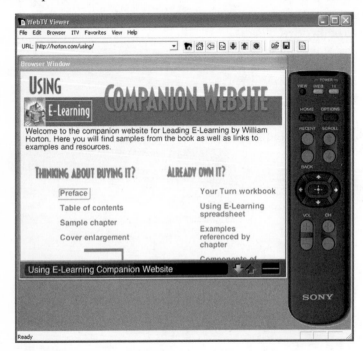

Page displayed in the WebTV testing browser for MSN TV

The MSN TV browser is limited to basic HTML with some JavaScript and Cascading Style Sheet features. Furthermore, MSN TV does not scroll pages horizontally, but squeezes the page to fit the available width. Most standard Web fonts are not supported.

If you suspect your learners are likely to use some kind of television browser to access your e-learning, think about providing an alternative version of your learning material optimized for the limitations of the television screen.

Palm OS and Pocket PC

www.palmsource.com or microsoft.com

The Palm OS and the Windows Pocket PC OS have versions of browsers adapted for the small screens and wireless connections of handheld devices. Palm users can choose a variety of browsers including Handspring's Blazer 2.0 and ILINX's Xiino. Pocket PC users have a version of Internet Explorer already built in.

These browsers support different combinations of HTML, compact HTML (cHTML), Wireless Application Protocol (WAP), and Wireless Markup Language (WML). If you will be delivering content to one of these handheld devices, you must test, test, and test some more.

Page displayed in a Pocket PC emulator

Due to the slow connection speed and small screen, these devices are probably not suitable for media-rich content. Rather, they may be more useful in delivering information and simple assessment questions.

CHOOSING A BROWSER

Whether you are targeting a browser for your e-learning development, specifying one for a corporate or university IT standard, or just picking one for your own e-learning, what issues might sway you to choose one browser over another? In particular, what features in your e-learning will work across browser brands, versions, and operating systems? Let's look at the various issues, and then discuss how you can go about making a choice.

Picking for yourself

If you are picking a browser for your own use, here are a couple of recommendations:

▶ If your IT department has set standards for an operating system and browser for your office machine, follow those standards on your personal machine if you are planning to access your organization's e-learning.

▶ If you will be taking e-learning from a third party, such as an online university, follow their browser recommendation.

What you need to know first

Before you choose or recommend a browser, do a little research to determine the constraints on your decision. Here are some important questions to ask.

▶ Does your IT department have standards for which browser to use at work? These standards are often necessary to ensure compatibility among all software components.

▶ If you buy courses, do they specify a browser? Some courses are very fragile and work only with a particular browser running on a specific operating system.

▶ What operating systems do your learners have? Some browsers are not available for all operating systems.

▶ What browsers do learners have installed already? If you are not in a position to specify a browser, then your development team will have to live within the limits imposed by your learners' browsers.

Capabilities to consider

Here is a laundry list of capabilities to consider when choosing a browser for your learners—or determining how a browser's capabilities will affect your e-learning design.

HTML compatibility

Well, all browsers support HTML, right? Yes, but does the browser fully support the official W3C version of HTML? The current versions of both Netscape and Internet Explorer say they fully support HTML 4.01. However, the browser for MSN TV says it supports most of HTML version 4.0.

Another issue is how strict is the browser's support of HTML? That is, if an HTML

> **Some browsers are more lenient**
>
> HTML code elements are called tags. These tags usually occur in pairs—an opening tag and a closing tag.
>
> Internet Explorer is more forgiving to developers who forget closing tags, such as a closing TABLE tag. Usually the page will form just fine. However, that same page loaded into some versions of Netscape will fail to form.
>
> This is not a bad thing; it just means that developers should not be lulled into complacency because their pages look fine in Internet Explorer. They should validate their HTML to ensure their code is well-formed (all closing tags are present and no tags are incorrectly nested).

coder omits a DOCTYPE definition or uses LANGUAGE instead of TYPE to indicate the scripting language used in a page, will the page still display?

If you have designed pages to takes full advantage of a browser's features, you need to be concerned whether the newest version of your browser will still support those features. This issue has come up for us with the newest version Use these and other lists of capabilities as a starting point. Add capabilities you need and strike out ones you do not. Sort the list to reflect your priorities. Make it your own. of Netscape (7 at the time of this writing). Prior versions of Netscape (3 through 4.7) allowed using JavaScript to put informative text into the status bar of the browser window. The newest release, however, does not.

The ALT (alternative text) property is another troublesome area where a newer browser has failed to continue support for a particular feature. Commonly used within image tags, the ALT property allows developers to assign meaningful descriptions to images to aid screen readers and those who have set their browsers not to display images. All versions of Internet Explorer and all versions of Netscape—until version 6—supported ALT text.

Operating system

Not all versions of all browsers are available for all operating systems. What might that mean for e-learning developers? If your target audience includes those using UNIX, for instance, you may not be able to design for the latest features of Netscape. If your audience includes users of Apple's OS X, then you should avoid exploiting the latest features of Internet Explorer.

There is another kink to this issue. Even the same version of browser may not display information in the same way from one operating system to another. (Remember the screen captures earlier in this chapter?) Even such mundane issues as bullet lists and graphic placement can cause display problems on various operating systems. Testing is the only assurance and conservative design the only solution.

IE displays other files

In organizations that have standardized on the Microsoft Office Suite, many of the network resources will be in some Office format (Word, Excel, Access, PowerPoint). These formats can be displayed within Internet Explorer without being converted.

6

Web browsers

File formats displayed

Another issue for e-learning developers may be the file formats a browser can display without assistance from separate viewers or plug-ins. Some browsers display only text, but most will display Graphics Interchange Format (GIF) and Joint Photographic Experts Group (JPEG) graphics unassisted. Recent versions of IE and Netscape will display Portable Network Graphics (PNG); however, they don't support exactly the same features of this format.

Additionally, some browsers can display vector graphics. A vector graphic contains a description of the graphic in terms of lines and areas rather than defining each pixel of the graphic, such as in a bitmap. Vector graphics files are usually smaller that bitmap files. The two main vector file formats for the Web are Vector Markup Language (VML) and Scalable Vector Graphics (SVG). At the moment, only Internet Explorer can display VML files and only Amaya can display SVG files.

For most e-learning purposes, GIF and JPG graphics are adequate. PNG, VML, or SVG support may be important, however, if the subject matter is highly graphical and you need compact files that are still of the highest visual quality.

Interface features

Just like other applications you use every day, a browser should have a well thought-out look and feel. It should include productivity features to make performing common tasks easier and more reliable. Here are some interface features that should be simple, clear, and efficient:

- **Keyboard shortcuts** for the most common actions, such as going forward and back or for setting a bookmark

- **Bookmarking facility** to allow users to easily save the Web addresses of favorite or frequently used pages

- **Context menus** for common operations, such as opening a link in a new browser window

- **Status bar** to display tips as well as the full Web address of hypertext links within a page

- **Visual cues** to indicate whether a Web site is on a secure server—especially important when data is being obtained from a learner

Security

To what extent does a browser facilitate secure transactions for e-commerce and confidential material? Ideally, the browser you choose should at least support 128-bit encryption as Internet Explorer, Netscape, and Opera all do.

Another issue involves how a browser supports server security. Consider this scenario: Suppose your Web server uses either the Windows NT 4 or 2000 operating system. Now suppose that you wish to protect certain Web pages. An easy way to do that is to place those pages into a separate directory within the Web site and use the NT internal security scheme to control access. That is, each potential user of the protected pages is a documented user of the server, or a member of a particular group. When a user tries to access one of those protected Web pages, a dialog box asks for their user name and password. If the user is accessing the page with Internet Explorer, all is well and the user simply enters the correct information. However, if the user is accessing the page with Netscape, the login process will fail. To overcome this, the server administrator has to allow user names and password to be transmitted "in the clear," that is, unencrypted. Yikes!

Media players

Media players, sometimes called plug-ins, enable browsers to display media they cannot display natively. For instance, a video clip embedded in a Web page requires a media player to display it within the browser. Media players are available to display all kinds of media, such as Acrobat PDF files, audio files, video files, Flash Shockwave.

 To learn more about plug-ins, go to netscape.com.

Another good site to visit is cws.internet.com/ 32plugins.html.

However, not all media players are available for all browsers and all operating systems. Your choice of media for use in e-learning may depend on whether there is a media player available for your target browser and operating system. For more on media players, see chapter 7.

Browser scripting languages

Browsers differ in the client-side scripting languages they support. The term *client-side* just means that the script runs on the browser machine instead of the server machine. Client-side scripts are snippets of programming located within a Web page or in a separate file referenced by the Web page. Through the use of scripts, developers can add interactivity and visual effects to otherwise static Web pages. The two main client-side scripting languages are JavaScript and VBScript, a variant of Microsoft's

Visual Basic language. Netscape supports JavaScript while IE supports both JavaScript and VBScript.

If you must provide e-learning to both main browsers, there are some JavaScript incompatibilities of which you need to be aware. IE and Netscape do not implement all the elements of JavaScript in the same way, nor do they support exactly the same set of elements. These inconsistencies are due primarily to the differences in each browser's Document Object Model, or DOM. (We will discuss the DOM a bit later.) To get around these differences, you may need either to avoid inconsistently supported programming elements or to write scripts for each browser version and use a "browser sniffer" routine to determine which script to use.

What do these differences mean to developers of e-learning? Not a whole lot. Rich interactivity can be achieved just as effectively in JavaScript as in VBScript. Just be sure to test courses with the targeted browsers to spot programming errors or unexpected results.

Document Object Model

The *Document Object Model* describes the structure of a Web page, such as the elements or tags on a page, the number of elements, the order of the elements, the properties of these elements, and finally, how each element or tag looks when it is displayed. For instance, a DOM lets scripts refer to the color of a word in a link within a bullet list embedded in a table on a page. By using scripting languages (JavaScript or VBScript) and Cascading Style Sheets to control these tags and elements, developers are able to create sophisticated dynamic effects.

With more of the DOM exposed (accessible to programming), there are more possibilities for creating rich interactions. Different browsers expose different elements of their DOM; therefore, certain interactivities are not possible on every browser—or they must be programmed differently.

Java support

Java is an object-oriented programming language used to create both full-featured programs and small interactive applications called applets. Web developers commonly use Java applets to play media or to allow users to interact with a Web page such as in a game or puzzle. The attractive thing about Java applets is that they do not require players or viewers to work. What these applets do need, however, is for the browser to support the correct Java virtual machine. A *Java virtual machine* takes the Java code (which is supposed to be independent of the operating systems and processor) and translates it into a format understood by the particular operating system and processor.

Java applications and applets are, thus, cross-platform compatible among all machines with a Java virtual machine—in theory. Of course, that compatibility gets a little shaky when learners have different versions of the Java virtual machine and when the applet has to call on the operating system to play media. If your developers want to use Java applets directly on a Web page, they need to test those pages with all the target browsers. If you must provide cross-platform, cross-operating system interactivity, you may find it easier to use Macromedia Flash. It does require a player; but, the player is readily available for most platforms and browsers.

Dynamic HTML support

Dynamic HTML (DHTML) is the ability of the browser to format a page precisely and to adjust the page's appearance after it has loaded. For instance, using DHTML you can program a button to display or hide information. Imagine designing a Web form that reconfigures itself based on choices made by the user.

Dynamic HTML is dependent on a browser's DOM. Each browser has a slightly different DOM, however. Therefore, in order to create an effect like expanding and collapsing text that works across browsers, it may be necessary to write slightly different versions of the programming scripts to account for the differing DOMs of your target browsers.

XML Support

Internet Explorer and Netscape can read documents coded in XML as well as those in HTML, but they differ in how that document is displayed. Netscape can display an XML file only if a Cascading Style Sheet (CSS) is linked to it. Internet Explorer can display an XML file with either a CSS style sheet or an XSL style sheet linked to it. CSS is discussed below and XSL is explained in chapter 23.

If training content will be stored as XML for eventual display as a Web page, you may want a browser that can easily display the XML-encoded information without the need for pre-transforming it on the Web server.

Cascading Style Sheets

Style sheets allow formatting (e.g., fonts, colors, spacing) to be defined separately from the content rather than in each individual tag. This formatting can be stored in a separate file and applied consistently throughout a range of individual pages. Cascading Style Sheets are one such formatting scheme.

Cascading Style Sheets work like this: Suppose you want every first-order heading (<h1>) on your Web page to be red, 20-point bold Arial. Before the development of style sheets, you had to write the following HTML each time you used an <h1> tag:

```
<h1><strong><font face="Arial" color="red"
size="20">This is a red, bold, Arial first-order
heading</font></strong></h1>
```

But CSS lets you specify this style for all instances of the <h1> tag at one time by creating what is called a selector, like this:

```
h1 {
   font-weight: bold;
   font-size: 20pt;
   font-family: Arial;
   font-color: red;
}
```

With this style definition in place, you only have to use the regular <h1> tag to apply it.

You can place this style information in the <head> of a document. But it is more useful to put definitions like this into a separate file with a .css extension and link to it from each page where you want this style to appear.

You can use CSS selectors to control formatting and to precisely position items on a page. However, not all CSS properties are supported by all browsers on all platforms. The WebReview Master Compatibility chart (webreview.com/style/css1/charts/mastergrid.shtml) is a good place to look to determine which browser version on each platform supports a particular property or value.

Customizability

How customizable is the browser? Can you add a logo and choose a different color scheme? You may want to brand the browser for the students of you university or customers of your company. You may want the browser to act as a marketing tool by featuring your logo and theme colors. Or, you may want to limit the features available to just those needed for e-learning.

Network installation

Can you download a copy of the browser installation program and make it available over the network to employees, customers, and students? If your organization must support numerous learners, it may be more efficient for the IT department to install the necessary browser, players, and viewers from a centralized copy of each application.

Accessibility

▷ Although there are no explicit accessibility standards for e-learning alone, e-lea.
does fall under accessibility standards for information technology and Web content
(see chapter 22). If your organization provides e-learning to U.S. federal agencies or
their subcontractors, your content must be accessible by those with common
disabilities. You need a browser that helps make content accessible. For instance,
which screen readers work best with your browser? What other accessibility features
does your browser support? Can users navigate using voice commands?

Internet Explorer in Windows works well with the accessibility aids built into
Windows as well as third-party accessibility aids that work through the Windows
operating system. Opera, which is available for several operating systems, works well
with screen readers for the blind. Though you may not develop primarily for Opera,
you may want to test on Opera.

> **We don't need no stinkin' server**
>
> Browsers can view Web content residing on a CD-ROM, a local computer, a network
> computer, and a Web server. As long as the Web content does not require processing by a
> Web server, it can be located anywhere the learner can browse and open files. (Server
> processing might be necessary to capture data entered on a form or to record test results in a
> remote database.) This makes browsers, with the players and viewers they support, an
> efficient way to provide a common interface to a variety of network resources.

What you should specify

When it is time to formalize your choice of browser, there is more to it than just
shouting "Netscape only!" To specify a browser, you must make three decisions.

Decision	Description
Brand	The main brands are Microsoft Internet Explorer (IE) and Netscape Navigator. Other special-purpose alternatives are Opera, Lynx, AOL, as well as browsers for wireless devices.
Version	Browsers continually evolve through a seemingly endless series of versions. Do not say "Netscape 6 or later" when what you really mean "Netscape 6.2.3 or later." Later versions usually add capabilities and fix bugs found in earlier versions. Usually. Sometimes a new version will drop support for capabilities found in earlier versions, causing your content to suddenly stop working or develop a nervous disorder.

| Operating system | The capabilities of a browser depend heavily on resources provided by the computer's operating system. A version of a browser on Macintosh may perform differently than the same version on Windows or Linux. |

ALTERNATIVES TO STANDARD BROWSER PROGRAMS

It is hard to imagine any sizeable e-learning solution that does not in some way require a Web browser. However, the conventional browser program need not be the focus of learners' attention or the conveyor of 100% of your content.

Standalone courses

Not all e-learning content is sipped from a Web server using a Web browser. You may choose to develop your course as a file that learners can obtain on CD-ROM or download and play locally. Your standalone course could be packaged as a self-contained program, or it may play through a separate media player. These courses are ideal for learners without frequent access to networks—people in remote locations and those who travel frequently.

Standalone courses can be built in a tool like Authorware, Flash, or Director from Macromedia or Quest from Mentergy. (See chapters 14 and 17 for more about these authoring tools.) Each of these authoring tools comes with a standalone player for displaying content created in the tool. Or, you may choose to develop your course in a conventional programming language such as Java or Visual Basic.

Though such courses work without network access, they can incorporate components that let them obtain content and interact with Web servers. Web servers are not snooty; they'll talk to anybody who speaks HTTP.

Embedded browsers

If you want to offer Web pages in your training, some kind of Web browser software is necessary. The browser, though, need not be a standalone application. Instead, it could be a component within some other application. Here is an example of what we mean.

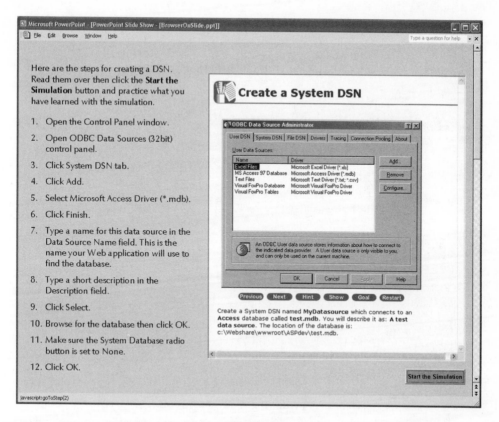

This PowerPoint slide contains an embedded Web browser control. When an instructor or learner clicks the Start the Simulation button, the practice activity is loaded from a remote Web server into the embedded Web browser, as shown. Individual learners could access the same page on their own using a standalone Web browser. You can also embed a Web browser in documents created with other Microsoft Office programs, such as Excel, Word, and Access.

Another alternative is to embed a Web browser into software. Suppose your organization wants to provide training on a software application it has developed. To maintain a cohesive look to the product, management wants the training to appear right in the application. You can accomplish this tight integration by embedding a browser control right into the user interface of the application. To access the training, users of the application only have to click a button or make a menu selection.

You can even go further as did Instron Corporation, which put most of the interface inside a browser control.

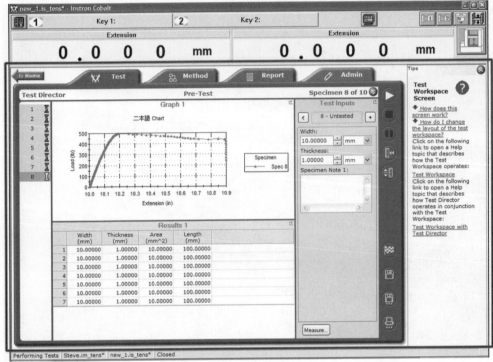

Copyright © 2001 Instron Corporation. All rights reserved. Everything within the border is being displayed using an embedded browser control—the tabbed pages as well as the just-in-time help in the right-hand panel.

Help viewers

Another way to offer e-learning content is to make use of the standard Help viewer that is provided as part of the Windows operating system. Using a Help authoring tool, developers can include Web content as well as the usual Help content locally stored on the user's computer. Here is an example.

In this help file for a small application, users find a Web-based tutorial in addition to the more common procedural information

Media players

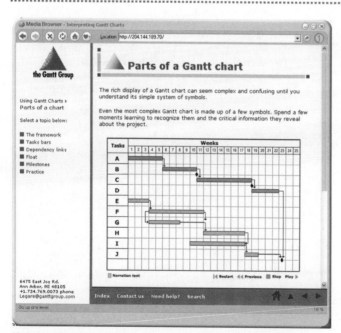

Here is a Web-based course displayed within the RealOne Player. There is a frame with the table of contents along the left side, a navigation bar at the bottom, and a main content frame at the right displaying an embedded Flash animation with voice-over narration.

Finally, you can offer e-learning content within a media player window. The RealOne Player from RealNetworks, for instance, displays Web content just like a standard browser—embedded media and everything.

Read more about media players in chapter 7.

WHAT NOW?

For most e-learning projects, the most critical piece of software is the web browser. That's why we provided you with lots of information about browsers. To put your knowledge to work, consider your situation.

If you ...	... And you are ...	Then, take these actions.
Can control what browsers learners use to take e-learning	Buying courses from outside suppliers	▶ Buy the course that best meets your goals. ▶ Document the browsers required by these courses. ▶ Help learners to obtain these browsers.
	Developing courses	▶ Specify the browser that best realizes the potential of your courses. ▶ Help learners obtain that browser.
Cannot control what browsers learners use to take e-learning	Buying courses from outside suppliers	▶ Survey to learn what browsers learners already have. ▶ Buy the best courses that run on these browsers.
	Developing courses	▶ Survey to learn what browsers learners already have. ▶ List the common denominators of capabilities among these browsers. ▶ Design to these limitations.

In deliberating the capabilities of Web browsers, keep in mind that browsers need not display all the content of your e-learning. Some content may be displayed by media players and viewers, which are the subject of the next chapter.

7 Media players and viewers

When we talked about browsers in chapter 6, we made a distinction between content that the browser can view natively and content that requires the assistance of another tool. Media players and viewers help browsers by playing dynamic media, such as audio and video. They also help browsers display proprietary file formats, such as Adobe Acrobat PDF or Macromedia Flash. For conciseness, we'll just use the term *media player*.

Within the tools framework, media players squat at the bottom of the Access column in the Media row—where they faithfully play media delegated to them by the imperial browser.

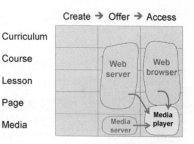

Not only can media players play media within the browser interface or embedded in a Web page, media players can also play media independently of the browser. For instance, you can type a Web address or file path into the open-file dialog box of many media players and play media directly, either from a Web server (chapter 8) or from a media server (chapter 13).

WHAT IS A MEDIA PLAYER?

If you are listening to an Internet radio station, previewing a CD on CDNow.com, checking out a preview for a new movie, or reading a document in Adobe Acrobat PDF, chances are you are using a media player.

For e-learning, media players are closely associated with Web browsers because they let learners experience more media than can be played directly by the browser. Some media players handle simple, linear media such as sound, music, and video. A second class of media players, sometimes called viewers, displays proprietary file formats. These formats tend to be more complex and may mix media and involve rich interactivity. Although general media players can play multiple types of media in multiple file formats, viewers typically display only their own special file format.

Players are often bundled with browsers and are automatically installed when the browser is installed. Some are tightly integrated with recent versions of IE and Netscape so that learners may not even be aware they are really separate applications.

 For Netscape, a media player is often called a *plug-in*. For Internet Explorer, it is called an *ActiveX* control. Media players that work in both browsers are usually Java applets.

HOW DOES A MEDIA PLAYER WORK?

When the browser receives a file it cannot play or when a learner double clicks the icon of a media file, the media player starts up and plays the media. But how does the browser or operating system know which player to use for different media?

When a player, like any new application, is installed on a computer, information is added to various operating systems files. This information includes the extension of the various file formats the application can open and where the application is located. This is so that when you click on a file's icon, the operating system can start the appropriate application.

 The extension is that part of the file name after the "dot." You can learn more about file types and extension in the appendix B.

In the case of a media player, the installation process installs the player into a known location so that any browser installed on the computer can find it and use it to display content. The browser knows which player to use based either on the browser's MIME table in Netscape, or on MIME-type information stored in the operating system files in IE running on Windows 98 or higher.

When the browser receives a file from the server, it examines the HTTP header that precedes the actual data of the file. This header specifies, among other things, the type of data that follows.

 If you aren't sure how a browser works, see chapter 6.

This specification includes the "Content-Type" of the data. The Content-Type consists of a general category and a specific type. If the Content-Type is text/html, the browser displays the data itself. If the Content-Type is video/mpeg, or any other type the browser cannot display, it consults its MIME table to learn what media player to use.

Here is an example of a Web page with embedded video along with the HTTP header information that was sent back from the server with the actual video file:

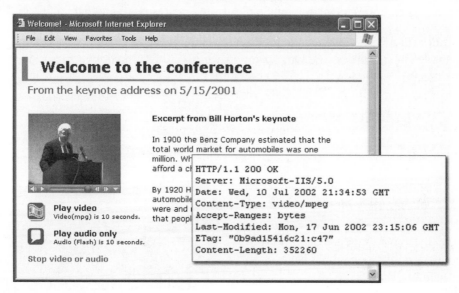

PLAYERS FOR AUDIO AND VIDEO

Several media players are available to handle audio, music, and video. Let's take a look at some of the most popular ones. We'll briefly discuss the media formats they support, where they can be obtained, and their unique features.

 I thought you said video talking heads were a waste of bandwidth?

 Busted!

QuickTime Player

By Apple Computer   **apple.com**   **Free for basic version**

The QuickTime Player, installed by default on Apple computers, plays a variety of audio, video, and graphic file formats both within a browser and as a standalone application. The current QuickTime Player does not play any of the Windows streaming media formats. It does, however, do a nice job as a standalone player for Shockwave Flash animations—no kidding!

The QuickTime Player can also serve as a media editor. For a small fee, users can upgrade their player so that it can perform such tasks as copying an audio track from one file to another or converting media files from one format to another.

The QuickTime Player is available for both the Windows and Macintosh operating systems. There is currently no QuickTime Player for either Linux or various other UNIX operating systems.

Windows Media Player

By Microsoft   **microsoft.com**   **Free**

Windows Media Player is installed by default on computers running recent versions of the Windows operating system. It can play media in a separate window or in place on a Web page displayed in IE.

Windows Media Player plays a number of audio and video file formats, though not as many as the QuickTime Player or the RealOne Player. It does not currently play QuickTime native files, Real Media native files, or any graphic or animation files.

The Windows Media Player is available for the Windows, Macintosh, Solaris, Windows CE, and Pocket PC operating systems.

RealOne Player

By RealNetworks   **real.com**   **Free for basic version**

The RealOne Player plays a wide variety of media—including video, audio, graphics, and entire Web pages—as well as RealNetworks' native formats. It also plays QuickTime files, Windows Media formats, and most Flash animations.

Like the QuickTime Player and the Windows Media Player, RealOne can play media in a separate window or in place on a Web page displayed in IE or Netscape.

The RealOne Player is currently available only for Windows. Macintosh users can download the less capable RealPlayer 8. UNIX users can download a "community supported" RealPlayer that is not formally associated with RealNetworks.

WinAmp player

By Nullsoft   **winamp.com**   **Free**

WinAmp specializes in playing a vast array of audio file formats—more than any other player. With Winamp3, you can also play common video file formats including MPEG, AVI, Windows Media, and Nullsoft's proprietary NSV format. Netscape 6+ users are likely to have this player because it is bundled with the browser. WinAmp is a standalone player and does not play inline audio files. If you have a lot of legacy audio files that for some reason will not be converted to a more recent, Web-friendly format, WinAmp is a good choice.

The free WinAmp player is available for Windows. There is currently an alpha release for Macintosh System 8.5 or later (but not OS X).

VIEWERS FOR PROPRIETARY CONTENT

Some media players are used to display proprietary formats produced by various computer programs. These formats are typically compound formats rather than simple media, such as audio and video. These media players are sometimes called viewers or readers.

Because viewers are so closely allied with the format they are designed to display, your choice of viewer is imposed by the design decisions you make for your e-learning product. If you decide to develop content in Macromedia Flash, then you need to ensure learners have the Flash Player installed on their computer. Likewise, if you plan to convert documents to Adobe PDF file format, then learners need Acrobat Reader.

Flash Player

By Macromedia **macromedia.com** **Free**

One of the most widely used viewers is Macromedia's Flash Player. The Flash Player displays content produced in its Flash authoring tool, or in other tools that can produce the Flash format (SWF), within a browser window. Content can include audio and video clips, graphics, complex games, assessments, entire lessons, or a whole course. According to a news release from Macromedia, a March 2002 study by NPD Research, the parent company of MediaMetrix, found that 98.3% of Web users have Macromedia Flash pre-installed with their browsers and can, therefore, experience Macromedia Flash content without having to download and install a player.

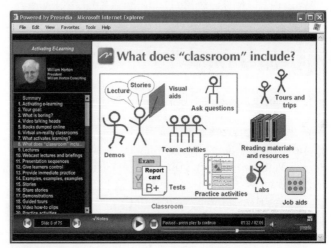

An online briefing being played by the Flash Player within Internet Explorer. This example shows slides converted to Flash by Presedia Express (chapter 18) and features Bill on vocals.

There is a Flash Player available for various combinations of IE, AOL, or Netscape browsers and most operating systems. Check with Macromedia for a list of compatible Flash Players for each operating system. We will talk more about Flash in chapter 17.

Acrobat Reader

By Adobe **www.adobe.com** **Free**

Another very popular viewer is Acrobat Reader that displays documents in Adobe's Portable Document Format (PDF), which preserves the layout and appearance of the original document. According to the same NPD Research study cited for the Flash Player, 75% of Web users have the Acrobat Reader installed on their computers. And it is available for most popular operating systems.

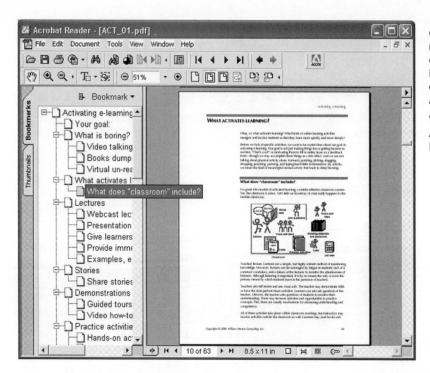

Online guide made by converting a Microsoft Word document to Acrobat PDF.

Viewed in the Adobe Acrobat Reader window.

7

Media players and viewers

The Acrobat Reader can display PDF documents in a separate window or within a browser. In either case, learners have the ability to search and navigate the file. If the author of the file permits it, learners can also select text and graphics. You can read more about Acrobat in chapter 18.

Microsoft Office viewers

By Microsoft   microsoft.com   **Free**

Microsoft provides viewers for Office products including PowerPoint, Word, Excel, and Visio. These viewers let those who do not have Office installed on their computers look at files created with the various Office applications.

Learners using Internet Explorer 5 or later will see the Office documents within their browser window. Those with Netscape and Opera will see the content in a separate window.

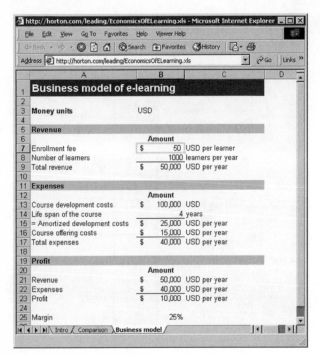

A Microsoft Excel spreadsheet displayed directly in Internet Explorer.

Microsoft's Internet Explorer can display Microsoft Office documents directly within the browser window if the Microsoft Office suite is installed.

Office viewers are available for the Windows operating system and some versions of the Macintosh operating system.

Other viewers and players for proprietary media

Other multimedia development tools and e-learning authoring tools have players for their private file formats. These include:

Tool and player	Vendor	Web address
Authorware	Macromedia	macromedia.com
Director	Macromedia	macromedia.com
Quest	Mentergy	mentergy.com
ToolBook	Click2learn	click2learn.com

CHOOSING MEDIA PLAYERS FOR E-LEARNING

Why would you choose one player over another? Let's look at what you need to know first. With that in mind, we'll look at all the issues that may contribute to your decision.

What you need to know first

As with browsers, the IT department may dictate which players can be used on company computers. In that case, your choice of rich media formats may be limited. In planning your project you may have to work backward and design for whichever media your learners are able to experience with the approved players. The good news is that you are aiming at a fixed target.

 First, decide what media you need, and then consider media players that let learners best experience these media.

You probably cannot totally control or fully identify what media players learners will have. So what do you do? First, inventory what your learners are likely to have. For instance, what operating system do they have, what browser are they using, and what players do they already have installed? Then design your e-learning to employ the media most of your learners will be able to play.

Capabilities to consider

Here are some capabilities to consider when choosing a suite of players for your learners—or determining how to design e-learning for the players your learners already have.

File formats played

Each player has its own *native* formats for which it is optimized. Some display only one format. The RealOne Player is optimized for playing RealAudio and RealVideo formats, the Windows Media Player for Windows Media formats, and the QuickTime Player (you guessed it) for QuickTime. In addition, most players can play some generic formats such as MPEG video or MP3 sound. However, not all players play the same mix of media. The Windows Media Player does not play RealAudio or RealVideo formats and the QuickTime Player does not play Windows Media formats. Players for proprietary formats display only that one format. The Acrobat Reader reads only Acrobat PDF files and the Flash Player plays only Flash SWF files.

Operating system compatibility

Not all players are available for all operating systems. QuickTime, for example, is not available for UNIX operating systems. Furthermore, some players are not available for particular versions of an operating system. Version 9 of the Windows Media Player, for example, is available for the Macintosh OS X operating system. OS 9.x users must use version 7.1.

Browser compatibility

Browser compatibility comes into play if you want learners to experience rich media within a Web page rather than in a standalone player. You will also need to determine in which browsers the player can display content. For example, there is currently no Windows Media plug-in for Netscape 6 browsers.

Advertising

Because most media players are free, some creators of these players may defray their costs by incorporating advertising within their players' user interface. For e-learning, this is more than an aesthetic issue. Such advertising can be distracting—especially if it lures learners away from the subject at hand. When choosing a player, you may want to determine whether you can eliminate or minimize the distractions caused by these ads. To do so may mean paying the company that provides the media player some kind of customization fee, or buying a deluxe version of the player.

Playback controls and feedback

Not only should an interface be legible, it should also possess the right set of playback controls and readouts. Here is a checklist of desirable playback elements that help learners remain informed and in control.

Function	Control	Readout
Play	●	●
Stop	●	●
Pause	●	●
Rewind	●	●
Position in stream	●	●
Volume	●	●
Title, author, copyright		●

Function	Control	Readout
Technical specifications of stream		●
Mute	●	●
Source	●	●
Buffering status		●

These recommendations cover streaming media, such as audio and video. Other media require analogous controls and readouts.

Footprint

The size of the media player's window may also be an important issue for your e-learners. True, most players can be minimized so that they do not take up any screen space. However, in that mode, the playback controls are not immediately available. Here are the Windows XP versions of several common media players in their most compact form playing an audio file.

Windows Media Player

QuickTime Player

RealOne Player

WinAmp player

Customization and branding

Your e-learning content probably has a certain look and feel that distinguishes it from e-learning provided by other organizations. You may wish to extend this branding effort to the programs that support your e-learning, such as media players. In addition to specifying what features to allow, some media players can be customized through the use of *skins*. A skin is like an interface style sheet and can radically change the look and feel of a player.

This is the WinAmp audio player that downloads with Netscape Navigator. It has a special skin that carries the Netscape logo in the upper-left corner.

Here is the same player but with a skin promoting the University of Oklahoma. (It is bright red.)

Skin by Mike Metevelis (winamp.com)

When customizing the visual appearance of a media player, take into account the size and legibility of the control devices. If they are too small, they will be difficult for your learners to manipulate. This is an important consideration if you are designing content for learners with hand-eye coordination difficulties, such as children or the elderly. Here are two examples that illustrate how changing the skin of a player can greatly alter the legibility of an interface.

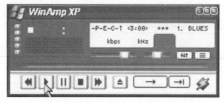 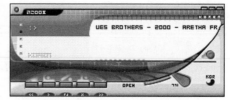

Skin by Karem Erkan (winamp.com)   Skin by Sungjee Yoo (winamp.com)

Inline display capabilities

Can the media player display media in place on the Web page so no separate player window is required? Can you control whether the media plays immediately when the page loads or requires some learner interaction? Each player has its own display and operation parameters that determine how the media appear and behave when embedded within a Web page. But, the player must be able to recognize them.

Can you control whether learners see a playback bar with a slider and VCR-like buttons? Is the playback bar visually pleasing? Do you have a choice of which controls to display. These various parameters are set within the HTML of the web page.

Here is an example of an inline video clip being displayed using an embedded QuickTime Player. Notice the playback slider and control buttons.

Remember, not all players can be embedded within a Web page. For example, WinAmp exists only as a standalone player.

Codec availability

One requirement for smooth media playback is the availability of the appropriate codec. What is a codec, you ask? *Codec* stands for compression/decompression. Video and audio are compressed with a special program to save space and speed transport over the network. When the media is viewed, the viewing software uses a matching program that decompresses the media for playback. A codec is the recipe for both compressing media and decompressing it. There are multiple codecs available. Some are common and are included along with media players. Other codecs are proprietary and require the learner to find and install them. Furthermore, not all players can use all codecs.

If you have no control over which media players learners will use for audio or video, be sure to use a common codec when compressing your media. If, however, you wish to use a proprietary codec, be sure to recommend a compatible media player and links to the codec and instructions for installing it.

Automatic updates and codec downloads

Vendors are continually updating their products, making improvements, fixing bugs, adding bugs, renaming bugs. Keeping up with these new versions can be a chore for developers, learners, and course administrators. To ease this burden, many vendors provide an automated update service. When a learner is connected to the Internet, the media player checks the update Web site to determine if the currently installed version is the most recent version available. If not, the media player displays a dialog box offering to download and install the update. Media players without automatic updating may still include a "check for updates" command on their menus.

In addition to updating software, many players offer to download a missing codec. When players are installed, not every possible codec is installed with it—only the most common ones. If the appropriate codec is not installed, the media player displays a dialog box offering to download the appropriate codec. Most of the popular media players handle this chore automatically.

Saving media

Can the players save media on the learner's system for playback or viewing later? You may want learners to be able to replay the media without having to download it again. Or, you may want to prevent them from making copies of the media.

Accessibility aids

Some media formats and players simplify making media accessible by those with common disabilities. The QuickTime movie format lets developers add text captions to audio and video segments. The QuickTime Player can display these text captions and make them available to screen readers for the blind. The RealOne Player also supports supplemental text captioning and descriptive audio.

In these media players, accessibility options may not be enabled by default. If these features are important to your learners, be sure to tell them how to enable them.

Media server compatibility

If you plan to offer streaming media, you'll likely want to match the media player and file format to the media server you plan to use. As an example, if you are using Windows Media Services to stream Windows Media files, then the Windows Media Player is probably your best choice; likewise, the QuickTime Player can take full advantage of the QuickTime Streaming Server.

Price

Some media players are offered in two versions: a basic version for free and a deluxe version costing between $20 and $40 USD. The deluxe version may play more formats, play at higher quality, allow more interface customization, and provide some simple editing capabilities. One example of the dual-version player is QuickTime. The free version is a highly capable player. The deluxe version adds handy editing features.

What you should specify

When it is time to choose media players, you will need to make several related decisions.

Decision	Description
File formats to play	You need to match the media file formats to the capabilities of the player. If you are planning to use only QuickTime or Adobe Acrobat files, then your choice of players is simple. If, however, you will be using MPEG video and MP3 audio, your field of possible vendors broadens.
Browser	Not all players are available for all browsers. Know what your learners will be using before specifying a brand.
Operating system	You need to know the operating system of your learners. For example, Windows Media Player offers one version for Mac OS X and another version for Mac OS versions 8.1 through 9.x.
Brand	The main players for video are Windows Media Player, QuickTime Player, RealOne Player, and the WinAmp player. Proprietary file formats usually require a corresponding player.
Version	Players continually evolve through a seemingly endless series of versions. Do not say "Acrobat Reader" when what you really mean is "Acrobat Reader 5 or later." Later versions usually add capabilities and sometimes fix bugs found in earlier versions.

MAKING PLAYERS EASIER TO USE

Make it easy for learners to check whether they have the players and viewers needed to take your e-learning. Provide an easy-to-find technical requirements page. For each player and viewer needed, include a link to a test page that checks to see if the required media player is installed.

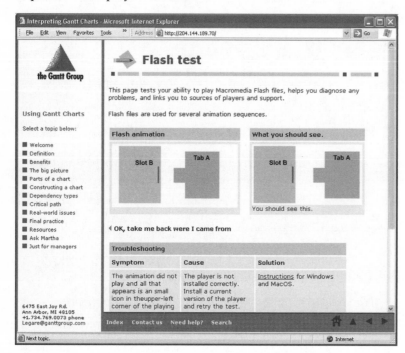

This page lets learners verify that they can play Flash files. It also helps them diagnose and correct problems.

ALTERNATIVES TO MEDIA PLAYERS

Are there alternatives to media players? The obvious and rather flippant answer is: "Don't use media requiring players." If that position is too extreme for you but To ensure compatibility across operating systems and browsers, say along with me: "Test and test again."

you still want to have tighter control over how learners will experience rich media, then consider this approach. Integrate your video and audio into Flash movies using Flash MX and then embed the movies within your HTML pages. Using Flash for all your media needs will reduce the operating system-browser-player matching game.

Another alternative is to use Java applets. Some programs will save their files as Java applets. There are other programs, such as IBM's HotMedia, that allow developers to embed various video, audio, and graphic files into a presentation that is published as a Java applet. Java applets rely on the Java virtual machine installed on the learner's computer rather than on a variety of players and viewers.

WHAT NOW?

To put the ideas of this chapter into action, you need to make decisions and take actions. Here are some recommendations for how to proceed.

If you ...	Then ...
Are still designing your e-learning	Consider which media you need: video, voice-over animations, interactive simulations, games, documents, spreadsheets, virtual reality worlds, and so forth. Identify the file formats required by these media and list the players available for these file formats.
Are at the point of picking media players	Use the criteria in this chapter as a starting point. List your requirements. Check for additional media players beyond the ones listed here. Using the process listed in chapter 20, make your selection.
Have already picked your media players	Map the file formats each player can display to specific tools that can create those file formats. Create a guide for authors about what to use—and what not to use. Develop templates, style sheets, custom menus, and code snippets, needed to simplify inserting rich media into your e-learning.

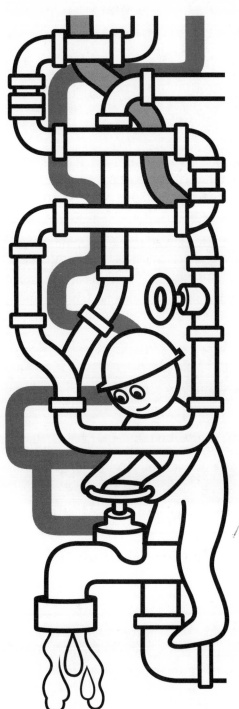

Tools for offering e-learning

Tools for offering e-learning make sure that the e-learning you create can be accessed by learners—conveniently and efficiently. Tools for offering e-learning provide several functions:

▶ **Making e-learning available over a network**. Sometimes this activity is referred to as *publishing* a course. As its name suggests, publishing makes the course public.

...stering your e-learning offerings. ...on tasks include enrolling learners in ...es, assigning administrators and ...ructors to courses, collecting fees, and ...urning out required reports. Even online ...ourses involve a lot of paperwork. Tools in the Offer column of our tools framework help with this paperwork.

► **Controlling and tracking access** to the courses, lessons, and individual objects you offer. Tools may be needed to restrict access to registered learners and log which modules they have taken and completed. Offering may also require recording scores on individual tests and other graded activities.

Offering tools are the fuzziest group of tools in this book. Vendors are continually packing more and more features into their products to become that one and only tool you will ever need. To further blur the boundaries of this category, some of these tools overlap into the Create column by providing authoring capabilities. So, pay careful attention to the specific capabilities the tool provides—not to the label attached to it by the vendor.

Offering tools include several main categories:

► **Web servers** to deliver Web pages and other media requested by a Web browser (chapter 8)

► **Learning management systems** to administer courses and students (chapter 9)

► **Learning content management systems** to assemble and offer courses made up of reusable content modules (chapter 10)

► **Collaboration tools** to enable fluid communication among distributed learners (chapter 11)

► **Virtual-school systems** to conduct instructor-led learning over the network (chapter 12)

► **Media servers** to deliver sound, video, and other dynamic media efficiently over the network (chapter 13)

The tools in this section tend to be the most expensive and technically complex of the tools and technologies we cover in this book. And they are the most likely to be outsourced to an application service provider or portal. Even so, it is important to understand what they offer.

8 Web servers

Web servers, like browsers, are core technology for e-learning endeavors. If e-learning is offered on the Internet or an intranet, some kind of Web server software is required. Those who design and administer e-learning may never have to directly choose or set-up a Web server, but they cannot escape the limitations of Web server software. LMSs and virtual-school systems may be more chic, but it is the sweaty web server that dos the heavy lifting.

WHY YOU NEED TO KNOW ABOUT WEB SERVERS

You probably will not directly pick a Web server for e-learning. Web servers are usually chosen as part of an organizational IT strategy that goes beyond the needs for e-learning.

It's unlikely that you will be directly involved in picking a Web server for e-learning. Web servers are usually part of an organization's IT strategy that goes beyond the needs of e-learning. Yet you still need to know about Web servers, because they may constrain your choice of other tools. And that's because many of those tools—such as a learning management system (LMS), learning content management system (LCMS), or virtual-school system—rely on capabilities provided by the underlying Web server.

Web servers also provide many capabilities directly useful for e-learning—especially for projects offering a small number of voluntarily taken, learner-led courses about informational subjects.

Finally, even if someone else is providing the server for you, you may still need to know which of its features to enable, which to disable, as well as how to optimize the server for the unique needs of e-learning.

WHAT WEB SERVERS OFFER

The term *Web server* has several meanings. It refers to the piece of software that dispatches Web pages to browsers. It also can mean the physical machine on which that software runs. Both definitions share the notion of the Web server as a computer on the Internet or intranet, which serves up content and performs other services as requested by other computers on the network.

Where Web servers fit

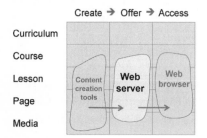

The Web server is the bull's-eye on the tools framework. It is exactly in the center. The Web server enables the essential middle levels of the offering process, but it often goes unnoticed because it sits in the background of other tools.

The Web server is a conduit between course authors and learners. Course authors upload their course content to the server, which makes it available to learners who request and display specific parts through their Web browsers (chapter 6).

In addition, Web servers may include other common Internet services, such as e-mail, newsgroups, and FTP sites.

Relationship to other components

Web server software is part of a system of hardware and software that is necessary to offer e-learning. Imagine that server system as a stack of blocks. Higher-level blocks or components depend on lower-level ones.

At the bottom, we find the server hardware. The server hardware is a high-speed, high-capacity computer that is physically connected to the network. This hardware is the basis for the capabilities provided by all the software that runs on it.

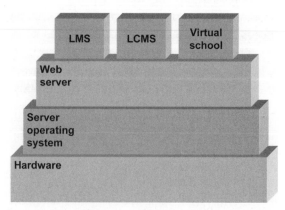

Atop the server hardware runs a *server operating system* that is honed to provide general services over a network. The server operating system handles such tasks as dispensing files to people in the office, queuing up jobs going to a shared printer, and routing e-mail messages. The server operating system is sometimes called the *server platform* because it provides a foundation on which the Web server software rests. The server operating system could itself be called a server because it serves other machines on the network.

Atop the server operating system, we find the Web server. A Web server, then, is a more specialized program that runs above the server operating system. It dispatches Web pages and other related media in response to requests from remote computers. Although the Web server is a separate piece of software, it is often sold as part of the server operating system. For example, Internet Information Services is part of the Microsoft Windows 2000 Server.

Finally, atop the Web server may go additional pieces of software such as an LMS, LCMS, or virtual-school system. These tools use capabilities provided by both the server operating system and the Web server software. Hence, they must be compatible with the Web server, server operating system, and server hardware beneath them.

Interdependencies among layers

In the real world, the term Web server is variously used to refer to just the layer labeled "Web server" in our diagram, to that layer and the server operating system together, or to the combination of these two with the server hardware. The reason for the confusion is that the layers are not entirely independent. To see the dependencies, consider some examples of Web servers, server operating systems, and hardware.

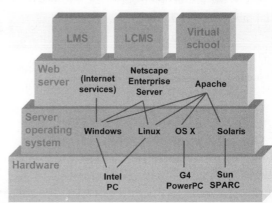

Three popular Web servers are Windows Internet Information Services, Netscape Enterprise Server, and Apache. Their relationships with operating systems are both economic and intimate. Windows Internet Information Services is not even a separate product. You can't buy it separately; it is built into Windows 2000 Server. Netscape Enterprise Server has versions available for Window and Linux operating systems. Apache is the most independent of servers. Versions are available for Windows, Linux, Macintosh OS X Server, and Sun Solaris operating systems. For all but the Windows version, Apache servers are typically included as a free part of the operating system and even integrated with it.

Dependencies continue downward with the hardware. Windows server operating systems, with few exceptions, run exclusively on computers with Intel processors. Linux can also run on these computers and on some other hardware not shown here. The Macintosh OS X Server runs only on Macintosh G4 PowerPC systems. Likewise, Sun's Solaris operating system runs on Sun SPARC systems.

What this means is that companies usually buy the Web server, server operating system, and hardware as a package. And they standardize their choices to limit the number of combinations they must maintain. Their chosen combination becomes the platform (the blocks analogy, get it?) on which to offer e-learning.

HOW WEB SERVERS WORK

The Web server uses Hypertext Transfer Protocol (HTTP) to receive and acknowledge requests. This protocol is just a set of rules for how a Web browser requests information and how the server packages and sends it back. Because this protocol is standardized, any browser works with any Web server.

Simple static content

To see how a Web server works, let's step through a simple transaction. Say your browser requested the URL "http://horton.com/evaluating," either because you typed this into the browser's location or address window or because this was the destination of a link you clicked on (1).

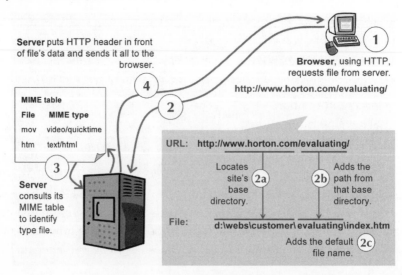

By magic more profound than we can explain, that request wends its way across the Internet to the Web server housing the horton.com site (2). The Web server, which actually hosts several separate Web sites, checks to see where it keeps the home directory for "horton.com." In this example, it is the directory "d:\webs\customer\" (2a). Notice that the URL does not end with "horton.com." It also contains "/evaluating/." So, the server knows it has to look deeper in its directory structure and adds this additional part to the home directory to get "c:\webs\customer\evaluating\" as the file location (2b).

At this point, the server notices that something is missing, the name of a particular file. The path "c:\webs\customer\evaluating\" is a directory in which there are many files. How does the Web server decide which one to send? It checks the properties for this Web site to see what was designated as the default file name to use when none is specified. In this case, the default file is "index.htm" (2c). So now the Web server looks for "c:\webs\customer\evaluating\index.htm" and finds it.

Before the Web server sends the file back to the browser, however, it performs one more chore. It figures out what kind of data the file contains (3) and passes that information back to the browser along with the page (4).

You would think that after serving up millions of Web pages a server would know that files whose names end in ".htm" are HTML text files. A Web server makes no assumptions. To determine the kind of data in each file, the server looks up the file's extension in what is called a *MIME table*. This table says that files ending in ".htm" are of type

```
HTTP/1.1 200 OK
Date: Wed, 18 Sep 2002 18:03:16 GMT
Server: Apache/1.3.26 (Unix)
mod_ssl/2.8.10 OpenSSL/0.9.6g
Last-Modified: Mon, 12 Aug 2002 16:26:03
GMT
ETag: "e540e-e8e-3d57e19b"
Accept-Ranges: bytes
Content-Length: 3726
Connection: close
Content-Type: text/html
```

"text/html." The server then prepares an HTTP envelope or header for the file, like the one pictured here. This header describes the file, including its type. Finally, the server sends the header and file to the browser that requested the file.

Dynamic content

If all Web servers ever served up were static pages, they would be much simpler, and e-learning would not be possible. It is dynamic content that makes up e-learning and most other really useful Web content. The term dynamic does not mean that the pages contain video and animation but that the content sent back to the browser is not always the same. Dynamic content makes it possible to customize pages to what learners need, to score tests, and to engage learners in rich simulations.

How then does the server produce dynamic content? There are several ways the content delivered to the browser can change from user to user. One way is through the use of server pages. These are conventional HTML pages with parts that get filled in only when the page is requested. If you look at such a page, you would likely see familiar HTML tags until you get to the changeable section. There you would see scripts to generate the missing content. Common scripting schemes are Active Server Pages, JavaServer Pages, or Cold Fusion. These scripts generate content by manipulating data and sending the results to the browser as plain HTML.

Here we refer to the requesting entity as a Web browser. It could also be any kind of Web client capable of using HTTP to talk to the server. It might be a collaboration tool or a media player.

This data may come from different sources such as entries in a database or information entered into a Web form. Here is an example to illustrate the concept. A learner completes a multiple-choice question and clicks the Submit button. The learner's answer is sent to the server for processing by a specialized script. The script takes the learner's answer and consults a database containing information about this question. The script compares the learner's answer to the correct answer, calculates a grade, posts the grade to the learner's personal record, and generates feedback based on the learner's score. Finally, the script fills the score and feedback information into a server page and sends it back to the browser as pure HTML.

Here is another example. It is an Active Server page viewed in Dreamweaver MX. This page provides feedback in a game about nutrition.

The little icons with ASP written on them

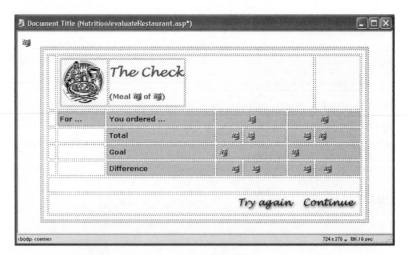

indicate where separate scripts run when the page is processed by the server. These scripts replace themselves with meaningful content before the page is sent to the browser.

Here is a portion of what the page looks like "under the hood." It shows the code that adds rows to the table just before the row titled "Total."

```
<%
totalSubstanceAmount = 0
totalSubstance2Amount = 0

Types.MoveFirst
Types.MoveNext
do while not Types.EOF
     theID = Request.Form(Types("Category"))
     if theID > 0 then
             cmdTemp.CommandText = queryPreamble & theID & ")"
             Foods.Open cmdTemp, , 0, 1
             theDescription = Foods("Description")
             theSubstanceAmount = Foods(theSubstance)
             if numberOfCriteria = 2 then
                     theSubstance2Amount = Foods(theSubstance2)
             else
                     theSubstance2Amount = 0
             end if
             Foods.Close
     else
             theDescription = "Nothing"
             theSubstanceAmount = 0
             theSubstance2Amount = 0
     end if
     Response.Write("<tr><td> </td>")
     Response.Write("<td class='gray'>" & Types("Category") & "</td>")
     Response.Write("<td class='gray'>" & theDescription & "</td>")
     theValue = formatNumber(theSubstanceAmount, theSubstanceFormat)
     Response.Write("<td class='grayRight'>" & theValue & "</td>")
     Response.Write("<td class='gray'>" & theSubstanceUnits & "</td>")
     if numberOfCriteria = 2 then
             theValue = formatNumber(theSubstance2Amount,
theSubstance2Format)
             Response.Write("<td class='grayRight'>" & theValue & "</td>")
             Response.Write("<td class='gray'>" & theSubstance2Units &
"</td>")
     end if
     Response.Write("</tr>")
     totalSubstanceAmount = totalSubstanceAmount + theSubstanceAmount
     totalSubstance2Amount = totalSubstance2Amount + theSubstance2Amount
     Types.MoveNext
loop
%>
```

Here is how the page appears in the browser after the scripts have run.

The check - Microsoft Internet Explorer					

The Check
(Meal 1 of 3)

For ...	You ordered ...	Carbohydrate		Protein	
Appetizer	Salmon, smoked	0	grams	18	grams
Soup	Tomato soup w/ water, canned	17	grams	2	grams
Pasta	Macaroni and cheese, home rcpe	40	grams	17	grams
Entrée	Beef roast, rib, lean + fat	0	grams	19	grams
Side	Potatoes, mashed, recpe, w/ milk	37	grams	4	grams
Beverage	Beer, regular	13	grams	1	grams
Dessert	Apple pie	60	grams	3	grams
Bread	Rolls, dinner, home recipe	20	grams	3	grams
	Total	187	grams	67	grams
	Goal	At least 260 grams		At least 55 grams	
	Difference	-73	grams	12	grams

Try again   Continue

Another way the server can generate dynamic content is by running a program on the server. This program generates a response, which the Web server dutifully passes back to the browser. Such programs range from simple scripts to complete server applications. They may be implemented as ActiveX server components or Java servlets.

What else Web servers do

Delivering requested files and data is the most important duty of Web servers, but that's not all they do. Web servers provide a wide range of services such as logging requests and their responses, reporting errors, uploading files from authors, and. enforcing security restrictions.

QUICK TOUR OF A WEB SERVER

A correctly functioning Web server is invisible. The only time you might notice it at all is when there is a problem and you get a message that the server could not find the requested file or that a necessary database was offline for vacation.

This tour is completely optional. It's not intended to be some sort of user's manual. I just want to give you a look behind the scenes.

To the person who sets up and maintains the Web site—the Webmaster or Web site administrator—the Web server is quite visible. Let's take a guided tour of a Microsoft Internet Information Services Web server as seen by its administrator.

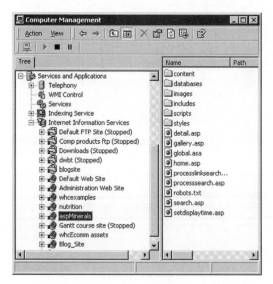

The key task of the server is maintaining Web sites. Here you can see the sites defined on this server. Each one is represented by an item in the tree view in the left pane. The area in the right pane shows the subfolders within the selected site.

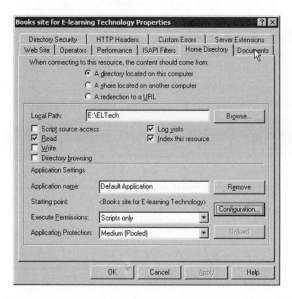

As the tabs indicate, each site has a number of options or properties that the administrator sets.

The most important one is the home directory of the site. In this example it is "E:\ELTech."

Also important are security settings that determine what browsers can do with content in the site. In this example, all the browser can do is read the files.

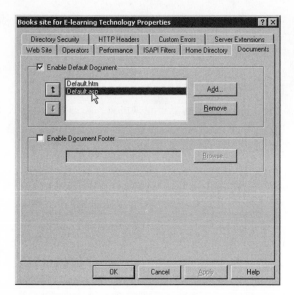

Another tab lets the administrator set the default file name, that is, the file that is sent if the browser does not specify one. The administrator can set up a list of names for the server to try.

Additional security options control who can access the site and what they can do there. Such options can enable encryption or require identification certificates from clients.

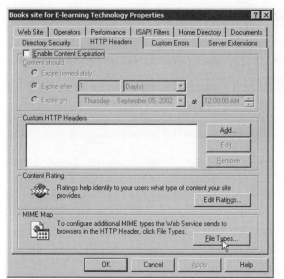

The administrator can adjust the way the server generates HTTP headers sent back to the browser. For example, the administrator can specify when content expires. The browser will not reread expired content from its cache but will re-request the content from the server. The administrator can also specify that content on this site is for adults only ("Sex 101"?). This site does not have any custom HTTP headers.

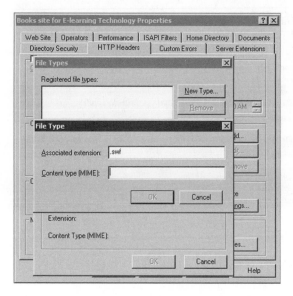

By opening the File Types dialog box, the administrator can edit the MIME table that identifies the file types associated with file extensions.

The administrator can also adjust how the server responds to errors, such as when the browser requests a page that does not exist on the server. For instance, the administrator can specify a custom Web page to send in response to each anticipated error.

POPULAR WEB-SERVER SOFTWARE

Although there are dozens of Web servers available, you really only need to know about two main ones—Apache HTTP Server and Internet Information Services. They account for well over 90% of the servers in use and are the only ones widely supported by tools that run atop Web servers, such as LMSs, LCMSs, collaboration servers, and virtual-school systems—the very chapters following this one, as a matter of fact.

Apache HTTP Server

By Apache Software Foundation   **apache.org**

The Apache HTTP Server is the most widely available and most widely used server. According to the June 2002 Netcraft (netcraft.com) survey of 38 million active Web servers, 64% were running Apache. Could that be because it is capable, available for all operating systems, and reliable? Or, could it be because it is free?

This procedure of making source code available is called *open source licensing*. Those who get the code modify it to add features and fix bugs. They then make the changes available to the supplier and other users.

Free? Well, sort of. The Apache HTTP Server is made available by the Apache Software Foundation, and the source code is free to developers who take it and make it run on their operating systems. Some operating system vendors include the Apache HTTP Server in the package with their server operating systems. Check the fine print in the ads for the Red Hat Linux Server or Macintosh OS X Server.

Another advantage of the Apache server is that versions are available for even the most obscure operating systems, including Windows 3.1, Windows 95, Windows 98, Windows NT, Windows 2000, Macintosh OS X, Linux, Solaris, Novell NetWare, Net BSD, Free BSD, AIX, Digital UNIX, HP/UX, SCO UNIX, IRIX, VMS, AS/400, OS/2, and Be OS. Next month there will probably be a version that runs on your microwave oven!

"Apache" is a contraction of "A PAtchEY" Server because it grew out of fixes to an earlier server.

An Apache HTTP Server v 1.3 running on Windows 2000. The administrative interface is a freeware package called Toolkit for Apache by Innerdive Solutions (innerdive.com).

Internet Information Services

By Microsoft   **microsoft.com**

Microsoft, starting with one of the endless series of service packs (bug fixes) to Windows NT Server, made its Internet Information Services (IIS, for short) Web server available free. Of course, IIS is free only if you purchase Microsoft's server operating system. The tradition of integrated Web services continues with the Microsoft Windows 2000 Server. Now IIS makes up about 25% of active Web servers, according to the June 2002 Netcraft survey (netcraft.com).

Though only available for Windows server operating systems, Microsoft's IIS is widely supported by vendors of other server software, such as LMSs and other e-learning management and collaboration systems.

IIS has some key advantages because it is well integrated with Microsoft's databases, XML tools, scripting languages, collaboration systems, e-commerce tools, and other enterprise-level technologies. And Microsoft has made administering Web sites a point-and-click operation, even remotely.

Other Web servers

There are other Web servers you may need to know about. These Web servers range from freebee class projects in computer science to special-purpose, high-performance, industrial-strength enterprise systems. Some are no longer under development. Others are only for obscure operating systems.

 Why consider any other Web servers? After all, Apache and Microsoft account for over 90% of active servers, and they are the only two Web servers that work with common LMS, LCMS, collaboration, and virtual- school tools. Hmmm.... Maybe Bill and Kit own some Zeus stock!

You may need to know about these other servers because one of them may be all your organization has available to host your e-learning—at least until you can justify your own server. Or, you may want to do some name dropping around the company water cooler.

Zeus Web Server

By Zeus Technology   **www.zeustechnology.com**

The Zeus Web Server, available for most UNIX-based operating systems, is designed for especially high-traffic sites. It currently accounts for between 1% and 2% of active servers.

AOLserver

By AOL Time Warner   **www.aolserver.com**

The AOLserver is an open source Web server provided by AOL (America Online). It is available for a number of UNIX-based operating systems. It touts itself as an ideal Web server for high-traffic sites.

Netscape Enterprise Server

By Netscape   **netscape.com**

Netscape Enterprise Server is a high-volume Web server for Windows and Solaris server operating systems. These servers were widely deployed in big businesses during the end of the last century.

Lotus Domino server

By IBM   **lotus.com**

IBM's Lotus division has evolved the Domino server through several versions now. Though primarily a support for collaboration and Lotus Notes, the Domino server does contain a capable Web server and is widely deployed in large and medium businesses.

Sun ONE Web Server

By Sun Microsystems   **sun.com**

Formerly known as the iPlanet Web Server, the Sun ONE Web Server is available for Windows, Solaris, Linux, and some other UNIX operating systems. It is marketed as an application server platform, especially for running server-based applications written in Sun's Java language.

Even more

To find even more Web servers, you can start with the not-quite-up-to-date list at serverwatch.com. Also check the sites of the server operating system or hardware you are using (microsoft.com, sun.com, ibm.com, apple.com, and so on). Or, search the Web for "Web server software." You'll have to filter out a lot of irrelevant hits, but you'll find some gold among the dross.

CHOOSING A WEB SERVER

If you are involved in selecting a Web server or specifying how it is to be set up, you need to understand your options and the features that are especially important for e-learning. As we point out these options and features, we are going to be talking about Web servers in the larger sense—as a platform composed of hardware, operating systems, and server software. Remember the building blocks?

What you need to know first

Before you pick a specific Web server you need to do some research and make some decisions.

▶ **What is your company's policy toward servers**? Has it standardized on a particular Web server already? Does it have servers and licenses available for your use? Because many corporations standardize on a single server operating system, you may be limited to the Web server bundled with that operating system or ones compatible with it. This limitation may, in turn, constrain your choice of other software that runs on this server.

▶ **What capacity do you need**? How many users will you have? How many pages will they request per hour? What other files will those pages require downloading? What is the mix of media the server must serve? Knowing the answers to these questions will help you decide how many servers you'll need, what capacity disk drives to purchase, and whether you'll need a separate media server.

▶ **What other software must run on the server**? Will you need to run an LMS, LCMS, collaboration server, virtual-school system, or some other software atop or along side the Web server? The Web server will need to be compatible with these additional pieces of software.

Capabilities to consider

What capabilities should you look for in a Web server? Which should you remember to turn on when you install it? Let's run down a list of the most important features.

Responsiveness and capacity

Does the server have the raw speed and efficiency to handle frequent requests from many learners? Can it handle hundreds—or even thousands—of hits per second? Although the speed of the underlying hardware and the number of other tasks performed on the machine affect server speed, raw speed and efficiency of the server software are core capabilities. The WebBench test (etestinglabs.com) is a widely used measure of Web server performance.

Integration with other servers

Does the server integrate with an LMS, LCMS, virtual-school system, collaboration server, media server, e-commerce, or other specialized server software? Or, do these services require a separate machine?

Integration with the operating system

Is the Web server tightly integrated with the server operating system? Does it take advantage of features of that operating system? For example, Microsoft's Internet Information Services is built into Windows 2000 Server and simplifies access to the Microsoft Internet Server Application Program Interface (ISAPI) for programming the server, to Open Database Connectivity (ODBC) for connecting to databases, to Active Server Pages (ASP) for dynamic content, and Extensible Markup Language (XML) components for single-source publishing.

 Don't let all these abbreviations get you down. Just skim over them in the data sheets of products, and don't be afraid to ask for definitions.

Scripting and programming

Does the server support programs or scripts for dynamic content? Can it process dynamic pages using Active Server Pages, JavaServer Pages, or Cold Fusion? Does it run scripting languages such as JavaScript, Visual Basic, and Perl as well as languages like Java (J2EE)? Does it make it easy to use software components such as Java beans and Java servlets? Does it have tools to transform XML data into HTML Web pages? Can it retrieve and format data in databases, using tools such as ODBC, JDBC, ADO.NET, or PHP?

Rich security model

If your e-learning site involves e-commerce or must deal with confidential or secret information, such as employee records or courses on forthcoming products, you need a secure server. Ask whether the server lets you protect files from unauthorized access and changes. Does it make it easy for authors to create and revise pages and for learners to read them while preventing hackers from deleting or damaging them? Does the Web server (or the server operating system) provide features such as Secure Sockets Layer (SSL), digital certificates (X.509), a certificate server, and secure HTTP (S-HTTP).

Server running too slow?

If the server is too slow, bring the following suggestions up with the IT department or server administrator:

▶ Add more memory.

▶ Install a faster processor.

▶ Increase the speed of the network connection.

▶ Add more processors.

▶ Provide more direct database access.

▶ Eliminate other activities on the server. Move FTP and media services to another server.

▶ Disable services you do not need.

▶ Share and balance the load among multiple servers.

Virtual servers

Can you set up many unique sites on the same server? Can you change the properties of each site individually? Can you allocate network bandwidth and other resources to sites individually? Can you set different security constraints on each site?

Bundled services and products

Besides an HTTP server to dispatch Web pages, what other services or products does the Web-server package include? Look for:

▶ FTP for uploading files to the server

▶ E-mail server (SMTP, POP3, or IMAP) for basic e-mail capabilities

▶ News server (NNTP) for online discussions

▶ Chat server (IRC) for crude instant messaging

▶ Media server for streaming audio and video files

▶ Firewall to block undesirable files

▶ Network management tools for remotely administering the server

▶ Database server, such as mySQL, which is included on several Linux systems

ALTERNATIVES TO WEB SERVER SOFTWARE

For most e-learning projects, there is no practical alternative to a Web server. You may outsource the hosting of your e-learning, but there will be a server somewhere.

Okay, okay, there are a couple of exceptions. Some higher-level tools work directly on top of the server operating system without benefit of a separate Web server. Most of these get by without a separate Web server because they have built in Web serving capabilities.

Another alternative to making content available through a Web server is to deliver content directly to browsers and other media players by writing it onto CD-ROMs or letting learners download it to their local disks. Web browsers are quite capable of reading files from local disks.

Or, you could install a Web server directly on the learner's machine along with the e-learning content. Windows XP Professional includes a simplified version of the Web server found in Windows 2000 Server.

WHAT NOW?

To learn more about Web servers, read the tutorials at serverwatch.com. You can practice setting up Web sites using Personal Web Server for Windows 98 or the Internet Information Services built into Windows XP Professional. Read the documentation for a Web server. Documentation for the Apache Web Server is available from apache.org. Even if you do not understand everything you read, you will get an appreciation of what IT departments do for a living.

Once you understand how Web servers work and how they can contribute to e-learning, you are ready to proceed.

If you ...	Then ...
Are still designing your e-learning	▶ Consider what other tools will run atop your Web server: LMS, LCMS, collaboration server, virtual-school system, and a media server. You will need to pick products that all work together. ▶ Decide what parts of your e-learning you will outsource.
Are at the point of picking Web server software	▶ Learn whether your IT department has a policy restricting what Web server you can choose. ▶ Compile a list of requirements for your Web server imposed by products that must run atop it. Combine those requirements with the general criteria of chapter 21 and those in this chapter to guide your choice.
Have already picked your Web server software	▶ Set up the server for e-learning. Consider the needs of other e-learning software running on the same server. Activate and deactivate various features as needed. Also set up security to control access to your e-learning.

Remember, the Web server is valuable on its own—and as a platform for more specialized tools like a learning management system, which is covered in the next chapter.

9 Learning management systems

A learning management system simplifies the process of administering education and training. It is a complex system used by managers, administrators, instructors, and learners to schedule, register, bill, and track

Remember, buying an LMS is not a substitute for having a learning strategy.

learners through courses and other learning events. It lets learners find and register for courses, launch online courses, monitor their competencies, and gauge their progress through a course or program of learning. Finally, it helps administrators manage training programs and compile statistics and reports.

WHAT AN **LMS** DOES

LMSs help create and offer courses and curricula. They reside at the top of the Offer column of our tools framework. Their primary function is to offer a collection of courses. They may also include capabilities for assembling individual courses into organized curricula or certificate programs. At the course level, LMSs provide an ability to launch and track performance within courses.

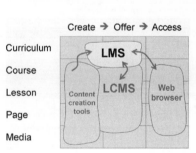

Pure LMSs work primarily at the curriculum level, tracking what courses learners have taken. Some systems track classroom training events as well as online training. Others can also assemble courses into certificate programs, tracks, or curricula.

The LMS integrates courses created in content creation tools (Web-based and course authoring tools). It may also integrate courses delivered by a Learning Content Management System (LCMS). In these cases, the LMS finds

Yeah, yeah. LMSs are all the rage today, but we conducted effective training programs for centuries without them. The lack of an LMS is **not** an excuse for failing to educating people.

the course and redirects the learner to the LCMS, which actually launches the course and tracks the learner's progress. The LCMS then reports completions and grades back to the LMS.

LMS vs. LCMS vs. VIRTUAL-SCHOOL SYSTEM

Although the capabilities of high-level e-learning systems overlap considerably, it is important to keep the core function of each tool in mind as you consider the ones you need for your project. In the following table, we compare the functions of *pure* LMSs, LCMSs (chapter 10), and virtual-school systems (chapter 12).

Issue	Pure LMS	Pure LCMS	Virtual-school system
Why do you need one?	To manage learners who are taking whole courses.	To assemble courses from smaller units of content.	To run an online school with instructor-led classes.
What levels of content do they manage?	The curriculum and course levels.	The course, lesson, page, and media levels, especially if delivered as learning objects.	The course, lesson, page, and media levels, as well as collaborative events and online meetings.
What else do they manage?	May manage classroom courses and certifications.	May manage competencies at a very detailed level.	Classroom meetings, seminars, and other events, like those found in university programs.
What do they help you reuse?	Whole courses in multiple curricula.	Lessons, pages, and media in multiple courses.	Courses in multiple curricula. May reuse content at lower levels.
How do they adapt content to the learner?	Present a menu and catalog of courses. Some suggest courses based on a learner's profile.	Some analyze a learner's progress at the level of individual objectives.	The instructor manually adapts content to individual learners.

Issue	Pure LMS	Pure LCMS	Virtual-school system
What do they track about learners?	Needs, preferences, and abilities. They also track course starts, completions, and test scores.	Starts, completions, scores, and progress through courses, lessons, and pages.	Preferences and learning needs. Most track activities such as those normally entered in a grade book.
What kinds of reports do they produce?	Learners, curricula, courses, and grades.	Courses, lessons, test, and activities.	Learners, courses, lesson, tests, activities, and meetings.
How are courses authored?	Courses are imported into LMSs. Authoring tools are not built in.	Authoring tools are built in or available as an add-on. LCMSs also let you import existing content.	Few virtual-school systems have sophisticated authoring tools. However, they all let you import content.
How do they assess learning?	LMSs have built-in test creation and administration tools for course- and curriculum-level assessments.	LCMSs have built-in test creation and administration tools. Tests can be tracked at the page, lesson, and course level.	Tests and quizzes are usually tracked as separate activities—not as part of a specific lesson or page.
Who provides navigation controls for the course?	LMSs launch complete courses that use their own navigation schemes.	Modules of content appear in the LCMSs navigational framework.	Modules of content appear in the virtual-school system's navigational framework.

There are few pure systems. Many products incorporate features from all three categories. As a result, they are less distinct and the various products are more versatile—and more cumbersome and expensive.

QUICK TOUR OF AN LMS

The following screens illustrate some of the main functions of an LMS. They are from a product called The Learning Manager (thelearningmanager.com).

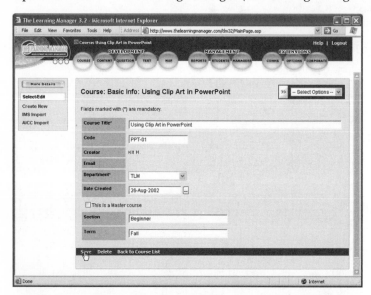

Here the administrator adds a course to a curriculum. Administrators can define multiple curricula.

The course need not be on the same server. It can be anywhere on the Internet.

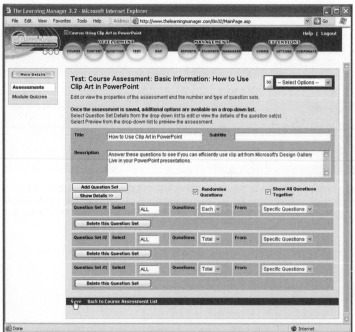

The instructor or course author creates questions that are grouped together into assessments. Assessments can be attached to courses or to individual modules. (The Learning Manager has some LCMS features.)

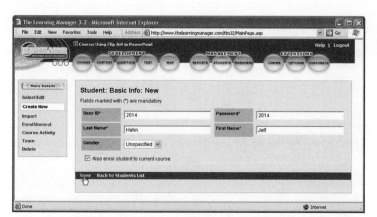

The administrator registers learners.

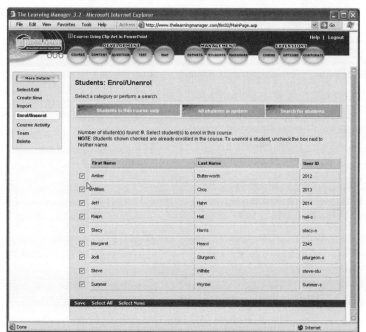

Once learners are registered in the system, the administrator can enroll them in specific courses or groups of courses.

The administrator may also enable learners to enroll themselves in courses.

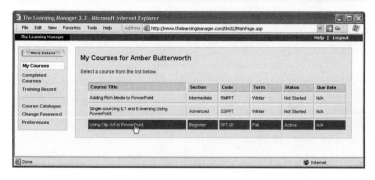

After logging in, learners see a list of courses in which they are enrolled.

9

Learning management systems

Learners can view details about courses in which they are enrolled or about which they are curious.

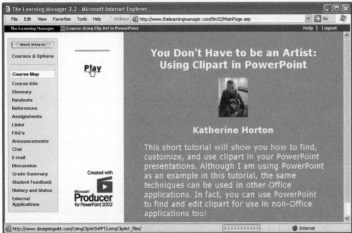

Learners use the system to launch the course.

Although the course may appear in the same browser window as the LMS, it is accessed from its own location.

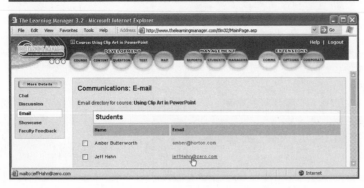

Learners, instructors, and administrators can communicate with one another via chat, discussion forum, or e-mail (as in this example).

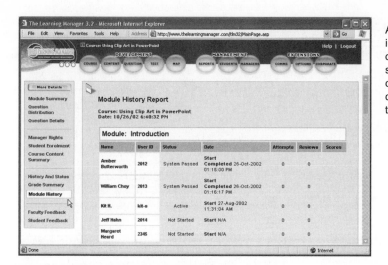

Administrators and instructors can view many different reports. This report shows the learners currently enrolled in a course and their progress in the course.

HOW AN LMS WORKS

Behind the scenes, an LMS is a Web-based database application that tracks learners and the courses they have access to or have completed. Through an integrated, Web-based interface, an LMS lets administrators perform common tasks, such as registering learners, adding courses, enrolling learners into courses, launching courses for learners, recording course completions and grades, and generating reports.

The actual structure of the system varies from product to product but LMS databases typically track learners and courses. Course records include the Web address to launch the actual course which may be stored separately. The database also defines

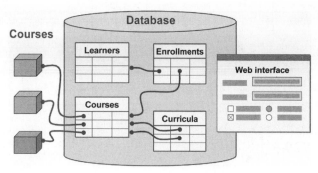

curricula as sequences of courses and tracks or records enrollments—that is, the learners assigned to each course.

LMS PRODUCTS

Estimates vary but the number of products calling themselves LMSs or claiming to include an LMS component is somewhere between 50 and 150. Here is a list of 60 or so products you can start investigating.

 In the early part of the 20th Century, there were this many automobile manufacturers.

If your favorite LMS is missing, check the lists of LCMSs (chapter 10) or virtual-school systems (chapter 12) as many of these tools also contain learning management capabilities.

Product	Vendor	Web address
ABC Academy	Danish Probe	danishprobe.com
Active Learner	Resource Development Corporation	www.resourcedev.com
Aspen Learning Management Server	Click2learn	click2learn.com
Boniva Learning Management	Boniva Software	boniva.com
Compliance Suite	RMS Systems	rmssystems.com
Conductor	Sage Corporation	conductit.com
DigitalThink Learning Management	DigitalThink	digitalthink.com
Docent Enterprise Learning Management Server	Docent	www.docent.com
DOTS Learning Management System	WebRaven	webraven.com
eLearning Server 3000	HyperMethod Company	www.hypermethod.com
Enterprise Training Management System	SystemSoft	systemsoftinc.com
GeoExpress	GeoLearning	geolearning.com

Product	Vendor	Web address
How To Master LMS	Infosource	howtomaster.com
IntraLearn SME, XE, and LSP	IntraLearn Software	intralearn.com
IntranetU	Applied Technology Consultants	profitfromlearning.com
iPerform Learning Management	Integrated Performance Systems	ips-inc.com
KnowBase Networks Learning Management System	KnowBase Networks	knowbasenetworks.com
Knowledge Centre	Meridian Knowledge Solutions	meridianksi.com
KnowledgeBridge LMS	Websoft Systems	websoft.com
KnowledgeHub	Element K	elementk.com
KP Learning	KnowledgePlanet	knowledgeplanet.com
LearnCenter	Learn.com	learn.com
LearnerWeb	MaxIt	maxit.com
Learning Management Services	Edcor	www.edcor.com
LMS by John Matchett	John Matchett Limited	www.jmlnet.com
LUVIT Education Centre	LUVIT	www.luvit.com
Manager's Edge	Mentergy	mentergy.com
Mentor LMS	Educate-Global	www.educate-global.com
MySmartForce	SkillSoft	skillsoft.com
OnTrack for Training	DKSystems	www.dksystems.com
Oracle iLearning	Oracle	oracle.com/ilearning
Panurgy LMS	Panurgy	epanurgy.com

9

Learning management systems

Product	Vendor	Web address
Pathlore Learning Management System	Pathlore	www.pathlore.com
Pinnacle LMS	LearnFrame	learnframe.com
Plateau Enterprise Learning Management System	Plateau Systems	plateau.com
PROFIS	Profis Web Corp.	profis.ca
Quelsys SPM	Quelsys	www.quelsys.com
Saba Learning	Saba	saba.com
Sun Enterprise Learning Platform	Sun Microsystems	sun.com
SyberWorkss	SyberWorks	syberworks.com
Syntrio	Syntrio	www.syntrio.com
TBK Tracker	Platte Canyon Multimedia Software	plattecanyon.com
TEDS	TEDS	teds.com
The Learning Manager	TLM	thelearningmanager.com
THINQ TrainingServer LMS	THINQ	thinq.com
TopClass LMS	WBT Systems	wbtsystems.com
Total Knowledge Management System	Generation 21	generation21.com
TRACCESS	Frontline Group	built2learn.com
TraCorp LMS	TraCorp	tracorp.com
Trainee Tracker	SofTrain	traineetracker.com
Trainersoft Manager	Trainersoft	trainersoft.com
Training Partner 2000	Geometrix Data Systems	trainingpartner2000.com
Training Wizard MX	Gyrus Systems	gyrus.com

Product	Vendor	Web address
TrainingDepartment.com	TrainingDepartment.com	trainingdepartment.com
ViewCentral:eLearning	ViewCentral	viewcentral.com
Virtual Training Assistant	RISC	risc-inc.com
Vuepoint Learning System	Vuepoint	vuepoint.com
WBT Manager	Integrity eLearning	ielearning.com
WebMentor LMS	Avilar Technologies	avilar.com
WebTrain	WebTrain Services	www.webtrain.com.au
Xtension LMS	Xtend	xtention.net
YnotManage	YnotLearn	ynotlearn.com

To find more LMSs, go to horton.com/tools, or search the Web for "LMS" or "learning management system."

CHOOSING AN LMS

Before talking to vendors, talk to management, your learners, and (close the door first) yourself. Make sure you know exactly what the LMS must accomplish. Then, and only then, should you start the selection process.

What does LMS really stand for?

Lots More Spending
Lost My Syllabus
Less Money for Staff
Learners Made to Suffer

You decide.

What you need to know first

Before you go shopping, do a little research and thinking to answer these questions:

▶ **What must you manage**? How many learners, courses, classes, sessions, enrollments, administrators, and vendors must you track? How often do these items change? Some LMSs are designed for large organizations. So, unless you have 5,000 employees, you may find that some LMS vendors are not interested in you.

▶ **Who are the learners**? Are you teaching employees, customers, vendors, distributors, partners, or fee-paying students? Knowing your audience will help you determine, among other things, whether you need e-commerce capabilities and whether you can outsource or must host the courses yourself.

▶ **How much detail must you track**? For example will you track just the final grade for the course or grades of individual activities within the course? The answer to this question will influence whether you purchase an LMS or an LCMS or both.

▶ **What standards and regulations apply**? What records must you keep and what reports must you produce? Be sure to evaluate the library of reports and the method used to secure learner data for each LMS.

▶ **What is your organization's learning or knowledge management strategy**? How do you want your organization's staff, customers, suppliers, and partners to get the knowledge and skills they need? If your e-learning endeavor is part of a larger knowledge management strategy, then the choice of LMS is probably an enterprise decision, rather than a departmental one—with more stakeholders to think about.

Capabilities to consider

Once you are sure you need an LMS and know what it must do for your organization, it's time to look at specific capabilities and issues that will influence your choice of product. Be forewarned. Picking an LMS is not a quick process. It is a team effort that may take months to complete. There are a number of factors to consider.

Costs and commitment

How much money and time can you invest in this tool? How much are you spending to perform these activities now? How much are you willing to spend? Keep in mind that most LMSs are not Some LMSs are offered, not as separate products, but bundled with content and authoring tools. shrink-wrapped, off-the-shelf products. Most require considerable time and money to set up and customize.

Costs vary widely. You may pay $5,000 USD for a bare-bones LMS with no support. You may pay millions of dollars to implement an enterprise-wide system that involves consulting, customization, and an ongoing relationship with the vendor. According to Bryan Chapman of BrandonHall.com, acquiring and operating an LMS for five years costs an average of $472,000 ($94,000 per year) for 8000 users. At William Horton Consulting, our combination crystal ball, Ouija board, and supercomputer uses this formula to estimate the cost of getting an LMS up and running: $100,000 USD plus $50 per user. For annual maintenance, we throw in another 20%. Your results may vary.

Because of the potential cost and difficulty of implementing an LMS, you must gauge your commitment to the particular product. A large-scale implementation is a long-term commitment.

Managing enrollments

An LMS must streamline and simplify the process of taking and administering training. Managing enrollments is the heart of this effort. Here are some capabilities to consider:

▶ **Automated administration**. Can learners register and withdraw themselves? Are confirmation notices, reminders, conflict and prerequisite checks, waiting lists, approval requests, completion notices, certificates, and diplomas handled automatically?

▶ **Automatic billing**. Can fees be charged to credit cards, corporate purchase orders, departmental account numbers, or a basic enrollment plan?

▶ **Batch registration**. Can learners be registered as a group by designating a specific department or other group? Can batches of learners be registered using a tab- or comma-delimited file as might be produced by a separate database system?

▶ **Resource management**. Does the system track and allocate resources needed for learning? This may involve scheduling time on a conferencing system or reserving classrooms and audiovisual equipment.

Setting up courses

Although a pure LMS may not need tools to author courses, it should make importing or registering them as swift and reliable as possible. Here are some capabilities to consider that can simplify the process of getting courses into your new system.

 Make a list of potential course vendors, and ask the LMS vendor: "Exactly what must I do to import courses from each of these vendors?" Get the answer in writing.

▶ **Packaged courses**. Can the LMS import courses formatted as an IMS or SCORM package? Does the LMS unwrap the package and install components correctly?

▶ **Metadata**. Can the LMS read standard metadata to create a complete description in the course catalog? Which metadata scheme does it understand: IEEE, IMS, or SCORM?

▶ **Classroom courses**. Can the LMS handle classroom courses too? Is it easy for administrators to enter grades and other information for classroom events?

 Standards like SCORM, AICC, IEEE, and IMS are covered in chapter 22.

▶ **Course location**. Can the LMS handle online courses hosted outside the organization as well as those on the local intranet? Can it launch and run courses outside the firewall as well as those on the same machine as the LMS?

▶ **Multiple vendors**. Will the LMS accept courses from all vendors, only courses that are AICC- or SCORM-compliant, or only those from the vendor of the LMS? Yep, some only handle their own courses.

▶ **Other learning resources**. Can the LMS handle other forms of learning resources, such as CD-ROMs, books, videotapes, and audiotapes? Can it handle one-shot presentations and briefings in addition to structured, formal courses? Can it track mentors and coaches assigned to individual learners or whole classes?

Connecting to related systems

Few LMSs stand alone. Their value depends on integration with other aspects of the organization. Although integration with other information systems is important for all tools, it is especially critical for LMSs. The process of integrating LMSs with existing organizational information systems may double the overall cost of the LMS and has proved a source of dissatisfaction in many installations. An InformationWeek (informationweek.com) article of May 13, 2002, appropriately titled "E-Learning Struggles To Make The Grade," documented how Cargill, Inc. switched LMS vendors after considerable expense because of the original LMS's inability to interface with their internal systems.

Streamlining administration

A good LMS reduces the effort required to administer large, complex learning programs. It also lets administrators and educators focus on learning and economics instead of trivial administrative tasks. Does the LMS support the following capabilities?

▶ **Automatic tracking**. Does the LMS automatically track and record enrollments and withdrawals, course launches, course completions, course evaluations, and grades?

▶ **Reports, reports, reports**. Does the LMS produce the exact reports you need? (Some offer 800 different reports right out of the box!) Can you easily modify predefined reports to meet your needs? Can you define your own custom reports? How hard is it to program the LMS to record additional data of interest to you?

▶ **Simple user interface**. Is the user interface for administering the LMS simple and clear? Some LMSs have a very simple student interface but leave administrators puzzling over cryptic codes.

▶ **Remote administration**. Can the LMS be administered remotely, say from Waikiki beach via a handheld wireless device? How about a laptop computer over a modem line from a hotel in São Paulo?

▶ **Flexibility**. The LMS must have the flexibility to enable learning as it really needs to occur. The administrator must be able to handle exceptions and special cases. For example, can the administrator:

- Set up free courses that do not require a user name and password?

- Authorize guest accounts?

- Grant anonymity? If privacy is a concern, let learners be anonymous to one another. In special cases (unions, for example) learners can be anonymous to instructors and administrators.

▶ **Batch changes**. Is it possible to make multiple changes to records by selecting multiple learners or courses and then specifying the changes to make to all selected learners rather than having to change each course or learner record individually?

Offering curricula and certificates

Offering individual courses may not be sufficient for your organization. You may need to define complex programs of learning to qualify for a specific degree or certificate. Can the LMS:

▶ **Define course paths**? Does the LMS allow you to define a course path, that is, a sequence of courses required for a certification or degree? Such sequences may have prerequisites and electives and may include testing.

▶ **Track certifications**? Does the LMS record learners who have completed required programs of learning? Does it remind those whose certifications are about to expire that it is time to renew? Can it report compliance with regulatory requirements for training and retraining?

▶ **Map curricula**? Can the LMS automatically generate a curriculum map showing the organization of the course sequences and let the learner jump to an individual course by selecting it on the map.

Linking learning to enterprise goals

Unless you view education as entertainment or a corporate perquisite, you probably want to know how it contributes to the overall ability of your organization to do its job. Organizations are concerned that their staff and students acquire the required skills. They are looking for an LMS that can tie courses to these organizational needs.

Keep in mind that organizational goals may be articulated in separate information systems, such as an enterprise resource planning (ERP) system. Furthermore, these other systems may be able to analyze the effect of learning and tie it back to the articulated organizational goals.

In considering an LMS, ask how it can help you identify what skills and knowledge are needed, what skills and knowledge potential learners already possess, and what learning will close that gap. Ask whether the LMS has tools to help you:

▶ Analyze jobs to identify what skills and knowledge they require

▶ Measure current skill and knowledge levels

▶ Calculate the skill or competency gap between what people know and what they need to know

▶ Rate courses for their ability to close this gap

▶ Plan curricula or certificate programs to bring skills and knowledge to required levels

▶ Match the needs of individual learners to available courses

▶ Monitor skills and knowledge after learning

If your organization has implemented a specific method of measuring competencies, say 360-degree feedback, your LMS should promote that method.

Providing a course catalog

We once worked as consultants to a company where supervisors routinely spent their lunch breaks searching for training courses for their employees, and internal training departments spent hundreds of thousands of dollars developing duplicate courses— all because there was no easy way to learn what courses and other learning resources were already available. That is a problem an LMS can solve.

A unified course catalog makes clear what resources are available for learners. Most LMSs include a catalog. Look for one that makes it easy for your learners (and their supervisors, advisors, or parents) to find the courses they need. A good course catalog should:

▶ **Reveal pertinent data**. The course catalog displayed by the LMS should make clear exactly what the course offers and what it requires. What would you want to know before signing up for a course? Here are some items to look for:

  ▪ Course objectives—what the learner will gain

  ▪ Credits received

  ▪ Jobs or other courses that require this course

  ▪ What the knowledge, skills, or attitudes the course teaches

  ▪ Cost of the course

  ▪ Time required to complete the course

  ▪ Who can take the course

  ▪ Prerequisites and how to meet them

▶ **Simplify search**. Does the course catalog let learners search for courses by subject, name, job role, degree program, and format (WBT, CD-ROM, and classroom)?

Furthering the learner experience

The LMS should make the learning experience simple rather than frustrating, and efficient rather than wasteful. In many ways the LMS should be almost invisible to learners. If they consciously notice it or spend much time dealing with it directly, it is probably wasting their time. A learner's efforts should be focused on the courses launched from the LMS. So, how can the LMS make the learner's experience better?

▶ **One login for multiple courses**. Once learners have logged in, the LMS should not require them to enter their name, user ID, e-mail, or other recorded information again. If learners are eligible to take multiple courses, the LMS should switch between courses without an additional login.

▶ **Distinctiveness from the course**. If the LMS only launches courses, it should make clear to learners when they are dealing with the LMS and when they are dealing with the course. The learner should never wonder whether a feedback button on the LMS offers feedback on the LMS or the course.

▶ **Assistance meeting technical requirements**. Does the LMS make it easy to help learners obtain necessary players and viewers, set up their browsers, and test their systems?

Content authoring and management

Although a pure LMS only launches and tracks individual courses, you may also need the ability to create and track components below the level of the course. Some LMSs include content management features, such as:

▸ **Module tracking**. Can the LMS track units of learning smaller than the course? Can courses be defined as a sequence or collection of lessons or even of individual pages?

▸ **Assembling courses**. Can the LMS assemble online courses from existing content, such as PowerPoint slides, Microsoft Word documents, Web pages, Flash animations, and other media files?

▸ **Testing**. Does the LMS let you create tests and assessments? Does it let you import tests created in other test-creation tools? Can external tests use AICC or SCORM protocols to report their scores to the LMS?

If you need extensive and sophisticated content-management capabilities, consider a learning content management system (chapter 10).

Enabling collaboration

Because pure LMSs only launch courses, they typically do not contain collaboration features, leaving it to the individual courses to provide those capabilities. Some LMSs, however, do provide collaboration for use at the school or curriculum level. These collaboration features might include chat, e-mail, or discussion forums. For more collaboration tools and capabilities, see chapter 11.

Including virtual-school capabilities

LMSs designed to assist instructor-led e-learning may include features for conducting classes. An LMS with many of these capabilities might be considered a virtual-school system. In fact, some of the virtual-school systems started out as simple LMSs.

Some key virtual-school system features included in LMSs are:

▸ **School metaphor**. Does the LMS organize learning along the lines of the familiar school environment? For example, is the LMS called a *campus*, are reading materials provided in a *library*, and are the instructors called *faculty*?

▸ **Classes**. Can learners be grouped into classes that take the same course on the same schedule? Can the LMS provide a study-group chat or discussion facility?

▶ **Grade book**. Does the LMS provide a streamlined way for learners to submit assignments to the instructor to grade, for the instructor to return the corrected assignments to learners, and for instructors to record the grade in the database?

For more virtual-school systems, see chapter 12.

ALTERNATIVES TO AN LMS

If you have determined that you need the capabilities of an LMS, don't stop with this chapter. Investigate LCMSs and virtual-school systems, too. Many of the tools in those categories contain LMS features that may meet your needs. So, before you plunk down your cash on an LMS, run through this list of alternatives.

If you ...	Consider this alternative
Have only a few dozen courses and a few hundred learners	A clerk with a spreadsheet or simple database
Want to custom tailor courses to the needs of individual learners	Learning content management system (chapter 10)
Create and maintain multiple courses covering aspects of one subject area—and you want to reuse content	Learning content management system (chapter 10)
Offer lots of instructor-led e-learning courses	Virtual-school system
Already have an ERP, HRIS, or CRM system	Training management modules within these systems
Need to create a large online university with hundreds of courses, hundreds of instructors, and thousands of learners	Combine an LMS, an LCMS, and a collaboration system. Add custom programming to tie the pieces together and add custom features.

Don't forget, some ERP systems, such as those from SAP and PeopleSoft, include learning management modules. In other words, you have choices.

WHAT NOW?

Learning management systems are complex tools, expensive to purchase, and an elusive category. If you need one, you need to learn more about them.

▶ Compare specifications and data sheets for a dozen LMSs. Get these from the vendor sites.

▶ Experiment with trial versions. Getting a trial version, especially for one of the bigger systems, is challenging, and getting it to run is even harder. Start with one of the smaller systems. Try setting up the kind of learning program you might need for your organization.

▶ Scan the LMS's documentation to gauge the breadth of features it offers.

If you ...	Then ...
Are still designing your e-learning strategy	▶ Learn what aspects of training you need to track and to automate. ▶ Decide whether you need an LMS, LCMS, virtual-school system, or some combination. ▶ Decide whether you want to host or outsource learning management functions.
Are at the point of picking an LMS	▶ Learn what other systems the LMS must communicate with. ▶ Using this chapter as a guide, list and prioritize your requirements. ▶ Using the process in chapter 20, make your decision.
Have already picked your LMS	▶ Set it up to work the way you want it to. Most LMSs can be customized. ▶ Learn the LMSs full range of capabilities. Plan how you will use them to meet your needs. ▶ Streamline the processes of entering learners and courses.

While pure LMSs deal with courses and curricula, learning content management systems help you create and conduct courses composed of reusable modules. LCMSs are covered in the next chapter.

10 Learning content management systems

A learning content management system (LCMS) simplifies the task of creating, managing, and reusing learning content, that is, the media, pages, tests, lessons, and other components of courses.

WHAT AN LCMS DOES

LCMSs manage learning content by maintaining items of content in a central repository. From this database, instructional designers can organize, assemble, approve, publish, and deliver courses and other learning events. An LCMS lets authors create, store, and refine learning objects or other units of content. It helps learners locate and take just the learning they need at the moment.

Learning content management systems sit slightly left of center in the tools framework. They facilitate administration and authoring at the course, lesson, and page levels. As the name suggests, LCMSs are closely related to content creation and display tools.

The content managed by LCMSs may come from content creation tools, especially Web-site creation tools and media editors. LCMSs may provide courses to an LMS that tracks students and the courses they are enrolled in. Courses in an LCMS may be accessed and navigated through a Web browser. If the

LCMS does not provide testing capabilities, it may deliver tests created and administered by a test-creation tool.

So, with a full-featured LCMS, your organization can:

▶ Efficiently create semi-custom courses

▶ Manage complex projects involving many authors and different types and levels of content

▶ Create derivative courses and other forms of content

▶ Track course access at the level of the individual module or learning object

▶ Deliver content in different formats, such as via the Web, on CD-ROM, on mobile devices, and as paper workbooks

QUICK TOUR OF AN LCMS

To help you put a face on one of these systems, let's take a tour of Preceptor by K2Share (k2share.com). These screen shots illustrate the main functions of an LCMS.

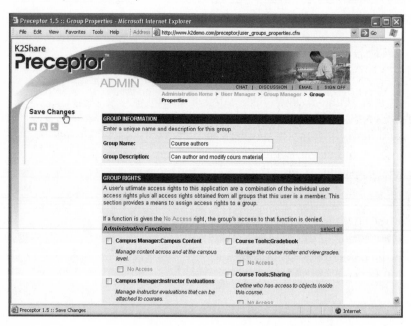

LCMSs simplify the process of building, administering, and reusing learning content. To that end, the LCMS can define administrators, moderators, course authors, learners, and more—each with a different set of privileges.

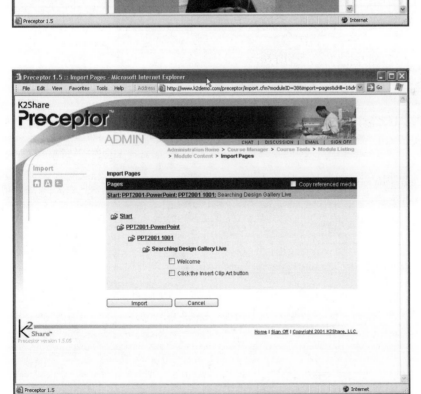

Course authors build the individual pages using a built-in page editor to enter text, import graphics and other media, and lay out the pages.

Course authors can reuse pages in different lessons and reuse lessons in different courses.

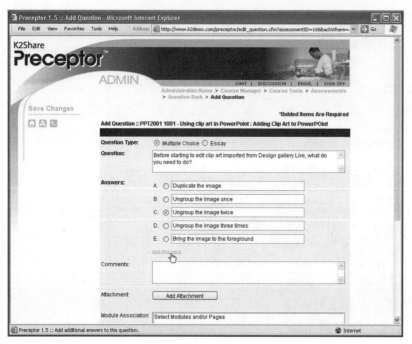

LCMSs may provide tools for constructing test questions and assembling test questions into assessments, both of which can be reused freely.

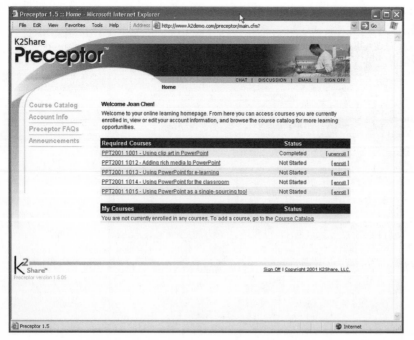

Learners log into the system to see the courses in which they are entered or to which they have access.

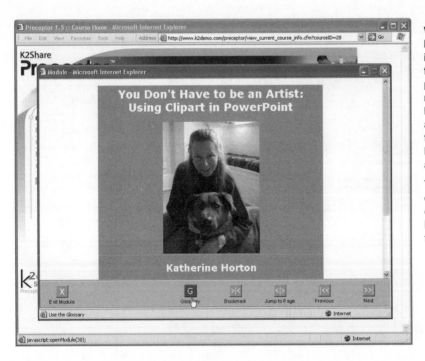

When learners launch a course, it is displayed in a framework that provides navigation buttons, and access to special features, such as bookmarking and a glossary.

The course author did not need to create these buttons or features.

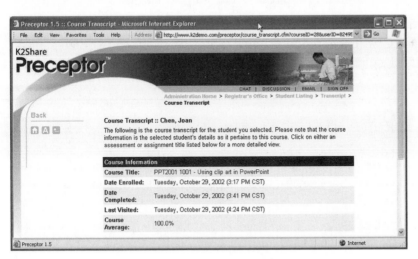

The LCMS tracks access to the course, course completion, and scores for individual tests.

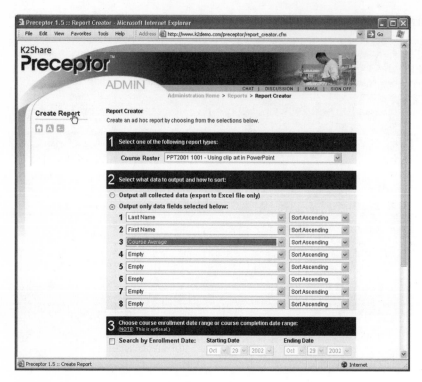

LCMSs provide many reports. Some even allow administrators to define custom reports.

LCMSs have more features than those shown, but this tour outlines the main capabilities of one LCMS. Other products will look different and offer a different mix of capabilities.

How an LCMS works

No two LCMSs are exactly the same, but central to most of them is a repository of components needed to generate courses. Look inside an LCMS and you are likely to find:

▶ **Raw ingredients for courses**, such as HTML pages, XML data, media components, and other raw materials

▶ **Test questions** that can be used to measure accomplishment of a learning objective

▶ **Definitions of learning objects** that combine raw ingredients and tests to completely accomplish a learning objective

▶ **Definitions of lessons and courses** that specify how to combine learning objects and other ingredients

▶ **Templates and style sheets** to control the appearance of a course and customize it for various delivery mechanisms

▶ **A framework for navigation and user interface**, including menus and course maps

For each of these items, the LCMS may also store metadata, which describes the items in detail.

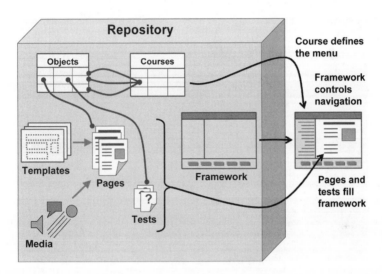

This diagram illustrates how these components are related to one another. Authors and other content developers create the media, tests, and other raw ingredients and enter them into the repository. Using templates or starting from scratch, they combine media to form pages. Then they define learning objects in terms of a learning objective and the ingredients needed to accomplish that objective. Lessons and courses are defined in terms of the learning objects they contain. Authors may also define a framework to control navigation and provide a user interface for the course.

When a course is needed, a copy of the framework is made. From the course definition, a menu is generated for the course. As learners select from the menu, pages, tests, and other components are displayed in the framework.

 What does LCMS stand for?

Lets Close More Schools
Less Content, More Spending
Learners Consistently Made to Suffer

You decide.

POPULAR LCMS PRODUCTS

The list of learning content management systems is long and includes tools with a wide range of capabilities, some of which go beyond the bounds of a pure LCMS.

Product	Vendor	Web address
Aspen Learning Content Management Server	Click2learn	click2learn.com
Centra Knowledge Center and Knowledge Server	Centra	www.centra.com
CentreLearn	CentreLearn	centrelearn.com
Docent Enterprise Learning Content Management System	Docent	www.docent.com
e-Education Suite	WebsiteASP	omniupdate.com
ePath Learning ASAP	e-Path Learning	epathlearning.com
Evolution	Outstart	www.outstart.com
FlexTraining	Online Development	flextraining.com
GeMS SWIFT	Gemini Learning Systems	gemini.com
Intellinex LCMS	Intellinex	www.intellinex.com
iPerformance	Online Courseware Factory	courseware-factory.com
IPRESS and KBridge	KnowledgeXtensions	www.knowledgextensions.com
Jupiter Suite	Avaltus	avaltus.com
K2Share Preceptor	K2Share	k2share.com
KM Studio	KMGP	kmgpinc.com
Knowledge Pathways	Global Knowledge	globalknowledge.com
KnowledgeBridge LCMS	Websoft Systems	websoft.com
KnowledgeOne Content Manager	LeadingWay Knowledge Systems	www.leadingway.com

Product	Vendor	Web address
KP Publishing System	KnowledgePlanet	knowledgeplanet.com
LogicBuilder	LogicBay	logicbay.com
Lumenix	Handshaw	handshaw.com
Quelsys SPM	Quelsys	www.quelsys.com
ROCKET KM	Eedo	eedo.com
SmartBuilder	Suddenly Smart	suddenlysmart.com
Techniq LCMS	Vitalect	vitalect.com
Theorix-LCMS	e-com inc.	www.theorix.com
TopClass LCMS	WBT Systems	wbtsystems.com
Total Knowledge Management System	Generation 21	generation21.com
Vuepoint Content Creator & LCMS	Vuepoint	vuepoint.com
X.HLP	X.HLP	xhlp.com
Za: The Intelligent Content Engine	Adaptive Tutoring	www.adaptivetutoring.com

If your favorite LCMS is missing, check the lists of LMSs (chapter 9) or virtual-school systems (chapter 12) as many of these tools also contain content management capabilities. Also search the Web for "LCMS" or "learning content management system" or go to horton.com/tools.

CHOOSING AN LCMS

Choosing an LCMS is hard work and requires a broad perspective. For this task, pull together a team drawn from your instructional designers, media developers, and IT specialists. Include potential learners, too. Let this team help you research your needs, specify selection criteria based on those needs, and evaluate candidate products.

What you need to know first

Before setting out on your shopping expedition, you need to make a few strategic decisions. These decisions will help you identify candidate products.

▶ **What do you want to reuse**? How much do you reuse content in your learning programs? How much should you be reusing? At what levels: courses, lessons, pages, or media components? If few components are candidates for reuse, then you may need to look at another type of tool, such as an LMS (chapter 9) or a virtual-school system (chapter 12).

▶ **How much content must you manage**? How many courses, lessons, topics, and media components do you need to create and track separately? For instance, if you plan to reuse a large number of graphics, video files, and other media elements, you need to make sure that the LCMS you select efficiently manages content at that level of granularity. Another implication resulting from this decision is the kind of database that is required. If your needs are modest, then something like a Microsoft Access database may be all that is required. If your needs are extensive, however, you may need an enterprise database system like Oracle or SQL Server.

▶ **Who will create the content**? How many authors and media specialists will contribute to the project? If multiple people will be checking content elements in and out, then the LCMS will need some kind of source control capabilities to track changes and ensure that files are not overwritten.

▶ **How divergent are the training needs of learners**? How precisely can you articulate these needs? If needs are diverse, you may want to look for an LCMS that will adjust course modules on the fly based on such criteria as a pretest or a gap analysis.

▶ **Must you offer multiple versions of the same content**? Do you need to deliver content to paper, mobile devices, CD-ROMs, electronic performance support systems, as well to the Web? Do you need to provide content that is compliant with multiple standards—for instance, AICC or SCORM communications standards (chapter 22)? Some LCMSs make it easy to publish modules and courses targeted to various delivery media.

▶ **How detailed do you need to be**? To what degree or level do you need to manage development and learning processes? To what level do you need to track learners' navigation and performance? LCMSs vary in the levels of the content they can track.

Capabilities to consider

Now that you have answered the key questions, it is time to list needed capabilities. So, what issues should you consider?

Workflow management and productivity

Development of complex courses composed of reusable objects requires careful project management and teamwork. In evaluating an LCMS, look for several kinds of workflow management tools.

▶ **Project management**. Can the tool help you plan and track required tasks, resources, budgets, and milestones? Can it create a consolidated to-do list of tasks remaining to be performed?

▶ **Collaborative authoring**. Can content be created, edited, and assembled by a team of instructional designers, subject-matter experts, media developers, reviewers, quality assurance testers, and project managers working in concert? Does the tool prevent accidental overwriting of components by requiring participants to check components in and out?

▶ **Revision tracking**. Can authors flag deletions, additions, and changes for approval or rejection? Can they maintain multiple versions of courses, lessons, and learning objects? Can provisional versions of objects be rolled into a released version after testing and approval?

▶ **Metadata labeling**. Metadata is descriptive information about units of content, making them easier to find and evaluate. Does the tool make it easy and economical for authors to enter metadata for units of content? For instance, can all metadata be entered through dialog boxes? Does the system infer as much of the metadata as possible, for example, the size and file format of units? Can the LCMS export metadata descriptions of courses for inclusion into course catalogs?

▶ **Instructional model**. Does the tool structure content in such a way that it promotes instructionally sound design? Does it do so without limiting designers to a single instructional model or theory? What instructional design theory or model does the tool encourage?

▶ **Testing environment**. Can courses be tested thoroughly before letting students see them? Can authors create, preview, and test their courses locally before uploading them to the server, or can authors work directly on the server?

Adaptive learning

Can the LCMS adapt learning to the specific and immediate needs of learners? Can it adjust the object presented to a learner, suggest a recommended sequence, deliver the best media to use, as well as format the visual appearance of the object? Can it adapt content based on factors such as the learner's preferences or demonstrated learning style, on assessment results, on prior learning, on the learner's job role or department, or on a search query by the learner? Does the LCMS continuously adjust the learning program to reflect the learner's demonstrated progress?

Multiple forms of learning

Can the LCMS produce training appropriate for various delivery mechanisms? For example, can it render pages appropriate for a high- or low-speed network connection, CD-ROM or DVD, a mobile device such as a Palm Pilot or Pocket PC, or a printed document? Can it produce versions accessible by those with common disabilities? Can learners print out individual pages, lessons, and entire courses?

Additionally, if online connections are difficult or expensive, does the LCMS allow learners to download large chunks of the course and take it offline? Are the results of assessments held and uploaded to the server when the learner is online again?

Learner's user interface

The LCMS provides the user interface for the course. This framework lets the learner navigate the course and provides access to special features. In considering the framework, ask how well it suits the way learners need to take the course. Does the LCMS:

- ▶ Automatically generate course menus, index, map, search page, and navigation buttons? Does the menu or table of contents show where the learner is in the course, which units the learner has started, and which the learner has completed?

- ▶ Provide one- or two-click access to most popular features, such as the main menu, index, course map, home page, e-mail, discussion forum, help, search, and exit?

- ▶ Create courses with the navigation mechanisms specified by the ASTD E-learning Courseware Certification standards (chapter 22)?

Reuse of content

For maximum reuse of content, you should be able to include pages, tests, and media components in multiple courses or learning objects. Learning objects should also be reusable in multiple lessons or courses. So, ask LCMS vendors whether their product:

▶ Lets authors reuse blocks of text, test questions, scripts, style sheets, graphics, icons, pictures, and other media freely.

▶ Tracks and reports which components have been incorporated into each learning object and course.

▶ Reveals interrelationships among components. Does it flag the dependencies for a particular module? Does it identify orphaned elements, dangling links, and missing components?

▶ Enables authors to easily find individual objects and other components. For instance, can authors use search keywords to locate content to include in their courses?

Importing media

Can the LCMS incorporate a wide range of media formats, such as:

▶ Pictures (GIF, JPEG, PNG, SVG)

▶ Animation (Flash, Director Shockwave)

▶ Sound, (MP3, Real Audio, Widows Media Audio)

▶ Video (MPEG, QuickTime, Real Video, Windows Media Video)

Can the LCMS import or include common office document formats, such as:

▶ Microsoft Word

▶ Microsoft PowerPoint

▶ Microsoft Excel

▶ HTML Web pages

▶ Adobe Acrobat PDF

Importing objects and courses

Can the LCMS import learning objects or entire courses formatted as IMS or SCORM packages? See chapter 22 for more information about these standards.

Can the LCMS automatically compile courses or objects by importing HTML? Does it compile a course menu, table of contents, map, or index from <META> tags containing keywords, <TITLE> tags naming the page, headings, and body text? Does it check HTML and links for errors?

Exporting courses

How easy is it to get content out of the system and into another system? For instance, can producers export the course and import it into another system of the same brand? Can they export it as a SCORM or IMS package that can be imported into a different vendor's system?

The LCMS should allow the export of an entire course. The exported file should contain everything needed to use a particular course. Other authors should be able to take this exported file and import it onto their own servers where it will be automatically unpacked and installed and the media files will be restored and put into the correct location on the destination server. Remember, your relationship with the vendor may sour, or their financing may evaporate. It is best to be prepared for change.

Course structure

The authoring component of the LCMS should make organizing complex courses simple. Make sure the LCMS you are considering gives authors control over the structure of the course. Ask whether the LCMS:

▶ Allows the creation of an outline of the course or object with placeholders that can be filled in later. Authors should be able to continue editing in this outline view.

▶ Permits nonhierarchical structures.

▶ Enables authors to group units of material several levels deep and allows authors, instructors, and administrators to select and organize these groups as units.

▶ Supports any number of levels and any number of components per level.

▶ Allows authors to mix pages and lessons at the same level.

▶ Automatically aggregates, for each unit, characteristics and components from lower-level components the unit includes. For instance, a higher-level unit automatically includes items from its lower-level units, such as:
  - Pretest questions
  - Posttest questions
  - Index terms and search keywords
  - Lists of requirements
  - Objectives lists
  - Summaries

If the LCMS does not support this feature, putting together a complex course will be more tedious.

Authoring in familiar tools

Does the LCMS let authors create pages in an external HTML editor like Dreamweaver or FrontPage, in a word processor such as Microsoft Word, or in a presentation tool like Microsoft PowerPoint? Does the LCMS allow authors to enter HTML directly? Furthermore, can authors preview the HTML as it will be seen in a browser?

Synchronous events

Can learning objects contain synchronous events, such as class meetings, role-playing activities, and mock debates? Does the LCMS contain the necessary collaboration mechanisms? Does it integrate easily with collaboration tools?

Standards and regulatory compliance

Does the LCMS make complying with standards, regulations, and laws easier? Does it produce learning objects and courses that meet the various AICC, IMS, and SCORM specifications? Does it produce content that meets accessibility requirements such as those of the W3C Accessibility Initiative or Section 508 of the Rehabilitation Act of 1998? For more information about these specifications and standards, see chapter 22.

Consistent appearance

Can the author can set formats, page layouts, colors, and fonts for an entire course or other collections of objects in one operation. The course author should not have to design the appearance of each page individually. All basic page characteristics should be specified in one place and inherited throughout the course.

Models and templates

What types of pages, test questions, media combinations, activities, and other learning experiences can authors easily create? Does the LCMS provide instructionally sound and aesthetically pleasing fill-in-

Templates are as much a ceiling as a floor. While they support competence, they prevent excellence.

the-blank models for common kinds of displays and activities? Does the tool include

The templates that work in one tool may make it hard to move content to another tool later on.

templates, wizards, or other aids for creating common kinds of pages, such as introductions, summaries, resources, or objectives? Can authors create their own templates for lessons, pages, colors, buttons, fonts, and other recurring components?

Costs

LCMSs tend to be a bit on the expensive side, you see. According to Bryan Chapman of BrandonHall.com, acquiring and operating an LCMS for five years, supporting 8,000 learners and 30 authors costs an average of $537,000 ($107,000 per year). In his survey, costs ranged from $150,000 to $1.9 million with a median of $430,000. At William Horton Consulting, our equally approximate formula estimates the cost of installing and firing up an LCMS at $100,000 USD plus $30 per user. Annual maintenance costs add another 20%.

Remember that the purchase or license price is just the beginning. To this you must add the cost of setting up and customizing the system and the cost of administering it.

Learning management capabilities

LCMSs classically compose and deliver individual courses, leaving higher level issues of student enrollment and administration to LMSs. However, some LCMSs include learning management capabilities. They may:

▶ Let students, register, pay for, and withdraw from the course

▶ Base courses and learning objects on skills-gap analysis

▶ Track and report rolled up information at the course and curriculum level

▶ Define curricula, certification programs, and other course sequences

▶ Interface to other organizational information systems

For more learning management capabilities, see chapter 9.

Collaboration capabilities

Collaboration capabilities are the province of collaboration tools and virtual-school systems, but some LCMSs include simple collaboration capabilities, such as:

▶ Ability to include collaborative activities in learning objects

▶ E-mail, chat, and discussion tools to support collaborative activities

▶ Interface to online-meeting and collaboration tools

For more collaboration capabilities, see chapter 11.

Virtual-school capabilities

If the LC you M with your S is instructor-led or facilitated e-learning, you probably want an LCMS that includes virtual-school capabilities, such as:

▶ School metaphor and organization with a syllabus, class meetings, homework, final exam, and templates to create learning objects for each of these items

▶ Communication and collaboration tools so instructors can lecture and advise students and students can submit work and ask questions

▶ Grade book for instructor-graded activities

For more virtual-school capabilities, see chapter 12.

ALTERNATIVES TO AN LCMS

LCMSs are complex and expensive. Not everyone needs one. Not everyone who needs one can afford one. Before you spend your budget on an LCMS, consider whether one of these alternatives might work better for you.

If you ...	Consider this alternative
Need to manage raw media components for multiple purposes rather than just for e-learning	A generic content management system, such as: ▶ IBM Content Manager (ibm.com) ▶ Microsoft Content Management Server (microsoft.com) ▶ SparkPlug (13amp.net) ▶ TeamSite (interwoven.com) ▶ Vignette (vignette.com) ▶ LightSpeed Astoria (lspeed.com) If you are interested in generic content management, read the book *Managing Enterprise Content* by our good friend Ann Rockley.
Need to track grades and completions for entire courses only	LMS (chapter 9)
Just want to record grades and test scores for individual activities within the course	Course authoring tools (chapter 14) or testing and assessment tools (chapter 16)

WHAT NOW?

Learning content management systems are quite complex. If you need one, you must do some careful research. Here are some suggestions for learning more about LCMSs.

▶ Compare the specifications and data sheets of a range of LCMSs. Get these from the vendor Web sites. While you are there, look for recorded demos.

▶ Experiment with trial versions. Getting a trial version, especially for one of the bigger systems may be a challenge. So, start with one of the smaller systems. Try setting up a simple course you might need for your organization.

▶ Read the documentation for an LCMS. Note the range of capabilities.

If you ...	Then ...
Are still designing your e-learning	▶ Decide how you want to modularize your e-learning and what modules you want to reuse.
	▶ Investigate the various forms in which you need to deliver content.
Are at the point of picking an LCMS	▶ Using this book as a guide, list your requirements for content management.
	▶ Follow the process in chapter 20 to make your selection.
Have already picked your LCMS	▶ Invest time and effort to operate the LCMS.
	▶ Set up workflow and quality-control features that take advantage of the LCMS' capabilities to reuse content.

Some LMSs and LCMSs have collaboration capabilities. The next chapter discusses collaboration tools in greater detail.

11 Collaboration tools

Collaboration tools help people work and learn together at a distance. They let participants share their ideas, and even their shrugs, sighs, and smiles. They are essential for collaborative e-learning, e-mentoring, and knowledge management initiatives.

This category spans a wide range of tools, from simple text-based e-mail clients to complex online meeting tools. Providing a complete collaborative environment may require you to combine several separate tools and technologies.

HOW COLLABORATION TOOLS WORK

Most collaboration tools work the same way. Typically, someone creates a message in a collaboration tool called a client. The message then goes to a collaboration server that relays the message to other clients. The content can be almost anything—a simple e-mail composed in Microsoft Outlook, a reply to a chat message, a drawing on a whiteboard, a statement made in audio conferencing, or a frame of video in video conferencing. Regardless of its form, the message is sent to the server, which relays it to each of the client tools that should receive it. The client tools then display or play the message for their users. Let's look at several characteristics common to collaborative tools.

Client-server relationship

Collaboration tools typically require communication between two kinds of software to enable a dialog among participants. First there is the *collaboration server*. It runs on a Web server on the Internet, an intranet, or a LAN. Its function is to coordinate the flow of messages among participants. The second type of

207

collaboration software runs on each participant's system. It is called a *collaboration client*, and it enables the participant to receive and send messages to other participants by way of the server.

E-mail software is a simple example of this client-server relationship. Centralized e-mail servers route and dispatch messages that are then opened, read, and answered using e-mail clients. The e-mail server may be a specialized software package, such as Microsoft Exchange Server, or it may be a built-in part of a standard Web server. This built-in server component is typically called an *SMTP server*, which stands for Simple Mail Transfer Protocol. The client part is the *e-mail reader*, such as Microsoft Outlook.

Some collaboration servers and clients provide multiple collaboration tools, whereas others specialize in one particular tool. A number of servers and clients are designed as matched sets where a specific brand of server requires the same brand of client. Other standards-based collaboration tools allow learners to pick servers and clients from different vendors. Let's look at some of these variations in more detail.

Variations on the client-server theme

Some collaboration servers work only with corresponding client tools. For example, learners using a Centra system would use a Centra client to communicate through the Centra server. Other collaboration servers follow standards such as H.323 (discussed later) that are understood by standards-compliant clients. For example, if your e-mail server uses the Simple Network Mail

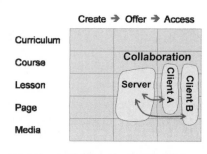

Protocol (SNMP), then users have a choice. One user may choose Microsoft Outlook as their mail reader (client), and another may choose the mail client in the Netscape browser.

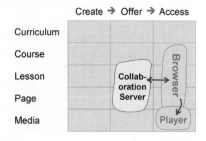

Other collaboration servers, especially ones for textual media, require no specific client and can be accessed with a Web browser. To display other media, these servers use a media player. Such a setup is called a *thin client* architecture because most of the software is in the server and little is in the client.

Another variation omits the server altogether and enables collaboration clients to communicate directly with each other. Tools like Groove are called peer-to-peer (P2P) collaboration tools because most of the communication goes directly from one client to another without passing through a server. We say most because a server may still be used to register the addresses of potential collaborators so they can find each other.

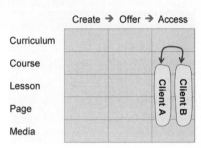

Collaboration tools can also be categorized based on whether they enable synchronous or asynchronous collaboration. Let's take a closer look at this aspect of collaboration tools.

Synchronous vs. asynchronous collaboration

Collaboration tools can link participants synchronously or asynchronously. Synchronous communications, also called conferencing, occur in real time. That is, all participants have to be online at the same time. Synchronous communication media include chat, application sharing, whiteboards, audio conferencing, and video conferencing.

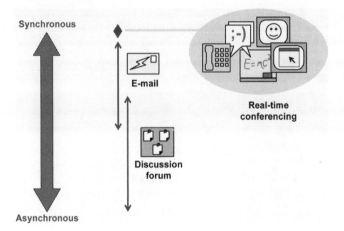

Asynchronous communications, on the other hand, do not require participants to be online at the same time. Participants do not have to wait for a specific person to be online to send that person an e-mail message. They just send it, confident that eventually it will reach the desired person and the person will respond. With asynchronous communication, participants send messages when it is most convenient for them. Asynchronous media include e-mail and online discussion forums. Note, however, that discussion forums are less synchronous than e-mail because there is less expectation of a speedy reply.

11

Collaboration tools

COLLABORATION TOOLS AND CAPABILITIES

Collaboration tools make it possible for distant learners to communicate freely and to work together on common tasks. Let's take a look at these tools and how they are used in e-learning.

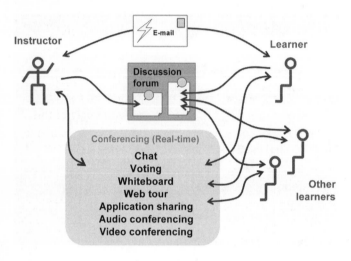

The simplest tool is *e-mail* between the instructor and learner. Often e-mail messages are broadcast, typically from the instructor to all learners to announce a change or an event.

Learners and instructors can also post messages on an online *discussion forum* or bulletin board. Others can then read and reply to these messages.

Several collaboration tools provide real-time exchanges among the instructor and learners. For example, participants can use *chat* or instant messaging to exchange text messages—something like instant e-mail. The instructor may also use a polling tool to encourage *voting* on issues and other types of choices.

Another group of tools help distant learners share a common experience. A *whiteboard* lets learners share a graphic and take turns marking it up. The instructor may conduct a *Web tour* to take all participants to the same Web sites. Through *application sharing*, the instructor lets learners see and interact with a computer program, a window, or a document.

Here we talk about individual forms of collaboration and the tools that support them. Later in this chapter we talk about online meeting tools that include several forms of collaboration in a single tool.

When network speed allows, learners can use *audio conferencing* much as they would a telephone conference call to talk with the instructor and each other. Those with very fast networks can use *video conferencing* to see the instructor or to swap video images of each other.

Let's look at each of the collaboration tools individually and see how you might include them in your e-learning. We will explain what it is, how it works, and what you need to implement it.

E-mail

E-mail is the oldest collaboration tool and, for many tasks, still the most effective. It is simple, reliable, inexpensive, omnipresent, and familiar. Anyone who can use computer technology can use e-mail, and almost everybody has an e-mail address.

Here's how e-mail works. When you write an e-mail message and hit the Send button, that message goes to an e-mail server that reads its destination address and sends it over the Internet to the mail server that corresponds to that address (the part of the address after the @ sign). The receiving Web server holds the message until the person the e-mail is addressed to (the part of the address before the @ sign) logs into the server and downloads the message.

Originally e-mail was limited to simple text messages, but today most e-mail readers, like those from Microsoft and Netscape, can use HTML for formatting messages.

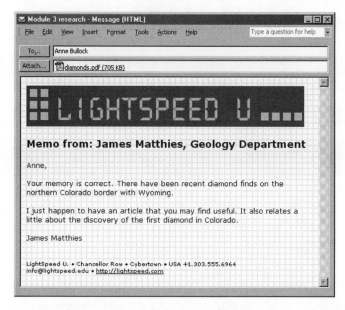

This e-mail message is formatted in HTML and has an Adobe Acrobat PDF file as an attachment.

That means e-mail messages can use the same rich mixture of media as Web pages. Most e-mail readers also allow senders to attach other file formats to their messages, such as a word-processing documents, slide presentations, photos, or spreadsheets.

How e-mail is used for e-learning

Learners use e-mail to ask questions of instructors, facilitators, administrators, and technical support staff. Learners may also use e-mail to discuss issues with fellow learners and to submit assignments.

Instructors typically use e-mail to give assignments, make announcements, and answer questions. Instructors may structure assignments around e-mail, for example, requiring learners to conduct an e-mail interview of an expert.

Most e-mail systems display the sender, date, and subject of the message along with any specific flags. For an e-learning class, flags might identify types of messages, for example, announcements, assignments, questions, answers to questions, or submissions.

E-mail correspondence courses

The simplest and earliest form of e-learning has its roots in the postal correspondence courses of the 19th and 20th centuries. In the e-mail version, the instructor sends an assignment to the learner by e-mail.

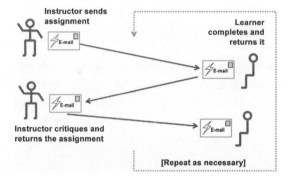

The learner then completes and returns the assignment by e-mail. The instructor critiques the learner's work and returns it (you guessed it!) by e-mail. And the cycle repeats again and again, with a typical course consisting of 10 to 20 assignments. Such courses are by necessity simple; however, they work well for subjects that require a human instructor to evaluate the learner's work but do not require face to face contact.

Popular e-mail tools

There are tools for sending e-mail over the Internet and embedded tools for sending messages among members within a closed system.

Internet e-mail tools

Internet e-mail tools use standard protocols to route messages across the Internet. Messages are written and read in e-mail clients and delivered by e-mail servers.

Internet e-mail servers include Sendmail (www.sendmail.org), Eudora WorldMail Server (eudora.com), Microsoft Exchange Server (microsoft.com), and MailSite (rockliffe.com). For more mail servers, go to serverwatch.com.

Popular Internet mail clients include Microsoft (microsoft.com) Outlook and Outlook Express, Eudora (eudora.com), and Netscape Mail included with the Netscape browser (netscape.com). For more, go to emailman.com.

Web-based e-mail services, such as hotmail.com, and products such as SquirrelMail (squirrelmail.org), let people read and write mail messages using their Web browsers.

Protocols used for e-mail include Simple Mail Transport Protocol (SMTP), Post Office Protocol 3 (POP3), and Internet Message Access Protocol (IMAP). The server and client have to use the same protocol.

11

Collaboration tools

Microsoft Outlook as an LMS

In an article appropriately titled, "Innovative Use of Email for Teaching," Albert Huang tells how to use the Microsoft Outlook mail client as a simple learning management system. (The article appeared in the November 2001 issue of *Communications of the ACM*. Footnote fanatics, that's volume 44, number 11.) The key to the technique is using Outlook's ability to automate message routing. Huang uses it to schedule delivery of assignments to students and route their submissions to folders on his system. If you want to set up something similar:

▶ Define a mailing list including all the members of the class plus the instructor for confirmation.

▶ Design assignments as e-mail messages to learners. Set them up so that learners submit their answer by replying to the original message.

▶ Use delayed delivery to schedule when assignments are transmitted to learners.

▶ In the subject header, include an ID for the assignment. That way the reply will contain this ID in the header too.

▶ Request delivery and read receipts to verify when students receive and read time-critical assignments.

▶ Set up rules to route assignments to folders based on their subject headers, with an additional rule to notify the instructor when each arrives.

Embedded e-mail tools

Embedded e-mail tools are found in internal systems, such as virtual-school systems. This kind of e-mail is sometimes called course mail. The system exchanges messages among learners, instructors, administrators, and others known to the system but not to the whole Internet. Some closed e-mail systems do, however, have a bridge for exchanging messages with the public Internet mail system.

Closed e-mail systems typically do not require a separate e-mail client, relying either on a general collaboration client or the Web browser.

Capabilities to look for in e-mail tools

E-mail is used for many purposes beyond e-learning, but here are some capabilities that are important to participants in e-learning.

▶ **File attachments**. Can you insert or attach files created in other programs to an e-mail message?

▶ **HTML formatting**. Does the tool make it easy to format e-mail messages using buttons or commands similar to a word processor? Can you embed other media, such as graphics, video, and animation?

▶ **Message sorting**. Can you organize messages using different criteria like message data, subject, or sender?

▶ **Multiple folders**. Can you create folders to organize received messages? Is there a limit to the number of folders you can add?

▶ **Automatic routing of messages**. Can you define rules to automatically route received messages to different folders? Is there a limit to the number of rules you can define? Can you easily change and reorganize the rules?

▶ **Message receipts and flags**. Does the tool allow you to request notification when the recipient opens the message? Can you attach a flag or marker to a message to indicate that the message is urgent?

▶ **Automatic archiving**. Will the tool allow you to automatically remove, compress, and archive messages based on message date, subject, sender, or other criteria?

▶ **Backup and restore**. Does the tool perform scheduled backups of messages? Does the tool make it easy to restore messages in the event of a disk failure or some other problem?

▶ **Address book**. Does the tool have an address book? Can you automatically import names into it, for instance from the course roster or some kind of structured list?

▶ **Familiar interface**. Is the tool easy to use? If it is an embedded system, is the interface similar to e-mail programs such as AOL or Microsoft Outlook?

Online discussion

Online discussions are intellectual watering holes that attract individuals with like interests but distant locations to a free exchange of ideas. They are a direct offshoot of the social and professional exchanges that take place on Internet list-servers and newsgroups. They go by a variety of forms and names: *newsgroups, net news, discussion groups, computer bulletin boards,* and *discussion forums.*

Most online discussion software implements threading. *Threading* is a way of displaying messages and replies to messages in an easy to follow format. So when you enter discussion, you see an indented list of messages. Usually the left-most message is the main message of the thread or topic and the messages indented under it are the replies or comments to the main message. Some replies may have replies of their own.

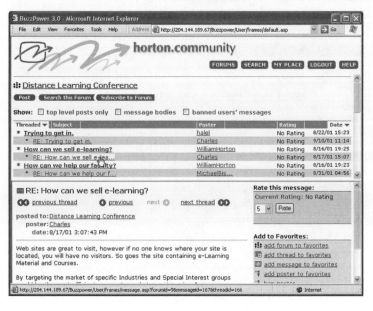

This is a typical online discussion from the perspective of a participant.

The online discussion displays conversations (threads) as indented lists of subject headers. To add to a conversation, the participant selects a message.

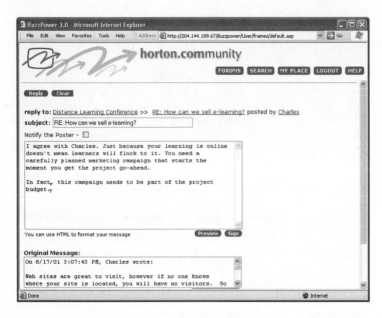

The discussion displays the message and offers the participant an opportunity to reply to it by filling in a few fields on a form. The participant fills in the form, typically entering a name, a subject header describing their message, and the content of the message. Replying to a forum message is much like replying to an e-mail message.

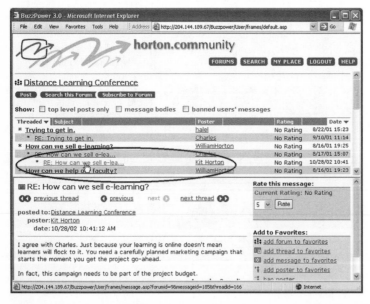

After the participant sends the message, it appears in the list of messages, indented under the appropriate message.

This pattern of indented messages is called a *thread*. Having the messages organized in threads greatly simplifies the task of following conversations. Perhaps this is why online discussions are a favorite part of many e-learning and knowledge management projects. Learners frequently cite the discussion as the best part of the course, and it is not unusual for conversations to continue months after the formal end of a course.

How online discussions are used in e-learning

Online discussions are commonly used in e-learning and knowledge management. In online discussions, learners participate in a conversation by sharing and replying to each other's text messages, even though they cannot be available at the same time.

Online discussions are especially valuable when learners are too busy to attend class meetings in person or online, when learners are scattered over 24 time zones, and when learners are too shy or lack language fluency to collaborate effectively in real-time conversations. Here is a typical implementation of an online discussion in e-learning.

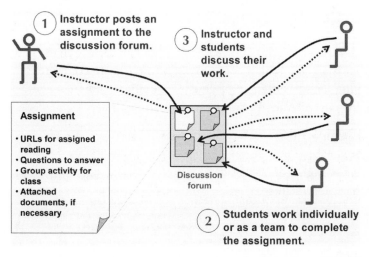

Learning starts as the instructor posts an assignment to the discussion forum (1). The assignment may include URLs or hyperlinks to assigned readings, questions to answer individually, and group activities. Assignments may also include attached reading and other necessary materials.

Learners read the assignment (2). They may work on it individually or in teams before posting their completed solutions back to the discussion forum, where the instructor and other learners review, discuss, and evaluate them (3). A typical course may consist of 6 to 12 assignments.

Such discussion-based courses and activities work well for subjects that involve collaboration, teamwork, and negotiation among multiple learners but do not require advanced multimedia.

In addition to providing the structure to an entire course, online discussions can augment other forms of e-learning. They are especially useful in extended role-playing, brainstorming, group-critiquing, and team-design activities. They can also be used for:

▶ Out-of-class questions and answers

▶ Continuing class discussions

▶ Coaching and supporting other learners

11

Collaboration tools

Popular online discussions tools

Let's look at some of the ways you can provide online discussions in your e-learning projects.

List servers

E-mail list servers (listservs) are a popular tool for online discussions. They relay e-mail messages among members of a mailing list. Each list contains the e-mail address of its members. The list itself also has an e-mail address. Every e-mail sent to the mailing list is in turn sent to all members of the mailing list. A reply to a message from a list member is sent to all members of the list. In short, everybody on the list gets a copy of every message sent to the list.

E-mailing lists are easy to use. Anyone who knows how to read and write e-mail messages can use one. Other than an e-mail reader, no other software is required. The disadvantage is that e-mailing list servers can inundate list members with messages. And there is no easy way to spot separate threads or conversations.

Popular e-mail list servers include: LISTSERV (www.lsoft.com), Majordomo (greatcircle.com), and Lyris ListManager (lyris.com). For more, go to serverwatch.com.

 Some list servers offer *digest* formats that organize messages into threads to avoid overwhelming listserv participants. That way, participants only get one message per day that contains hyperlinks to the individual messages.

News servers

There are currently more than 20,000 public Internet newsgroups where people from around the globe discuss interests both common and obscure. The software that makes these discussions possible is called a *news server*. News servers throughout the Internet swap copies of their newsgroups. That way, people can interact with a newsgroup from their local server or the one provided by their Internet services provider. The only tool needed to participate in a newsgroup is a news reader such as Outlook Express (microsoft.com), Mozilla's News and Mail reader (mozilla.org), or Agent (forteinc.com). For more readers, go to users.erols.com/foxdm/newsgrp.htm or search for "newsgroup readers" using your favorite search engine.

News servers rely on a standard protocol for exchanging messages. This protocol, called Network News Transfer Protocol (NNTP), ensures that news servers and news readers work interchangeably.

Some news servers include DNews (netwinsite.com) and CoffeeLink News Server (burton-computer.com). For more, go to serverwatch.com, but be careful because some of the products listed there are no longer supported.

Discussion servers

Discussion servers are Web-based applications that run on a Web server. They host the online discussion and participants interact through their Web browsers. There are many online discussion servers ranging in price from free to $10,000 USD and above. Here are just a few: DiscussionApp (server.com), DBabble (netwinsite.com), Phorum (phorum.org), UBB (infopop.com), and Snitz Forums (snitz.net).

Discussion servers are also built into general-purpose collaboration tools, such as Microsoft Exchange Server and Web Crossing (webcrossing.com). Simple discussions can be set up using tools in Microsoft FrontPage. Discussion servers are also a part of some virtual-school systems, LMSs, and LCMSs. To find more discussion servers, search the Web for "discussion server," "discussion software," "discussion board," or "discussion forum software."

Collaborative blogging tools

Blogs (short for Web logs) create an easily revised online journal. The blog can have multiple authors, say the students in a class or a team working on a project. Blogs provide an easy way for a few participants to carry on an asynchronous conversation. However, as a discussion tool, blogs are limited because they do not support threading. For more on blogging tools, see chapter 16.

Capabilities to look for in online discussion tools

Discussion tools are used for many purposes beyond e-learning and have evolved a rich list of capabilities. Let's look at the ones most important for e-learning.

▶ **Ease of use**. Discussion tools should be easy for learners and instructors to use. This is especially true for part-time or occasional students who are not continually interacting with the discussion tool. Therefore, you need to determine how easy it is to perform the basic processes of logging in, writing and posting a message, finding a particular message, and replying to a message. For instance:

- Do the controls for simple tasks stand out? Or are they buried among those for advanced features?
- Can participants easily compose messages? Is the window large enough they can see more than a few lines of their message?
- Does the tool provide buttons to format text and to insert smileys (emoticons)?
- Does the tool preview formatted messages the way they will appear to recipients?
- Is the interface for composing and posting discussion forum messages the same as that for e-mail messages?

- ▶ **Administrative features**. Can administrators, instructors, and facilitators easily start forums and threads, change privileges, archive messages, hide and reveal forums and threads, and delete messages? Can they filter out bad words and limit the size of attached files? Can administrators easily set up names and passwords for learners and make them the same as in other tools used by learners? Does the tool support several layers of administration? That is, can certain groups be assigned certain administrative tasks?

- ▶ **Moderation features**. Does the tool allow moderated as well as unmoderated discussion forums? In moderated forums, a moderator must approve messages before they are seen by others in the discussion.

- ▶ **Rich messages**. Can messages include HTML for formatting? Can they include pictures? Can other file formats be attached to messages?

- ▶ **Threading**. Does the discussion tool arrange messages in threads that can be examined separately, expanded and collapsed, and printed separately? Can threads be archived separately? Online discussions should show the structure of separate threads of conversation.

- ▶ **Message lists**. Does the tool make it easy to focus on messages and conversations of interest? Can participants clearly see the subject and sender of a message before opening it? Can they filter and sort messages by sender, subject, date, and whether they are already read? Can participants search for message by sender, date, subject, or text of the message?

Chat and instant messaging

Every day 90 million AOL users get together in chat rooms and instant messaging sessions to whine, pontificate, flirt, and who-knows-what. Chat provides an immediate, spontaneous exchange of messages, much like instantaneous e-mail or a textual phone conversation. Other names for this capability are *text messaging* and *instant messaging*.

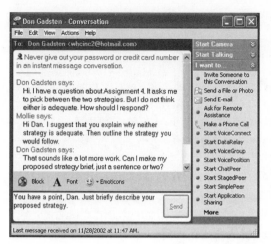

A conversation conducted in an MSN Messenger instant message window.

Conversations in chat involve participants using chat clients to add bits of text to an ongoing conversation. The chat client has two main areas. One, usually at the top, displays the ongoing conversation. Each participant's statements are identified by their name followed by a colon and then the words of their message. Names may be pseudonyms, but each is unique. At the bottom is another area in which the participant types his or her message. This new message is not added to the conversation until the participant presses the Send button, allowing the participant to revise it.

When the participant presses the Send button, the chat client sends the message to the chat server which in turn relays it to all the clients involved in the chat. These clients each add the message to the display of the ongoing conversation.

Chat sessions can appear in several forms and use several different software programs. They can be placed directly in a Web page using a Java applet or some other kind of embedded application, or they can be conducted with a separate chat or instant messaging application.

Chat vs. Instant messaging

If you are a linguistic purist, please forgive us for lumping these two forms of real-time messaging together. Unfortunately, the terms are used pretty much interchangeably in the data sheets and menus for e-learning tools you are likely to evaluate. We use chat to include the more spontaneous, intimate forms of instant messaging.

11

Collaboration tools

Here are some examples of these various methods of conducting chat.

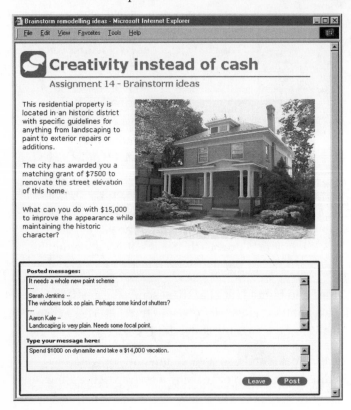

Chat capability may be embedded directly into a Web page as an integral part of an activity to promote discussion within the context of the subject.

This example uses Macromedia's MultiuserServer and the Director Shockwave Player.

In this example, learners are using a separate chat program with its own window. The chat session is a scheduled event and is the center of attention. This classic mode of chat may be based on the original Internet Relay Chat (IRC) protocol or the more recent T.120 protocols that allow users a choice of chat client.

Instead of classic chat, this exchange is taking place in an instant messaging application that looks almost the same. Some use the term instant messaging for learner- initiated conversations and chat for instructor-initiated conversations.

How chat is used for e-learning

In e-learning, chat can be used for real-time conversations about the subject of the course, for example as part of a brainstorming, team-design, or role-playing activity.

Chat can also be used for other kinds of communication common in conventional classroom training, including study groups where small groups of learners tutor one another, instructor office hours, team meetings for assignments, and even passing notes in class. During lectures and other real-time presentations, chat is an effective way for participants to ask questions and provide feedback to the presenter.

Because chat conversations are text-based, many learners prefer it because it leaves a written record they can consult later.

Popular chat tools

Chat servers range in price from several thousand dollars to free. Here are some server products to check out.

Product	Vendor	Web address
Chat Blazer	Chat Blazer	chatblazer.com
ChatSpace Community Server	Akiva	akiva.com
DBabble	NetWin	netwinsite.com

GlobalChat ROOMS	GlobalChat	globalchat.com
Lucid Chat	Lucid Chat	lucidchat.com
VolanoChat	Volano	volano.com

Chat capabilities are also included in many general-purpose conferencing and meeting tools, such as Centra, WebEx, and Microsoft Exchange Server, as well as some virtual-school systems, LMSs, and LCMSs.

Capabilities to look for in chat tools

Social chat is quite different from chat used for learning. In evaluating chat servers and clients, you should consider the capabilities needed to promote effective e-learning.

▶ **Structured sessions**. Can the instructor or administrator schedule chat sessions? Can the instructor set up numerous chat rooms, that is, areas where only certain people can participate?

▶ **Sending messages**. Can learners see enough of the conversation window to understand the context of a message? Can they scroll the window? Can they set the color and font of their contributions to the conversation? Can they save and print the conversations?

▶ **Required client**. Does the server require a client or does it work in a Web browser? Can the chat client be embedded on a Web page, in a Flash animation, and elsewhere in e-learning content? Does the chat server follow the T.120 protocol so learners have a choice of chat clients to use?

▶ **Informal sessions**. Can participants easily set up informal chat sessions like in instant messaging? Can they define a buddy list so they are notified when someone on their list is online and available for chat? Such features are especially valuable for peer-coaching and for instructors holding office hours.

▶ **Predefined messages**. Can participants prepare messages ahead of time to be injected into the conversation at the click of a button? For example, the instructor may want to have the statement "I'm not sure I understand. Can you elaborate please?" ready to go. Can participants inject smileys or emoticons into the conversation?

▶ **Public and private chat**. Can participants interact with individual participants as well as with the whole group? For example, in an online meeting can chat be set up for messages from the presenter to all learners, from learner to presenter, from presenter to individual learner, and from learner to learner?

Voting

Online voting asks questions and reveals responses of participants. It is like those keypads used in satellite video courses for distant participants to indicate their choices.

 Online voting tools are also called virtual response pads, polling, surveys, and virtual show of hands.

Online voting is quite simple. First, learners are presented with a question, typically with a list of answers from which to choose. Learners vote by clicking on an answer. An application on a Web server tabulates the answers and displays vote totals as a bar graph. Totals may also be stored in a database for later analysis.

How voting is used for e-learning

Voting requires participants to form an opinion, an act that requires them to think about an issue. It can also reveal the opinions of others—sometimes a humbling and sensitizing activity in itself. And voting activities can reveal changes of opinion, perhaps in response to various arguments or behaviors.

Online voting is useful to:

▶ Analyze the audience's background and interests

▶ Uncover attitudes, feelings, and biases

▶ Measure and monitor understanding as the course progresses

▶ Force thought and discussion

Because voting tools can effectively collect data about attitudes, emotions, and opinions, they are useful in soft-skills training, especially when linked to a chat session or a discussion group related to the issue being voted.

Forms of voting

There are two main forms of voting: synchronous and asynchronous. Synchronous voting is real-time voting. Typically at some point in a meeting, the instructor poses a questions to the audience, gives them a few seconds to decide and vote, and then reveals the vote totals.

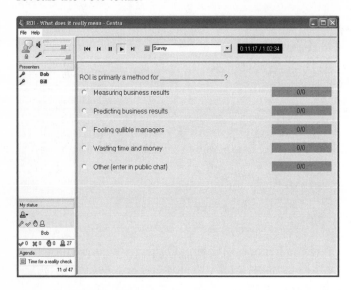

Here is a voting activity from an online meeting Bill (the co-author) conducted in Centra.

Before the class began, Bill entered the question into the tool. At a specific point, he displayed the question and asked learners to vote.

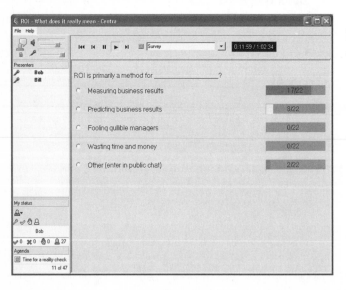

After the voting was completed, Bill revealed the results to the class.

Asynchronous courses can uses polls, though on a more leisurely basis. Voting is open over a period of days, months, or even indefinitely.

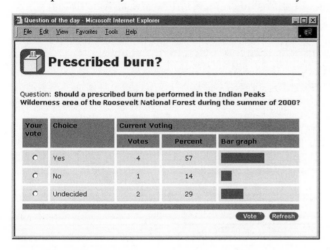

Here is an example of an asynchronous voting activity used in a course for foresters. After examining case study materials, learners are asked to apply what they learned to a complex decision.

Popular voting tools

Tools for online voting include The Survey System by Creative Research Systems (surveysystem.com), Poll Pro by AdComplete.com (pollpro.com), and the Multicity Value Package (multicity.com). Keep in mind that products for voting tend to be designed for wide-scale opinion surveys. However, they can be adapted for use in e-learning. And if you are blessed with programming talent, you can easily build your own using a database and tools like Macromedia Dreamweaver MX (macromedia.com), Adobe GoLive (www.adobe.com), and Microsoft VisualStudio .NET (microsoft.com). Voting capabilities are commonly built into online meeting tools like those from Centra, WebEx, and PlaceWare.

To find more voting tools, search for "online survey software" or "Web polling tools" or variants on these.

Capabilities to look for in voting tools

Here are some voting capabilities to look for that are especially important in e-learning.

▶ **Question types**. Even though the term "online voting" may make you think of simple yes/no questions, you should not be limited to that kind of question. Can the instructor ask other types of questions, such as pick-one, pick-multiple, open-answer, point-along-a-scale, or place-on-a-map or -diagram?

▶ **Rich media**. Can voting questions include links, graphics, and other media?

▶ **Question creation**. Can voting questions be created offline and saved? Can questions be reused in later sessions and other courses?

▶ **Question revelation**. Can the instructor choose when to reveal questions and results to participants? For example, the instructor may want learners to vote without being influenced by how others vote or may want to keep voting open and visible until a consensus emerges.

▶ **Use of results**. Can results be saved in a database and later analyzed in statistical reports? Can results be printed? Can evaluation results for individuals be saved to an LMS as if the voting questions were test questions?

Web tour

In Web tours, the leader navigates the Web while participants follow on their Web browsers. This feature is also called *Web safari, co-browsing, synchronized Web browsing, Web browser sharing,* or *follow me.*

An example of a Web tour using the online meeting tool Groove (groove.net). The tour leader is showing the Web site for the book *Evaluating E-learning* (horton.com/evaluating).

How Web tours are used for e-learning

Web tours are ideal for:

▶ Demonstrating and teaching the use of Web-based applications and services

▶ Analyzing company products and services

▶ Teaching how to look up information online

▶ Introducing online job aids

▶ Showing and discussing navigation, user interface, graphical design, icons and other aspects of Web sites

Popular Web tour tools

Web tour capabilities are part of many online meeting tools. If your online meeting tool does not have a Web tour feature, you can accomplish much the same effect by using the application sharing feature instead. We discuss application sharing a bit later.

Capabilities to look for in a Web tour tool

For e-learning, Web tours need just a few basic capabilities.

▶ Does the learner's browser quickly follow the browser of the instructor so the tour is not out of sync with the instructor's commentary?

▶ Can the leader let participants lead the tour?

▶ Do learners' browsers resize and scroll to mimic changes on the leader's browser?

▶ Are audio, video, and other media displayed on the leader's Web page experienced by all participants?

Whiteboard

Whiteboard is a collaboration tool that simulates the communication that occurs when the instructor draws on a wall-mounted whiteboard and then invites a student to contribute to the drawing.

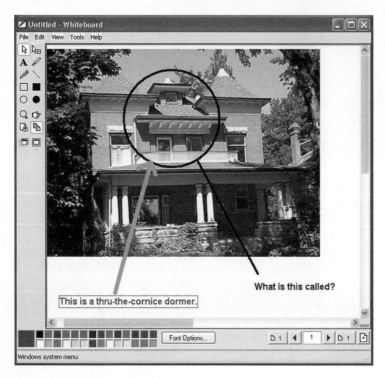

In this example from a course on architecture, the instructor starts the whiteboard session by showing a photograph of a dwelling.

Then the instructor circles one part of the house and asks a learner to identify it.

Next the instructor turns control over to the learner who, using a different color ink, draws an arrow to the feature and labels it.

The tool used here is Microsoft NetMeeting.

Like chat, voting, and other real-time collaborative activities, an application running on a Web server mediates the messages coming from various participants. For instance, if the leader uploads a graphic for discussion, the server application broadcasts the graphic to all the participants so that everyone sees the graphic in the whiteboard client application running on each participant's computer. As each participant annotates or makes additions to the graphic, the additions are transmitted back to the server and immediately broadcasted to the rest of the participants.

How whiteboards are used for e-learning

Whiteboards are valuable for discussing visual subject matter such as engineering diagrams, numerical charts, architectural plans, product photographs, organization charts, and works of art. They also work in visual brainstorming and collaborative design where participants add ideas to a sketch or diagram.

Popular whiteboard tools

Although some standalone whiteboard tools like Groupboard (groupboard.com) do exist, the whiteboard capability is most often found as part of an online meeting tool. If your online meeting tool does not have this capability, you can achieve a similar effect by using the application sharing feature instead.

To find more whiteboard tools, search for "whiteboard tools."

Capabilities to look for in a whiteboard

For e-learning, the whiteboard needs a balance of power and simplicity. Here are some capabilities to consider when evaluating a whiteboard tool.

▶ **Drawing tools**. Does the whiteboard include a rich selection of drawing tools similar to those found in drawing programs that instructors and students have used before? Can users draw basic shapes such as lines, arrows, rectangles, ovals, stars, dots, and diamonds? Can they set the color and width of lines and the color of shapes? Can they highlight areas to call attention to them during a presentation? Are there an adequate number of colors so annotations by different participants will remain legible and distinct, regardless of the background?

▶ **Editing**. Can participants edit notes and drawings without having to delete and redraw them? Can they erase an annotation without erasing the underlying graphic?

▶ **Multiple pages**. Can the instructor create multiple whiteboard pages, each with its own annotations that are saved with the page?

▶ **Saving drawings**. Can whiteboard drawings and annotations be saved for replay or reuse? Can they be saved in file formats you can reuse for other purposes? Can annotated drawings be e-mailed to participants or saved by them?

▶ **Efficiency and speed**. Does the whiteboard transmit just changes to the shared space, or the entire screen? This may be an issue for participants with slow connections.

▶ **Importing images**. Can images in common file formats (GIF, JPEG, and Windows Metafile) be imported or pasted in? Can participants draw on these images to annotate and label them? Can the presenter load graphics ahead of time?

Application sharing

Application sharing lets the presenter share programs, windows, or the entire screen with participants. Participants see exactly what is displayed on the presenter's screen. In some systems, participants can take control of the display—with the presenter's permission, of course.

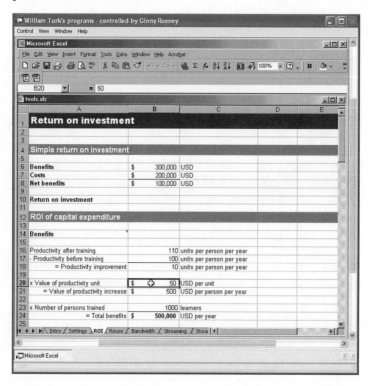

Here is the learner's view of a shared spreadsheet application. The learner has control and is entering information into the spreadsheet, even though the spreadsheet program is running on the presenter's computer.

The tool used here is Microsoft NetMeeting.

Application sharing is especially valuable when combined with document- and file-sharing to demonstrate real work and to collaborate on designs. Application sharing can also substitute for Web tour, whiteboard, and presentation capabilities by enabling the presenter to share Web browser, drawing program, or presentation program respectively.

How application sharing is used for e-learning

Application sharing is often used to teach and demonstrate computer programs. The instructor typically demonstrates the program and then transfers control to a learner to repeat the demo.

Using application sharing, learners can experience a program they do not have on their own machines. This capability is especially valuable for pre-release training of sales representatives. It is also valuable when the program is too expensive to provide copies for each learner, as in the case of a data analysis or charting tool.

Popular application sharing tools

Application sharing is not commonly available as a separate program. It generally comes in online meeting tools. To find tools with this feature, search the Web for "application sharing."

Capabilities to look for in application sharing

Application sharing is pretty straightforward. Essentially, someone agrees to share a window and all the participants get to see it. With permission from the sharer, participants can also interact with the contents of the window. There are just a few issues to think about when selecting a tool for application sharing.

▶ **Efficiency and speed**. How quickly do learners' screens refresh? Do demonstrations appear smooth even to learners with slow-to-moderate connections? Like whiteboard tools, application sharing tools must transmit changes efficiently so that remote displays do not lag behind the leader's display.

▶ **Split screen**. Does the tool support a split-screen feature? In some systems, the learner's client program may display the shared application in split-screen mode so the learner can follow along on a local copy of the application. This is sometimes called the *do-as-I-do* feature.

Presentations

Sometimes it seems that 90% of classroom training consists of looking at PowerPoint presentations and listening to the instructor drone on about each slide. Such lectures may not be the best form of instruction, but narrated slides are an essential fixture in learning today—so much so that most online meeting tools include ways to make live presentations over the Web.

11

Collaboration tools

How presentations are used for e-learning

In e-learning, online presentations are used much as they are in the classroom, namely for lectures, especially for visual subjects. They allow presenters to reuse proven classroom presentations. They are also useful in providing instructions for complex online activities.

Presentations can be one-way or two-way flows. A one-way flow occurs when the presenter shows slides and talks but learners can only watch and listen. Two way exchanges allow learners to ask questions, make comments, and otherwise contribute to the presentation.

For one-way presentations, you do not need a collaboration tool. You could use the online broadcast capabilities built into PowerPoint or tools for converting PowerPoint

Here is a presentation Bill (the co-author) conducted over the Web. The area to the right shows a PowerPoint slide. Bill provided the narration for the slides using voice over IP (VoIP). Learners asked questions using chat.

presentations to Web-deliverable formats. Chapter 18 discusses some of these tools. If learners are not going to interact with the presenter, there is no reason to tie up precious meeting time. Just record the presentation and let learners play it at their convenience. Then use meeting time to discuss the presentation.

Popular tools for presentations

Presentation tools are not common as standalone products. However, most online meeting tools have presentation capabilities. If your online meeting tool does not provide this capability, perhaps you can present slides using the online meeting tool's application sharing capability.

Capabilities to look for in a presentation tool

For effective e-learning, the online presentation should be just like being in the room with the presenter—or better. When evaluating presentation tools, ask whether it provides these capabilities.

▶ **Display area**. Is the display area large enough that the presentation is legible? Is it small enough to fit the screens of most participants without scrolling? Or, can the display area be adjusted by the learner?

▶ **PowerPoint features preserved**. If presenters use PowerPoint slides, what features are preserved? Fonts? Sounds on layers? Animations and transitions?

▶ **Other content**. Can presenters include other content, such as Web pages, sound clips, video sequences, Flash animations, and other media?

▶ **Whiteboard features**. Does the tool provide whiteboard capabilities for marking up slides?

▶ **Narration**. How is commentary communicated, by VoIP or conference call? A conference call leaves more bandwidth available for slides but may tie up a phone line.

▶ **Questions**. How do participants ask questions, answer questions, and make comments? If learners have no ability to interact, the presentation does not need a collaboration tool. Just record the presentation and make it available to learners to take on their own.

▶ **Uploaded files**. Can presenters import their presentations without delay? Or do they have to do this well before the session starts?

▶ **Recording**. Can the presentation be recorded and played back with a common media player? Or do learners need the collaboration client used to record the presentation?

Audio conferencing

Audio conferencing lets participants talk with one another. It is a feature found in many collaboration software packages. Audio conferencing essentially uses the Internet to conduct a conference call (VoIP). With audio conferencing, presentations can be more spontaneous. Participants can attend to visual matter without having to read text at the same time.

How audio conferencing can be used for e-learning

Audio capabilities are especially useful in e-learning where verbal communication or quick exchanges of ideas are important, that is, when there is not time enough to write everything down or where the spontaneous expression of thought is paramount. Much like presentation tools, audio conferencing allows one-way or two-way flows.

One-way (presenter to learners) audio communication is useful for:	Two-way (among all participants) audio conferencing is useful for:
▶ Narrating visual displays, such as slides ▶ For presenting material orally: to lecture, pontificate, inform, suggest, recite, read, or advise	▶ Question-and-answer sessions ▶ Mock debates ▶ Brainstorming ▶ Role-playing

Popular audio conferencing tools

Although dedicated audio conferencing tools such as Robust Audio Tool (www-mice.cs.ucl.ac.uk) do exist, most audio conferencing is found as part of many online meeting systems. In addition, instant messaging systems, such as those from Microsoft and AOL, now let participants send voice messages as well as text.

To find more audio conferencing tools, search for "audio conferencing tools."

No form of one-way communication is collaboration, but one-way audio can be combined with a back channel of chat or e-mail to close the loop. And speeches can be followed by discussion in chat or a discussion forum.

Sometimes it is just not technically practical or wise to provide all participants with speaking capabilities. But they should still be able to contribute to the collaboration.

Capabilities to look for in an audio conferencing tool

For effective audio collaboration, sound must be clear and well controlled. Here are some capabilities to consider.

▶ **Sound quality**. At low network speeds is the sound clear and understandable? Does it arrive with minimal delay? Does it stay in sync with the visuals displayed? For example, does the speaker appear to be pointing to the third bullet item while taking about the first one?

If you use multiple active microphones, make sure the system provides duplex audio so the listener does not have to wait for the speaker to finish before beginning to speak.

The technical term for audio conferencing with more than a few speakers at once is *pandemonium*.

▶ **Modes and control**. Does the tool let designers and instructors set up appropriate uses of audio? Can they easily broadcast lectures, "pass the microphone" to individual speakers, give speaking rights to a small group, or open up the meeting so anyone can talk at any time?

▶ **Standards**. Does the tool follow the H.323 telecommunications standard, which allows learners to choose their own clients?

▶ **Choice of voice technology**. Is audio conferencing conducted over the Internet using VoIP or by telephone conferencing? VoIP lets participants use their network connection to transmit voice rather than having to use a separate phone link. Phone conferencing, on the other hand, preserves precious network capacity for transmitting other media such as pictures of slides or shared applications. For phone conferencing, ask whether the collaboration tool can integrate with PSTN (Public Switched Telephone Network) and PBX systems, depending on which you plan to use.

I learned the value of using the telephone for audio conferencing when my computer crashed in the middle of a presentation. Using the phone line, I told learners what happened and continued the presentation while I switched to my backup computer.

Video conferencing

Video conferencing lets participants see and hear each other. It promises complete interpersonal communication—voice, gestures, body language, facial expressions—everything.

With video conferencing, participants see the person talking as a person. They can see three-dimensional objects, movements, and gestures. They can see a smile or a glare. They can notice a wink or a nervous twitch. They notice passion and nervousness.

How video conferencing is used for e-learning

Video conferencing is used mostly for presentations while a back channel of chat or audio conveys questions and comments from learners. In this mode, video conferencing is useful to:

▶ Introduce the presenter, helping participants to picture the presenter as a human being (It requires about 20 seconds of video.)

▶ Demonstrate physical procedures and psychomotor skills

▶ Reveal three-dimensional shapes and spatial

Video conference in Microsoft NetMeeting using VoIP

relationships by a video "walk" around physical objects

▶ Add realism and impact by demonstrating that something, a new product for example, really exists

▶ Communicate human emotion through facial expressions, gestures, body language, and tone of voice

Popular tools for video conferencing

Separate video conferencing tools are available, such as Vic by the Network Research Group at Lawrence Berkeley National Laboratory (www-nrg.ee.lbl.gov); however, most video conferencing tools used in e-learning are built into advanced collaboration tools like Microsoft Exchange Collaboration Server (microsoft.com) and Centra (www.centra.com). To find more, you can search the Web for "video conferencing tools."

Capabilities to look for in a video conferencing tool

 Most of the time, all you get from video is a small grainy, blurry, jerky, off-center picture of a poorly lit, awkward, self-conscious presenter.

In considering video conferencing tools for e-learning, ask whether the system has the capability to make video a learning experience, not just a novelty or worse—a frustrating experience. Here are some issues we think are important.

▶ **Technical requirements**. The quality of video conferencing depends on network speed, the quality of the video camera, the speed of the presenter's computer, and the speed of participants' computers. The technical requirements for video conferencing are high—as are the expectations. To meet these high expectations, you will need:

- A professional quality video camera attached to an IEEE 1394 (or other equally fast) port on a…

- A computer powerful enough to capture and encode the video stream and transmit the encoded video to a…

- A media server that will broadcast the video to participants who have…

- High-speed network connections.

▶ **User interface**. How well is video integrated into the interface? Does it appear in a pane of the main window? Or does it appear in a separate floating window with its own controls? How large can the video window

 Use video at your own peril. When e-mail starts running slow on the network, who do you think they are going to blame? "Yep, it's got to be all that video being used for e-learning."

be? Is it large enough that the learner can see important details and facial expressions?

▶ **Bi-directional**. Does the tool just transmit video from the presenter to other participants? Or can it transmit video from any participant to all the other participants? And can it do so without totally clogging or crashing the network? Sure?

▶ **Standards**. Does the tool follow the H.323 telecommunications standard, which lets learners choose their own client?

ONLINE MEETING TOOLS

As important as individual tools are, they become even more valuable when used together to conduct an online meeting. Fortunately, there are general-purpose tools for conducting online meetings and discussions. To varying degrees, these tools include the individual collaboration capabilities we've looked at, all wrapped up into one convenient package.

Quick tour of an online meeting tool

Here is a tour of an online meeting tool. Though tools vary, they provide similar capabilities. The example shown here uses a tool called Groove from Groove Networks (groove.net).

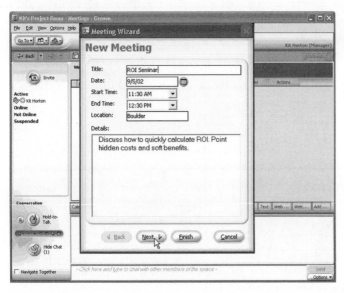

Kit starts by setting up a meeting. She picks a time for the meeting and describes it.

She sends an invitation to a participant. The invitation will arrive as a pop-up window on the participant's desktop. It can include a voice message or other attachment.

The participant clicks the link on the pop-up invitation to join the meeting.

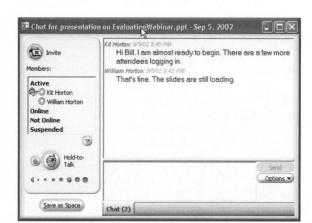

Once in the meeting, participants can communicate using chat, as shown here.

They can also communicate using audio by pressing the mouse button over the Hold-to-Talk button.

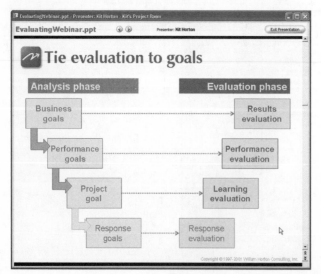

During the meeting, participants view PowerPoint slides while Kit narrates using telephone conferencing. VoIP is also available.

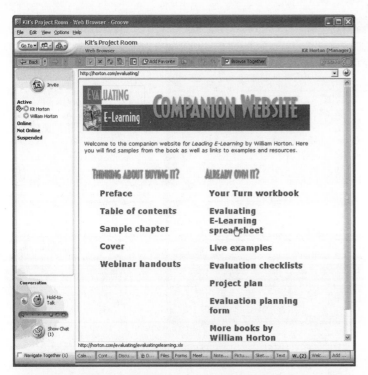

Kit leads participants on a Web tour. Here she shows the Web site for the book *Evaluating E-learning* (horton.com/evaluating).

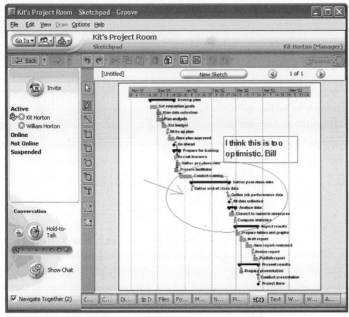

Here, participants share a Gantt chart using the whiteboard feature. Kit uses the drawing tools to highlight and comment on aspect of the chart.

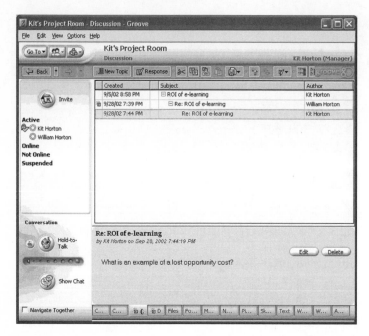

In the project discussion forum, participants discuss ongoing issues about the project or lesson at times convenient to them.

Indentations show that the messages are threaded.

In e-learning, online meeting tools are often called *virtual-classroom systems*. We've avoided this term because it's so close to *virtual-school systems*, which go far beyond the scope of individual meetings. Virtual-school systems are covered in the next chapter.

Popular online meeting tools

Here are some well known online meeting tools. Where both an e-learning and general version are offered, the e-learning version is listed here.

Product	Vendor	Web address
Aspen Virtual Classroom Server	Click2learn	click2learn.com
Campus Crossing	Web Crossing	webcrossing.com
Centra Symposium	Centra	www.centra.com
Convene	Convene	www.convene.com
eRoom	eRoom Technology	eroom.com
Enterprise Communications Platform	Interwise	interwise.com

Product	Vendor	Web address
Exchange Server and Exchange Conferencing Server	Microsoft	microsoft.com
FirstClass	Centrinity	www.centrinity.com
Groove	Groove Networks	groove.net
Groupboard	User Data Connections Limited	groupboard.com
GroupWise	Novell	novell.com
iCohere	iCohere	icohere.com
LearnLinc	Mentergy	mentergy.com
Lotus Domino server and Notes	IBM	lotus.com
MeetingPlace	Lattitude Communications	meetingplace.org
OfficeClip	Cosec Corporation	officeclip.com
PlaceWare	PlaceWare	placeware.com
QuickPlace	IBM	lotus.com
Sametime	IBM	lotus.com
vClass	Elluminate	www.elluminate.com
WebEx Training Center	WebEx	webex.com
Windows NetMeeting	Microsoft	microsoft.com

11

Collaboration tools

Capabilities to consider in online meeting tools

In addition to the capabilities listed for each collaborative tool, online meetings have other capabilities. Here are some we think are important for e-learning.

Floor control

Floor control is the process of managing the meeting. It is also called *choreography* or *baton passing*. The meeting leader must be able to control the meeting by calling on others to participate and by restricting who can speak or take other actions.

Good floor control features let the meeting leader determine the degree of participation by others, for instance:

- ▶ Who can speak

- ▶ Whose comments are seen by the class

- ▶ Who can annotate a presentation

- ▶ Who can show slides or present other media

- ▶ Who can launch applications

Floor control features typically provide a dynamic list of learners currently online. Learners can signal that they want to speak by "raising their hands" (in reality, pressing a button), causing an icon to appear in the dynamic roster next to the learner's name on the instructor's monitor.

Some tools only allow one leader at a time while others allow multiple leaders.

Meeting setup

Setting up meetings should be quick and efficient. Ask whether the leader can prepare the presentation without having to log into the server, typically by using a local utility program. Do the leader and participants have to upload all materials ahead of time, or can they share files as the need arises? Can a meeting setup be saved so the leader does not have to repeat this work for the next meeting that needs the same setup?

Online persona

For online meetings you may want to let participants pick their nickname, handle, avatar, or picture that others see as their representation in the meeting. You may also want a place to post a biography. In some cases, you may want to let learners participate anonymously—to comply with union rules, to accommodate multiple levels of management in a single meeting, or to discuss a sensitive, confrontational subject.

Calendar and schedule management

Online meeting tools should let administrators easily set up events, including inviting and scheduling participants. Some meeting tools contain a group calendar that can be synchronized with the learner's personal calendar, such as Outlook.

Recording

In some online meeting tools, live sessions and presentations can be recorded for later playback. Tools vary in what gets captured: presentations, chat, application sharing, Web tours, audio, video. If such recordings use a standard video format, they can be played back in a common media player. They can also be edited and updated using a video-editing program.

Display

The online meeting tool should provide a large enough display area for all types of activities. For instance, slides, Web pages, and other content should appear in an area large enough to avoid small text or extensive scrolling. Some tools provide an option to display slides, Web pages, and other content full screen rather than in a window or part of a window.

Breakout rooms and groups

A *breakout room* or *breakout group* allows leaders to divide a large meeting into separate meetings, each with its own leader. They let instructional designers deploy small-group activities the way they would in classroom workshops. The success of online breakout rooms depends on several capabilities.

- ▶ **Number of rooms**. Can the leader set up enough separate rooms to accommodate a large group?

- ▶ **Different content**. Can each breakout room have access to different presentations, documents, and other resources? Does each have its own whiteboard, application sharing, Web tour, and presentation capabilities?

- ▶ **Look-in by leader**. Can the overall leader observe ("look over the shoulder") and participate in the separate breakout meetings?

- ▶ **Dynamic reassignment**. Can participants be moved from one breakout room to another after the session begins? Can leadership within a room be reassigned by the current room leader or by the main meeting leader?

- ▶ **Sharing work**. Can the work done in a breakout room, for example a marked-up whiteboard, be shared with the whole meeting?

Presenter feedback

In online meetings, participants need to be able to provide continual feedback to the presenter or leader. Some tools provide buttons participants can click to express an emotion, such as laughter or applause, or to pace the presentation by requesting that the presenter slow down, speed up, or review material. Most systems provide at least a chat channel for private messages to the presenter ("Hey teach, your hair is on fire!").

Collaborative creation

Good meeting tools let participants work together on real or example projects. In a typical collaboration scenario, one person starts by creating and uploading a file. Another person can "check it out" to work on it locally. While it is checked out, only this person can modify it; however, others can see the modifications as they are being made. When the person is done, he or she checks the document back in so someone else can make changes.

In another scenario, participants review a document. This review may occur as part of a meeting or outside the meeting. In a document review, the document is sent to a series of "reviewers" sequentially. Each reviewer makes comments and changes and then passes it along to the next person in the review or approval chain.

Collaborative creation requires capabilities to:

▶ Send files simultaneously to other participants, with the transfer taking place in the background

 Some of these features are built into Microsoft Word. Take a look at the Track Revisions, Compare and Merge, and Online Collaboration features.

▶ Select reviewers and route a single document among them

▶ Let all participants see when the document is edited by the leader

▶ Track revisions and approvals of each reviewer

▶ Automatically synchronize different versions when resuming a meeting

COLLABORATION CLIENTS

Online collaboration tools may require learners to download and install a corresponding piece of software called a *collaboration client*. Clients for collaboration tools are components that run on the learners' computers to enable them to interact.

They are the learners' interface to the online meeting tool. Clients communicate with one another by way of a collaboration server, which takes care of routing messages among all the participants in a collaboration activity.

For most e-learning applications, collaboration clients are usually paired with a particular collaboration server or online meeting tool. Notable exceptions include e-mail readers, newsgroup readers, and online discussions that appear directly in a browser window. These generic collaboration clients include:

Product	Vendor	Web address
ChatZilla (IRC chat client)	Mozilla.org	mozilla.org
Mozilla Mail and Newsgroups reader	Mozilla.org	mozilla.org
Outlook Express (mail and newsgroup reader)	Microsoft	microsoft.com

CHOOSING COLLABORATION TOOLS

Because collaboration tools involve so many different media and capabilities, and because they come as standalone tools or capabilities built into composite tools, picking the right tool can be tricky. First, decide what collaboration capabilities you need, and then pick the collaboration clients and server to implement them.

What you need to know first

Before shopping for collaboration tools for e-learning, clearly understand where you are now and where you want to go.

What do you have already?

Before you consider buying any collaboration capabilities, learn what capabilities you have already. For instance:

▶ Your organization probably has e-mail service. What other collaboration tools does the organization have? Check with your IT department.

▶ If you have a Web server, what collaboration capabilities does it include? Sometimes these collaboration capabilities are not turned on or installed when the server is set up. Could you use these capabilities without degrading the server's performance for its current mission?

▶ Does your organization have a collaboration product or service now? Ask around. Does the sales department, perhaps, use a service to conduct sales briefings? Does technical support use a system to assist in solving problems? If your e-learning needs are modest, could you share these existing systems and services?

What are other collaboration needs?

You may be implementing collaboration just for e-learning, but you should consider other uses of collaboration. You may involve other departments and functions, such as human resources, customer support, sales, marketing, vendor relations, and others where efficient human-to-human communication is crucial.

For example, can you pool your needs for collaboration with those of other groups to justify a sophisticated collaboration system? Ask who else needs collaboration, such as:

▶ Other departments that want to put their education or training online

▶ Internal technical support, to keep internal IT working

▶ Sales and marketing, to communicate with sales representatives, customers, and potential customers

▶ Purchasing, to communicate with suppliers

▶ Customer support, to diagnose and solve problems for customers

Other groups may be able to share the cost and support your purchase request. Analyze their needs before you start shopping for specific products.

Capabilities to consider

Collaboration is essential to productivity and a key component of many e-learning and knowledge management strategies. The choice of collaboration tools is an important commitment for an organization. In many ways, this choice is no different than choosing other forms of software, but it does warrant a few special cautions.

IT standards

Your choice of collaboration tools may be limited by standards put in place by your IT department. If no standards exist, you may want to make your choice of collaboration tools a part of IT standards so that the whole organization uses compatible tools.

Platform

What combination of operating system and hardware does the collaboration server support? Not all tools work on all systems. Make sure these requirements are compatible with the requirements of other software that must run on the same machine.

Client required

What kind of client does the server require?

▶ Is the client easy to download and install?

▶ Is it available for all operating systems including Windows, Macintosh, Linux, Palm, Pocket PC, and so forth?

▶ Is the required client proprietary or generic? For example, if a video conferencing server follows the H.323 standard, then learners can download a generic client. You can find a list of these clients at the OpenH323 Project site at www.openh323.org/h323_clients.html.

▶ How will the client affect the features learners can use? For example, those using the NetMeeting client with the Microsoft Exchange Server see scheduled events automatically entered into their Outlook calendars.

Meeting size

How many people can participate in events and conversations? Is the tool designed for one-on-one exchanges? Is it suited for small seminars of 5 to 10 participants, classes of 10 to 30, or briefings for thousands of participants?

Data storage

Where are shared files, such as presentations, stored? Are they on a central server so presenters can present from any location on the network? On the presenter's workstation so the presenter can revise them offline? Or are they copied to all participants' workstations for quicker response? Each storage location poses issues of security, network traffic, and conflicting versions.

Learners' needs

The choice of collaboration tools is partly a decision about technology. It is also a decision about human factors. What human factors should determine your choice of collaboration tools? Here are just a few.

- ▶ **Language fluency** limits the use of real-time conferencing that requires people to understand and respond immediately, and accents limit the use of audio conferencing and video conferencing because these technologies rely heavily on voice.

- ▶ **Typing skills** are required for chat and instant messaging to be spontaneous and fluid.

- ▶ **Technical expertise** could be a barrier if participants must install required hardware and software themselves.

- ▶ **Connection speed** limits the use of media such as voice and video that require high bandwidth.

- ▶ **Geographic distribution and work schedule**s could limit their participation in any conferencing events that require everyone to be online at the same time.

You can probably think of other human factors that will help you narrow your choice of collaboration tools.

Product or service

Some online meeting tools are available as outside services, so you do not have to install and run them on your own network. Some vendors of online meeting tools offer a product you can install as well as a service to which you can subscribe.

WHAT NOW?

There are several places you can look to find the collaboration capabilities you need for your project and your organization. Here are some recommendations for how to proceed.

If you are in any one of these situations …	Consider these sources of collaboration capabilities
All you need is simple text-based collaboration (e-mail, discussion, chat) and if you must keep costs to a minimum.	Tool bundled with your Web server or server operating system (See chapter 8)
You need advanced capabilities offered by specific tools. You need to customize capabilities or combine capabilities offered by individual tools. Tools will be used throughout your enterprise for a wide variety of purposes, such as providing e-mail to the entire organization.	Individual tools for specific capabilities (Some of these are listed in this chapter where individual capabilities are discussed.)
Your organization needs to conduct online meetings and collaboration for a variety of purposes. E-learning is one of the purposes but cannot justify a tool on its own. You have aspirations to knowledge management that cannot be fulfilled by a system designed expressly to offer learning events.	Online meeting tools (Online meeting tools tailored for seminars and other learning events are sometimes called virtual-classroom systems.)
Your e-learning efforts are complex and varied. Classes require several coordinated meetings. Your learning is formal with grades and outside work as well.	Virtual-school system (or an LMS or LCMS that includes collaboration). See chapters 9 and 10 for more information on these tools.

Virtual-school systems, the subject of the next chapter, combine features found in LMSs and LCMSs with the collaboration tools discussed in this chapter. If you plan to use a school or university metaphor for your e-learning, the next chapter will be especially interesting to you.

11

Collaboration tools

12 Virtual-school systems

Virtual-school systems enable the delivery of instructor-led and facilitated e-learning. They are really a hybrid category of tool that combines capabilities from learning management, content management, and collaboration systems. Now you can see why we discussed those technologies first.

Virtual-school systems differ from online meeting tools in several ways. Online meeting tools tend to be a collection of collaboration tools enhanced for e-learning. They tend to be session-oriented. Virtual-school systems, on the other hand, tend to be more course- and curriculum-oriented even though they may share the ability to conduct online meetings.

 In academic settings, virtual-school tools may go by the name course-management systems. We avoid that term here because some course management systems merely automate certain aspects of classroom training, such as grade collection and submission of homework. And, the acronym CMS is easily confused with content management system.

WHAT VIRTUAL-SCHOOL SYSTEMS DO

Virtual-school systems are one of the largest blobs on our tools framework. That's because virtual-school systems include tools for course authors, administrators, instructors, and learners. At the curriculum level, the administration tools may overlap similar functions in LMSs; however, the collaboration tools tend to be more specific than those in generic collaboration packages. Compared

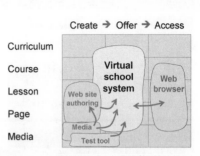

to systems created by assembling separate components, the value of the virtual-school system is that it provides a complete package of features needed to assemble, administer, and conduct e-learning courses. And, virtual-school systems promote consistency.

Virtual-school systems help course authors develop courses by assembling content and organizing it into lessons and other instructional units. They help instructors conduct courses by making it easy for them to post assignments, assign grades, route messages among participants, and conduct online discussions with the class. Virtual-school systems simplify routine administrative chores such as recording test scores, tracking activities, and reporting results. To students they offer a consistent, convenient way to obtain materials, post assignments, and interact with their instructor and classmates.

Though virtual-school systems provide many of the capabilities needed for creating and offering e-learning, you may need to create advanced page content and specialized media, such as animations, audio, and video. If the virtual-school system lacks advanced testing capabilities, you may need a testing tool to provide that level of assessment.

 You pay for the convenience of packaged virtual-school systems. They may possess fewer capabilities and may be more expensive than purchasing separate tools.

QUICK TOUR OF A VIRTUAL-SCHOOL SYSTEM

The following screens are from Jones e-Education software by Jones Knowledge (jonesknowledge.com). These screens show just a few of the main features of a virtual-school system.

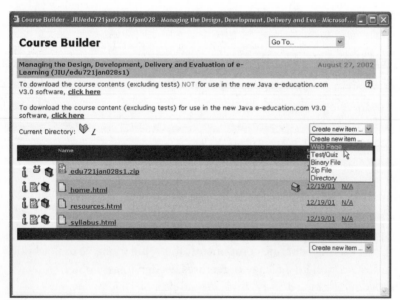

Virtual-school systems contain tools to assemble courses. Though not as rich as the authoring features of a pure LCMS, they do simplify the task of specifying the components of courses and lessons.

Here the author is adding a new unit of content to the course.

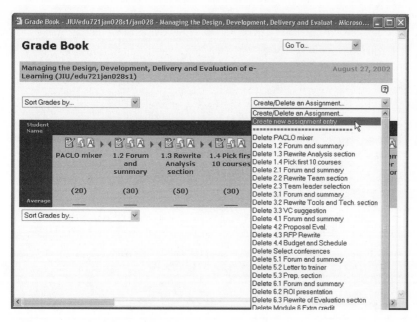

Instructors and facilitators can manage the process of instruction, including assigning grades for each assignment completed by learners.

Here the author is adding an assignment to the grade book.

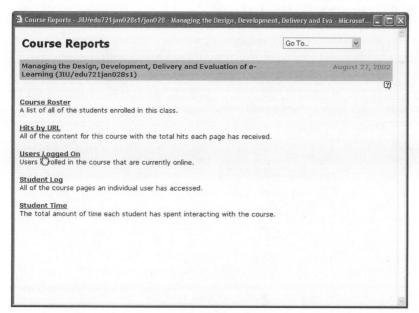

Instructors and administrators can view a variety of reports analyzing training activity and documenting progress.

Here the instructor is going to check to see who is currently working on the course.

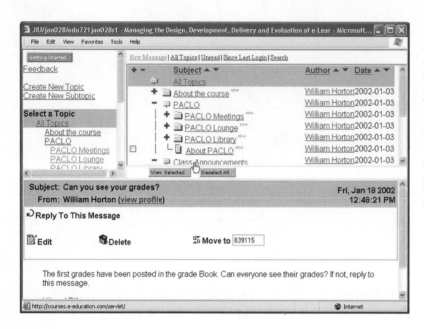

Participants can collaborate using e-mail, a discussion forum, chat, and a whiteboard.

Here the instructor has added a message to the class announcements thread in the discussion forum.

HOW VIRTUAL-SCHOOL SYSTEMS WORK

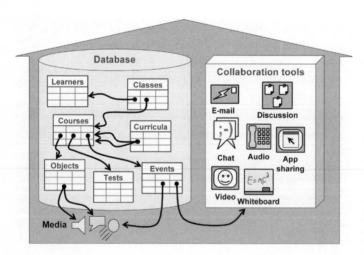

Virtual-school systems usually combine an extensive database that tracks all aspects of learning with a collection of collaboration tools.

The database lists and tracks connections among classes which are defined in the system as learners enroll in particular courses. Curricula are defined as sequences and dependencies among courses. Courses are defined in terms of lower-level objects, which may include specific media. Courses may also involve tests and meeting events, which may include media, such as presentation slides, and may also involve a mix of collaboration tools such as e-mail, discussion forums, chat sessions, audio conferencing, application sharing, whiteboard sessions, and video conferencing.

All of this is organized and presented to learners, instructors, and administrators within the metaphor of a conventional school.

POPULAR VIRTUAL-SCHOOL SYSTEMS

Here is a list of virtual-school systems aimed at both academic and corporate organizations. Some of these systems are designed for enhancing classroom training but can also be used to deliver entire courses online.

Product	Vendor	Web address
Aspen Virtual Classroom Server	Click2learn	click2learn.com
Blackboard	Blackboard	blackboard.net
Convene	Convene	convene.com
eCollege Campus	eCollege	ecollege.com
e-education	Jones Knowledge	jonesknowledge.com
Enhanced Distance Learning Environment (EDLE)	IBM	ibm.com
FirstClass	Centrinity	www.centrinity.com
Integrated Virtual Learning Environment (IVLE)	Centre for Instructional Technology, National University of Singapore	ivle.nus.edu.sg
Jenzabar's Internet Campus Solution	Jenzabar	www.campus.com
Lotus Learning Space	IBM	lotus.com
.LRN	dotLRN	dotlrn.org
Serf	Serfsoft	serfsoft.com
TopClass Virtual Classrooms	WBT Systems	wbtsystems.com

Product	Vendor	Web address
Virtual-U	Virtual Learning Environments	vlei.com
WebCT Campus Edition	WebCT	webct.com

If your favorite virtual-school system is missing, check the lists of LMSs (chapter 9) or LCMSs (chapter 10) because many of these tools also contain some virtual-school capabilities.

To find more virtual-school systems, search for "virtual school" or "virtual classroom." Keep in mind that many of the systems you find are highly customized implementations. A lot are aimed at one-time class meetings and not the full range of activities commonly found in a school.

CHOOSING A VIRTUAL-SCHOOL SYSTEM

Virtual-school systems are complex and expensive. Buying one is, well, complex and expensive. There are many factors to evaluate and many perspectives to consider.

What you need to know first

Before ordering demos or hitting the Web sites of vendors, take a few minutes to define your needs and goals. Ask yourself these questions.

▶ **What kind of school do I want to create**: Online university, K-12, or corporate training center?

▶ **How large will my school be**? How many students will take how many courses composed of how many sessions taught by how many instructors presided over by how many administrators?

▶ **Will my school be totally online**? Or, will the virtual-school be used to add online activities to classroom courses? Or, will you mix online and classroom courses?

▶ **What other tools do I already have in place**? Do you have content management, course management, student information, online meeting, or collaboration tools already installed? Would a virtual-school duplicate or conflict with such tools? Can it be connected to them?

▶ **What are the technical skills and professional flexibility of my staff**? Can they adapt to new ways of creating, organizing, and teaching courses? Or, must the virtual-school mimic existing ways of doing things?

Capabilities to consider

What follows is our list of virtual-school capabilities grouped by the people who benefit from them: administrators, course authors, instructors, and learners. Use this list to help you evaluating virtual-school systems.

For administrators

A virtual-school system, like its brick-and-mortar counterpart, requires a great deal of administration. Administrative capabilities are especially important to administrators of learning programs.

▶ **Ease of use**. What documentation, training, and customer support is provided by the vendor to help learners, authors, instructors and administrators get started? Ease of use may be just as important as the features provided.

▶ **School-wide announcements**. Can the virtual-school send announcements to all instructors, instructional designers, administrators, or learners involved in a course? Can it send announcements to alumni of a course or of the school?

▶ **Automation of basic tasks**. Does the system automate enrollments, billing, grade reports, and other common operations? Can you override these automated features when necessary to handle exceptions and special cases?

▶ **Security levels**. Does the virtual-school recognize different roles of users and provide tools to help them function in their roles? Roles might include student, instructor, teaching assistant, discussion forum moderator, course author, instructional designer, sponsor, alumni, administrator, or guest.

▶ **Range and use of collaboration**. Does the virtual-school system provide a rich mix of collaborative tools? Are the tools easy to use—both for learners as well as for authors, instructors, and administrators? Does the system provide chat rooms, discussion forums, online poling, and other collaboration capabilities centered on a specific:
  - Course
  - Class (particular group of learners at the same place in the course)
  - Curriculum or degree program
  - Non-learning event (a learner lounge, for example)

- Faculty or staff member
- Department (such as technical support)

If the necessary collaboration tools are not provided by the system, can third-party tools be easily integrated?

▶ **Course sequences**. Can the virtual-school system create curricula, that is, sequences of courses with prerequisites and electives leading to a degree or certificate?

▶ **Flexible definition of a class**. Does the virtual-school system allow classes of any length, containing any number of modules, having any number of students, with any number of instructors (including zero), and containing any mixture of online and classroom activities from all online to all classroom? The virtual-school should certainly be able to create classes that mimic classroom courses in all aspects except the delivery media.

▶ **Community**. Does the system build a community by allowing outside-the-course communication among students, faculty, administrators, and alumni? Does it make it easy for alumni to stay involved by contacting teachers, attending virtual reunions, and donating money? Does it provide a virtual student union for cross-course discussions? Does it let students set up clubs with Web sites, chat meetings, and discussion forums?

▶ **Advertising**. Can the organization sell and position advertising within its online campus and courses?

I know some schools really, really need the money, but how much learning takes place with a twirling, pulsing banner ad on the screen?

For course authors

Course authors create learning events and assemble them into lessons and courses. Here are some capabilities to help them with these tasks.

▶ **Authoring tools**. Does the system have course authoring tools? Does it support authoring by those with little experience creating online courses? Does it limit those with extensive experience? Can authors assemble content from a variety of common document formats such as HTML, Microsoft Word, PowerPoint, Excel, and Adobe Acrobat PDF? Can they create new content without knowing HTML?

▶ **Pedagogical assistance**. Does the system assist instructors and designers in creating instructionally sound and aesthetically pleasing courses, displays, and activities? Does it provide fill-in-the-blank

Watch out! Forms and templates that work in one tool may make it hard to move content to another tool later on.

forms, templates, models, and advice to guide those without formal instructional design training?

▶ **Blending**. Does the system enable you to define programs that include a mixture of different types of learning events? Types of learning events can include classroom sessions, Web-based activities, CD-ROM content, audio and video conferencing, and online discussions.

▶ **Synchronous and asynchronous courses**. Does the tool work for both synchronous (real-time) and asynchronous courses? Some tools require the course to be organized around real-time online class meetings. Others may lack the collaboration features for online meetings.

▶ **Testing and assessments**. What kinds of assessments can you create? Are you limited to simple multiple-choice and short-answer tests? Or are sophisticated matching, drag-and-drop, and other types of assessments possible? Can the virtual-school system use tests created and administered by a separate tool, integrating scores on these tests into its own database?

For instructors

A virtual-school system should help instructors and facilitators more efficiently teach and aid learners. Capabilities for instructors and facilitators include:

▶ **Faculty and staff support**. Does the virtual-school provide support for faculty and staff or does it make creating this support easy? Such support can include:

- Tutorials and documentation on their individual roles
- Sample courses
- Rosters so they can contact one another
- Teachers' lounge with chat, discussion, and other collaboration tools
- Staff meetings using audio or chat

▶ **Streamlined grading**. Can instructors grade submissions and add comments right on the screen? Does the system provide a spreadsheet-like grade-book for entering scores that automatically calculates totals and averages? Are results recorded and automatically routed back to the learner? In addition to these basic features, does the system:

- Provide access to Web-based plagiarism-checking services?
- Allow instructors to change grades at any time? (All changes should be logged.)
- Make it easy for instructors and facilitators to assign extra work to individual learners, for example, optional assignments, make-up work, and extra-credit assignments?

▶ **Scheduled release of material**. Can instructors schedule when material is revealed to learners and when it is hidden?

For learners

Without learners, there would be no schools. Learners need more than raw content. A virtual-school system should provide:

▶ **Study aids**. Does the course interface supplied by the system provide study aids for taking notes, highlighting material, bookmarking locations, and other actions common to classroom learning and textbooks? Can students create a journal to record their insights, decisions, frustrations, and changes of opinion?

▶ **Library**. Is there a school library where you can provide links to books, reports, Web sites, presentations, experts, and other resources valuable for research on the subjects taught by the school? Does the system make it easy to create subject-specific glossaries?

▶ **Résumé and portfolio-building**. Are there tools within the virtual-school to help learners develop a résumé and portfolio? Does it guide them in writing a résumé and posting it to the Web? Does it help them make samples of their work available online to prospective employers—or just to amaze their boss or parents? This is a rare feature, indeed, but can be very motivating to learners.

▶ **Learner contributions**. Does the system enable learners to prepare lessons or presentations and link them into the course so that the whole class can see them?

▶ **Automated assignment submissions**. Does the virtual-school system automate the process of submitting assignments? Can learners have a folder or drop box on the server to which they can post assignments? Does the system electronically acknowledge and record all submissions, completions, tests, discussion postings, or anything else the learner completes? Virtual-school systems should automate the submission process, including:

- Scanning for viruses
- Forwarding submissions to the assigned grader
- Returning grades to the learner
- Archiving assignment and any comments by graders
- Producing a report of all submissions and grades

For more in-depth capabilities specific to learning management, learning content management, and collaboration systems, review chapters 9, 10, and 11 where these systems are discussed.

ALTERNATIVES TO VIRTUAL-SCHOOL SYSTEMS

Getting the right mix of capabilities in a virtual school is complex. Doing so for a modest budget is epic heroism worthy of a comic book series. Before purchasing a virtual-school system, consider some alternatives.

One alternative to the virtual-school system is to build your own by combining an LMS, an LCMS, and collaboration tools. In fact the Aspen virtual-school system by Click2learn is a combination of three such products, each of which is offered separately by Click2learn.

Another alternative may be to buy just an LMS or LCM that includes the virtual-school capabilities you need. If you are shopping for a virtual-school system, you definitely should check out LMS, LCMS, and collaboration tools.

WHAT NOW?

To build your virtual school, you must put the ideas of this chapter into action. Here are some recommendations for how to proceed.

If you ...	Then ...
Are still designing your e-learning	Make a complete list of the capabilities you will need to create the kinds of learning experiences in your instructional design. Consider what kind of environment your learners will need. Will they need synchronous or asynchronous collaborative mechanisms? Will they need facilitation or instruction? Do they need the motivation of a classroom atmosphere?
Have selected other tools but not a virtual-school system	Make a list of the capabilities your current tools have. Compare this list to all the capabilities you anticipate needing. Is there a gap? Are there capabilities not currently being met that overlap the main capabilities of a virtual school? If not, then you may be better off purchasing separate tools and integrating them with those you already have.

12

Virtual-school systems

Are at the point of picking a virtual classroom	Use the criteria in this chapter as a starting point. List your requirements. Check for additional virtual-school systems beyond the ones listed here. Using the selection process in chapter 20, select your virtual-school system.
Have already picked your virtual-school system	Investigate the tool's every capability and how it can be used for the kinds of e-learning you want to create. Publish a guide for your administrators, instructors and facilitators, and course authors, pointing out how to make the tool do what you need it to do. Then use the virtual-school system to educate your administrators, instructors, and facilitators.

13 Media servers

Conventional Web servers deliver HTML Web pages on request. Because most Web pages consist of text and simple graphics, this is not too difficult a chore. A moderately powerful Web server can handle hundreds of requests per second. But when the media requested are large audio and video files, a conventional Web server may begin to cough, wheeze, and collapse from the exertion required.

The chores of handling many requests for large media files are best handled by a media server, which specializes in high-bandwidth audio and video.

WHAT MEDIA SERVERS DO

Media servers do just what their name implies: They dispense media files as requested by Web browsers and media players. Because media servers must deal with "heavy" media, they may need to run on a separate, dedicated machine rather than on the same machine as the regular Web server. That machine can be a computer or a special-purpose appliance.

Media servers complement Web servers by relieving them of the tasks of serving up heavy media files. A Web page from a Web server can include media served by a separate media server; however, learners experience the media as if they were an integral part of the page.

Media servers squat at the bottom-middle of our tools framework, thus symbolizing their role: the middle between creating and accessing media. They are an essential part of the media pipeline from creation to display. Media editors create media, the media server offers it, and media players let learners experience the media. This flow from creator to learner may require coordinating tools. For

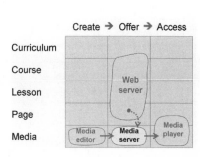

example, if you are using Real Network's video format, you need a Real server and Real player to complete the flow.

QUICK TOUR OF A MEDIA SERVER

Let's take a quick tour of the media server that is part of the Microsoft Windows 2000 Server and learn how to set it up to serve media files.

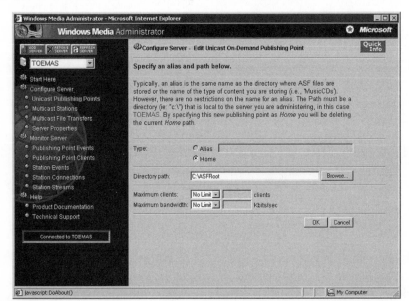

We start by defining a folder where the media files are to be kept. This is called an *on-demand publishing point*. Once this is defined, the media server knows where to look first for requested media files.

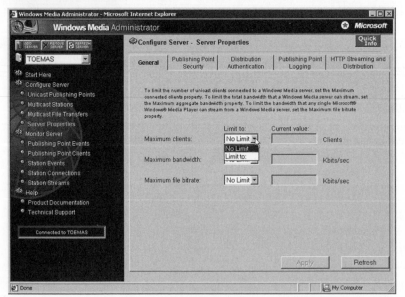

For this publishing point, we set parameters such as how many people can request files at the same time, how much bandwidth is allocated to this publishing point, and what the maximum requested stream rate per file can be.

These settings help balance the needs of different courses or projects.

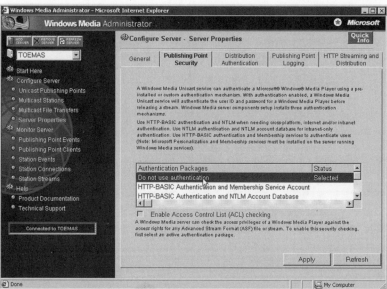

If desired, we can secure the media files using one of several authentication schemes.

Authentication schemes make sure that only authorized people and systems can view the media files. Media server security should complement the security scheme used by the Web server that handles other aspects of the course.

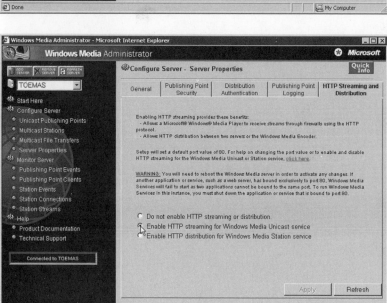

We can enable access to media using the HTTP protocol. This is especially important for people accessing media from behind a firewall. They may only be able to access content coming through port 80, which is the default HTTP port.

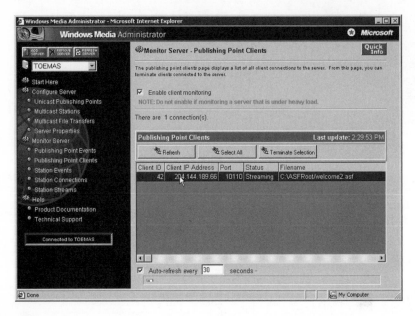

Once the server is running, we can monitor activity. In this example you can see that there is one user connected.

These are just a few of the basics. Media servers offer many more controls and capabilities, and servers differ considerably in how you manage their capabilities.

HOW MEDIA SERVERS WORK

What happens when someone requests a media file from a media server? The details may vary slightly, but the sequence is something like this.

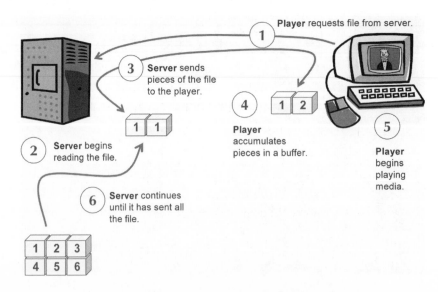

1. The media player or browser requests the media file from the media server.

2. The media server reads the first part of the file.

3. The media server begins putting the file into packets and sends them down to the browser.

4. The media player unpacks the first few packets and starts queuing up the first part of the file. This is called *buffering*.

5. The player begins playing the media.

Meanwhile the server continues sending packets until the complete file has been sent.

As you can see, media servers work much like Web servers (chapter 8) except that they specialize in delivering media formats, especially streaming audio and video, instead of just text and graphics.

13

Media servers

Streaming? What's that?

What exactly is streaming, and how does it make media appear to download quicker? In the conventional way of downloading a file, you must wait for the whole file to arrive before it can begin playing. *Streaming* is a more recent approach. It is designed especially for playing heavy media over a network. With streaming, the file begins playing as soon as the first few packets arrive.

Streaming means that learners spend less time waiting for a file to begin playing. Streaming may, however, require special media server software, which adds complexity and expense to the project. And, it may only work for file formats designed with streaming in mind. That is, for a file to stream, it usually needs to be encoded or processed in a special way before being placed on the server.

Also keep in mind that the quality of the playback still depends on the connection speed. High-fidelity playback requires a fast connection.

Streaming media formats include Windows Media Format from Microsoft, RealVideo and RealAudio (from RealNetworks), MP3, Sony ATRAC3, and QuickTime 4 (from Apple). The Macromedia Shockwave format for Flash, Director, and Authorware files is an inherently streaming file format and does not require a separate media server.

WHAT MEDIA SERVERS REQUIRE

Serving up media requires a dedicated machine with a very fast network connection and plenty of disk space, in addition to the media server software. Let's do the math to see what you need.

Network connection speed

Serving lots of media to lots of learners simultaneously requires a connection capable of transporting all the bits learners have requested. Let's work through a simple example. (Bits and bytes are explained in the appendix.)

The basic formula for computing network speed is:

$$\text{Number of learners} \times \text{Stream rate} = \text{Network speed required}$$

Start by assuming you have 100 learners who have requested a 33.6 Kbps stream. The required network speed is:

$$100 \times 33.6 \text{ Kbps} = 3360 \text{ Kbps or about 3.4 Mbps}$$

If you have another 50 learners accessing a 100 Kbps stream at the same time, you need even more network speed:

$$50 \times 100 \text{ Kbps} = 5000 \text{ Kbps or 5 Mbps}$$

If you expect both to be served simultaneously, you must add the two requirements together:

$$
\begin{array}{r}
3.4 \text{ Mbps} \\
\underline{5.0 \text{ Mbps}} \\
8.4 \text{ Mbps}
\end{array}
$$

Such a rate would require six T1 lines or 131 channels of a fractional T3 line. Just to review, a T1 line can sustain a data rate of about 1.5 Mbps (24 channels of 64 Kbps each). A T3 line carries 672 channels of 64 Kbps each for a data rate of about 43 Mbps.

Disk space

The media server must store the media it is to serve. Therefore, you must ensure that the computer has sufficient storage capacity or disk space. The formula for this calculation is relatively simple:

$$\text{Length of media in seconds} \times \text{Stream rate} = \text{File size}$$

For example, let's say you have a 100-second audio clip that streams at 80 Kbps. That would require a file size of:

$$80 \text{ sec} \times 100 \text{ Kbps} = 8000 \text{ Kbits}$$

To convert bits to the more common bytes, divide by 8:

$$8000 \text{ Kbits} \div 8 \text{ bits per byte} = 1000 \text{ KB or 1 MB}$$

A 1-megabyte file is not bad, but you have to multiply the size of this file by the number of such files you expect to have. Let's say you expect a thousand such files. That means you need this much space:

$$1 \text{ MB per file} \times 1000 \text{ files} = 1000 \text{ MB (or 1 gigabyte)}$$

You would need to repeat this chain of calculations for each set of files your media server must handle. You might also want to account for backup copies of media as well.

POPULAR MEDIA SERVERS

Well-known media servers include the following products. To find more, search the Web for "media server."

Product	Vendor	Web address	Price
Darwin Streaming Server	Apple Computer	apple.com	Free, with no per-stream license fees
Helix Universal Server	RealNetworks	RealNetworks.com	$1999 USD (standard)
QuickTime Streaming Server	Apple Computer	apple.com	Free, with no per-stream license fees
SGI Media Server*	Silicon Graphics	sgi.com	Check with vendor
Torrent OSA streaming media appliance*	Starbak Communications	starbak.com	Check with vendor
VideoCharger	IBM	ibm.com	Check with vendor
Windows Media Services	Microsoft	microsoft.com	Free with Windows 2000 Server operating system

* Includes both hardware and software packages.

13

Media servers

CHOOSING A MEDIA SERVER

Media servers are highly specialized pieces of software. Picking one requires mapping your specific needs to the capabilities provided by available products.

What you need to know first

Before you start evaluating media servers, take a few minutes to ask yourself some questions about your needs and goals.

▶ What media will you use: graphics, animations, sound, or video? What mix of these media will you serve?

▶ At what rate will learners request these media files? That is, how many media files will be requested per hour (or some other unit of time)?

▶ How long and how large will these files be?

▶ What specific file formats will you use?

▶ What speed connections do learners have? Slower connections benefit more from streaming.

Capabilities to consider

Here are some questions you might want to ask to help you decide which media server to use for a particular project.

 Media servers can also handle non-streaming formats such as WAV, AVI, and JPEG.

▶ **Formats handled**. What file formats does the server handle? The servers from RealNetworks, Apple Computer, and Microsoft are optimized for their own media file formats. You probably would not standardize on Microsoft's media formats and then buy the RealNetworks media server.

▶ **Performance**. Can the media server keep up with requests from learners? What is the capacity of the server? How many files of what size can the server deliver over what period of time? Some can handle the requirements of a 100-channel Internet TV station without breaking a sweat. Others may be scaled for more moderate loads. As a general rule for e-learning, a media server should have a raw capacity of 100 Mbps or higher and should be able to maintain thousands of simultaneous connections.

► **Reliability**. Can the server keep its poise under bombardment by media-hungry learners? Or does it sputter, stutter, and crash. Look for features to provide error correction and recovery, such as forward error correction (FEC) and packet loss recovery. Also look for skip protection, which can be enhanced by adjusting the amount of buffering for files being sent to learners.

> **A package deal**
>
> As with Web servers, media servers can be thought of as a package that includes both hardware and software. Many aspects of the hardware determine how efficiently the media server software delivers media. For instance, how many processors does the server have? How fast are they? How much memory does the server have? How many network interface cards are installed? In short, when evaluating performance, consider everything.

► **Standard protocols**. Does the media server support standard multimedia and streaming protocols such as real-time streaming protocol (RTSP) or synchronized multimedia integration language (SMIL)?

► **Dynamic customization**. Does the media server adjust to the learner's connection speed by selecting from multiple versions of a file? Can it automatically generate these reduced-size versions of the original file or allow you to store the data for multiple connection speeds in one file? (This ability may also depend on the format of the media being served.)

► **Security**. Does the server protect sensitive information? Can it require authentication of learners and encryption of media streams? Can it enforce a Digital Rights Management scheme?

► **Multicasting**. Can the media server send a single stream of content to multiple network destinations at one time (*multicasting*) rather sending separate streams to each destination (*unicasting*)? If only one copy of the media file is sent to multiple client computers, it requires less bandwidth than a unicast broadcast.

► **Encoding tools**. Does the media server include tools for encoding and compressing media files? Does it also include tools for capturing and streaming live broadcasts? Do these tools use codecs (compression/decompression modules) that learners already have on their machines? Can the server dispense these codecs to learners who need them?

► **Updating players**. Does the server automatically update players in the field? Can it send an e-mail notification including update instructions to those whose players are not up to date? Can it perform mass updates of all the players within an organization?

ALTERNATIVES TO MEDIA SERVERS

Media servers are esoteric and potentially expensive. Before buying one, consider a couple of alternatives.

If you use only a few media beyond text and graphics, you may be able to get by with a conventional Web server as long as your files are small and encoded in an inherently streaming format, such as Shockwave Flash (SWF) or MP3 audio.

Our advice is to outsource the serving of audio and video unless you have a lot of video and audio. Serving media requires dedicated hardware and very fast network connections. To find media service providers, search the Web for "streaming media providers" or "Internet broadcasting service providers."

WHAT NOW?

To put the ideas of this chapter into action, you need to make decisions and take actions. Here are some recommendations for how to proceed.

If you ...	Then ...
Are still designing your e-learning	▶ Investigate what media learners can really play.
	▶ Decide what media types you really need.
	▶ If you need video or audio, decide what formats you will use, i.e. QuickTime, Windows Media, Real, etc.
	▶ Determine how many files you will need to stream, at what rate, over what period of time.
	If you are delivering more than a few media files to a few learners, you will probably need to select a media server.
Have selected audio- and video- creation and editing tools but not a media server	▶ Make a list of the streaming formats your tools can create.
	▶ Investigate media servers that can handle these file formats.

Are at the point of picking a media server	▶ Carefully determine the load the server must sustain now—and in the near future. ▶ Calculate the amount of disk space required now—and in the near future. ▶ List other criteria for the media server. ▶ Match your needs to the technical specifications of your candidate products. ▶ Decide whether or not to outsource media hosting.
Have already picked your media server	▶ Set up the server for the media formats you are using. Tune it to match the anticipated number and connection speeds of learners. ▶ Prepare your media files. This may require specially compressing or encoding them or creating different versions for different network speeds. If you are not going to administer the server yourself, be sure to clearly communicate your requirements to the person who will be administering it.

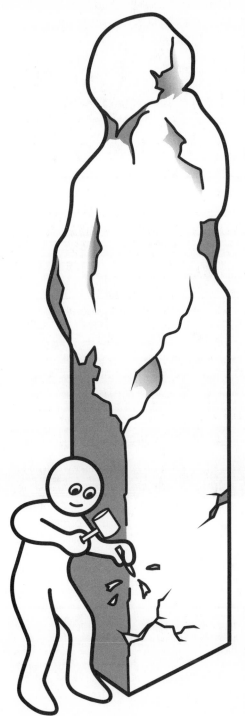

Tools for creating e-learning content

Before the Web, somewhere between the Cretaceous period and the Internet, tools were invented to create and edit what became e-learning content. Such tools and their descendents are the subject of this section.

Creating e-learning refers to the process of authoring and integrating content. It can take place at each level of content. That is, you can create raw media elements; integrate them into pages, displays, and learning objects; link those to create lessons; aggregate the lessons to create courses; and link courses to create a curriculum.

In this section we will talk about tools for creating e-learning. The chapters in this section cover:

	Create →	Offer →	Access
Curriculum			
Course			
Lesson			
Page			
Media			

(You are here)

▶ **Course authoring tools** expressly designed for creating e-learning. Such tools simplify the process of implementing instructional strategies, creating menus and navigation schemes, and authoring pages—without extensive technical knowledge (chapter 14).

▶ **Web site authoring tools** for creating HTML pages and linking them to produce entire Web sites. Such sites could be courses or material associated with courses. By including scripting, dynamic display effects, and connections to databases, these tools can create highly animated and interactive e-learning content (chapter 15).

▶ **Testing and assessment tools** for creating and conducting assessments. These tools create true-false, multiple-choice, short-answer, text-entry, matching-lists, and other kinds of computer-scored tests. Some track performance and generate reports (chapter 16).

▶ **Media editing tools** for creating, editing, and "Web-readying" drawings, icons, photographs, animations, sounds, video, and other media included in e-learning (chapter 17).

▶ **Conversion tools** for transforming documents, presentations, graphics, and other content to formats that can be used in e-learning and on the Web (chapter 18).

In addition to the tools covered in this section, you may want to check out some tools in the Offer column that overlap into the Create column of our tools framework. Some LMSs (chapter 9), LCMSs (chapter 10), and virtual-school systems (chapter 12) contain components for authoring pages, lessons, and courses and for integrating courses into curricula.

14 Course authoring tools

The increased use of e-learning has spawned tools to simplify the authoring process and remove it from the realm of the technologist or Web master. Although there are many tools for creating Web pages and other media, there are only a few tools solely for creating e-learning. This chapter is about those tools. Other tools that can be coerced into creating e-learning content are covered in other chapters of this section.

Looking at our tools framework, you can see that we have placed course authoring tools in the Create column, spanning the Page, Lesson, and Course rows. If you compare this diagram to the one for Web site authoring tools, you see that there is some overlap in the Page and Lesson rows. That's because many of the tools in this category include editors for authoring individual pages as well as

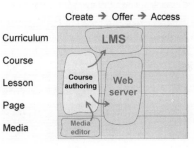

the ability to import content created outside the program, perhaps by a Web site authoring tool. And these tools are optimized to aggregate or link individual pages into lessons—something that you must do manually in most Web site authoring tools.

Though highly capable, course authoring tools do not stand alone. They usually require media editors to create needed graphics, icons, animations, and video segments. Some may let you use the sophisticated page-editing capabilities of Web site authoring tools to polish individual pages.

Course authoring tools typically rely on other software to offer the courses they produce. For example, the courses may be lodged on a conventional Web server or managed by a learning management system.

WHAT COURSE AUTHORING TOOLS DO

Course authoring tools are special-purpose tools for creating e-learning courses. They typically create pages and add text, graphics, and other media as well as provide a framework to organize pages and lessons so learners can navigate reliably. Some include tools to incorporate testing and feedback so learners can monitor their progress. Others include scorekeeping and reporting capabilities so instructors and administrators can monitor learners' progress. A few even contain project-management features to help control the sprawl of files and tasks required on even simple e-learning efforts.

Course authoring tools differ in the types of e-learning they create, the specific capabilities they incorporate, the file formats they produce, what browser they support, and skills they require.

QUICK TOUR OF A COURSE AUTHORING TOOL

Let's take a look at how you might use a course authoring tool to create e-learning content. These examples use Trainersoft 8 (trainersoft.com).

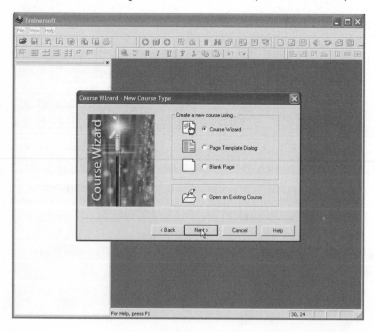

The author starts a new course by using the Course Wizard, which automatically creates the basic course structure.

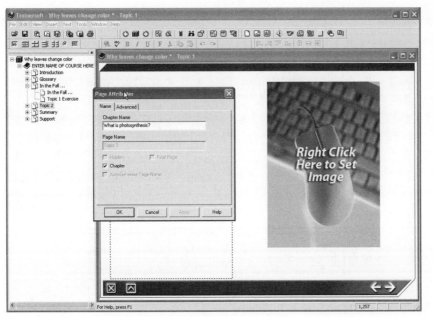

As the author adds pages, they are assigned to a table of contents that determines the structure of the course. The author does not have to manually link pages to create the structure of the course. This table of contents will later appear as menus to the learner.

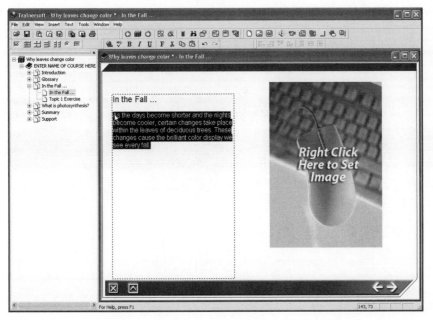

The author completes a page by filling in the placeholders on the page. These placeholders prompt the author to enter text, graphics, and other media. The author can add media beyond those specified by the template.

Here the author selects a picture to include on the page.

This graphic was created in a separate graphics tool.

Trainersoft allows a wide range of graphic formats, not just those optimized for the Web.

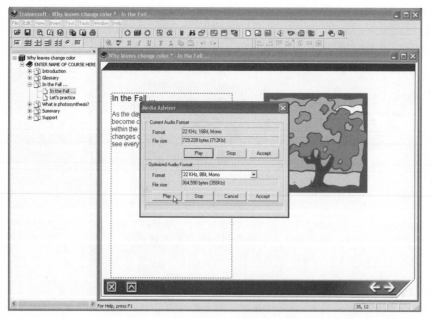

The author can position more text, pictures, animations, tests and other media on the page. Here, the author adds an audio clip containing narration.

Other media can be added as well.

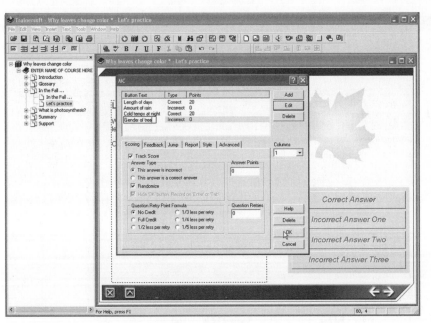

To create tests, the author picks types of test questions, enters the questions, and specifies how their answers are to be evaluated and the feedback displayed to the learner.

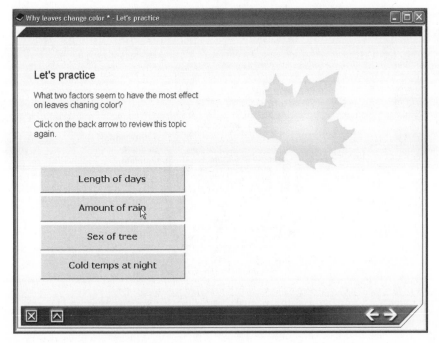

Here's how the test appears to the learner.

Selecting answers triggers scoring of the answers and displays feedback.

Performance Report				
Course Name	Employee	ID#	Department	Score
Why leaves ...				
	Abconn, Robert	15894		100
	Bonner, Martha	11635		100
	Davenport, Rick	23695		100
	Drexler, John	95565		100

Course authoring tools may include simple reporting capabilities, for example, to show which learners have taken specific courses and how learners scored on tests.

HOW COURSE AUTHORING TOOLS WORK

Course authoring tools differ in their detailed operations, but they all strive to let authors quickly build, test, and refine components of e-learning. Authoring follows a common cycle of activities.

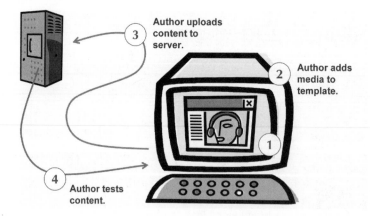

3 Author uploads content to server.

2 Author adds media to template.

1

4 Author tests content.

First, the author selects a template containing placeholders for specific media (1). Authoring tools may come with predefined templates or they may let authors define their own. The author then fills in the placeholders with text, graphics, tests, and other media (2). The author integrates this new page or lesson into the course, saving it to the server (3). With a couple of clicks, the author switches roles and tests the content from the viewpoint of the learner (4).

It is the speed and ease of this cycle that justifies using a course authoring tool rather than more generic tools.

POPULAR COURSE AUTHORING TOOLS

Here are some popular authoring tools that are representative of the different types of applications available.

 Looking for Dreamweaver here? It's in the chapter on Web site authoring tools. It is also mentioned later in this chapter as an alternative to course authoring tools in this chapter.

Authorware

By Macromedia   macromedia.com   **About $2700 USD**

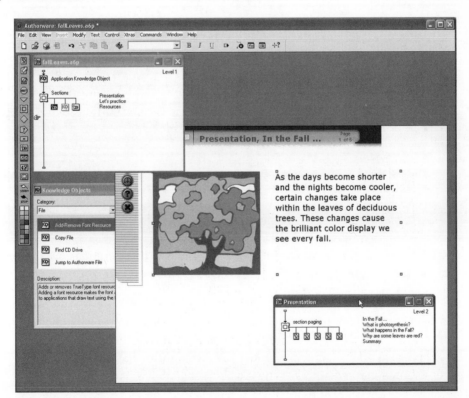

Authorware is a prominent authoring tool for e-learning. Originally designed to create disk-based CBT (computer-based training), Authorware has been adapted to create modules

 Authorware is the COBOL of e-learning. Everybody predicts its demise, but it still delivers lots of paychecks.

that, with the help of a proprietary plug-in, can play in Web browsers. And, because of its rich scripting language, authors can use Authorware to create highly interactive, branching simulations. To reap the benefits offered by Authorware requires specialized training and practice. There is no built-in instructional design model with this tool; however, there are a number of pre-built objects for different parts of a course, such as a login screen, that can save authors a great deal of time when building lessons.

DazzlerMax

By MaxIt   **maxit.com**   **About $500 USD**

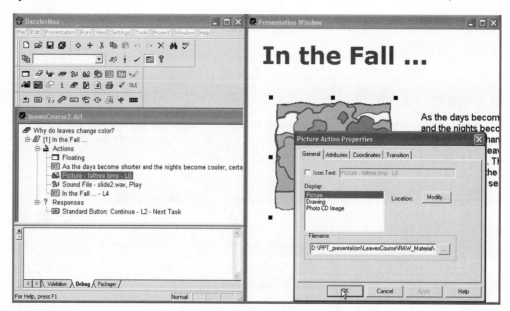

With DazzlerMax, authors create courses with drag-and-drop operations. DazzlerMax does not use scripting or icon-flows for creating interactivity. Courses do not need a media-player or viewer.

DazzlerMax provides templates, but does not restrict authors to these templates. Authors can modify templates and import any kind of Web content browsers can display. MaxIt also offers a template library for DazzlerMax that provides a wide variety of instructional sequences.

DazzlerMax can create software simulations that monitor mouse movements and clicks. It can store results of activities and tests and use them to guide navigation and other actions.

DazzlerMax prides itself in the degree to which it follows AICC and SCORM communications standards. Course authors can record test scores, for example, without having to write their own scripts. DazzlerMax can communicate with a variety of LMSs.

Lectora Publisher

By Trivantis   lectora.com   **About $1600 USD**

Lectora Publisher helps creates courses as dynamic HTML. Lectora provides wizards for creating buttons, page backgrounds, and overall course structures. It can also import and incorporate other components, scripts, and media that can go on Web pages.

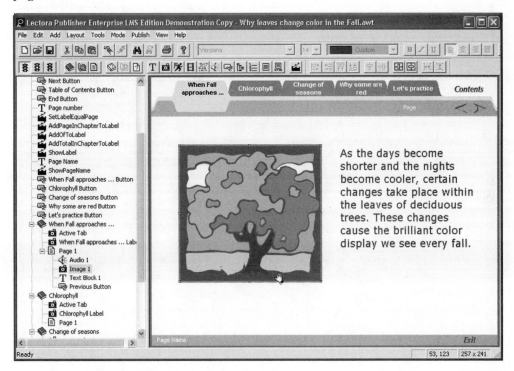

Authors organize the course in outline view and can import lessons, pages, and media components from other courses. Lectora Publisher can generate a table of contents. A course outline can be saved as a template.

Lectora Publisher includes sophisticated testing capabilities. Tests can mix true/false, multiple-choice, matching-lists, drag-and-drop, fill-in-the-blank, and essay questions. Tests can appear on one page or be displayed one question per page. Tests can be automatically scored, with feedback on individual questions. Tests can be timed, and questions can be selected from question banks. Results can be submitted by e-mail or AICC and SCORM communications standards.

Variables can hold data used to control the path through the course. Objects can be shown and hidden and optional text displayed. Lectora Publisher can generate a reference list of works cited in the course and can print out a course, lesson, or individual page.

Lectora also produces authoring tools for building courses for mobile devices, such as the Pocket PC and Palm Pilot.

Quest

By Mentergy   **mentergy.com**   **Contact Mentergy**

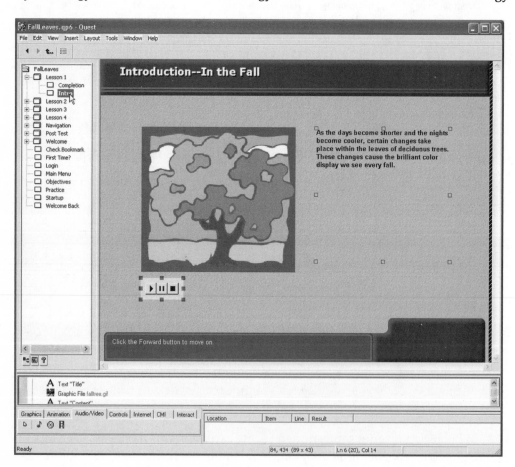

Quest is a comprehensive tool for authoring multimedia e-learning to run on Windows computers. It contains complete templates for pages, lessons, and entire courses. Quest can create ActiveX controls that can be experienced on Windows systems. These controls can be embedded in Web pages, the user interface of application programs, or PowerPoint presentations and Word documents. This makes Quest especially valuable for those creating embedded learning.

ToolBook

By Click2learn   **click2learn.com**   **About $2600 USD**

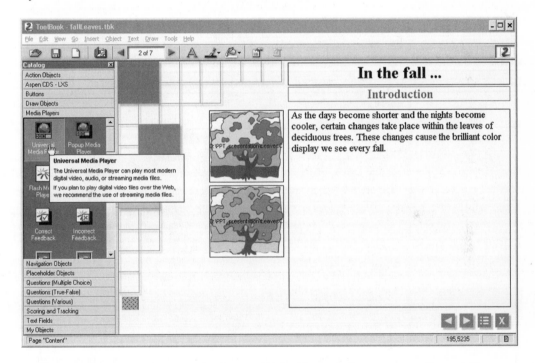

Click2learn sells two course authoring packages that produce courses that can be tracked using their Aspen Learning Platform or other AICC or SCORM 1.2 compliant LMS. One is ToolBook Instructor, which started out as a CBT tool but has made the transition to the Web. ToolBook Instructor has a very rich scripting language that allows authors to produce simulations as well as highly interactive e-learning lessons. It can produce interactive courseware that runs without plug-ins. Authors can build just about any interactivity using whatever instructional design approach they wish.

The second tool from Click2learn is ToolBook Assistant. Assistant provides the means to create standards-compliant, highly interactive lessons and courses—with no programming—using an array of predefined templates that target various training needs. The two tools have a common file format and can be used together. With Instructor, authors can create custom objects and templates and add them to special catalogs for use in both tools.

Trainersoft 8

By Trainersoft Corporation   **trainersoft.com**   **About $2100 USD**

Trainersoft 8 is a popular authoring tool for e-learning. Using wizards, novice authors are guided to select the right pre-designed template to meet their training needs—whether it is a quick-start guide or a standard course with multiple lessons.

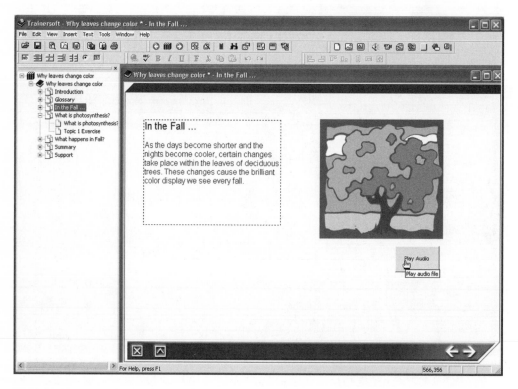

The built-in templates provide the structure for the course along with placeholders and prompts for needed text. Authors can enter text using features similar to those in a word-processor. They can also add such objects as graphics, rich media, a Web browser control, scripting, and test questions. There is also a rudimentary screen capture utility which authors can use to take single or multiple snapshots of the desktop or a running application.

Trainersoft 8 organizes content using a book metaphor, where the book is the course, a chapter is a lesson, and a page is a topic. The main navigation mechanism for authors and learners is the table of contents. Authors can control whether the learner sees this table of content as well as what portions of it are visible. Authors can even compile an index to help learners access specific pages within the course.

Trainersoft 8 saves content as HTML or as a self-running Windows program. When saving as HTML, authors have the option of sending test scores to an AICC compliant LMS like Trainersoft's companion product, Trainersoft Manager 2.

Web Course Builder

By ReadyGo   **readygo.com**   **About $500 USD**

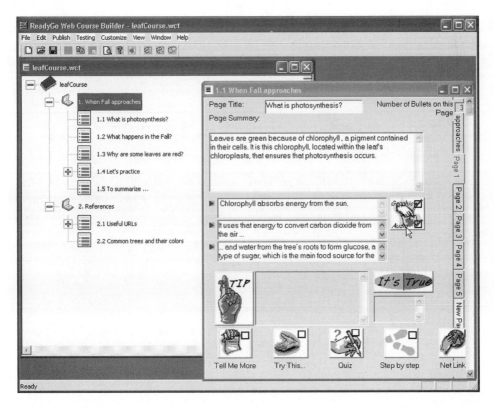

With ReadyGo Web Course Builder, the focus is on simplicity of authoring. Course authors create pages by filling in dialog boxes, not by editing visual images of pages. Web Course Builder uses predefined templates to control layout. Templates are provided for entire courses and for common course components, such as bullet lists, in-depth explanations, tests, surveys, glossaries, and frequently-asked questions (FAQ) pages. Web Course Builder does not include media editors but authors can import any Web-viewable media created externally. PowerPoint users will appreciate its ability to import titles and bullet lists from PowerPoint slides.

Authors can reorganize courses by dragging and dropping icons in an outline view. They can also copy and paste lessons, pages, and other components between courses. Web Course Builder automatically generates a table of contents, navigation buttons, and indexes. It also contains a spell checker and can print a text version of an entire course, chapter, or page.

Web Course Builder runs on Windows but can produce courses in HTML and JavaScript that even display in early Netscape 3.0 and Internet Explorer 3.0 browsers on most operating systems.

Others

This list is just a sample of the array of content authoring tools available. For a list of more tools to evaluate, go to horton.com/tools. You can also search the Internet using phrases like "e-learning authoring tools" or "list e-learning authoring tools" (with and without the hyphen) or a similar combination of terms.

ALTERNATIVES TO STANDARD COURSE AUTHORING TOOLS

Besides dedicated course authoring tools, there are several alternatives for creating courses. These include combinations of other categories, online help tools, multimedia tools, as well as authoring capabilities built into other categories. Let's see when you might choose each of these alternatives.

Combinations of other tools

Instead of using a single program to create courses, many authors combine tools from other categories. Usually these combinations involve a tool for authoring presentations with one for creating tests or activities.

Macromedia Dreamweaver MX (macromedia.com) together with its Learning Site and CourseBuilder extensions forms a popular combination for authoring e-learning courses and lessons. Within Dreamweaver, authors can use the Learning Site extension to create a special learning Web site that provides the navigation structure for a lesson. During the site-creation process, the author creates placeholder pages for HTML, rich media, and interactions (from the CourseBuilder extension). The author also selects the navigation model and the course template.

If the author chooses to track tests and activities, the Learning Site extension presents a dialog box to help choose or create a tracking database and set up the necessary connection to the database. Authors can also choose to add an administration component to their learning site to handle registrations and monitor student activity. Because of its capabilities, some people refer to this Learning Site extension as an "LMS-lite."

Other combinations of Web site authoring tools (for presentation) and testing tools (for assessment and interactivity) are possible. Just mix and match from these lists:

Web site authoring tool	Testing and assessment tool
Microsoft FrontPage (microsoft.com)	QuestionMark Perception (questionmark.com)
Adobe GoLive (www.adobe.com)	Hot Potatoes (halfbakedsoftware.com)
NetObjects Fusion (netobjects.com)	Quiz Rocket (learningware.com)
Macromedia Dreamweaver (macromedia.com)	Test Generator (testshop.com)
See chapter 15 for details.	CourseBuilder (for Dreamweaver only) (macromedia.com)
	See chapter 16 for details

Those of you sitting on gigabytes of PowerPoint presentations may want to employ a tool like Presedia Express (presedia.com) that converts PowerPoint slides to a Web-ready Flash presentation and add simple tests as well. (See chapter 18 for more on Presedia).

We could continue listing possible combinations for a few more pages, but you get the drift. With a little creativity, you may be able to combine tools to create a suitable authoring environment for you.

Help authoring tools

Help authoring tools, though not optimized for creating highly interactive presentations, have some very attractive features that qualify them for creating e-learning content—especially e-learning that must be embedded in a software product. They are also well suited for courses that are information-rich and follow a cognitive model of instructional design.

Help is an online document designed to assist users of computer programs. Tools for creating online Help specialize in creating such documents and integrating them into the computer program they serve. Most such tools target Microsoft Windows applications, which have established standard forms and expectations for online help.

Typically, Help files contain short topics of practical, procedural advice. In Help files the emphasis is on quick access to individual topics. As a result, these tools contain features that make the content of Help files quick and easy to find and display. They also make it easy for authors to set up sophisticated indexes and rich navigation schemes.

Prominent Help authoring tools include RoboHelp from eHelp (ehelp.com), AuthorIT (authorIT.com), and Doc-To-Help from ComponentOne (componentone.com). They range in price from $199 to $900 USD—somewhat less expensive than dedicated course authoring tools.

In considering online Help tools, be sure to ask questions such as these:

▶ **What file formats can the tool create**? Many online Help authoring tools can produce several different forms of online help for use in different generations of Windows programs and non-Windows programs. These include the original WinHelp format, which was compiled from Microsoft's Rich Text Format (RTF); HTML Help that can be compiled into one file or remain as a cluster of linked files; Help 2.0, which is based on an XML structure; JavaHelp from Sun; and WebHelp from eHelp.

▶ **How well does the tool integrate with popular HTML editors**? Tools for producing HTML help sometimes let you use your favorite HTML page editor, for example, Dreamweaver or FrontPage, to prepare individual pages.

▶ **What project management capabilities does the tool provide**? Does it give authors version control and audit trails? Does it provide access control through user and group accounts? Does it incorporate a built-in task scheduler? Because writing Help files is usually a collaborative effort, many Help authoring tools have good project management capabilities that benefit authors of e-learning as well.

▶ **Does the tool support multiple output formats**? For instance, if you need to publish the same content in a paper tutorial and in online training, does the tool allow you to do both from the same content?

Multimedia tools

In chapter 17 we discuss multimedia tools. Some of them are viable alternatives to traditional e-learning authoring tools. Macromedia Flash, in particular, has built-in behaviors, available extensions, and a robust scripting language that authors can use to create highly interactive e-learning lessons and courses. In addition to Flash, Macromedia Director and Adobe LiveMotion can also be used to produce multimedia e-learning courses.

 Building an entire course in a multimedia tool is like growing and roasting your own coffee—an expensive luxury. Buy a course authoring tool and focus creativity on creating learning experiences, not on self-indulgent multimedia.

Software-development tools

Interactive e-learning is software, so why not jump into the deep end of the pool? The same tools that are used to develop other kinds of computer programs and database-driven Web sites can be used to develop e-learning. Popular software development tools include:

 If using a multimedia tool is like growing and roasting your own coffee, using a software-development environment is like mining your own ore to smelt your own steel to make your own nails to build your own house.

▶ Visual Studio .NET from Microsoft (microsoft.com)

▶ Sun ONE Studio from Sun Microsystems (sun.com)

▶ VisualAge for Java from IBM (ibm.com)

If you take this road less traveled, take along good companions such as the tools by companies like Platte Canyon Multimedia Software Corporation (plattecanyon.com).

Authoring capabilities of other tools

Many LCMSs, LMSs, and virtual-school systems have authoring capabilities. For instance, the Vuepoint Learning System (vuepoint.com) provides a template-based authoring environment, called Content Creator, where authors can enter content directly or import it from MS Word, PowerPoint, and HTML pages. It also supports rich media such as Flash, RealMedia, and Windows Media. Authors can selectively designate their modules as learning objects, which can be reused in other lessons and courses. They can also create reading trails as well as indexes to enhance information accessibility.

Vuepoint is just one example. Other management systems include authoring capabilities as well. Before you buy a dedicated course authoring tool, examine the authoring capabilities provided by other tools you are using.

CHOOSING AN AUTHORING TOOL

Choosing an authoring tool requires more than counting bullet points in brochures. It requires identifying the tool that best meets your requirements. Here we first take a detailed look at what you need to know before you start evaluating a tool. Then, we delve into even more detail as we discuss the features you need to consider before choosing course authoring tools.

What you need to know first

Before you start evaluating tools, take some time to ponder your project and poll your team. You need to know:

- ▶ **What types of e-learning you plan to create**. Some tools are optimized for creating tutorials or just-in-time lessons that may be embedded within another type of electronic document like a Help file. Other tools are better-suited for creating complex simulations. Still other tools are ideal for creating traditional linear or branching lessons and assembling the lessons into a course.

- ▶ **The technical and tactical knowledge of your team**. Some tools may be very easy for novices to use but too restrictive for experienced authors. Others may be easy to use—once you know how. Some provide an abundance of templates but restrict authors to these templates. Some provide instructional design guidance, and others impose instructional design shackles.

- ▶ **The target browser**. Some authoring tools may produce content optimized for a specific browser running on a specific operating system. Other tools may give you the option to select the level of cross-browser and cross-operating system compatibility that suits your environment.

- ▶ **The amount of development you will be doing yourself**. If you plan to outsource the creation of pages and lessons, you may be less interested in a tool's page authoring capabilities and more interested in its course-level features such as its ability to import lessons created in other tools.

- ▶ **Restrictions imposed by your IT department**. If the authoring tool produces content that requires a special media player, you may need to check with the IT department to ensure that learners can easily obtain these players through your organization's firewall.

▶ **Other technology decisions**. You may need to select an authoring tool based on the kind of server and server-side technology the operating system supports. If your organization is already using an LMS or LCMS, you may need to ensure that the authoring tool produces content compatible with these systems.

The selection of the appropriate authoring tool or suite of tools for your project must be based on the needs of your learners, the expertise of your development team, the concerns of your IT department, and the goals of your e-learning effort.

Capabilities needed to create e-learning

Authoring is a complex, multi-layered activity. We're going to discuss features needed at three levels: the course, the lesson, and the page. Please remember that we are not suggesting that one tool should have all these capabilities. Some tools are better at a particular level than others. Other tools combine features from multiple levels. What you must do is pick the capabilities that are important for the levels in your project then choose a tool that supplies most of those capabilities. If necessary, consider additional tools to meet the balance of your needs.

 Evaluate the tool against your own requirements. Do not settle for a walkthrough of features given by a sales representative. Actually try out the tool for yourself using your own content.

Creating courses

Authoring tools should help producers create the framework and infrastructure of courses. In general, issues at this level are not related to content but to consistency and reuse.

▶ **What file formats are produced**? The end products of authoring tools vary. One tool may publish a Web site of HTML pages. Another tool may publish the course as a Java applet. Still another tool may save the course in a proprietary format. The file format of the course may be a concern, especially if you plan to change authoring tools some time in the future—and you need to retrieve your content.

▶ **Does the tool produce content optimized for the Web, for CD-ROM, or for both**? Are the courses produced by the tool ones that work well over the Web? Tools designed for CD-ROM may perform slowly and erratically over the Web.

▶ **Does the tool require a proprietary player for learners to play content created with the tool**? If so, is the player readily available for all the browsers and operating systems on which you need to deliver courses? If learners will be accessing the e-learning from behind a firewall, they may have difficulty downloading a player, viewer, or applet.

▶ **Does the tool provide a complete course framework**? Or, must you create the entire framework from scratch? Some tools, when creating a new course, allow you to choose a template that contains placeholders for all the parts of a course.

▶ **Can pages automatically jump out to external content**? Does the tool allow authors to escape the restrictions of the development environment by filling slots with redirect pages that take learners to other content? A redirect page has special HTML in the head of the document that tells the browser to immediately go to a specific Web address without any intervention by the learner.

▶ **Can authors diagram an entire course before creating or importing content**? Does the tool allow visually oriented authors to create a graphical representation of the planned course and populate it with placeholder lessons composed of placeholder pages? Can authors create links to nonexistent pages, to empty templates (created at linking time), or to placeholder pages? Does the tool create fully linked navigation bars based on this plan?

▶ **What access or navigational aids can the tool create**? For instance, can it automatically compile a course menu, table of contents, map, or index from titles, headings, and indexing keywords? These access aids are very useful for both authors and learners; therefore, it is important that they be easy to create and maintain from existing information contained in each page.

▶ **What standards does the tool support**? Does the tool support AICC or SCORM communications standards? Can it produce courses that have demonstrated their ability to communicate with LMSs that support those standards? Can the tool create an IMS manifest and save it along with its content in a new location? Can it bundle all the pieces into a ZIP file for easy distribution to a SCORM compliant LMS? If an LMS or an LCMS is in your future, these are important considerations. For more information on standards, see chapter 22.

▶ **Are there limits on course size**? Does the tool have arbitrary limits on the number of levels, numbers of items, or sizes of items that may be included in a course? If you plan to develop highly complex or long courses, a restriction on the number of pages or the size of a page can hamper your development efforts.

▶ **Can authors easily add metadata**? Does the tool have a convenient mechanism for adding descriptive labeling to courses, lessons, and other components? Can the tool generate an index or an alphabetical list for both authors and learners to make it easy to find these components? Metadata is descriptive information about content (See chapter 22).

▸ **Can the tool publish courses in multiple forms**? For instance, can it publish content optimized for CD-ROM, fast Internet, slow Internet, paper, or wireless delivery from a single source? If you have to supply courses for offline viewing or provide content for different network speeds, you certainly want to avoid manually creating multiple versions of the course to meet those needs.

▸ **Does the tool simplify the task of publishing content**? Is publishing content a one-click operation? If files are large, can the tool automatically handle the compression, transmission, and decompression of the files to a server? Most tools have some kind of FTP utility that enables the transfer of files to a Web server. Some tools, however, bundle all the directories and files into one compressed file, thereby saving time in the upload phase.

▸ **Can authors specify their own directory structure**? Does the tool allow authors to reorganize and rename directories? Does it allow them to specify which assets will be stored in which directory? If you are offering multiple courses that use common interface graphics, scripts, or style sheets, you want to be able to avoid duplication of these assets by placing them in a known directory or group of directories.

▸ **Can authors specify the look and feel of a course in one place**? Does the tool have the ability to set default file extensions, templates, colors, and fonts for an entire course or other collection of objects from a set of master preference pages? Does the tool make it easy to change these preferences? Does the tool support cascading style sheets and allow you to import an existing style sheet or specify a new one at the course level? The ability to specify course-wide preferences will shave days or weeks from your production schedule.

▸ **Does the tool have project management capabilities built in**? Can it help you plan and track progress on individual pages and other components? Will the tool help you plan and track required tasks, resources, budgets, and milestones? Course development is a highly complex task and, as such, must be tracked with the same degree of diligence as any other project undertaken by your organization.

▸ **Does the tool support collaborative authoring**? Can content be created, edited, and assembled by a team of instructional designers, subject matter experts, media authors, reviewers, quality assurance testers, and project managers working in concert? Is there a check-in and –out feature to prevent accidental overwriting? Does the tool offer revision tracking and version control?

▶ **Can authors preview content before publishing it**? Can authors create, preview, and test their courses locally before uploading them to a server? Is the preview accurate and complete? If some of the content is from the Internet, will it correctly appear in the preview if the author has an Internet connection? Most tools provide some preview capabilities, but the accuracy of that preview can vary greatly. Problems may not be spotted until the content has been published, requiring the content to be corrected and republished—which is sometimes a time-consuming task.

Creating lessons

Capabilities at the lesson level assist in assembling and organizing pages and learning objects. They influence the structure of lessons within a course but not the supporting infrastructure (menus, index, and search). They support the assembly of existing content but do not contribute to its direct creation, as do the features discussed later.

▶ **Can lessons be built from preexisting content**? Can authors assemble content from a variety of common document formats such as HTML, Microsoft Word, PowerPoint, Excel, or Adobe Acrobat PDF? If the content is HTML, does the tool also allow authors to import dependent files as well, such as scripts, style sheets, and graphics?

▶ **Does the tool enforce any particular instructional design model**? Can this model be overridden? Many authors of e-learning come to the job from different backgrounds. They may come from documentation, software design, or marketing. Therefore, a tool that helps them structures content to promote instructionally sound design may be useful. However, if your authors are learning specialists with an instructional design background, a tool that limits them to a single instructional model or theory may be too restrictive.

▶ **Does the tool support a free-form course structure**? Can authors have any kind of page or content at any level in the course? Can authors group units of material several levels deep? Can courses have any number of levels and any number of components per level? Are nonhierarchical structures, such as branching and adaptive sequences, possible? Can branching be determined by assessments or other kinds of choices? The more choices an author has to organize content, the more useful the tool is in creating many different kinds of e-learning such as simulations, tours, and games.

▶ **How easily can authors rearrange content**? While developing your e-learning content, you may need to reorganize and reorder lessons and pages. Does the tool make it easy to do so by dragging and dropping icons in an outline view, or by selecting an item and clicking a nudge button? Can the tool update links to any dependencies like graphics, scripts, or style sheets? Any tool you choose should allow you to easily make alterations to the structure and update any dependent files.

▶ **Can authors easily override elements of the course-wide template or layout**? Is it possible to hide or override features on the master template? Can authors add lesson-wide elements that are inherited downward to new lesson pages? Although course-wide templates ensure consistency throughout an entire course, the ability to override them is essential for flexibility and creativity.

Creating pages

Capabilities at the page level increase efficiency in assembling media into HTML pages or learning objects and in entering text and importing other media.

▶ **Does the tool support page-level templates**? Can authors use templates, wizards, or other aids to speed creation of common kinds of pages, such as introduction, summary, resources, or objectives? In addition to enforcing visual consistency, templates can provide instructionally sound and aesthetically pleasing fill-in-the-blanks models for common kinds of displays and activities. They should clearly flag variables or placeholders that the author fills in and provide examples of what to fill in.

▶ **Can authors create all content through a visual interface**? Does the tool have a rich catalog of drag-and-drop behaviors and objects that meet the needs of most authors? Authors are more productive if they do not have to constantly change editing modes (from visual to code-view and back again) when creating complex interactions. Keep in mind that the visual interface may offer too much freedom to some authors and may be too restrictive to others.

▶ **Does the tool have wizards for importing a variety of media**? Can it insert media elements so that they play on various browsers and platforms? Does the tool size media appropriately? Embedding media into a Web page is more than entering a Web address. Each kind of media has special parameters unique to its file type. Without some kind of wizard or helper, the process can be tedious and error-prone.

▶ **Can authors pick files for links rather than type file names**? Many errors creep into pages when authors have to type file names and Web addresses to create links. Any time a file name is required (to build a Web address, for instance), does the tool let the author browse with a file-open style dialog box, drag-and-drop files into a link box, or point-and-click to identify the file?

▶ **Can the tool's functionality easily be extended**? Does the tool have an internal macro or scripting language for creating custom behaviors and objects? Are there third-party add-ins available to automate specialized tasks? No tool can meet every need. Look for one that can be easily customized and augmented to meet your specific needs.

▶ **Can text be entered and formatted efficiently**? Does the tool offer basic word-processing capabilities? For instance, does it allow the author to easily change font characters like size, face, emphasis, and color? Does it support common formatting structures like a bullet lists, numbered list, or tables? Can an author easily align text or select a style?

▶ **Can authors preview pages in various browsers**? Does the tool allow the author to automatically test pages in every browser installed on the author's computer, or does it try to approximate the display characteristics of a generic browser?

▶ **Can authors enter bibliographic citations and references**? Can citations and references be automatically collated to create bibliography or reference pages? Can images have associated references? Does the tool interface with bibliographic programs such as EndNote (endnote.com)? Learners expect to see footnotes and citations when reading a textbook. Such references indicate the book has been written with some degree of academic rigor. E-learning should be just as rigorous.

▶ **Does the tool make it easy to meet accessibility requirements**? Does it encourage and simplify incorporating alternative media? Does the tool simplify defining labels for all elements on a page? Is all text accessible by screen readers for the blind?

▶ **Can authors create and edit content in a familiar external tool**? Does the tool allow authors to define a particular editing program for every file type they can use, for example Microsoft Word for text or Adobe Photoshop for graphics? Can authors activate a favorite media editor from within the authoring tool? Authors should not have to break off what they are doing to open a new program, make the edit, save the file back to the correct location, then go back to the course authoring tool to re-import the file.

▶ **Does the tool enforce keyword lists**? Can the tool allow authors to assign keywords to pages or objects from a master list of approved keywords? In any large project where multiple authors are writing content, it is difficult to ensure consistency in keywords and index terms. A tool that allows these terms to be easily predefined helps ensure that learners—and authors—reliably find pages and objects they seek.

▶ **Does the tool make it easy to add footers to identify pages**? Can the tool automate insertion of page footers and other areas containing identifying information, such as the owner, copyright notice, and revision date? Can this identifying information be revised in one place and updated throughout the course?

▶ **Does the tool have a library of reusable components**? Can these elements include scripts, images, text passages, or other media? If elements in this library are updated or changed, will the changes propagate throughout the course? Can these frequently used elements be converted to mini-templates or objects that authors can drag from a palette when needed? Any feature that helps automate repetitive tasks enhances productivity.

▶ **Can authors easily create templates for frequently used elements**? Can authors easily build templates from scratch for lessons, pages, colors, buttons, fonts, and other recurring components? Can these templates be derived from existing elements? Can these templates be made available to other authors building other pages in the current course or other courses? The ability to easily create templates is valuable. To be able to build them from existing examples that have been used and validated is even more valuable and time efficient. To be able to use these templates across projects is a real boon to productivity and consistency.

▶ **Can authors easily add metadata**? Does the tool make it easy to enter page- or object-level metadata? Is all metadata editable through property dialog boxes? Can the tool automatically infer certain items from characteristics of the object being edited? Metadata is descriptive information about content. (See chapter 22.) If metadata and packaging standards are important to you, then you want to make sure the tool streamlines the entry of this kind of information.

▶ **Does the tool validate links**? Can the tool check all links on the page. Does it allow authors to create or upload missing files if necessary? Not only do authors need to verify links for typographic errors, but they also need to check for moved and missing resources. Validating links is not a one-time effort. Periodically it may be necessary to reopen courses in the authoring environment and check their links.

▶ **Does the tool save page content as XML**? Can the content of pages based on templates be saved as XML or into a database? Can XML be imported into templates? Are authors limited to entering content into a rigidly structured form or page template? Can authors enter content into something like Microsoft Word and then have the tool extract the XML?

Also consider the criteria listed for Web site authoring tools (chapter 15). After all, most e-learning is a special-purpose Web site.

WHAT NOW?

To pick authoring tools for e-learning, you need to make decisions and take actions. Here are some recommendations for how to proceed.

If you ...	Then ...
Are still designing your e-learning	Make a complete list of the capabilities you will need to create the kinds of learning experiences to carry out your instructional design. Also consider the technical expertise of your authors. What can they most productively use?
Have selected other tools but not course authoring tools	Investigate the authoring capabilities of these other tools. What's missing? Can you best fill the gap with a course authoring tool or with tools from some other categories?
Are at the point of picking a course authoring tool	Use the criteria in this chapter as a starting point. List your requirements. Check for additional course authoring tools beyond the ones listed here. Using the process in chapter 22, make your selection.
Have already picked your course authoring tool	Investigate the tool's every capability and how it can be used for the kinds of e-learning you want to create. Publish a guide for your authors, pointing out how to make the tool do what you need it to do. Create templates for pages and other units.

We dived right into this section on tools for creating courses with course authoring tools. Next, we are going to step back and look at another group of tools that are essential for creating e-learning—Web site authoring tools.

15 Web site authoring tools

Despite their lofty educational pretensions, many e-learning courses at their heart are just special-purpose Web sites. Many are created by Web site authoring tools. Web site authoring tools build and link individual Web pages to create a Web site. They are the successors to the simple HTML page editors of several years ago. Most sport sophisticated capabilities to create and maintain complex sites of thousands of pages. Some let you create interactive animations and database connections without any programming.

Joining these veteran tools is a relatively new type of Web authoring tool called a *blog*. Blogs make creating ongoing Web journals simple enough for anyone.

On our tools framework, we put Web site authoring tools in the Create column, spanning both the Page and Lesson rows. They peek up into the course level, but lack the sophisticated collaboration and tracking capabilities needed to completely cover this square. However, with the database connections built into some of these tools, you can, with enough hard work and cleverness, extend the scope of these tools to cover courses and curricula.

Web site authoring tools do not work on their own. Their purpose is to create Web sites that are, in turn, offered by Web servers. To create these Web pages, they rely on media editors for the graphics, animations, and other media that appear. Sometimes they are used in conjunction with course authoring tools (and the course authoring capabilities of some offering tools) to prepare pages more efficiently than the Web site authoring tool can.

WHY CREATE E-LEARNING WITH WEB SITE TOOLS?

Your first reaction to this chapter might well have been, "This book is supposed to be about e-learning technology. Why would I be interested in Web site tools?" Before you fast-forward to the next chapter, give us a few minutes to list reasons why you may want to use Web site authoring tools to create your e-learning.

▶ E-learning is steeped in Web technologies. Tools that implement these technologies are needed at least sporadically throughout most e-learning projects—a Web page here, a registration form there.

▶ Because Web site tools are sold to large markets, their developers have lavished time and money on making them capable, reliable, and easy to use. And their prices are also lower than many dedicated e-learning tools.

▶ For courses conveying information and hard knowledge, Web site tools may be all you need, especially for the presentation component of courses.

▶ Web site authoring tools can be combined with media editing and testing tools to create a custom course authoring environment.

▶ Your e-learning may need to integrate with other Web offerings and knowledge management efforts that are authored in Web site tools.

▶ Web site authoring tools are fast becoming a standard item in the toolbox of knowledge workers—like a word processor or spreadsheet. For e-learning producers it is a staple.

QUICK TOUR OF A WEB SITE AUTHORING TOOL

Let's look at examples of some of the most important capabilities of Web site authoring tools and how they are used to set up and maintain a site. The tool shown is Macromedia Dreamweaver MX.

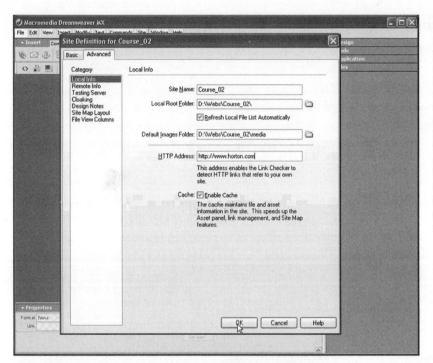

To create a new Web site, the author first defines the site by specifying characteristics such as where to store it locally, where to put it on the server, what its Web address will be, and what database connection it will use.

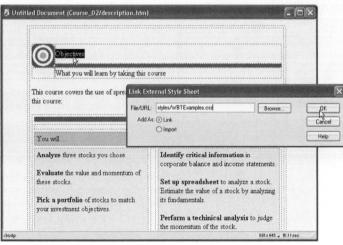

Authors create pages for the site by typing and formatting text, inserting graphics, and embedding other media. This visual style of editing allows authors to precisely size and position elements.

Authors can define and link style sheets to consistently format pages. Changes to the style sheet affect all pages linked to the style sheet.

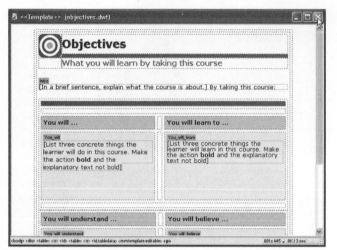

Authors can define templates for special kinds of pages—either from scratch or from an existing page, as in this example. The template has placeholders for components of content, such as graphics and blocks of text.

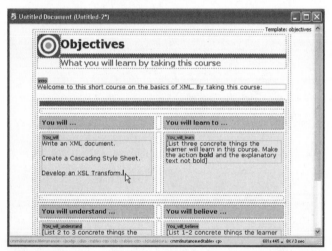

Once templates are defined, they can be used throughout a site for consistency among pages that are used for the same purpose. Here the template page for course objectives is being completed to create a new objectives page.

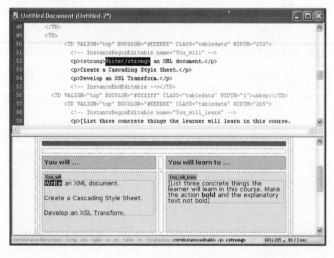

Authors can examine and modify the HTML behind pages. In this split view, the HTML is shown at the top and the visual display of the same page appears at the bottom. Changes in one view are immediately reflected in the other.

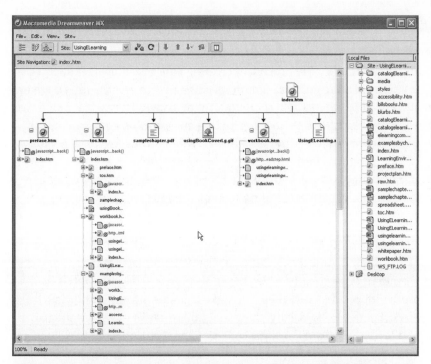

Authors are not limited to editing individual pages. They can view the entire site and link individual pages in a visual map view showing pages and links among them.

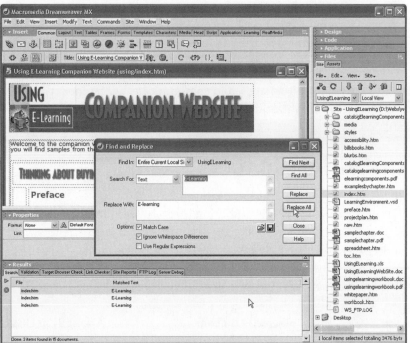

Authors can make changes throughout a site without having to open and change individual pages. Here the spelling of a word is being changed globally.

Other Web site authoring tools will differ in appearance and operation, but most provide the same basic capabilities.

HOW WEB SITE AUTHORING TOOLS WORK

Web site authoring tools simplify the process of creating complex Web sites such as those for e-learning. Visual page editors let authors edit a preview of the final page or other component without having to deal with underlying codes. They work much like modern word processors that allow the author to drag and position components on the page. If the page uses style sheets and dynamic HTML features, the preview may be quite lifelike, though some differences between browsers prevent absolute fidelity. Some Web site authoring tools come with code editors built in so that the author can quickly switch back and forth between editing the image of the page and editing its underlying codes.

Web site authoring tools create and manage large numbers of independent pages and their assets. They let authors work on the site as a whole, rather than just as a collection of independent pages. Authors can move and rename pages without breaking links or other dependencies. They can make changes throughout the site without having to edit pages individually. Such tools also make it easy to standardize layouts, colors, and icons, thereby ensuring a consistent and professional look throughout the site. Web site authoring tools also simplify creating navigation buttons and menus to implement a site-wide navigation scheme. And some have very robust scripting tools to enable authors to build sophisticated interactions that run either on the Web server or the learner's browser.

For developers of e-learning, Web site authoring tools make it possible to have total control over the way a course looks, behaves, and communicates with other systems. This is a popular approach for organizations with a capable Web development and programming staff.

POPULAR WEB SITE AUTHORING TOOLS

Here are a few of the best known Web site authoring tools. To learn more about any of these tools, please go to the vendor's Web site and conduct further research. (See if you can you tell if they used their own tool to create their Web site.)

Dreamweaver

By Macromedia   macromedia.com   **About $400 USD**

Dreamweaver MX is one of the most widely used Web site authoring tools. As a page editor, Dreamweaver is extremely full featured. In addition to injecting the basic HTML elements, Dreamweaver simplifies embedding media and creating tables, frames, forms, dynamic HTML. It automates the entire editing process and behaves very much like a word processor. Authors can choose to work in visual mode, in HTML-only view, or in a spit-screen view. And they can preview the page in any browser installed on their computer. One of the strong features of Dreamweaver is that it does not muck with your HTML code. It may tell you something is wrong, but it will not automatically try to fix it. Dreamweaver also has strong code editing tools, including auto-completion and debugging features.

Dreamweaver lets developers add utilities and advanced capabilities to the program through the use of extensions. These are prebuilt components that registered owners of Dreamweaver can download and install. There are extensions for e-learning developers, e-commerce site designers, and overworked site builders who want to make everyday authoring tasks easier.

Dreamweaver MX has powerful site creation capabilities too. It strikes a balance between the visual, drag-and-drop approach to site creation and the geeky, touch-the-code approach.

 For authors of e-learning, extensions are available to add testing (CourseBuilder), learning management (Learning Site), and help with packaging standards requirements (Manifest Maker) from the Macromedia Exchange.

Dreamweaver MX does not have the visual site prototyping or design tools found in GoLive. It does have, however, very good editing tools to create database-driven Web applications and support scripting languages such as Cold Fusion, Active Server Pages, ASP.NET, JavaServer Pages, and PHP.

FrontPage

By Microsoft   microsoft.com   **About $170 USD**

FrontPage has many of the same features as Dreamweaver MX. FrontPage will feel familiar to users of Microsoft Office. Users format text the same way they do in Microsoft Word and draw graphics as they do in PowerPoint. FrontPage does not have strong code editing tools, such as auto-completion or debugging features. For that, authors can use Microsoft's Script Editor that is installed with Microsoft Office XP.

In addition to being a good page editing tool, FrontPage is a capable site creation tool. It includes customizable graphical themes to enforce site-wide consistency, link checking, and site-wide find-and-replace. As with other Office XP programs, FrontPage is tightly integrated with Microsoft's SharePoint collaborative technologies and helps a developer set up a team Web site for intranet or Internet users to store, find, and share information, documents, and Web pages. To take advantage of some of FrontPage's features, such as the threaded discussion and search facility, your hosting server must have the FrontPage extensions installed. With these, Web site administrators can easily get usage analysis reports.

GoLive

By Adobe   **www. adobe.com**   **About $400 USD**

Adobe GoLive (www.adobe.com) is a powerful page editing tool that is tightly integrated with PhotoShop and Illustrator. For that reason, GoLive is a good choice for designers producing marketing content, e-zines (electronic magazines), or other highly graphical content. Its standard editing tools are similar to Dreamweaver and FrontPage. It does have one interesting feature that the others do not: You can author QuickTime movies and SMIL presentations right in the GoLive interface without the need for an external editor. GoLive has code editing tools, including color-coding and a customizable tag database. As with some of Adobe's other products, GoLive supports extensions that add development and content support.

GoLive also has good site design and management tools, such as support for graphical site prototyping and site mapping, including staging pages for testing and annotating items in progress. With GoLive, you can also create JavaServer Pages, Active Server Pages, or PHP Web applications that exchange data with a database. Version control, check-in/check-out, and centralized storage are handled by Adobe's Web Workgroup Server; thus enabling multiple authors to work on the same project.

NetObjects Fusion

By Website Pros   **netobjects.com**   **About $150 USD**

NetObjects Fusion is a very full-featured, modestly priced site content editor. It possesses all the basic tools you need to create a complex, interactive Web site, such as a site diagramming tool, link checker, WYSIWYG editor, code editor, and database access tools. It is targeted at new Web site designers and is designed to be easy to use.

Others

Other popular WYSIWYG editors include:

Product	Vendor	Web address
HoTMetaL Pro	Corel	corel.com
Netscape Composer	Netscape	netscape.com
Amaya browser	World Wide Web Consortium	w3c.org

Though not as capable as the tools listed earlier, they offer simplicity. They may be all you need to complement other tools you are using.

ALTERNATIVES TO WEB SITE AUTHORING TOOLS

There are several other approaches you could take for Web-based e-learning content.

Course authoring tools

If your purpose is strictly to offer courses, there are specialized tools for creating courses and learning events. These tools remove course authoring from the underlying Web technologies needed to offer the course. You still need a Web server and additional offering software discussed elsewhere. You can read about course authoring tools in chapter 14. Course authoring capabilities are also found in LMSs (chapter 9), LCMSs (chapter 10), and virtual-school systems (chapter 11).

Help authoring tools

Tools for creating HTML-formatted online help can also be used to author Web sites. Though not ideal for sales and marketing sites, which require lots of glitz and a dash of glamour, these tools are very well suited to informational sites, especially large-scale, highly structured ones that need menus and an index for quick access. For more on Help tools, see chapter 14.

Conversion tools

Another option is to create your content in a program like Microsoft Word and then save it as HTML, use a conversion program like WordToWeb to convert it to HTML, or use Adobe Acrobat to save it as Acrobat PDF. Similar conversions are possible for PowerPoint. Chapter 18 describes these options. Conversions that preserve cross-reference links and Web links are certainly practical ways to create online textbooks and presentations.

Code editors

Hand-coding the HTML and other formats of a vast e-learning project may not seem very efficient or pleasant, yet it may be a reasonable alternative for teams blessed with an abundance of knowledge about HTML formatting. It is also practical when most of the site is dynamically generated from scripts, perhaps pulling content from databases. In such cases, most of the site is really programming code.

Code editing tools provide a mechanism for entering text and code. Most let you type in text and press buttons to inject common codes or tags required by HTML, XML, JavaScript, and other languages. They are especially useful for embedding scripts or programming code, such as JavaScript or VBScript. By automating the process of inserting tags, code editors reduce syntax errors caused by misspelling, mistyping, and forgetting closing brackets and tags.

With code editors, the author still has to know the codes and tags of the language being used; however, some code editors include online documentation explaining the intricacies and formats of the codes.

Code editors range from simple text editors like Notepad and SimpleText, which come with the Windows and Macintosh operating systems, to sophisticated programming environments like Microsoft Visual Studio .NET. Most Web site authoring tools include a code editor window.

CAPABILITIES NEEDED FOR E-LEARNING

For authoring e-learning Web sites you need page creation and editing capabilities as well as site management capabilities.

Page creation and editing capabilities

There are several issues to consider when choosing a tool to create and edit Web pages for e-learning.

▶ **What functions does the tool automate for the author**? Can you create and apply style sheets for precise, attractive formatting of pages? Can you create buttons and interactive behaviors without writing any code? Can it use dynamic HTML to create animations?

▶ **How easy is it to create and edit media**? Say you add a graphic to a Web page, but the graphic is too large, can you double-click or use a menu command to edit the graphic in place?

Use these and other lists of capabilities as a starting point. Add capabilities you need and strike out ones you do not. Sort the list to reflect your priorities. Make it your own.

▶ **Can you easily pick files for links**? Does the tool make it easy to point to a link's target or drag an icon to the target rather than having to type a full Web address?

▶ **Can you embed rich media**? Does the tool have wizards or other helpers to make it easy to embed rich media into a page? And will the code generated by the wizard be cross-browser compatible?

▶ **Can you set the level of browser compatibility**? That is, can you specify that you want the tool to create code that works in only one browser or in multiple browsers? Does the tool temporarily disable features not supported in your targeted browsers?

▶ **Does the tool maintain changes you make directly in the code**? For instance, if you do make adjustments to the underlying code, does the tool accurately display your changes and leave them in place, rather than trying to rewrite them to suit its own internal scheme? In Dreamweaver, this feature is called *roundtrip HTML*.

 Don't muck with my code!

 Amen, Brother Thorndon!

▶ **Does the tool create pages that display equally well with all browsers and all Web servers**? Or, is the tool tuned for one particular brand of browser, server, or operating system? For example, Microsoft FrontPage provides some very useful features that unfortunately work only in the IE browser and from a Microsoft Web server.

▶ **Will the tool check your code**? Can you validate your code to ensure that it is compliant with W3C standards? This becomes important if you want to maintain multi-browser compatibility and offer content to wireless devices.

▶ **Can you easily create page templates**? Can you turn an existing page into a template? Can you design a template from scratch? How easy and reliable is it to apply a new template to a page or to change a template and reapply it to all pages based on it?

▶ **Can you easily find and use recurring elements**? Does the tool let you place frequently used components like text, code, or images onto a palette for easy access?

▶ **Does the tool support XML**? Can you export content from templates into XML? Can XML be imported into a template? Does the tool double as a general-purpose XML editor? XML is covered in chapter 23.

▶ **Can you import from word processors**? Can your tool open files created in your favorite word processor? How much of the page layout and text formatting is preserved?

Site management capabilities

A Web site is more than a folder of pages. It has structure, menus, and coherence. Good Web site authoring tools include capabilities for creating and managing large, complex sites. In considering such tools, ask questions like these:

▶ **Can you diagram your entire site**? Can you create a visual representation of your proposed site and populate it with placeholder pages? Can you also create fully linked navigation bars based on this plan?

▶ **Can you automatically create navigation mechanisms**? For instance, can the tool automatically generate an overall course menu, index, glossary, and map from information about the components? Can it generate links from an outline? Can it generate a reading trail, navigation bars and buttons, and other navigational aids?

A reading trail designates a sequence of pages traversed when the reader jackhammers the Next button.

▶ **Do you have flexibility in directory structure**? Does the tool allow you to define a custom structure of folders and files, and to assign specific names for them?

▶ **Can you ensure a site-wide look and feel**? Can you set file formats, page layouts, colors, and fonts for an entire course or other collection of objects at one time in one place? Can you easily edit those choices if you change your mind?

▶ **What project management features does the tool provide**? Can it help you plan and track progress on individual pages? Will the tool help you manage required tasks, resources, budgets, and milestones?

▶ **Can developers test courses and lessons locally**? Can authors create, preview, and test their courses locally before uploading them to the server? Or, does the tool let them work directly on the server?

▶ **Does the tool simplify the task of uploading content to the server**? Is uploading content a one-click operation? If files are large, can the tool automatically handle the compression, transmission, and decompression of the files?

▶ **Does the tool enable collaborative authoring**? Can content be created, edited, and assembled by a team of instructional designers, subject matter experts, media developers, reviewers, quality assurance testers, and project managers working on different continents? Does the tool support check-in and check-out to prevent accidental overwriting?

▶ **Does the tool track revisions and multiple versions**? Does it have the ability to flag deletions, additions, and changes for approval or rejection? Can the tool maintain multiple versions?

▶ **What advanced capabilities can the tool add to your site**? For example, can the tool add a search facility, save data entered on forms, or enable you to construct discussion forums?

▶ **Does the Web site depend on proprietary server components**? Such server extensions may add needed capabilities, such as a search facility, but may not be available for all servers.

▶ **Does the tool simplify using server scripts**? Does the code editor help you write scripts to run on the server? Does it check the code? Can the code be color-coded? Does the tool provide a menu of predefined server behaviors that can be used for scoring tests and communicating with databases?

▶ **Can the tool ensure a consistent look across the whole Web site**? Does the tool support site-wide style sheets? Does it allow you to predefine custom buttons and behaviors and then drag and drop them on pages? Does it provide templates to predefine the layout and repetitive content of classes of related pages?

▶ **Can you find and replace text across the entire site**? Can you search for words or phrases in both the text and the HTML tags? Can your search use wildcards like a question mark to match any single character or an asterisk to match any sequence of characters?

▶ **Can authors search for content**? Can authors easily find individual pages, pictures, and other media components? Can authors use index/search keywords to locate already authored pages and other units to include in their course?

BLOGGING TOOLS

When blogging tools first arrived in 1998, people asked "What's a blog?" The word "blog" is a contraction of "Web log" and is used both as a noun as well as a verb. To *blog* is to write content to a *blog*. A *blog* is a Web-based personal diary with dated entries. The beauty of blogs and blogging software is that they enable a writer to concentrate on content by removing all the distracting details of publishing the content to a Web site. An author can simply write and publish in one easy step. Magic! No knowledge of HTML or FTP is needed.

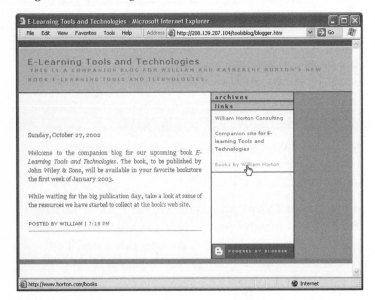

Here is the companion blog for this book. You will find it at horton.com/tools/blog.htm.

By design, blogs are best suited for the spontaneous thoughts and observations of an individual or team. They are not designed to facilitate rapid-fire back-and-forth discussion on a particular issue. To do that, you are better off using chat or a threaded discussion forum (chapter 11).

Quick tour of a blogging tool

Blogging tools are available as free or moderately priced services and as products you purchase and install on your own server. Here is a tour of a popular blogging service called BloggerPro from Pyra Labs (blogger.com).

Sounds like a bad stereotype of British slang: "Blimey, some bloody bloke blogged my site."

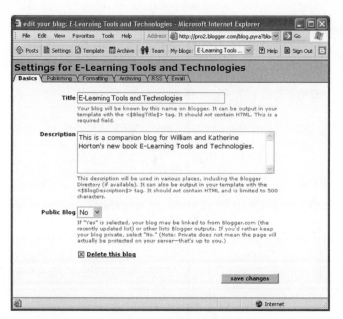

To start a blog, the author specifies a title and description. The author also specifies where the blog will be located and if a password will be needed to post or read messages.

15

Web site authoring tools

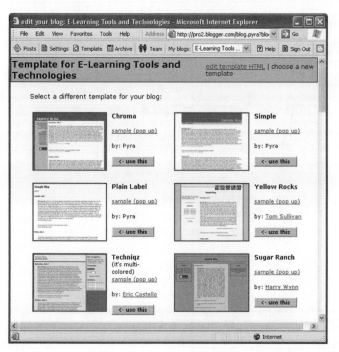

Next, the author picks a template to control the layout or color scheme of the pages. This template can be modified extensively.

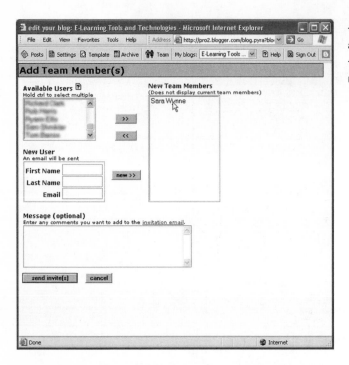

The author can then add coauthors and give them posting privileges.

The ability to have multiple authors makes blogs a collaborative tool.

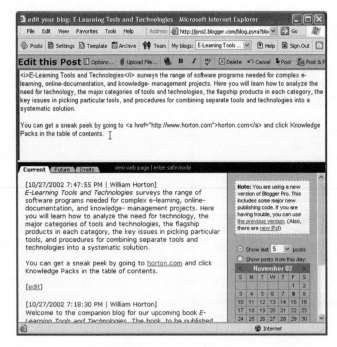

To post a message, the author types into a text field and clicks the Post & Publish button.

The new content is formatted, added to the existing blog, and posted to the specified location.

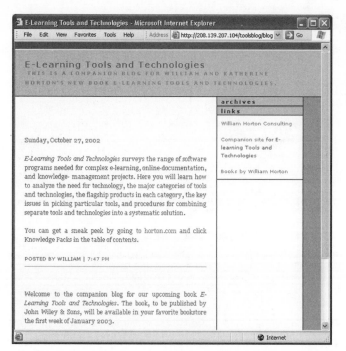

Here is the reader's view of the blog. The entry at the top is the most recent.

As the blog becomes long, older portions can be archived and links to the archives posted.

Most blogging tools allow posters to add graphics, links, and other HTML to their posts.

How to use blogs for e-learning

Blogs can provide a convenient way for learners to document learning experiences, such as interesting readings, the Web addresses of good examples, and questions and answers they have. Blogging tools remove any barriers to publishing to a Web site by allowing authors and learners to concentrate on content instead of technical operations.

Popular blogging tools

Blogging software is new, but several tools are available. Let's look at a few popular blogging tools.

Blogger

By Pyra Labs   **blogger.com**   **Free**

Blogger and BloggerPro are two of the best known blogging tools. They are services rather than shrink-wrapped products. Blogger is a free service and BloggerPro costs a nominal annual fee. Blogger and BloggerPro allow you to publish your blog to any server with FTP access.

Radio UserLand

By UserLand   **userland.com**   **About $40 USD**

Radio UserLand is a product rather than a service. Like Blogger, blogs can be sent to any server after being processed—in this case, processed right on your own computer. Another feature many users like is that Radio UserLand makes it easy to gather news from around the Web and post it to your blog. Radio UserLand users can also syndicate their content, allowing other Radio UserLand subscribers to display their posts making it is especially useful to sites that focus on news and commentary. Radio UserLand offers a 30-day free trial, after which you must purchase the software. Because the application is not Web-based, each author who contributes to your blog, must own their own copy of the application.

Manila

By UserLand   **userland.com**   **About $900 USD**

Manila allows a dispersed team of designers, writers, and graphic artists to work on a common Web site using a Web browser interface. This service is geared to project teams, training classes, and even large, far-flung families. Manila is sold as part of the UserLand Frontier content management system.

Others

Other popular blogging tools and services include these.

Product	Vendor	Web address
Free Open Diary	The Open Diary	freeopendiary.com
Blog Studio	Indigo Technology Partners	www.blogstudio.com
MoveableType	Moveabletype.org	moveabletype.org
Pitas.com	Pitas.com	pitas.com
TongueWag	TongueWag Limited	tonguewag.com
Big Blog Tool	Big Guy Media	bigblogtool.com

Capabilities to look for in a blogging tool

To use blogs in e-learning, you need to evaluate blogging tools with that purpose in mind. Here are some issues we think are important in choosing a blogging tool as part of your e-learning project.

▶ **Ownership and costs**. Are you buying a service or a product? You need to read the licenses carefully. When you buy a service, you typically pay a yearly fee as well as other charges, such as an excess storage fee or a fee for posts over a certain limit. Conversely, when you buy a product, you own it—along with all the set up and configuration problems that may come with it. Consider your needs and level of technical expertise.

▶ **Hosting**. Where is your blog hosted? If you do not have a Web site of your own, you may want to be sure that the blog tool you purchase (or subscribe to) has a free hosting service. Conversely, you may want to be able to host your content on a server of your choice. Not all tools offer this kind of flexibility.

If you do choose a free hosting service, consider how much you can customize the graphical appearance. Does advertising appear in your blog? If so, is there a service upgrade that removes the ads?

▶ **Security**. Security controls who can author and read a blog. If you are sponsoring a group blog, how do you ensure that only contributors that you have cleared can post to the blog? Likewise, how do you limit access to authorized learners?

▶ **Administration**. If you are using a blog as a collaborative tool, how easy is it to add new contributors to your blog, change the order of posts, approve posts before they are added to your blog, and archive outdated posts?

▶ **Search**. How easy is it for readers to find specific posts in a blog? Can they search by date, by subject, by title? If you have a long blog, the ability to find a particular piece of information is important.

▶ **Posting**. What is required to add new content to the blog? Can you post from any computer using the Web, or do you need a special application installed on your system? It may be more convenient for you to be able to post from anywhere. Does the tool check your spelling with a spellchecker? (Face it, everybody needs an editor.) Can you edit posts after adding them to a blog? Can you make posts through a firewall?

RELATED TOOLS

You choice of Web site authoring tools may affect or be affected by other technology decisions. For instance, site authoring tools are sometime closely allied with certain server technologies. GoLive supports authoring PHP server-side scripts. Dreamweaver MX makes it easy to author Cold Fusion Web sites as well as Active Server Pages. If your graphics and multimedia department are vested in Adobe Illustrator and Photoshop, you may want to pay special attention to Adobe GoLive. If you want to design e-learning assessments without purchasing additional test authoring software, you may want to choose Dreamweaver MX because the CourseBuilder extension for creating tests is a free add-on.

Although few Web site authoring tools directly integrate media editing capabilities, many can import and embed Web-ready media from popular media editors. Some Web site tools are bundled with media editors and sold as Web creation suites.

WHAT NOW?

To put the ideas of this chapter into action, you need to make decisions and take actions. Here are some recommendations for how to proceed.

If you ...	Then ...
Are still designing your e-learning	► Consider what forms of Web content you need to create: courses, administrative pages, textbooks, and reference materials. Also, consider how other Web content for your e-learning should be created. These insights can guide your decision about whether you need a Web site tool as part of your e-learning efforts or what kind of content you would use it for.
	► Also, decide whether you need a full-featured Web site authoring tool, just a blogging tool, or both.
Are at the point of picking a Web site authoring tool	► Use the criteria in this chapter as a starting point. List your requirements. Check for additional Web site authoring tools beyond the ones listed here. Then use the process in chapter 20 to make your selection.
Have already picked your Web site authoring tool	► Map your needs to specific tool capabilities. Create a guide for authors about what to use—and what not to use.
	► If you have chosen a sophisticated authoring tool, train your authors in its use.
	► Develop templates, style sheets, custom menus, code snippets, and insertable objects needed to make authoring e-learning easier.
	► Integrate this tool into your overall workflow.

When used in e-learning, Web site authoring tools are often combined with testing and assessment tools, like those covered in the next chapter.

16 Testing and assessment tools

Tests and other assessments measure the effectiveness of learning. Learners rely on tests to gauge their progress in a course. Instructors and course authors may use test scores to assign subsequent learning activities or just to measure effectiveness of e-learning.

Tests are seldom an end in themselves. They are usually just one element of a course or lesson yet a very important one. Testing tools simplify the chore of creating and conducting online tests.

In our tools framework, testing tools live in the bottom row of the Create column. We show them draping over the boundary between creating and offering because some of these tools contain features to conduct tests and record scores on a server.

In e-learning, test tools are used to supplement other kinds of content. For example, tests often find their way onto pages created with Web site authoring tools. Tests may also be added to courses and learning objects created in course -authoring tools, LCMSs, LMSs, and virtual-school systems that lack adequate test creation features of their own.

HOW TESTING TOOLS WORK

Testing tools vary in the way they work, but most follow a common cycle of developing, conducting, and reporting tests.

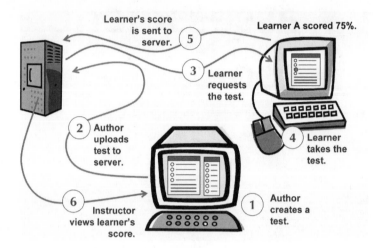

The process usually starts when the author uses the testing tool to create a test (1). The author defines the test by specifying questions and answers. The author then uploads the test to a server (2) from which learners access the test as part of their e-learning course (3). A learner takes the test (4). The results are reported to the learner and, if specified by the test's author, sent back to the server (5). The course author or instructor can periodically check results stored on the server to see how learners are progressing in the course (6).

QUICK TOUR OF A TESTING TOOL

Let's look at an example of using a testing tool to create and conduct a simple multiple-choice test. This example shows the process for creating a question, how the question appears to the learner, and the feedback a learner might receive. The tool used to create the question is Hot Potatoes by Half-Baked Software (halfbakedsoftware.com).

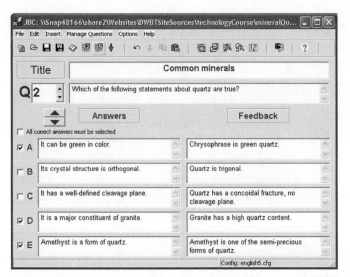

Using the multiple-answer question template, the author defines a question.

The author enters the question, possible answers, and feedback for each.

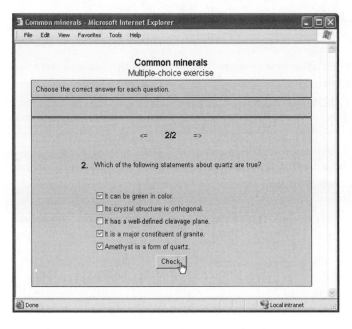

The test is saved as a Java applet that can be embedded in a Web page. Here the student has answered the question and is about to have the applet grade it.

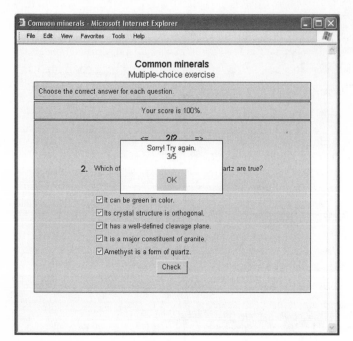

Here is the feedback for a correct answer.

POPULAR TESTING TOOLS

Though other categories of tools may create test questions, often the best results occur when you use a tool especially designed to create and administer tests. Here are some popular testing tools. Some are self-contained products, some are add-ons for other products, and some are Web-based services.

Perception

By Questionmark   **questionmark.com**   **About $5000 USD**

The best-known testing and assessment tool is Perception. It comes in two versions. Perception for Windows allows you to create, offer, and administer assessments using a Windows application, a database, and a local area network. Perception for the Web includes the same PC-based applications as well as a server component that allows you to create, edit, offer, and administer tests from anywhere using a Web browser.

Perception allows you to build questions in a number of different formats called question types. They include true-false, drag-and-drop, multiple-choice, one-choice, matching,

The Windows application allows you to create more kinds of questions than the browser-based version, but it requires application licenses for additional test authors.

and ranking. You can organize questions into topics and subtopics, shuffle choices, and include question-specific graphics and styles. Topics can be assigned specific outcomes so that you can provide topic-based feedback based on the score achieved for each topic. Questions can be selected by assessment, by topic, or by a combination of tags assigned during the creation process.

Perception automatically uploads tests to your Perception sever where learners can access them and, if desired, receive instant feedback. The server application automatically scores, tabulates, and stores the answers in a database (Microsoft Access for small installations and Oracle or SQL Server for large, enterprise installations). Administrators can easily log into the secure server application to manage enrollments and to view and print reports. For added security, you can also purchase the Perception Secure Browser which helps eliminate cheating on tests.

CourseBuilder for Dreamweaver

By Macromedia   **macromedia.com**   **Free**

CourseBuilder is a free extension for Macromedia Dreamweaver. Once installed in Dreamweaver, you simply drag a question type to your Web page and replace the placeholders with your unique content. CourseBuilder includes a number of question types including drag-and-drop, single-choice, multiple-choice, true-false, text-entry, and exploratory exercises.

By setting an option, you can track learners' scores and send them directly to an AICC-compliant learning management system such as Lotus LearningSpace, or save the information in a database, such as Microsoft Access, SQL Server, or Oracle 9i. By installing another free extension called Learning Site, you have a rudimentary course-creation and tracking tool.

Hot Potatoes

By Half-Baked Software   **halfbakedsoftware.com**   **About $100 USD**

Hot Potatoes is designed to create Web-ready self-assessments. With Hot Potatoes you can create multiple-choice questions, crossword puzzles, short-answer questions, fill-in-the-blank questions, matching questions, and jumble-sentence questions using one of the applications in the Hot Potatoes suite. The Masher, another tool in the suite, automatically compiles batches of Hot Potatoes test questions into units with the same appearance settings, forward and back navigation buttons linking the questions, and an index for the unit.

Hot Potatoes does not have any administration features other than the ability to e-mail scores to the instructor via a server script. It is best suited to creating self-assessments.

Quiz Rocket

By LearningWare   **learningware.com**   **About $1400 USD**

Quiz Rocket lets you create five different question types and surveys and then upload them to your server as Flash files. You can then aggregate the questions into tests using its Web-based administration utility. You can then choose to receive e-mail notification and summary scores, have users' results written to the database of your choice, or both.

RandomTest Generator Pro

By Hirtle Software   **hirtlesoftware.com**   **About $100 USD**

RandomTest Generator Pro is a Windows application that lets you create screen, paper, or Web-based tests using randomly selected questions you have created and stored in a Microsoft Access database. Question types include multiple-choice, one-choice, true-false, fill-in-the-blank, and essay. You can use graphics, animations, and sounds in any test question. And tests may be read aloud by the software using built-in text-to-speech capabilities. Students can get immediate feedback as well as have their test answers e-mailed to the instructor for grading.

Test Generator

By Fain & Company   **testshop.com**   **About $250 USD**

Test Generator comes in several versions: single-user, LAN, Web, and portable. All but the Web version are Windows applications. The Web version is an Internet-based test creation and delivery service hosted by Veracicom, an application service provider.

With any of the versions you can create eight types of questions, group questions into test banks, conduct the tests, record scores automatically, and generate reports.

Test Generator can import audio, video, and image media for use in tests. It can import and export users, tests, or lists of questions to and from other Test Generators or formatted files. It can also randomize questions in a test. Prices vary from $250 for the desktop version to $500 + $50 per test author and test taker for the LAN version.

TestLinc for LearnLinc

By Mentergy   **mentergy.com**   **About $400 USD per user**

TestLinc is a tool for use within the LearnLinc virtual classroom environment to create, deliver, and administer tests. Using a browser interface, you can create multiple-choice, multiple-response, true-false, fill-in-the-blank, formula, and short-answer/essay type questions. TestLinc also lets you deliver tests, evaluate and distribute the results, and generate numerous reports

HostedTest.com

By HostedTest.com   **hostedtest.com**   **$3000 (varies)**

HostedTest.com lets you create and edit questions, combine them into tests, and administer students using a Web browser. Question types include multiple-choice, one-choice, short-answer, and long-answer. HostedTest.com gives you a great deal of control over the appearance of your tests. You can embed them within your own site, link to them, or have student go directly to the site. HostedTest.com is a Web-based service. Pricing varies by how many graded tests are taken. The minimum subscription fee is $3000 for 1000 test-takers.

Unit-Exam.Com

By Unit-Exam.Com   **unit-exam.com**   **$50/monthly + $1/test**

Unit-Exam.Com has a complete set of Web-based forms that allow you to create and edit questions, combine them into tests, and conduct tests using a Web browser. Question types are limited to multiple-choice, one-choice, and true-false. Unit-Exam.Com is a Web-based service rather than a product. Unit-Exam.Com's pricing is based on a monthly service fee of $50 plus a per unit-exam charge of about $1 per graded exam.

Others

Here are some additional products, portals, and services that may be incorporated into an e-learning project.

Product	Vendor	Web address
Brainbench	Brainbench	brainbench.com
ExamsOnline.com	ExamsOnline.com	examsonline.com
ITcertinfo.com	MediaTec Publishing	www.ITcertinfo.com
Prometric	Thomson Learning	prometric.com
Vue Testing Services	VUE	www.vue.com

ALTERNATIVES TO TESTING TOOLS

What are your alternatives to using a testing tool? The flip answer is "Don't test." Nevertheless, learners need to know whether they understand and have mastered the material presented. Are there other ways to do that?

One alternative to dedicated testing tools is the testing features of a course authoring tool, LCMS, LMS, or virtual-school system. If you are buying one of these tools anyway, consider whether its testing capabilities are adequate for your purposes.

 Design the game so that winning requires demonstrating mastery of the subject material, not just eye-hand coordination or a good vocabulary.

Another alternative to formal testing is games. Several software packages are available to create engaging games to help learners evaluate their progress and add spice to e-learning as well. Here is a list of some software packages to consider.

Product	Vendor	Web address
Gameshow Pro Web	LearningWare	learningware.com
PuzzleMaker	Discovery.com	school.discovery.com/teachers
Web Author	University of Pennsylvania	ccat.sas.upenn.edu/plc/larrc/webauthor.html
Interactive Exercise Maker	Mellon Tri-College Language Grant	lang.swarthmore.edu/makers

A final alternative to purchasing a testing program is to develop your own question types using JavaScript or some other scripting language. If you are blessed with programming talent, building your own test questions maybe the best approach for you, especially if you need to go beyond the types of tests found in existing testing tools.

CHOOSING TESTING TOOLS

Here are some guidelines and features you should consider when choosing a standalone testing tool or service. In fact, you may want to review these issues before selecting other tools that include testing capabilities.

What you need to know first

The big question you need to answer before selecting a tool is "Why am I testing?" If you must satisfy a regulation or legally certify that learners have mastered certain information, then you need a tool that includes a server component to store questions, administer the tests, and analyze results. Security is mandatory. If you use an LMS, you may need to be able to transfer those results to the LMS.

On the other hand, if you are using tests and assessments for self-evaluation only, then a simple tool with no database backend is probably all you need.

Capabilities needed for testing

Capabilities needed for effective testing fall into four categories: question creation, test creation, test deployment, and test administration. Let's look at each of these features in turn.

Question creation

What kinds of test questions can the tool create and what kind of feedback can it deliver for each question? Here is a list of specific issues.

▶ **Variety of test types**. How many different types of test questions will the tool allow you to create? Will it let you create true-false, pick-one, pick-multiple, text-entry, matching, click-in-picture, drag-and-drop, and essay questions? The more ways you can ask a question, the more precisely you can assess learning.

▶ **Text-entry matching**. Can text-entry questions be evaluated by exact match, partial match, or match to items in a list? Can synonyms be defined for match words? Can match targets include wild card characters, such as an asterisk (*) to match a sequence of characters or a question mark (?) to match any individual character? Can regular expressions be used to specify patterns for matches?

 Regular expressions provide a language for expressing rules to determine whether two similar pieces of text match.

▶ **Custom-designed questions**. Can you define custom question types that use the tool's scorekeeping module?

▶ **Rich media**. Can you include graphics, audio, video, etc., in any test question? This feature sometimes varies with the type of question.

▶ **Feedback**. Can you specify any amount of feedback for both right and wrong answers? Can you include links to remedial information? Can you include rich media?

▶ **Hints**. Can you write hints for each question? Can you write hints for each answer? Hints are useful teaching tools.

▶ **Tags for questions**. Can questions be tagged with cataloging information to aid in organization and recall? For instance, can you select only questions that have a certain tag for a particular test?

Test creation

How much control does the tool allow you over how the learner experiences the test? Here is a list of issues to consider.

▶ **Test completion choices**. Can you specify specific actions learners can take upon successful or unsuccessful completion of an automatically scored test?

▶ **Multiple tries**. How many times can learners take the test and which scores are recorded? Does the testing service charge for retaking tests?

▶ **Time limits**. Can you set time limits for individual questions, the entire test, or both? Is the timer visible to learners? Does the tool give those with disabilities extra time if so requested?

▶ **Number of questions per test**. How many questions can be included in one test? Can more than one question appear on a page?

▶ **Number of questions stored in test bank**. Is there a limit to the number of questions you can keep in one test bank? If the system does not support test banks, how many questions can be added to the database?

▶ **Randomization**. Can tests be composed of questions that are randomly selected from a pool of available questions? Can questions randomly be reordered each time the test is viewed by one learner? Can the choices in a multiple-choice question appear in different orders for different learners?

▶ **Layout templates**. Does the tool have a wide selection of prebuilt templates? Can you customize the templates or create your own?

▶ **Appearance**. Can you define the background color or graphic, the font face, the font size, the font color, and placement of the questions?

Test deployment

How do learners take the test? What happens after they complete it? Here are some issues to consider.

▶ **Embedded on page**. Can the test be embedded within one of your course pages, or must it appear outside your course structure?

▶ **Flexible scoring**. Are answers automatically scored? Can they be sent via e-mail to the instructor for grading? Can you define actions triggered by scores above and below a threshold, such as adding material, removing material, notifying the instructor, recommending prerequisite or review information, or generating a jump page with links to remedial content? Can instructors define a formula for calculating the learner's final grade?

▶ **Feedback consolidated**. Does the tool allow the test to collect feedback for each question and present it all at the end of the test?

▶ **Results**. Are grades e-mailed to learners, recorded in a database for retrieval, or both? Can learners print out test scores—to show bosses, spouses, children, and parents?

▶ **Format**. Can tests be delivered in different ways, for instance on the LAN, on CD-ROM, on paper, and via the Web?

▶ **Time management**. At the beginning of timed tests, does the tool warn learners of time limits? During the test, does it display time remaining? Can learners with disabilities request more time?

▶ **Complete reports**. Does the tool tell learners what they need to know? For example, does it include items such as their score, percentage correct, letter grade, class average, rank in class, and percentile in the class?

▶ **Offline testing**. Can test results be held on the learner's computer and transmitted back to the server the next time the learner connects to the network? How secure is this capability?

Administration

How easy is it to perform the administrative duties necessary to offer multiple tests to multiple learners in different departments, companies, or schools? Here are some issues to consider.

▶ **Group testing**. Can you assign learners to groups, say by department or job category? And can you then assign tests to a group rather than having to add each individual learner to the test roster. The model is much like the Users and Groups feature in Windows NT Server.

▶ **Levels of security**. Can you assign different security classifications to instructors, learners, and administrators? For instance, can instructors view and edit their own questions and tests but not those of other instructors?

▶ **Interoperability**. Can you easily export data from the testing database into an LMS or other course management system? Can the tool use SCORM or AICC communications standards to report scores directly to an LMS, LCMS, or other system? Can the LMS launch tests?

▶ **Reporting**. What kids of reports does the tool generate? Can you customize them? Can you design your own? Can these reports be exported to a spreadsheet or some other analysis program?

WHAT NOW?

To put the ideas of this chapter to the test (no pun intended), you need to make decisions and take actions. Here are some recommendations for how to proceed.

If you ...	Then ...
Are still designing your e-learning	▶ Decide what role tests will play in your e-learning. Why are you testing? To measure effectiveness of e-learning, to meet regulatory requirements, or just to help learners gauge their own progress? Will you test knowledge, skills, attitudes, or behavior? Will you record scores? What types of tests do you need?

Have selected other tools as part of your e-learning effort	▶ Investigate their capabilities for creating and delivering tests. Decide whether you need a dedicated testing tool or whether the capabilities of existing tools are adequate.
	▶ Also consider whether you want to host your testing services or outsource that part of testing.
Are ready to pick a testing tool	▶ Using the criteria in this chapter as a starting point, list your requirements. Check for additional testing tools beyond the ones here. Using the process in chapter 20, make your selection.
Have already picked a testing tool	▶ Create examples and templates to ensure tests are fair and instructionally sound, and that they integrate smoothly with the rest of your e-learning content. If the tool is at all complex, get training for test-authors.

Tests are an important form of e-learning content. So too are the graphics, animation, video, and other media created by the tools in the next chapter.

16

Testing and assessment tools

17 Media editors

Without media editors, e-learning would be like reading books off a TV screen. Media editors are the tools that create and refine pictures, sounds, animations, video, and other media that go in pages—everything but the text. Media editors comprise a motley assortment of subcategories and eccentric tools.

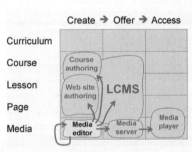

In our tools framework, media editors bubble and brew at the lower-left corner of the diagram, at the intersection of the Media row and the Create column. Media editors supply media components for other tools, such as course authoring tools, Web site authoring tools, and the authoring components of LCMSs, as well as other media editors. They may also be used to place audio and video components on a media server for better performance. Note that some media may require a specific media player for the learner to experience the media.

You may not need to read this chapter if...

▶ **It's not your job** and you plan to farm out media creation. You may want to specify file formats but will leave the choice of tools to subcontractors.

▶ **You are not ready**. You aren't far enough along in your planning to pick media, much less the tools to create them.

▶ **You are not qualified**. No offense, but you may want to leave the choice of media editing tools to staff members who will actually operate the tools.

A LITTLE STRATEGY FIRST

There are dozens of tools for editing media. Each is different, and many have overlapping capabilities. Picking these tools is complex and should not be done piecemeal. Before diving into the details of dozens of tools, take a few moments to think about how you will put these tools to work.

 Media editors are fun. That's not always a good thing. Managers may have so much fun trying out neat, cool, fun media editors that they forget about the goals of the project or their own e-learning strategy.

Media

Media editors create and refine media components that go into pages and learning objects. Various categories of tools are available for various media. Here are the categories and the types of media each typically handles.

Category	Media
Multimedia	Interactive animations with sound. These tools include capabilities for creating and combining separate media.
Graphics	▸ **Drawings**. Drawings are vector graphics defined as lines and areas. These graphics scale well. ▸ **Paintings**. Paintings are *bitmap graphics* defined as individual pixels (sometimes called *raster graphics*). Though paintings do not scale as smoothly as drawings, they can be precise down to the pixel level. ▸ **Photographs**. Photographs are commonly captured with digital cameras and transferred to the computer where they are edited with special photo-editing programs. Photographs are bitmap graphics.
Animation	Animations are drawings and paintings that display a sequence of images over a period of time. This moving picture may be derived from two-dimensional drawings (2-D) or from three-dimensional (3-D) models.
Audio	▸ **Sound**. Sound includes sound effects and voice narration. ▸ **Music**. Music may include background "mood" music as well as music used as the subject of the e-learning.

Category	Media
Video	Video captured by digital video camcorders can be uploaded, cut, spliced, and edited to produce video clips.
Virtual worlds	Three-dimensional scenes that learners can move through and interact with are created using Virtual Reality Modeling Language (VRML).
Media utilities	In addition to tools for these categories, you may need some special purpose media tools and utilities to create and convert media for e-learning. Among these are tools to capture screenshots and moving pictures of computer screens. Throughout this book you have seen numerous screenshots of Web pages and applications.

Now let's look at each of these media separately and answer questions such as: What is the medium? What tools can be used to create and edit it? What features or capabilities are important to consider?

File formats

Before picking any tools, consider what media you will use and what file formats you will need for these media. Then you can pick the tools to create and edit these file formats. By considering file formats, you can greatly reduce the number of media players and other add-ons that learners must download and install.

In many ways, the choice of file formats is more important than the choice of tools. It does not matter what tool you pick as long as the file it produces can be used by the next tool down the production line.

 This chapter mentions a lot of file formats. Appendix B will help you decode the TFLAs (three- and four-letter acronyms).

For each medium, consider a range of file formats. On one end of the scale are proprietary formats. These are ones that work only with a specific brand of add-on, browser, or operating system. On the other end of the scale are the browser-native formats. These are ones that can be displayed directly in any browser. In the middle are formats that may be proprietary but for which players are widely available.

	Browser-native		Widely available		Proprietary
Text documents	Basic HTML XML		PDF		Microsoft Word
Graphics	GIF, JPEG	PNG	SVG	VML	BMP, PSD
Sound		MP3		RealAudio	MS Media
Animation	Animated GIF Dynamic HTML	Flash		Director Shockwave	
Video		MPEG		QuickTime RealMedia	MS Media
Programming	JavaScript	Java			VBScript

This diagram shows where file formats common in e-learning fit along the browser-native/proprietary scale.

Each media type has its own common file formats along this scale. By picking formats on the left (or browser-native) end of the scale, you reduce the number of players and add-ons learners must install and you broaden their choice of browsers and operating systems. By picking formats from the right (or proprietary) end of the scale, you limit your e-learning to a proprietary player, browser, or specific operating system.

Here is a list of the different formats available for each type of media.

▶ **Text documents**. The browser-native format for text is HTML. Recent browsers can also display XML documents linked to a style sheet that specifies the format. Acrobat PDF, though proprietary to Adobe, can be widely used. Formats like Microsoft Word, Excel, and PowerPoint either require conversion or special viewers that are not universally available.

▶ **Graphics**. Browser-native formats include GIF and JPEG. Portable Network Graphics (PNG) is another option, though not as widely supported. Vector Modeling Language (VML) and Simple Vector Graphics (SVG) are supported in some browsers but not all. Many formats, such as BMP and Photoshop PSD are not widely supported on the Web.

▶ **Sound**. No browser-native solutions exist for sound, though MP3 is gaining wide support. RealAudio requires the RealMedia player, which is available for many systems. Microsoft's Media format can play within Internet Explorer for Windows and a player is now available for Macintosh and some UNIX systems.

▶ **Animation**. The browser-native format for animation is Animated GIF. Dynamic HTML (DHTML) also runs in browsers but forms of DHTML can vary somewhat among browsers. A readily available alternative is the Macromedia Flash format. A less widely available animation format is that used for Macromedia Director.

▶ **Video**. There are no browser-native video formats though most systems can play MPEG-encoded video clips. Other choices, though not as widely available, are the QuickTime and Real Media formats. On the proprietary end of the scale are Microsoft's Windows Media formats, though more players now recognize that format.

▶ **Programming or scripting**. JavaScript is the browser-native format. Java is close, but some slight differences between Sun's and Microsoft's implementations of Java may limit its use. On the proprietary end is VBScript, which works only in IE browsers on Windows systems.

New formats are being invented and deployed and new media players are making formerly proprietary formats more widely usable. As you consider each one, be sure to ask how it limits deployment of your e-learning.

Workflow

After you choose tools and file formats, the next step is to think about combining them into a coherent workflow to produce e-learning content. You may need some tools to produce intermediate versions of a medium, while others refine it and optimize it for the Web. For example, a vector drawing program, such as Macromedia FreeHand, may be more convenient for creating, scaling, and editing graphics, but you may require a bitmap editing program, such as Adobe Photoshop, to convert it to a format that works well for all browsers.

Rather than picking tools individually, take a few moments to sketch out how the various tools you pick will work together. Here is an example of how a group of media editing tools were chosen to work together.

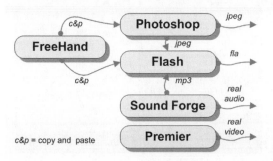

In this workflow, drawings are done in Macromedia FreeHand. Some are copied and pasted (c&p) into Adobe Photoshop to be polished and exported as JPEG graphics for inclusion in Web pages. Other Illustrator drawings are pasted into Macromedia Flash to be animated and output as Flash (fla) files. These Flash animations also incorporate MP3 audio produced in Sound Forge. Sound Forge is also used to create RealAudio files for lengthy voice narration segments. Adobe Premier is used to edit video segments that are saved in the RealVideo formats.

Before you buy any individual tools, sketch out your workflow to see how they will work together.

MULTIMEDIA TOOLS

Multimedia tools can capture, edit, or output multiple forms of media—graphics, animation, video. They go beyond the tools designed to capture, create, or edit a particular medium. Their purpose is to combine multiple media to produce one creation that can stand alone or be incorporated into an even larger production.

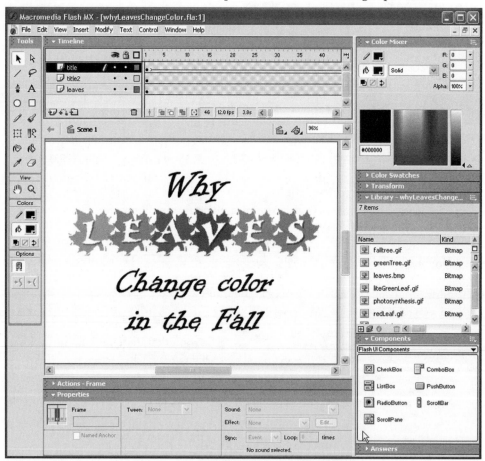

Macromedia Flash for authoring multimedia

In addition to integrating media, many of these tools have a built-in scripting language that allows you to add interactivity. Some of these tools are so sophisticated that they can be used to create highly complex games, simulations, and entire courses.

Popular multimedia tools

In this category you will find tools that combine media to create interactive, animated presentations. The following list represents a cross-section of such tools.

Director

By Macromedia   **macromedia.com**   **About $1200 USD**

Macromedia Director is the granddaddy of multimedia tools. It was originally designed for disk-based multimedia, but has kept up with the times and now exports to Web-ready formats too, including Java.

Director uses a theatrical metaphor. Action takes place on a stage, and the assets you create and import are called cast members. Using a multi-channeled timeline, you can import graphics, sounds, and video. You can also draw simple pictures and apply numerous transition effects to create very sophisticated animations. In addition to its considerable animation capabilities, Director also has a very complete scripting language called Lingo, giving you a wide range of creative possibilities.

Director lets you import 3-D models in the W3D format so you can manipulate and program them in your Director project. You can even create simple 3-D shapes within the program itself.

Flash

By Macromedia   **macromedia.com**   **About $500 USD**

Macromedia Flash is the leading multimedia tool designed with the Web in mind. Available for both Macintosh and Windows, Flash uses a timeline metaphor with multiple channels—layers, in Flash parlance—into which you can Technically, the Web-ready version of Flash (SWF) is called Shockwave Flash. Most people, however, just refer to it as plain Flash. We will follow this convention.

import all kinds of media, including vector illustrations in Windows Metafile, Adobe Illustrator, or FreeHand formats as well as audio, and video. These media can then be modified, synchronized, and scripted using the built in ActionScript language and preset behaviors. Finally, the project can be published in several formats—as Shockwave Flash (SWF), a QuickTime movie (some interactivity is supported), an animated GIF (no interactivity is supported), or a series of graphics.

Flash works well with Macromedia's drawing program FreeHand and can import each FreeHand layer as a separate Flash layer or cell. Illustrators often prefer FreeHand for its more conventional drawing tools. Not only can Flash import vector graphics, but it also has an array of drawing tools to create them. Because Flash stores graphics as vectors, Flash files are much smaller than many other similarly rich file formats.

If you use Flash, use it for everything

If you choose Flash for animation, consider using it for all your media needs. Doing so reduces the number of players learners need. Use Flash for:

▶ **Animations**. Flash uses a very compact vector file format.

▶ **Still graphics**. Draw your graphics in Flash and create a one-frame movie. These vector graphics are usually much smaller than their bitmap alternatives.

▶ **Photographs**. Huh? Try Flash's tracing feature to convert a bitmap graphic to a vector format. The impressionistic effect may be to your liking and the file size may be smaller than the native bitmap graphic.

▶ **Sound**. Flash can compress voice, music, and sound effects to the compact MP3 format.

Flash can be enhanced through the installation of a variety of free extensions. Of interest to e-learning developers are the Learning extensions that include several SCORM wrappers, the Questionmark Perception interactions, and the Learning Extension for common interactions.

Fluition

By Confluent Technologies   **fluition.com**   **About $100 USD**

Fluition for Windows and Macintosh is a SMIL editor that lets you synchronize graphics, audio, video, Flash, and other media to create a streaming media file. Leaners play the file using the RealOne Player, the QuickTime Player, or the Windows Media Player.

GRiNS Pro Editor for SMIL

By Oratrix   **oratrix.com**   **About $600 USD**

GRiNS Pro Editor for SMIL also lets you synchronize a variety of media which you can export for play by the RealOne Player, Internet Explorer 6, GRiNS Mobile SMIL player, and the GRiNS Player. GRiNS Pro Editor also has a timeline editor, animation editor, source code editor, and transition effects editor. It is available for Windows only.

> ### What is SMIL?
>
> SMIL stands for Synchronized Multimedia Integration Language. It is a markup language (like HTML) defined by the World Wide Web Consortium. SMIL is designed to choreograph multimedia presentations combining audio, video, text, and graphics. By using a single timeline for all of the media on a page, their display can be properly coordinated and synchronized. SMIL can be played by several of the streaming media players, such as RealOne and QuickTime, as well as by Internet Explorer 5.5+ for Windows. Tools for editing SMIL include Fluition, GRiNS Pro Editor for SMIL, and SMIL Composer.

HotMedia

By IBM **www-3.ibm.com/software/ad/hotmedia/** **Free**

HotMedia is a Java-based application for integrating rich media, such as video, audio, and 3-D animations, and saving the result as a Java applet to embed into a Web application—without the need for a plug-in or specialized server. You can combine graphics with synchronized narration and add hot spots or areas to which you can assign actions based on when a user hovers or clicks the target.

LiveMotion

By Adobe **www.adobe.com** **About $400 USD**

LiveMotion lets you create dynamic interactive content in a variety of formats including Flash and QuickTime. It has a scripting language called ActionScript and, like Flash, contains coding and debugging tools. LiveMotion is tightly integrated with other Adobe tools such as Photoshop, Illustrator, and GoLive. LiveMotion can be extended using Live Tabs. Unlike Flash, there is no specific support for e-learning courseware.

LiveStage Professional

By Totally Hip Software **totallyhip.com** **About $850 USD**

LiveStage Professional lets you create interactive QuickTime movies by combining video, sound, 3-D graphics, virtual reality models, Flash, and other media types that QuickTime can play. To that you can add text, interactivity, transitions, music samples, and MIDI music, all of which can be displayed in a custom-designed player that LiveStage calls a skin.

Producer

By Microsoft   **microsoft.com**   **Free**

Producer is a free application for owners of PowerPoint 2002 for Windows. It lets you combine graphics, audio, video, PowerPoint, and HTML files and synchronizes them on a timeline. In addition to importing existing media, Producer can also capture new video and audio. Projects are saved in the Windows Media format and streamed using the Windows 2000 Media server.

PresenterOne

By Accordant Technologies   **accordent.com**   **About $400 USD**

PresenterOne lets you integrate audio, video, PowerPoint slides, Web addresses, graphics, and e-mail feedback into an HTML frameset. There is no need for a media player unless you use audio or video. In that case, the learner will need either the RealOne or Windows Media players. PresenterOne has a number of predefined templates, and you can design your own templates. PresenterOne is available as an enterprise version and there is a free version as well.

Alternatives to multimedia tools

If you have a technically astute Web development team, you can provide many similar animations and multimedia interactivities using a Web site authoring tool like Macromedia Dreamweaver MX. Dreamweaver has a timeline feature that allows you to develop media-rich interactivities and animations using layers and Dynamic HTML. Adobe GoLive has a built-in SMIL editor for creating SMIL files for the RealOne Player.

Another alternative is to buy a special-purpose tool. For instance, rather than use a full-featured multimedia program to create a game, go for special game software. Instead of building a simulation from scratch, get a specialized simulation tool.

Choosing a multimedia tool

Multimedia tools differ greatly in the capabilities they offer and the skills they require. Deciding among them is not an easy job, especially if you are not a media specialist or a programmer. First, determine how you will use multimedia, and then seek the advice of practitioners.

What you need to know first

What kinds of learning experiences do you want to create? Do they need a game to lock in a concept? Do they need to practice using a simulation? How interactive does the content need to be? Does the multimedia experience need to stand alone or will it be part of another learning activity? Will you deliver your content via the Web or disk-based media? What network speed will learners use to access your multimedia?

In addition to considering the types of content you want to create, you need to evaluate the skills of your team. Can current team members quickly learn and productively use multimedia tools? Will you need to hire specialists?

Finally, you need to assess what raw materials you have to work with. Do you have presentations in PowerPoint? Do you have video or audio of existing classroom training you want to reuse? Do you have supporting content like technical illustrations, photographs, and 3-D models?

Capabilities to consider

Multimedia tools tend to combine capabilities found in specialized media tools. So if the tool you are evaluating provides tools for media creation (e.g., video, graphics, audio, tests), review the capabilities needed for the tools for each of these individual media. Capabilities you should evaluate for a multimedia tool include:

▶ **Synchronization**. How precisely can the tool synchronize media? For instance, can narration and animation be precisely timed? Can video be synchronized with other elements in the display, such as slides, Web pages, graphics, or text? Some tools do a better job than others when it comes to synchronizing media elements. Sometimes the quality of synchronization depends on which format the project is being exported to. For example, if you save the same SMIL project in the HTML+TIME format for viewing directly in Internet Explorer 5.5 and as a RealOne presentation, you may find that one version is better synchronized than the other depending on your particular media mix.

▶ **Built-in behaviors**. Does the tool have a set of ready-made actions you can just drag and drop into your project? Does it have commonly used code snippets? The more prebuilt behaviors, scripts, or other reused components a tool has, the more efficient you'll be using that tool.

▶ **Recording macros**. Does the tool have a way of recording repetitive actions and saving them as reusable objects, behaviors, or macros? Can you reuse them in the current project as well as in other projects?

▶ **Scripting**. Does the tool have a full-featured programming language to manipulate the objects you import and create? Everything you can do manually within a tool should also be achievable using the scripting language. Is the programming language proprietary, or is it based on an existing program language? The closer a scripting language is to an existing programming language, the easier it will be to learn. For example, experienced JavaScript programmers will find Flash's ActionScript language easier to learn than Director's Lingo language.

▶ **Templates**. Does the tool have a variety of built-in, well designed display templates for various uses? Can you create new templates for your specific project needs? Templates save time, simplify the creation process, and painlessly enforce a consistent look and feel or corporate identity.

▶ **Extensibility**. Can the capabilities of the tool be enhanced or customized through the use of extensions, plug-ins, or some other add-on? Many popular multimedia tool vendors like Macromedia and Adobe offer free extensions from their Web sites. These exchange sites encourage a community of users for the vendor's tools.

▶ **Media import**. How many different media formats can the tool import for use in your project? Can it import popular proprietary file formats? If you want to reuse existing content or if you create content for use in multimedia and elsewhere, your tool has to be able to import such content. Say your art department uses Macromedia FreeHand or Fireworks to create drawings and you want to use those drawings in an interactive animation. You would probably choose Macromedia Flash because of its support of FreeHand drawing layers. Conversely, if your team uses Adobe Photoshop or Illustrator, you may prefer Adobe LiveMotion.

▶ **File export**. Which Web-ready file formats does the tool export? Do learners require a special media player or a specific browser to experience your multimedia? Does the tool export Flash, Java, and streaming formats like RealMedia, Windows Media, and QuickTime?

GRAPHICS TOOLS

Graphics are the drawings, photographs, charts, graphs, diagrams, and icons used to guide and inform learners.

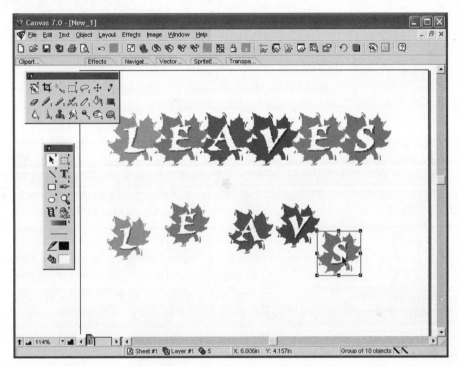

Deneba's Canvas for creating graphics

There are two ways to represent graphics in a computer: as vector drawings or bitmap paintings. A vector graphic contains a description or recipe for creating the graphic rather than defining each pixel of the graphic the way a bitmap does.

	Vector graphic	Bitmap graphic
Other names	Draw graphic	Paint graphic, raster graphic
How graphics are defined	As coordinates of lines and areas	As rows and columns of picture elements (pixels). The color of each pixel is specified.
Best used for	Line drawings with mostly solid colors	Photographs and paintings with intricate details and subtle shadings

	Vector graphic	Bitmap graphic
Advantages	Easier to edit Scales without distortion Produces smaller files	Displays consistently across different systems Uses file formats that are native for older browsers
Disadvantages	Displayed directly by only a few recent browsers—and not consistently Difficult to convert between vector formats	Generates large files for intricately detailed color graphics Editing requires redrawing

In evaluating graphics tools, also consider what Web and non-Web formats they important and export. The distinction between Web formats and non-Web formats is not as clear-cut as that between bitmap and vector graphics. Web formats tend to be standard, browser-native formats like GIF and JPEG that can be displayed directly by browsers. These formats are tuned for Web use, which means they store images in a way that reduces file size and thus download time.

Non-Web formats tend to be ones that originated before the Web. Most were designed for desktop publishing without great concern for file size. This category includes standard formats like TIFF and proprietary formats like those for Adobe Photoshop and Macromedia FreeHand.

Graphic file formats

A good place to start discussing graphics is with the various file formats you will encounter. These are numerous but, for our purposes, the list can be whittled down to four categories.

	Vector file formats	Bitmap file formats
Non-Web	Encapsulated Postscript (EPS) Adobe Illustrator (AI)* Windows Metafile (WMF)	Tagged Interchange File Format (TIFF) Bitmap (BMP) Photoshop file (PSD)*
Web	Vector Markup Language (VML) Scalable Vector Graphics (SVG)	Graphics Interchange Format (GIF) Joint Photographic Experts Group (JPEG) Portable Network Graphic (PNG)

* = Proprietary formats

Each of the tools discussed here has its own native file format, which is unique to that program. More important may be the extent to which each tool can import or export the above files formats, especially if you have legacy content you must edit and convert for use in your e-learning.

Popular graphics tools

Popular graphic tools include ones for creating all the popular Web-ready file formats—GIF, PNG, JPEG, and SVG. Some of these tools create and edit vector graphics, others create and edit bitmap graphics, and some do both.

 Always maintain your original artwork in the program's native file format. That way, each time you edit the graphic, you are editing and resaving the best version possible.

Canvas

By Deneba	deneba.com	**About $400 USD**

Canvas creates and edits vector and bitmap graphics. It has ample drawing and painting capabilities. One particularly useful feature is that Canvas can open and save more file types than just about any other graphics program. Canvas can also create presentation layout pages and generate simple animations. Canvas may not be the best at all the many things it does, but it is adequate for most purposes. Versions are available for both Windows and Macintosh.

Fireworks

By Macromedia	macromedia.com	**About $300 USD**

Fireworks is optimized for designing Web graphics and simple animations. The power of the program is that you can create and edit both vector and bitmap graphics, then save the results as PNG, JPEG, GIF, animated GIF, and Flash Shockwave.

FreeHand

By Macromedia	macromedia.com	**About $400 USD**

FreeHand is a direct competitor to Illustrator. It, too, has been around a long time and is currently shipping version 10. It can import and export a variety of file formats, including popular Web-ready formats. And it is closely integrated with other Macromedia tools, most notably Flash, which recognizes FreeHand layers, thus saving a lot of work preparing animations

Illustrator

By Adobe   www.adobe.com   About $400 USD

Illustrator is a venerable drawing tool that has kept up with the times. In addition to its vast array of drawing and layout capabilities, Illustrator has a number of productivity features, including an internal macro language that allows authors to automate repetitive tasks. It can import and export a variety of file formats, including popular Web-ready formats. And it is closely integrated with other Adobe tools such as PhotoShop and GoLive.

Paint Shop Pro

By Jasc   jasc.com   About $100 USD

Paint Shop Pro has been a favorite of Windows Help and application developers for a number of years. Like Illustrator and FreeHand, it has kept up with the times and is a full-featured program that can import and export a wide variety of file formats, including Web-ready formats. Paint Shop Pro is a good, general-purpose tool that can create and edit both vector and bitmap graphics.

Photoshop

By Adobe   www.adobe.com   About $600 USD

Photoshop is the bitmap editing program of choice for professional graphic designers and digital photographers. Its capabilities are optimized for working with photographs. Through its included ImageReady program, Photoshop can export a variety of Web-ready bitmap formats.

Visio

By Microsoft   microsoft.com   About $200 USD

Visio is a popular tool for creating all kinds of technical illustrations, from network diagrams to process flow charts to interior design and landscaping diagrams using Visio's built-in shapes. These diagrams can be included in your training course as Web-ready graphics or as HTML documents you can link to. Visio is available in a Standard ($200 USD) or a Professional ($500 USD) version.

WebDraw

By Jasc   **jasc.com**   **About $200 USD**

WebDraw lets you create Scalable Vector Graphics. Because SVG is the program's underlying format, designers can view and edit SVG source code directly—with the help of a built-in validator. WebDraw also has an animation timeline that can animate any object in the scene.

PowerPoint for graphics

By Microsoft   **microsoft.com**   **About $350 USD**

Microsoft PowerPoint is an essential classroom training tool, and it has the ability to export a presentation to HTML or drawings to Web-ready formats. You can use PowerPoint's drawing tools to create explanatory illustrations. Just draw your graphic, scale it to the desired size, right-click it, and then save the graphic in a Web-ready format like GIF, JPEG, or PNG.

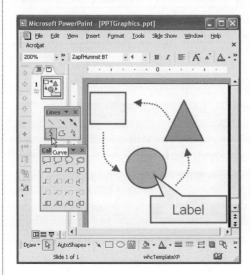

This graphic has been created using several of the many AutoShapes available. The graphic is then saved as a PNG file.

You can also use PowerPoint to:

▶ Edit clip art from Microsoft's Design Gallery Live, a free service to licensed users of Microsoft Office.

▶ Resize artwork before saving it to a Web-ready format, by pasting the graphic into PowerPoint, scaling it, compressing the picture to screen resolution, then saving the picture as a PNG, GIF, or JPEG.

Alternatives to graphics tools

Instead of the graphics tools mentioned here, you may want to consider other options, especially if your needs are modest. Here are some additional possibilities.

▶ Drawing tools in Microsoft Office, especially PowerPoint. See the sidebar PowerPoint for Graphics.

▶ Animation and multimedia tools, such as Macromedia Flash. Many such tools contain drawing capabilities. Just create your graphic as a one-frame movie.

Choosing a graphics tool

First of all, if you are not a graphic artist yourself, call someone who is to help you select a tool. Be forewarned, however. Artists are, well, artists. Their acceptance of a tool may be more subjective than objective. If the artist learned to draw using paper and pencil rather than a mouse and monitor, then how well a tool mimics paper and pencil may determine its acceptability.

Aside from the opinions of your artistic friends, here are some concrete issues to consider when selecting a tool.

What you need to know first

Before picking a tool, decide which Web-ready formats you need for your e-learning. Will you be using mostly photographs, screen snapshots, line drawings, or icons? Each type of graphic may require a different file format or setting. For instance, photographs are usually saved as moderately compressed JPEGs and screen snapshots as 16-color GIFs. Line drawings can benefit from newer vector formats such as SVG.

 Just because a tool can import a format does not mean it can do so perfectly for your artwork in that format. Test the tool's ability to import typical pieces of your source art. Success may depend on the version of the program that created the source art and the complexity of that art.

You also need to know the file formats of any source art you will be using. Many illustrations used in e-learning come from existing artwork. You may need to combine archived photographs in the Macintosh PICT file format with clip art in Corel's CMX format and technical illustrations in TIFF files.

Capabilities to consider

Once you know what file formats you will be working with, there are some additional capabilities to consider.

▶ **Vector and bitmap graphics**. Does the tool import, edit, and export both vector and bitmap graphics? Can it mix them freely and convert from one form to the other? If your source artwork exists in both vector and bitmap file formats, a tool that supports both may be a good choice for you.

▶ **File formats**. Can the tool import and export a wide variety of file formats? If your source artwork exists in many different file formats, you want a tool that can open all of them. If the archived file format is proprietary and you no longer use the old authoring tool, you need to convert that file to a more useful format. For instance, if all your archived vector art exists in Corel CMX files, you may want to open those files and resave them as Windows Metafiles (WMF).

▶ **Web-ready file formats**. Can the tool create graphics that work well over the Web, especially for learners with low-speed connections? Does it save as JPEG, GIF, transparent GIF, animated GIF, and PNG? You will be hard-pressed to find a modern graphics program that does not export to some kind of Web-ready format. However, not every tool gives you the same amount of control over the degree of compression in the Web-ready format. For example, when exporting to JPEG, some programs allow you to specify quality (amount of compression) only in terms of low, medium, or high. Other programs allow you to select a value between 1 and 100.

File-format entropy

When going from format to format, you may lose certain features only available in the original authoring program. Here's a case in point. If you convert a vector graphic with Bezier curves created in Macromedia FreeHand to a WMF file, you lose the Bezier curves and they are replaced with a multi-pointed figure as in this example:

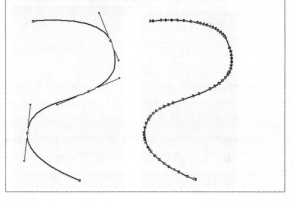

▶ **Digital watermarks**. Can the tool insert an invisible digital watermark to flag copyright ownership of the graphic? The Web makes it easy to copy and use graphics appearing in Web pages. Adding a digital watermark makes it easier to prove ownership of your graphics if they are used elsewhere on the Web.

▶ **Slices**. Can you export one large graphic as a series of pieces, each a predetermined width and height, and each in a separate file? Will the tool generate the necessary HTML to display the pieces? This is a very useful feature for Web designers who want to precisely place parts of a graphic, say for a tool bar, using tables or DHTML layers. Here is a simple example of a sliced graphic:

▶ **Drawing tools**. Can the tool draw and paint as well as edit existing graphics? Photoshop, for example, is a superb editing tool for photographs and other bitmap graphics. However, it is difficult to create precise drawings from scratch in Photoshop. Many artists, therefore, create the drawing in another program, such as Adobe Illustrator, then import the graphic into Photoshop for additional editing.

▶ **Layers**. Does the tool allow you to place various parts of a graphic on separate layers? Does it allow you to display specific layers and export them as a single Web-ready graphic? Layers are a way of organizing complex graphics by letting you place parts of a graphic that might be edited as a unit on a separate transparent sheet. Suppose you are drawing a series of six buttons in six different colors using the

This graphic has five layers, a base layer and four layers containing a different graphic. Only the cap and the base are selected. When that combination is exported, this is the resulting graphic:

same set of same icons. You draw each icon on a different layer and each of the six colored buttons on their separate layers. Then all you have to do is select the icon layer you need and the particular color of button you need and export them as one graphic.

▶ **Editable components**. Are text, shapes, and other components stored in an easily editable format within the graphic so that revisions are easy? For instance, if you use text within an illustration, does that text remain editable as long as the illustration is saved in the program's native format? Some graphic programs allow you to add text using very capable text tools; however, as soon as the text is created, it is converted to a bitmap which is not easily edited.

▶ **Animation export**. Can a series of pictures be exported as an animated GIF picture or a Flash animation? Graphics tools that support layers often allow you to export each layer as a separate frame in an animation and save the resulting file as an animated GIF (GIF89a format), a QuickTime movie, or Flash file (SWF format). Such tools can do double duty. They can create and edit graphics as well as simple animations.

▶ **Interface customization**. Does the tool allow you to rearrange palettes, create special keyboard commands for favorite menu selections, specify other productivity preferences, and then save these preferences? An interface customized for a particular project or a particular user is a boon to productivity.

▶ **Frequent action library**. Does the tool allow you to record repetitive tasks, save them as a macro or action to run whenever needed? Any time you can automate a repetitive action you save time and eliminate errors.

▶ **Graphics library**. Can you create symbols and other reusable pictures and save them in a special location for easy use in other graphics? When designing graphics for a course or a whole curriculum, the ability to store frequently used graphics, or graphic snippets, saves time and ensures consistency.

▶ **Web colors**. Does the tool allow you to define colors based on the same hexadecimal values used to specify colors in HTML? Are colors in the graphics identical to colors that are specified the same way in HTML?

 For a long time I had to use my computer's calculator to convert decimal red-green-blue color values to a hexadecimal number and vice versa. What a pain!

▶ **Custom palettes**. Can the tool define and store a custom color palette? Can it import a palette? One of the more important decisions you make when designing a course or a group of courses is the color palette. To make following the palette easier, your graphics tool should allow you to define a color palette and save it for use by everyone producing visual content.

▶ **Import from devices**. Can the program import graphics from digital scanners and cameras? Sometimes an artist may want to make initial sketches using paper and colored markers.

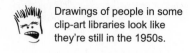 Drawings of people in some clip-art libraries look like they're still in the 1950s.

Clip art library

OK, OK, 99% of clip art is clichéd, hackneyed, and downright silly. However, with hundreds of thousands of pieces in a library, at least some are bound to be useful. Here are some clip art libraries to consider:

▶ Microsoft Design Gallery Live (dgl.microsoft.com)

▶ ClipArt.com (clipart.com)

▶ ClipArtNow (clipartnow.com)

Choose clip art formats you can easily ungroup, rearrange, and recolor to make them look like your own.

ANIMATION TOOLS

Animations are drawings in motion. They display a sequence of images over a period of time. They depict an illusion of motion like an old-fashioned flip book. Animation is a good medium for showing how things move and change—especially if the subject matter is visual. Animations range from simple two-dimensional cartoons to highly rendered 3-D scenes.

Like graphics, there are two basic kinds of animation: vector and bitmap. Animations composed of bitmaps, like animated GIFs, have larger files than similar animations created with a vector tool and saved in a vector format like SVG or Flash.

Popular animation tools

Because animations run the gamut from simple to complex, the tools that create them are equally as diverse. Here are some to consider.

 Some of the best animation tools, such as Macromedia's Flash and Director and Adobe's LiveMotion, are covered in the section on multimedia tools. Use multimedia tools for highly interactive animations.

Product	Description
3ds max By Discreet discreet.com About $3500	3ds max is a high-end professional tool for creating photo-realistic visualizations and animations suitable for film and television. Rendering can be distributed to other computers on the network.
Animation Applet By Ulead ulead.com About $40 USD	Animation Applet allows you to combine graphics, transitions, and visual effects to create Java animation applets. You can also add audio and simple interactivity.
Animation Master By Hash www.hash.com About $300 USD	Animation Master is an all-purpose, moderately priced 3-D animation tool. It is best suited to creating animations for disk-based applications where download time is not critical.
Bryce 5 By Corel corel.com About $300 USD	Bryce 5 is designed to create, render, and animate landscapes. It can distribute the task of rendering the image to other machines over a network, thus saving a great deal of time when creating a complex scene.
Cool 3-D By Ulead ulead.com About $45 USD	Cool 3-D builds simple 3-D objects and animates them using a timeline and built-in special effects. You can export projects as vector Flash files.
GIF Animator By Ulead ulead.com About $45 USD	GIF Animator imports a wide variety of graphic media, allows you to apply transitions and other effects, and exports the final product as an animated GIF (surprise, surprise), QuickTime, AVI, MPEG, Flash, sequential JPEG, or sequential PNG file.
Java Animator By Sausage Software sausage.com About $20 USD	Java Animator creates animations by defining a sequence of pictures and then converting them to a Java applet.
Poser By Curious Labs www.curiouslabs.com About $350 USD	If you can draw boxes and other simple shapes just fine but go completely catatonic at the thought of having to draw realistic-looking people, get Poser. Poser creates 3-D models of people, animals, and faces—and then animates them. It imports and exports a wide variety of media formats.

17

Media editors

Product	Description
Strata 3Dpro By Strata strata.com About $700 USD	Strata 3Dpro is very full-featured 3-D modeling, rendering, and animation program. Many libraries of pre-built 3-D models are available for Strata 3Dpro. You can save your projects at high resolution for print, as digital video formats for animations, as JPEG for Web images, as VRML for virtual worlds, and as Flash for playback by the Flash plug-in.
WebDraw By Jasc jasc.com About $200 USD	WebDraw is an SVG development environment we discussed earlier in the graphics section of this chapter. Because of its dedicated animation timeline, it warrants a mention in this section too.

PowerPoint as an animation tool

The layers and animation features in Microsoft PowerPoint can be used to create informative, voice-over animations. When saved as HTML, these animations are converted to DHTML that can be viewed in IE 5 or later. These same PowerPoint slides can be recorded as Windows Media formats using the presentation recording features of PowerPoint. Or the animated slides can be converted to Flash using Presedia or to Java using Impatica. Presedia and Impatica are covered in chapter 18 on converters.

ALTERNATIVES TO ANIMATION TOOLS

If your needs do not justify a dedicated animation tool, there are three alternatives to animation tools to consider.

▶ **Graphics tools**. Because many animations are composed of a series of pictures, most of the graphics tools discussed in this chapter have the ability to create GIF animations. For instance, using Adobe Photoshop and its companion program ImageReady, multi-layered graphics can be transformed to animated GIFs. Macromedia Fireworks can export files as either animated GIFs or as Flash files.

▶ **Multimedia tools**. You can use almost any of the multimedia tools like Macromedia Director, Adobe LiveMotion, and Macromedia Flash to create animations.

▶ **Web site authoring tools**. Tools for editing dynamic HTML pages can create simple animations. Both Macromedia Dreamweaver and Adobe GoLive can create Web pages with animations.

Choosing an animation tool

If animation is not your forte, then enlist the advice of an expert to evaluate these tools. But always keep in mind the needs of your organization and its projects.

What you need to know first

The most important thing to know before starting your evaluation is what role animation will play in your e-learning. Are you using animations to create a photo-realistic game environment or just to reinforce explanations of processes and procedures? Do you want to create an avatar or cartoon mentor? Your needs determine the kinds of animation tools to consider.

Another consideration is the legacy content you have to re-purpose for your project. For instance, if your course is about the operation of some complex machinery, you may have access to technical drawings in Autodesk's proprietary DXF format. In that case you will want to select a tool that imports DXF files, adds 3-D effects, and animates the result.

Capabilities to consider

Here are some capabilities you should consider when you evaluate animation tools. Some of these features may be found only in the high-end 3-D tools and in full-featured multimedia tools. Remember, the right tool for your project does not have to have every feature listed here.

▶ **Timeline**. Does the tool use a timeline metaphor? Timelines make it easy to build scenes and to synchronize precisely the appearance and movement of objects.

▶ **Pacing**. Does the tool allow you to easily change the frame rate of an animation? For example, if you change the rate, will the tool automatically reposition key frames to keep in synch with the new rate?

▶ **Onion-skinning and tracing**. Does the tool provide an onionskin feature that lets animators draw by tracing over a scanned pencil drawing or some other imported graphic? Can animators see dimmed images of preceding and following frames while drawing a new frame? Onion-skinning makes it easy to precisely move objects from frame to frame.

▶ **Layering**. Does the tool let animators assign shapes and other objects to easily manipulated layers? Some animations can become very complex with numerous objects per frame. Layers organize complex animations by grouping objects that might be edited as a unit on a separate transparent layer.

▶ **Interactive animations**. Can the tool create interactive animations by incorporating scripts or canned behaviors? Or is it limited to linear sequences?

▶ **Audio**. Can the tool import audio and synchronize it with motions? Audio can extend the effectiveness of an animation by adding another channel for information.

▶ **Transitions**. Does the tool provide a variety of transition effects (fades, wipes, dissolves)? Are they easy to apply? Transitions can help indicate passage of time, reinforce the spatial metaphor, and lessen visual shock.

▶ **Drawing tools**. Does the tool provide a rich set of drawing tools that behave like similar tools in drawing programs? If the tool just imports elements and doesn't provide the means to create additional elements, you will require other graphics tools.

▶ **Numeric and mouse editing**. Can animators describe shapes both by sketching them with the mouse and by entering precise coordinates from the keyboard? Some tools only allow manual creation and placement of objects in a scene. In 3-D modeling and animation tools it is critical to be able to numerically define and precisely place objects.

▶ **Canned content**. Does the tool allow you to save animation sequences or models and reuse them in other animation sequences? Can they be reused in more complex models and scenes? This is another productivity issue. If you are creating many animations about the same subject matter, for instance an airplane cockpit, then you'll likely be using certain elements again and again. A tool that allows you to save parts of an animation to a common library and reuse them in other projects saves time and ensures consistency.

▶ **Ready-made content**. Does the tool have a library of ready-made animations and 3-D models? For beginners and pros alike, it may be more efficient to modify an existing animation rather than create it from scratch. Many 3-D tools come with libraries of shapes, objects, and animations. Some of the more popular tools are well supported by third-party companies offering components for animation.

▶ **Import formats**. Can the tool import common graphic file formats, such as GIF, JPEG, Flash, or PowerPoint? Can it import video? Can it import proprietary formats from common drawing programs? Can it import fonts? Can it import 3-D formats like DXF, DirectX, or 3DMF (Apples QuickDraw 3D format)? If you have existing content, the ability to import a wide variety of file formats is an essential feature. Even if you don't, you still may want to create components of your animation in other more specialized tools. You may also want to outsource the creation of certain elements to subcontractors who pick their own tools.

▶ **Export formats**. Can the tool export animations in the format you need, such as Flash, SVG, animated GIFs, Java applets, QuickTime, MPEG, Windows Media Video, and RealVideo formats? Can the tool save or export 3-D models as VRML and as formats recognized by other modeling and animation programs? The greater the variety of export formats, the more flexibility you have in using your animations, either as standalone features or as components of other e-learning products.

Three-dimensional tools include numerous features that are beyond the scope of this book, such as lighting, viewpoint or camera control, and modeling and rendering technologies. Again, enlist the aid of an expert to help you sort through the feature lists of these tools. Also see the list of capabilities needed for creating 3-D virtual worlds.

AUDIO TOOLS

In this section we are going to look at tools used to capture, create, and edit sounds that provide narration, sound effects, and music. Many of the tools in this category can be used to edit all types of audio. Other tools are more specialized.

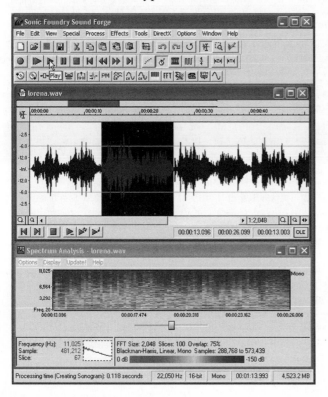

Here is a typical audio tool, Sound Forge from Sonic Foundry. This example shows a single-channel audio clip displayed as a waveform. A spectrum analysis is being performed on the clip to show the frequencies and overtones present in the recording.

The waveform (the spikey lines at the top) is important in gauging volume levels and precisely timing cuts.

The spectrum analyzer can help predict and monitor effects of compression on, say, a narrator's voice.

Popular audio tools

Audio tools capture analog and digital audio, refine it, and export it in a variety of digital formats. We are going to look at a few of the more popular tools for both Windows and Macintosh systems. These tools provide a mixture of sound- and music-editing capabilities.

Product	Description
Acid Pro By Sonic Foundry sonicfoundry.com About $350 USD	Acid Pro is a loop-based music creation tool for Windows that allows you to produce original, royalty-free music. You can create songs, remix tracks, develop music beds, and score videos and animations. Acid Pro also allows you to create and edit MIDI files and combine them with your audio tracks. It opens and saves a variety of file formats including RealAudio and MP3 files.
Cool Edit Pro By Syntrillium Software syntrillium.com About $250 USD	CoolEdit Pro is a moderately priced multi-track recording and editing program for Windows. Targeted at musicians, Cool Edit Pro can save files as MP3 as well as WAV. Cool Edit Pro has a more streamlined sibling, Cool Edit 2000, which has basic capabilities and costs about $70 USD.
MultitrackStudio By Bremmers Audio Design multitrackstudio.com About $100 USD	MultitrackStudio records and edits multiple tracks of audio and MIDI music. Available for Windows, it is targeted at home recording musicians. With this program you can record your own songs, as well as record tracks while playing along with previously recorded ones. It can export MP3 files.
Peak By Bias, Inc. bias-inc.com About $500 USD	Peak is a stereo recording and editing application for the Macintosh. You can use it to record audio directly or import all QuickTime-compatible audio formats. Peak exports a variety of audio formats including MP3. It also has a video track for precisely synchronizing image and sound.
Sonar By Cakewalk cakewalk.com About $500 USD	Sonar is a Windows-based tool that lets you record, edit, arrange, and mix MIDI and audio files. It is marketed as a music creation tool; however, it can handle sound effects and narration too. Sonar can import numerous audio file formats, as well as AVI videos.It can export MP3, RealAudio, and Windows Media Audio.
Sound Forge By Sonic Foundry sonicfoundry.com About $350 USD	Sound Forge is a stereo recording and editing tool for Windows. Plug-ins for special effects can be added. These include Sonic Foundry's Noise Reduction filter which saves time when working with less-than-perfect recordings. Sound Forge imports and saves a variety of audio file formats including QuickTime, MPEG 1 & 2, MP3, and Windows Media Audio.

Alternatives to audio tools

If you plan to use voice, sound effects, or music in your e-learning, you will need some tools to record, digitize, and edit that sound. To lighten your load of tools, you can use sound-editing capabilities in your multimedia and video-editing tools.

Many multimedia computers come with simple sound-editing tools already installed. These tools may be capable of recording and splicing together sounds and music.

Whatever happened to MIDI?

MIDI stands for Musical Instrument Digital Interface. In about 1995 it seemed destined to become the Web standard for music. Because MIDI represents the notes of music rather than the sound waves, tit is quite compact and well suited to slow network connections, but it does not produce CD quality sound.

MIDI is still around and doing good work, but it never became the promised Web standard for music. The reasons form a cautionary tale for e-learning developers.

MIDI, as we said, stores just the notes, not the actual sounds. To play the music, the browser or MIDI player needs to map the notes (for example B-flat) to simulated instruments (for example, an alto saxophone) for which the player has sounds. Unfortunately browsers and players never standardized the mapping, or virtual orchestra commissioned to play the notes. The result sometimes sounded as if the conductor had scrambled the parts assigned to instruments, giving the saxophone part to the violin and the drum part to the cello. At worst, it sounded like sundown at the zoo.

Meanwhile improvements in sound compression and network speed combined with a realization that not every Web page needed a musical background was enough to mute MIDI. Today Web sound formats like MP3, RealAudio, and Windows Media Audio (WMA) carry the bulk of music transmitted over the Web; however, MIDI is still used to compose music.

The moral of this cautionary tale is that great ideas sometimes fail, especially if the details aren't worked out. Have a Plan B.

Choosing an audio tool

Audio tools are not too difficult to understand and use. However, the field of sound editing is a bit esoteric, with a vocabulary all its own. Music introduces its own perspective and lingo too. Picking an audio tool may be harder than using it.

Seek advice from an expert. That person might be in your own company, teach at a local college or trade school, or work for a commercial studio. Ask what features will be useful on your e-learning projects and what issues novices tend to overlook when choosing such tools.

What you need to know first

There are a couple of decisions you need to make before you begin evaluating audio tools. First, how much and what kind of audio will you need to create? Are you just adding narration? Do you need background music to set a mood? Must you provide a complete soundtrack, mixing music, narration, and sound effects? Knowing what you need to create helps you narrow the range of tools needed.

Second, will you reuse existing audio recordings? For instance, do you have audio tapes of your instructors teaching a class? Does your organization have royalty-free music or sound effects left over from other multimedia projects? If you need to reuse existing audio, look carefully at what file formats the different sound editing tools import.

Capabilities to consider

Here is a list of some of the most important capabilities you should consider when evaluating a tool.

▶ **Basic editing capabilities**. Does the tool provide the editing features you need, such as:

- Mixing tracks, for example voice and background
- Adding transitions and cross-fading
- Adjusting volume and normalizing to equalize volume levels
- Reducing pops, clicks, distortions, and other forms of noise
- Shifting pitch and filtering certain frequency ranges
- Shortening and lengthening
- Looping and repeating
- Synchronizing separate sounds
- Down-sampling (reducing detail)

▶ **Import formats**. Can the tool import common sound formats, such as MP3, WAV, AIFF, AU, SND, RealAudio, QuickTime, and Windows Media Audio? Can it import video formats that include sound, for example Windows Media Video, AVI, and MPEG? If you must edit

---

sound effects library

Unless you have a resident Foley artist who creates sound effects, you will probably need a collection of sound-effects. Such collections provide a variety of common realistic and cartoon sounds you can edit, combine, and loop to add variety and realism to your work. These libraries can be somewhat pricey, so check whether your candidate tools provide a selection of sound effects. Popular sound-effects libraries include:

The Hollywood Edge (hollywoodedge.com)

Soundeffects.shop (www.soundoftheweb.com)

Ultimate Sound Archive (advances.com)

existing audio, purchased clip media, or video files, pay particular attention to the file formats the tool can import.

▶ **Output formats**. Can the tool save sounds in a variety of formats such as: MP3, QuickTime, Flash, Windows Media Audio, and RealAudio? Can audio be optimized for the Web? If the audio will be used in another program, such as a course authoring program, can the audio tool save the sounds in a format your course authoring program can import?

▶ **Number of tracks**. Does the tool let you edit enough simultaneous tracks? You may frequently need to combine multiple sound clips, for example subject sound, narration, ambient noise, and background music. Some tools lack multiple tracks or do not have enough tracks to build complex sound scenes.

▶ **Direct audio recording**. Can you record sound directly into the program? This is almost a must-have feature. Unless you are having all narration recorded in a studio, you must have the ability to capture audio. You also may need to capture audio from audio tapes, videotapes, or CDs.

▶ **Edit sound for video**. For video formats, can the tool edit the sound without altering the video? Can it display video so sound editors can check synchronization? If your project includes a lot of video, you may need to edit and augment the soundtrack. You may also wish to extract the audio from a video file and use the sound by itself.

▶ **Component library**. Does the program let composers create reusable modules or loops that can be recombined and altered to produce a wide variety of musical passages or sound scenes?

▶ **Filters**. Does the tool include a wide collection of noise-reduction and special-effects filters? Do the filters have good presets that correspond to most common tasks? Filters can help you improve the quality of audio recorded under less than ideal conditions. There are filters to

---

Music library

If you need background music, you can either compose it yourself or take it from a library of available music passages. Music libraries may include whole compositions or just short passages. They come in a bewildering range of musical styles.

Before you buy a music library, decide how you will use music and what style is most appropriate. As you consider candidate products, pay careful attention to licensing and usage fees. Some are licensed per use and others are royalty-free.

Popular music libraries include:

▶ The Hollywood Edge (hollywoodedge.com)

▶ Loops for ACID (sonicfoundry.com/loop_libraries)

▶ Royalty Free Music (royaltyfreemusicproduction.com)

remove crackles and pops, eliminate hums, add echo and reverberation, and otherwise refine and enrich sound.

▶ **MIDI support**. Does the tool include a MIDI sequencer? Can it capture musical compositions from an electronic keyboard or other instrument with MIDI output? For many musicians, playing music on a MIDI keyboard is easier than entering the notes using musical notation or a piano roll format.

▶ **Musical notation**. Does the tool let composers create and edit in standard musical notation? Will it print out compositions in standard music format? Can it convert scanned sheet music to MIDI?

▶ **Customizable tools**. Does the audio editor let you save settings in equalizers and other internal tools? Can you easily reload these saved settings? Every recording location has a unique character. If you are going to record in the same location time after time, you will be more productive if you can save all your custom settings and reuse them.

▶ **Batch processing**. Does the tool help you "can" repetitive actions and apply them to a group of files? For instance, you may need to down-sample 100 audio files, applying the same settings to each file.

VIDEO TOOLS

When we think of video in e-learning we usually think of streaming images of realistic situations: an employee interview, a trusted advisor speaking to a group, or maybe a scene from the factory floor.

Sony's MovieShaker video editing application.

Here the video editor can import clips, sequence shots, add transitions between them, include titles and special effects, and save the results in a range of formats.

The term video, however, goes beyond what video is used to show. Video is also a catchall term for a collection of file formats. For instance, some graphics programs allow you to create simple animations and export them to QuickTime—a video format. You would still think of the content as animation but what you have is a video file in the Apple QuickTime format. So, for the purposes of discussing video tools, we are going to treat video as a collection of file formats rather than just moving pictures.

Video file formats

For e-learning, there are several popular file formats for video. Here's a list of the most common video file formats along with a brief description and a note on whether it is a streaming format.

Format	Description	Streams?
Audio Video Interleaved (AVI)	An early de facto Windows standard. Not designed for the Web. Can be played with various players.	No.
Motion Picture Experts Group (MPEG)	MPEG is both a compression algorithm and a file format. There are various subtypes including MPEG-1 (used for video on CD-ROMs), MPEG-2, MPEG-3, and so on. Can be played with various players.	No, but can be highly compressed.
QuickTime movie (MOV, QT)	Proprietary Apple format for video, audio, music, and other media. Can use a variety of compression algorithms to balance quality and file size. Common file format on the Macintosh. Can be played with various players.	Yes, when specifically processed to do so. Requires a media server.
RealVideo (RV)	A proprietary format from RealNetworks. Requires the RealOne media player.	Yes, but requires a media server.
Windows Media Video (WMV)	Proprietary Microsoft format. Part of Windows Media Technologies. Requires the Windows Media Player.	Yes, but requires a media server.

17

Media editors

Popular video tools

The more popular editing programs cover the spectrum—from mainstream desktop editing tools to high-end special-purpose editing systems. Each of the video tools we list here has its own native file format unique to that program. However, the extent to which each tool can import and export other video formats may prove crucial if you have legacy content you must edit and convert for use in your e-learning.

Product	Vendor	Web address	Price (in USD)	Operating System
Avid Xpress DV	Avid	avid.com	$1700	Macintosh, Windows
Final Cut	Apple Computer	apple.com	$1000	Macintosh
Movie Maker	Microsoft	microsoft.com	Free	Windows XP
MovieShaker	Sony	sony.com	Free	Windows
Pinnacle Studio	Pinnacle Systems	www.pinnaclesys.com	$100	Windows
Premiere	Adobe	www.adobe.com	$550	Windows, Macintosh
Strata DV	Strata	strata.com	$500	Macintosh
Vegas Video	Sonic Foundry	sonicfoundry.com	$300	Windows
VideoStudio	Ulead	ulead.com	$100	Windows

To find more tools, search the Web for "video edit tool" or similar phrases. Also check video magazines, such as Videomaker (videomaker.com), and stop by horton.com/tools to see if we have listed some more recent ones.

Choosing a video-editing program

As with other special-purpose media tools, enlist the aid of someone who works in the medium. They can help you translate your needs into features found in such products. Here are some issues you will need to consider when selecting a tool for authoring video.

What you need to know first

Before you pick a video tool, first decide what video file formats are needed for your e-learning. Will you be using video within other authoring programs, such as Flash, rather than as a standalone component? If so, your video tool need not create Web-ready formats such as MPEG or Windows Media format.

Second, if you are planning to re-purpose existing film or video, you need to know its current format. For example, is it video on VHS tape, digital video (DV) cassette, or BetaMax cassettes? Or is it film in 16- or 35-mm format? Most of the popular video tools can import digital video from a digital camcorder directly, using the computer's IEEE 1394 connector. However, not every tool can import analog video. If it can, it will probably require additional hardware installed in the computer. Capturing film requires very fancy film-to-video machines—or, if your standards are low enough, just pointing a camcorder at the screen while playing the film.

Capabilities to consider

Once you know what file formats you will be working with, there are additional capabilities to look for in video tools.

▶ **Import from devices**. Can the tool import video directly from a digital camcorder? Can it import analog video (assuming the correct hardware is installed)? If you are shooting new video for your project, it is probably enough that the tool can import digital video. If you are shooting with film or BetaMax, try to see if your videographers can dub the video to DV tape. Then all you need is a digital camcorder and an IEEE 1394 connection on your computer.

▶ **Import from file**. What file formats can the tool import? Can it open AVI, QuickTime, and MPEG files? The more formats a tool can import or open, the more flexibility you have in source material to edit.

▶ **Output formats**. Can the tool output video in common file formats, such as MPEG, Windows Media Video, RealVideo, and QuickTime? Can the tool save video in a compact file size ready for streaming? Can it write to DVD? The more output formats a tool supports, the more flexibility you have in your training delivery, whether it is over the Web, over the LAN, from CD-ROM or DVD, or by an instructor in a classroom.

▶ **Streaming**. Can the tool export video in streaming formats? Does the tool have streaming video presets for all major streaming formats, including Windows Media, RealMedia, and QuickTime? Can you override the presets? Can you output versions for different bandwidths at the same time? The more presets a tool has, the less time you will spend in trial-and-error testing of various combinations.

Conversely, you may need to specify parameters individually to meet specific project criteria. The ability to batch-save video for multiple bandwidths saves a lot of time.

▶ **Appropriate codecs**. Does the tool compress video so it can be played back with a readily available, nonproprietary codec? Some tools have codecs that allow you to save video in a highly compressed file, thereby saving disk space and download time. However, these special codecs may be proprietary. That means you need to supply this codec to your learners for them to view the video.

▶ **Basic editing functions**. Does the tool provide the most needed editing functions, such as:

- Cutting and pasting sequences
- Cropping areas of the frame
- Titles and credits
- Transitions
- Resizing sequences
- Overlaying one sequence on top of another
- Color, brightness, and contrast adjustments
- Synchronizing with sound

For most Web-based video, basic editing capabilities are adequate. If, however, the same video will be used on CD-ROMs or broadcast on television where higher quality and advanced effects are expected, you need to look for additional features that support the higher quality requirements.

▶ **Sound editing**. Can the tool adjust volume? Can it normalize, equalize, and mix sound? Can it apply noise-reduction filters? Can you import existing audio tracks? Audio is an important part of a video. The ability to augment and enhance a video's soundtrack is essential.

▶ **Special-effects filters**. What visual, audio, and special-effects filters are available for the tool? Does it support third-party plug-ins? Several of the popular video tools extend their capabilities through the use of plug-ins and filters. For instance, VegasVideo allows you to use Sound Forge's Noise Reduction filters on the audio track. Premiere allows you to use some of the filters from Photoshop to create special effects. Avid has several add-on packages of special effect plug-ins.

▶ **Multiple tracks**. Can the tool simultaneously edit an adequate number of channels of video, graphics, and sound? The more sophisticated your project, the more editing tracks you need. For instance, you may need stereo audio channels, two to three video channels to facilitate intercutting among multiple clips, and several graphics channels for titles and visual filters.

▶ **Rendering on-the-fly**. Does the tool allow you to immediately view effects, transitions, titles, and transparency without waiting for the video to render?

VIRTUAL WORLD TOOLS

Virtual world tools create 3-D scenes that learners can view, navigate, and manipulate using a special 3-D viewer. These tools typically use Virtual Reality Modeling Language (VRML) to represent 3-D objects and their relationships.

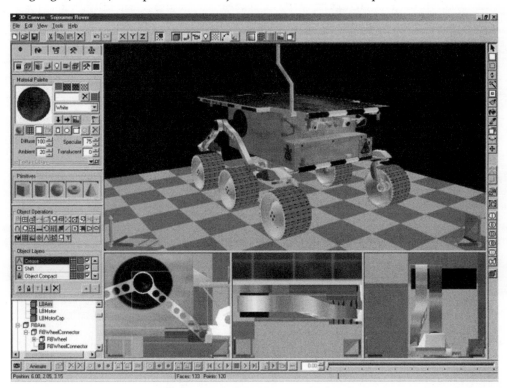

3D Canvas Pro by Amabilis (amabilis.com)

Virtual world tools represent 3-D environments as a scene graph, a tree structure that specifies the environment in terms of groups of groups of groups of objects. Groups like this are called nodes, and may move as a unit and have other characteristics in common, such as color or texture.

Virtual world models tend to be complex. Files may be large. They typically require a fast processor and display, to render quickly and enable smooth movement through the world.

Uses of virtual worlds in e-learning

You have probably encountered virtual worlds in popular computer games and wondered if you could use something similar in your e-learning efforts. True, you are not in the business of reducing scaly aliens to protoplasmic mist, but you may want to create activities that allow learners to move through 3-D environments or manipulate simulated physical objects. Here are some educational uses for virtual worlds:

▶ Inspect 3-D objects, such as crystals, machines, and manufactured products. The items examined may be ones that are too small, difficult, or dangerous to examine directly. They may be objects that are only planned and do not exist yet.

▶ Explore environments impossible to visit in real life, such as other planets, atoms, the bottom of the ocean, or the interior of a nuclear power plant reactor.

▶ Explore physical environments by reconstructing archaeological sites, rehearsing evacuations of buildings, driving big trucks through city streets, or previewing architectural plans.

▶ Practice complex and dangerous activities such as planning a military assault, training workers to use hyper-expensive manufacturing systems, and docking the Space Shuttle.

▶ Show complex physical and logical relationships such as multivariate data as shaded 3-D shapes, or statistical relationships as clouds of data points.

Popular virtual world tools

Here is a selection of tools for creating virtual worlds. Some are simple and others are complex. Some are expensive and others free. Some are for media authors and others for programmers.

Product	Vendor	Web address	Price (in USD)
3D Canvas Pro	Amabilis	amabilis.com	Free
AC3D	AC3D	ac3d.org	$40
Art of Illusion	Art of Illusion	artofillusion.org	Free
Cosmo Worlds	Silicon Graphics	sgi.com	Free

Product	Vendor	Web address	Price (in USD)
Dune	SourceForge	dune.sourceforge.net	Free
Internet Space Builder	Parallel Graphics	www.parallelgraphics.com	$80
mjbWorld	martinb.com	martinb.com	Free
SiteSculptor	Sculptware	sculptware.com	$1500
Spazz3D	Virtock Technologies	spazz3d.com	$100
trueSpace	Caligari	caligari.com	$200
VrmlPad	Parallel Graphics	www.parallelgraphics.com	$150

These are just a few of the many virtual world editors available. Some virtual world tools are aimed at programmers developing 3-D applications. They consist primarily of libraries of functions that can be used to create virtual worlds on-the-fly. For more about virtual worlds, search for "VRML editor," "virtual worlds," or similar phrases.

Alternatives to virtual world tools

If you only need to show a 3-D scene without letting the learner choose how to move through it, consider using a 3-D animation tool instead of a virtual world tool. Virtual world tools are necessary only if you want to let learners choose the path and pace of movement through the 3-D scene or manipulate objects in more than two dimensions.

If you are creating virtual worlds, consider using conventional computer-aided design (CAD) tools available in your organization. Tools like AutoCAD (autodesk.com) and Strata 3Dpro (strata.com) can be used to create VRML models as well as other 3-D representations of objects and scenes.

Choosing a virtual world tool

Virtual world tools vary considerably in the capabilities they provide and even in their definition of what constitutes a virtual world. Picking a tool requires finding a tool that lets you realize your vision for using virtual worlds in e-learning.

What you need to know first

First you need to understand what a virtual world is. No description will suffice. You just have to get in their and navigate. If you haven't explored such worlds, take a few hours to do so. (Search for "virtual worlds" in your favorite search engine.) Then download a free trial of a virtual world tool and try building a simple virtual world for yourself. Translating your 3-D visions into 3-D models takes some practice. Get a feel for what designers experience when they use such tools.

Will your virtual worlds include objects for which you have 3-D models or 2-D drawings? In what file formats can you save these source materials? You'll want to select a virtual world tool that can import these formats.

How else can you use the 3-D shapes you create for virtual worlds? Do you need to show them in static pictures and animations?

Capabilities to consider

Virtual worlds are rich, complex environments; creating them is difficult. It goes far beyond drawing or painting what a scene looks like. It requires specifying precisely the shapes, textures, colors, locations, and orientations of objects. It also requires specifying relationships among objects, such as how they move relative to one another, and how learners can interact with the objects.

▶ **Standards supported**. Does the tool create worlds using features of VRML 1.0 or 2.0? Or does it provide a subset of the features of one level or other?

▶ **3-D modeling functions**. Does the tool provide basic shapes, lights, and cameras for creating environments? Does it include a library of prebuilt objects?

▶ **Texture mapping**. Can objects be skinned with textures imported from GIF, JPEG, and other file formats?

▶ **Importing**. Can the tool import VRML 1.0, VRML 2.0, CAD files such as AutoCAD and Strata3D, TrueType fonts, and other 2-D and 3-D formats?

▶ **Animation**. Can models be used to create animation sequences as well as explorable worlds?

▶ **Views**. Does the tool let you view the scene you are creating from enough different directions? Does it provide standard views (front, top, and side) as well as let you define, store, and recall custom views?

▶ **Edit nodes**. Can you select a node on the scene graph or in the scene? Can you easily change properties of nodes? Can you copy and paste nodes? Can you save a node and its entire branch of the scene graph?

▶ **Manipulation**. Can you easily position, orient, move, scale, and transform objects?

▶ **Output**. Can the tool produce both VRML 1.0 and 2.0 formats? Does viewing the model require a special proprietary viewer or only a standards-compliant VRML viewer?

MEDIA UTILITIES

In addition to the general-purpose media tools we have talked about so far, there are special-purpose media tools for creating very specific media components or for use in particular subjects, such as learning to operate computer systems. These tools can round out your media editing toolbox.

Screen capture utilities

Screen capture utilities allow you to capture a part of your computer desktop as a static graphic. Typically, such tools allow you to capture the whole screen, a window, a region, or a scrolling page. You can perform some basic editing functions to crop, resize, change resolution, and recolor. Some let you add annotations and additional graphics. The resulting files can be saved in a variety of Web-ready and non-Web-ready formats.

Popular screen-capture tools include:

Product	Vendor	Web address	Price (USD)	Operating System
FullShot	Inbit	inbit.com	$50	Windows
HyperSnap-DX	Hyperionics	hyperionics.com	$40	Windows
SnagIt	TechSmith	www.techsmith.com	$40	Windows
Snapz Pro X	Ambrosia Software	ambrosiasw.com	$50	Macintosh

To find more, search the Web for "screen capture software" or "screen capture tool." Also check horton.com/tools for any additional tools listed there.

Screen recording utilities

Screen recorders do more than capture static screens. They capture a sequence of actions, for example, performing a task on the computer. Though capabilities vary, the best of these tools let you record video files of a screen, window, or region; add text, drawings, and cursor highlights; narrate during or after screen recording; splice videos and remove unwanted frames; add transitions and still images; and then export the movie as Real, Windows Media, QuickTime, AVI, or a self-running demo.

Product	Vendor	Web address	Price (USD)	Operating System
Camtasia	TechSmith	www.techsmith.com	$150	Windows
HyperCam	Hyperionics	hyperionics.com	$30	Windows
Snapz Pro X	Ambrosia Software	ambrosiasw.com	$50	Macintosh
Windows Media Encoder	Microsoft	microsoft.com	free	Windows

Software simulation tools

Software simulation tools go beyond recording screen actions to make them interactive. These tools create simulations of computer operations so learners can not only watch them but practice them as well. Along the way, learners receive hints and feedback on their actions. Some screen tutorial tools even record and report scores, storing the tutorials as Java, Flash, or some other format that can be included in e-learning lessons.

Product	Vendor	Web address	Price (USD)	Operating System
On Demand	Global Knowledge	kp.globalknowledge.com	--	Windows
RADAuthor	Global Competency Systems	radauthor.com	About $2500	Windows
RapidBuilder	XStream Software	xstreamsoftware.com	About $3000	Windows, Linux
RoboDemo	eHelp	ehelp.com	$900	Windows

Product	Vendor	Web address	Price (USD)	Operating System
TurboDemo	Bernard D&G	turbodemo.com	$900	Windows
ViewletBuilder	Qarbon	qarbon.com	$900	Windows
Virtual Professor	Productivity Center	prodctr.com	NA	Windows

You can also use more generic tools for creating a variety of simulations. One such tool is AgentSheets (agentsheets.com). You can also create simulations in Flash (See flashsim.com for examples.) or in other tools for creating multimedia, Web sites, and e-learning content.

TO FIND MORE MEDIA EDITING TOOLS

Online shopping sites (such as amazon.com, microwarehouse.com, etc.) are a good place to start when looking for a list of tools to consider. Search for the tools based on the media they create. Another way to find candidate products is to type a query into the address bar of your browser like "music composition software."

After preparing a list of candidates, go to the vendors' Web sites to get more detailed specifications and perhaps download an evaluation copy. After trying the tool yourself, you may want to check on the Web for product reviews. Simply type in the name of the tool and "review" into the address bar of your browser or in the search box of your favorite search engine.

WHAT NOW?

To put the ideas of this chapter into action, you need to make decisions and take actions. Here are some recommendations for how to proceed.

If you ...	Then ...
Are still designing your e-learning	▶ List all the media you need. Investigate what media learners can really play. Decide what you really need. ▶ Inventory assets you will reuse. Note the variety of file formats you will need to import into tools.

If you ...	Then ...
Are at the point of picking tools	▶ First decide what types of media editors you need for your media. Will one general-purpose multimedia tool suffice, or will you need separate tools for graphics, audio, video, and animations? ▶ If you need separate tools, pick a suite of tools that work together in your workflow plan. ▶ Test candidate tools with your source materials and workflow.
Have already picked your media editing tools	▶ Supplement your tools with clip art and extensions. ▶ Train your staff to use the full range of capabilities provided by your tools. Challenge them to find instructional uses for these capabilities. ▶ Locate newsgroups and other sources of community and support for users of these tools.

Another way to create content is to convert existing documents, presentations, spreadsheets, and other content. Content converters, which are covered in the next chapter, make reusing such materials quick and easy.

18 Content converters

If you have unlimited time, you can create all your e-learning content from scratch. If you have unlimited money, you can purchase content from others. If you don't have unlimited time or money, you may need to reuse existing presentations, textbooks, graphics, spreadsheets, and documents. Content converters can help.

Conversion tools transform one file format to another. Producers of e-learning use them to convert conventional formats used in day-to-day work into formats that can easily be shared and displayed over the Web. In addition to transforming one file format to another, converters are helpful when you need to maintain material in two or more forms. For example, you need to maintain presentations in PowerPoint slides for use in classroom training as well as in Flash or Java for use in e-learning. Converters are also helpful in making paper documents more widely available. By converting them to Web-ready formats, these paper documents can be posted on Web servers from which anyone on the network can download and read them.

In our tools framework, converters reside firmly in the Create column, spanning the Media, Page, and Lesson rows. Converters creep into the Course row for content that goes beyond the scope of a lesson. Once, converted, content may be placed on a Web server for viewing in a browser or a media player for the converted format.

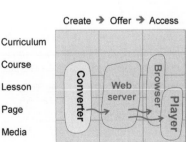

385

There are converters for various purposes; however, we are going to concentrate on products that convert raw materials likely to be used by e-learning authors.

HOW CONTENT CONVERTERS WORK

With converter tools, you author content in your familiar word processor, spreadsheet, presentation program, drawing program, or other tool.

You save the file as usual in the tool's regular file format (1a). Then you run the converter program to convert the native file to a Web-ready format such as HTML, Java, Acrobat PDF, or Flash (2). Or, if the converter is built into your authoring program, you can save directly as one of these Web-ready formats (1b).

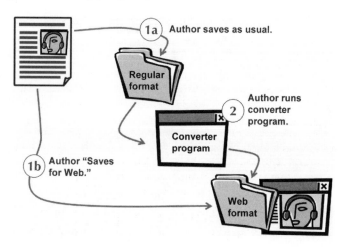

To see what the conversion process entails, we will demonstrate conversion of a PowerPoint 2002 slide presentation to a Java applet for inclusion on a Web page. The conversion tool is Impatica (impatica.com).

QUICK TOUR OF A CONVERTER TOOL

To see what the conversion process entails, we will demonstrate conversion of a PowerPoint 2002 slide presentation to a Java applet for inclusion on a Web page. The conversion tool is Impatica (impatica.com).

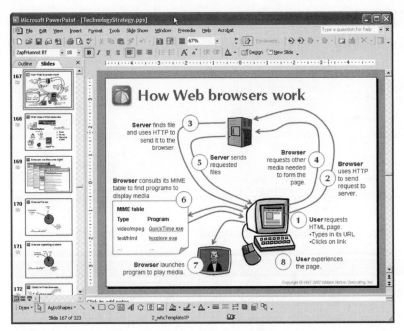

Here is a slide in the presentation. The slide is richly animated with wipes, fades, and other transitions. (And, yes, it is the basis of one of the pictures in this book.)

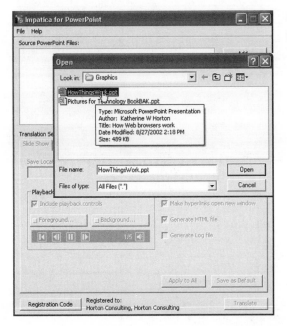

To convert the file, we started Impatica and told it to convert the file from PowerPoint to Java.

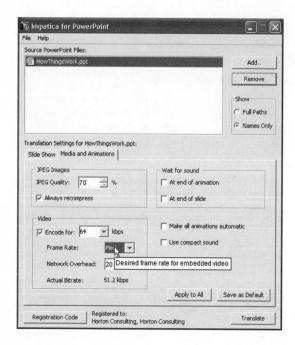

Next we set options for the conversion process and for the type of result we wanted. We then save the presentation as Java.

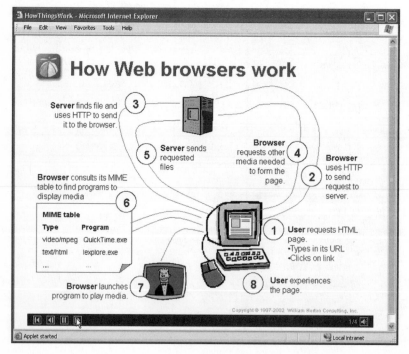

Here is the result. It can be displayed in 99% of available browsers. It is similar to the original but not a perfect match. Such differences are typical with PowerPoint conversion tools.

CONVERTERS FOR POWERPOINT

Throughout corporations and schools, countless nuggets of information, advice, and wisdom reside on tens of millions of PowerPoint slides. Making these slides more widely available has the potential to add great intellectual value. Fortunately, there are resources to help convert PowerPoint slides to Web-ready formats.

Save as Web Page command

The simplest conversion features are built into PowerPoint itself. The Save as Web Page command can convert slides to HTML. This method preserves all animations and audio, both slide-level and layer-level, plus links added to various slide elements. Such conversions, however, can only be viewed using Internet Explorer version 4 or later.

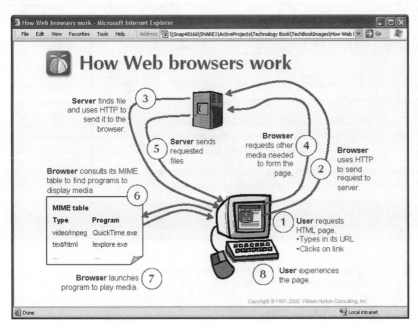

Here's what the slide in the tour above looks like when saved as a Web page in PowerPoint.

Some lines and arrows have been converted to filled shapes. Some of the graphics appear rougher.

18

Content converters

Record and Save a Broadcast command

A second built-in conversion feature is PowerPoint's Record and Save a Broadcast. With this command, you can record a narrated presentation that learners can access and play back over the Web. A wizard guides you in recording a presentation that can be exported in Windows Media Video format for immediate broadcast or saved to a server for viewing on demand. Both approaches require Windows Media Player to view the presentation. The recorded broadcast maintains the layer animation and the layer-level audio. It also lets you add narration as you record the presentation.

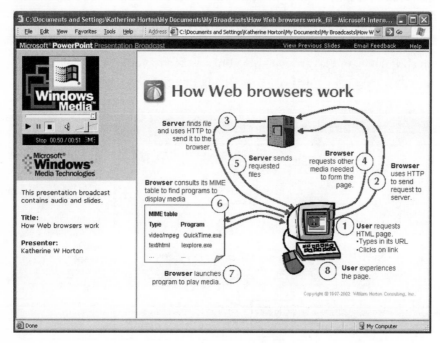

Here's what the slide in the above tour looks like when recorded as a broadcast.

Some lines and edges appear rougher.

If you are thinking about using the Record and Save a Broadcast feature, consider using Microsoft Producer for PowerPoint. It adds capabilities and lets you incorporate additional media in your presentation.

Impatica

By Impatica	**impatica.com**	**About $500 USD**

Impatica converts a narrated PowerPoint presentation to a Java applet. It converts many of the animation effects found in PowerPoint 2000 as well as sounds attached to layers or to the slide as a whole. It also converts videos embedded within the slide.

Impatica was the tool used in the conversion tour earlier in this chapter. Here again is what the slide in the quick tour above looks like when converted by Impatica.

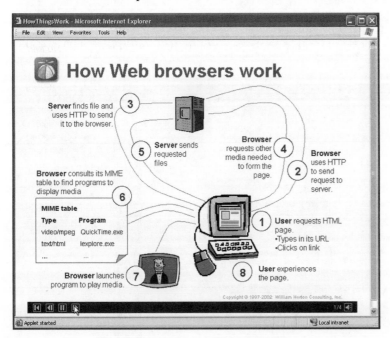

Arrowheads have vanished, some of the graphics appear rougher, the font face has reverted to Arial, and some animation effects are missing.

Presedia Producer

By Presedia	presedia.com	Contact Presedia for price

Presedia Producer is a service that can convert PowerPoint Presentations to Macromedia Flash. You record your narration for each slide using the Presedia add-in to PowerPoint. Using Presedia, you can record narration directly into a slide, import a narration file recorded elsewhere, edit audio once it has been added to the slide, time narration-to-animation sequence, and finally upload the PowerPoint presentation to the Presedia server for conversion.

Once converted, the presentation can reside on the Presedia server or be downloaded to your own server. Presedia accurately converts most of the PowerPoint 2000 custom animation effects.

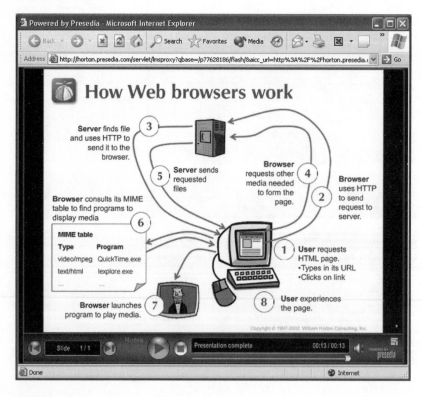

Here's what the slide in the above tour looks like when converted by Presedia.

Visual fidelity is good, but not all of the PowerPoint animation effects are converted.

More PowerPoint converters

Depending on your needs, you have additional choices for converting PowerPoint slides. For simple slides, you may want to use PowerCONVERTER (About $300, presentationpro.com). If you want to convert a presentation to a standard IMS package, use Microsoft's LRN Toolkit (microsoft.com/elearn). For more, check horton.com/tools.

Other PowerPoint converters, such as HotFoot by Interactive Digital Technologies (digitallava.com), are offered as part of a larger product or system. In addition, some LMSs, LCMSs, and virtual-school systems can import PowerPoint slides.

If none of these converters works for your slides, consider letting learners view the slides directly. Learners who have Microsoft Office (and a fast network connection) can view PowerPoint slides right in their Internet Explorer browser. Those who lack Microsoft Office can download a PowerPoint viewer from microsoft.com,

Issues to consider in choosing a PowerPoint converter

Here are the main things to look for when choosing a method or product to convert PowerPoint slides to a Web-ready format.

▶ **PowerPoint features preserved**. Does the conversion preserve layer effects, especially transitions and animations? Are the sounds that are attached to layers converted as well? How about artwork drawn on the slide or pasted in from another application? This capability is especially important if you plan to use the same slides in the classroom as well as online. The compromises required for a smooth conversion may be unacceptable for the classroom.

▶ **Destination file formats**. Does the tool produce HTML, Java, Flash, Windows Media, Real Media, or a combination of these formats? Are these formats ones that your learners can display? You may need to pick your converter to suit the media players your learners already have.

▶ **Narration synchronized with animation**. Some converters do not support tight synchronization between layer animations—including bullet lists—and audio. If your presentations use a lot of animation and transition effects to explain a concept, make sure the converter supports your hard work.

▶ **Product or service**. Is the converter offered as a product or a service? Who owns the tool? Do you subscribe to a service or pay a fee per presentation or per slide that is converted?

▶ **Features added**. Can the tool add any features not found in the native PowerPoint slides, such as tests or a table of contents? Some converters allow you to add multiple choice and polling questions that can report back to certain LMSs. Some tools create a table of contents of the slides so that learners can more easily navigate the presentation.

CONVERTERS FOR MICROSOFT WORD

Billions of documents already exist in word processing files. Converting these to Web pages should just be a button click by now. After all, most word processors, such as Microsoft Word, have a Save as HTML command. Issue settled? Not quite.

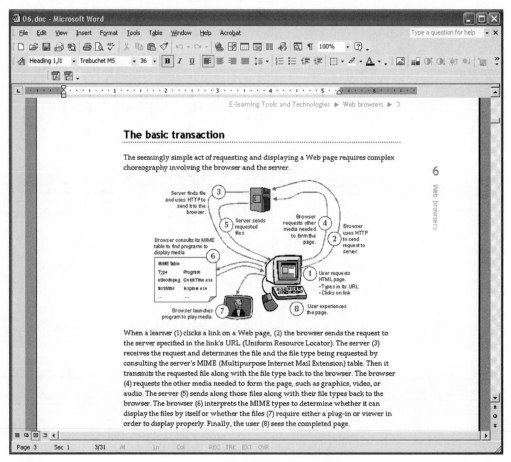

Document as it appears in Microsoft Word

Save as Web Page command

Microsoft Word can save documents as HTML. Microsoft Word 2002's Save as Web Page command can save Word files as HTML targeted to 3.0 and 4.0 browsers as well as files targeted to take advantage of the advanced features of Internet Explorer 5 or later.

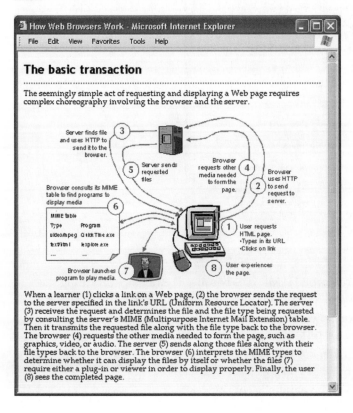

Here is a page from this book saved as HTML using Word's Save As Web Page command and viewed in Internet Explorer 6.

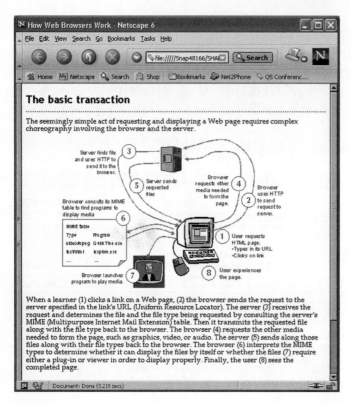

This is the same converted file viewed in Netscape 6.2.

Microsoft Word 2002 produces large HTML files because it embeds everything that Word needs to display the file in addition to what the browser needs to display the file. The files are not only large, they are complex and tricky to edit. Also, Word allows little control over the final format of the HTML file. For instance, you cannot specify page breaks, nor can you specify how certain Word-specific styles will be handled. To ensure that the resulting file is viewable in Netscape, you must specify Netscape as one of the target browsers in the Save As Web Page dialog box.

 To purify the HTML saved by Word, import the HTML file into Dreamweaver and apply Dreamweaver's Clean Up Word HTML command.

If you are using Word 2000, you can improve your conversions to HTML by using a free add-in from Microsoft called Export to Compact HTML. Files saved using this command omit the unnecessary Microsoft-specific code and are a bit easier for Netscape browsers to display. This add-in can also be run by itself to convert several files at once.

WordToWeb

....

By Solutionsoft   **solutionsoft.com**   **About $300 USD**

The built-in features of Microsoft Word are not the only way to get Word documents to the Web. There are some third-party converters. They include WordToWeb, which can automatically break a long document into separate pages based on the headings in the document. It links the pages together with graphical or text-based navigation links so the learner can page through the text. It can also create an online table of contents and convert a Word index into an online equivalent. WordToWeb runs on Windows.

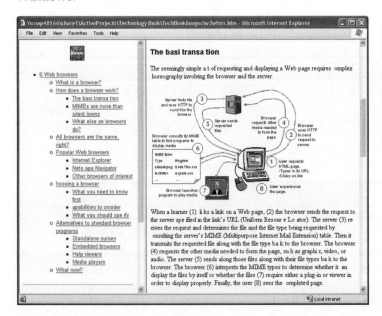

Here is a chapter of this book converted to HTML using WordToWeb.

The missing letters are not a defect. The evaluation version of this product, which we used for this example, drops out random letters.

HTML Transit

....

By Avanstar   **avantstar.com**   **About $5000 USD**

HTML Transit handles large-scale conversions and automatic updates of converted documents. You can specify source locations for standard business documents and HTML Transit will publish content from those source documents into HTML or XML directly to a Web server. When source content changes, HTML Transit updates the documents on the Web server. HTML Transit provides a great deal of control over the appearance and behavior of the resulting Web-ready files. HTML Transit is available for Windows.

More conversion tools and alternatives

Other tools for converting Microsoft Word documents to HTML are available. Here are a few more for you to consider.

Product	Web address	Price (in USD)
Filtrix	blueberry.com	About $190
Logictran RTF Converter	logitran.com	About $70
WordConverterExe	softinterface.com	About $470

For additional tools, search the Web for "convert Microsoft Word HTML" or something similar.

If none of the conversion tools do an adequate job for your documents, you have two more options. You can use Adobe Acrobat to give learners a facsimile of the document. Or let learners view Word documents directly. Learners require Internet Explorer and either Microsoft Office or a viewer for Microsoft Word, both available from Microsoft.

Issues to consider in choosing a converter for Word

Here are the main things to look for when choosing a method or product to convert Word documents to a Web-ready format.

▶ **Can you break up a long document?** Long documents with embedded graphics are large. If you are converting such a document, you need to look for a converter that allows you to break up the file into smaller pages.

▶ **Does the converter only work for recent browsers**? Or, can it be used with a wide variety of browser brands and versions? Not all conversions methods provide satisfactory results for older versions of Netscape or other browsers.

▶ **Can you control the layout of the HTML files**? If your conversion method does not maintain your document's layout, you need to map document styles to HTML styles to ensure a predictable result.

▶ **What conversion activities can be automated**? For instance, can you automate the conversion of hundreds or thousands of separate documents? Can you automatically reconvert documents that have been edited? If your library is large or if your documents change frequently, you need a tool that allows unattended batch processing.

▶ **Is the tool free, or does it have a substantial cost**? As with any tool, you must consider the total cost of the tool, including all fees and your time learning and using it.

ACROBAT: GENERAL-PURPOSE DOCUMENT CONVERTER

By Adobe	www.adobe.com	About $250 USD

For other document formats, you can use Adobe Acrobat to convert word processing documents, spreadsheets, slide handouts, drawings, and other images. In fact, the installation of Adobe Acrobat includes a print driver called Acrobat PDFWriter that appears to be another printer to your regular authoring programs.

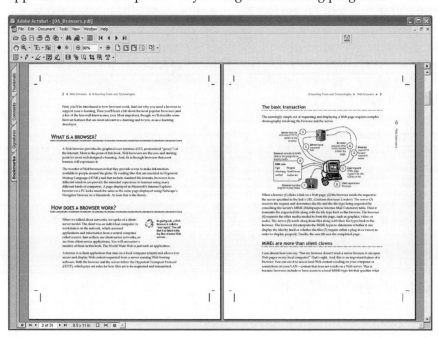

Here is an example of a draft of this book as Acrobat PDF.

The resulting document is almost a perfect visual replica of the same document printed to paper. Some minor differences may crop up, for example if the learner does not have the same fonts as the author, but these differences seldom render the document unreadable.

To view the document, consumers must have the free Acrobat Viewer, which is available from the Adobe Web site. To create Acrobat PDF documents, authors must purchase the publishing tools from Adobe. These tools are available for both Windows and Macintosh.

In addition to converting materials to a Web-ready format, Acrobat allows authors to add features, such as a hyperlinked menu and bookmarks, thumbnail images of pages, and reading trails through complex layouts. Authors can also add multimedia elements, such as narration and video clips.

FILE CONVERTERS AND BATCH PROCESSORS

Often when you are working with legacy content you need to convert or process multiple media files.

One of the most popular programs in this area is DeBabelizer from Equilibrium (equilibrium.com). It is like a Swiss Army knife. It is a multifunction tool that batch-processes bitmap graphics, bitmap animations, and video. Using its macro language, you can automate actions like cropping and resaving video, remapping colors of all the graphics in a folder, converting one file format to another, and so on. DeBabelizer costs about $700 and is available for both Windows and Macintosh. If your needs are more modest, then Adobe Photoshop (mentioned earlier) can automate editing actions and batch process directories of graphics.

There is not a similar all-purpose tool for vector media files. You can use Deneba's Canvas (deneba.com) to open a large variety of vector file formats and export them to another format.

For batch processing and converting audio files, Sonic Foundry's Batch Converter (sonicfoundry.com) is a valuable tool. You can chain together filters and actions from a list of common actions and apply them to a particular files or directories of files.

ALTERNATIVES TO CONVERTERS

Instead of converting documents and other files, you can give learners viewers for the original formats. Viewers are available for most major computer applications especially ones that do not save as HTML or other Web formats. Viewers are available for Microsoft Office formats. In addition, learners who have Internet Explorer and Microsoft Office on their computers can view Office documents directly in the browser.

WHAT NOW?

To put the ideas of this chapter into action, you need to make decisions and take actions. Here are some recommendations for how to proceed.

If you ...	Then ...
Are still designing your e-learning	List all the legacy content that might be useful in e-learning. Identify its current format and the format that will make it most useful for e-learning.
Have files to convert	First try the conversion features of your current tools. Then get trial copies of candidate tools that convert from your source format to your destination format. Try to convert your most complex example. Examine and test the results thoroughly. What compromises can you—or must you— make?
Have already picked conversion tools	Fine-tune your conversion process. Document which options and processes work for which types of files. For example: "Jan's slides have sound on layers, so select the Convert Layer Sound option."
Need to convert large numbers of files	Look for tools that convert batches of files or that have a built-in programming or macro language.

18

Content converters

Picking tools and technologies

Picking e-learning tools and technologies is one of the most critical and difficult decisions on a project. Tools are expensive, difficult to fathom, and constantly evolving. The process of picking tools can become more reliable and accurate by adopting sound strategies and methods. This section shows how to decide the kinds of tools and technologies that best fit your purpose, and then how to identify and select specific tools. The goal is an objective, comprehensive, systematic, fair, and methodical process of picking tools.

Picking a tool is primarily a filtering process. You start with many possible choices and narrow them down to the one that best meets your needs.

First, design a few knowledge products. By design, we do not mean build them, but specify them—on paper if necessary. Second, ask yourself how you want to deliver these knowledge products two years hence. Third, select tools that best realize your vision. Consider issues of capability, quality, and economy.

Keep in mind that technology moves rapidly. Don't base your decision on what's easy today. Anticipate advances that may occur by the time you completely deploy the project. Conversely, technology advances so erratically that projecting more than a couple of years ahead can be dangerous.

This section contains three chapters to help you select tools in a systematic and rational way. They cover:

▶ Strategies for picking technologies that suggests ways that organizations can acquire the tools and technologies they need to deploy e-learning (chapter 19)

▶ The process of picking tools that guides you in identifying candidate products, evaluating them, and selecting a specific product (chapter 20)

▶ General criteria for picking tools that offers a checklist of characteristics desirable in most of the e-learning tools you need (chapter 21)

This section will ensure that your choices are informed ones and that you can explain and defend them later.

19 Strategies for picking technologies

With so many categories of tools and so many choices in each category, you need a strategy to guide your choices. A strategy cannot pick a particular brand of tool. It can, however, help you filter the list of available tools and ensure your choices are informed and consistent.

Don't have an overall management strategy for e-learning? May I recommend another book by one of the authors of this book other than me? It is *Leading E-learning* and is available from its publisher, ASTD (astd.org), or from horton.com.

This section will help you develop a coherent strategy for selecting technologies and tools.

OVERVIEW OF A STRATEGY

To pick tools and technologies wisely, your organization needs a systematic process to identify, acquire, and implement specific products—a strategy that can be used to select tools and technologies consistently across the enterprise.

This chapter presents a strategy for picking tools. Use it as the basis for your own strategy. This strategy articulates the actions and decisions needed for acquiring tools. In this chapter we discuss

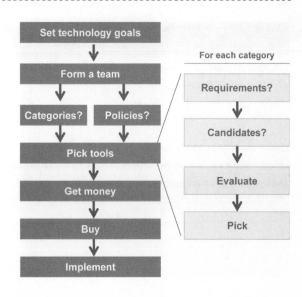

each of these actions and decisions in detail. The actions and decisions expanding from the *Pick tools* box in the diagram are covered in chapter 20.

The sequence shown here indicates, in general, when a step is completed—not when it starts. For instance, you need to begin thinking about implementation long before you buy anything. That's our subtle way of telling you to read this entire chapter before you begin putting the strategy into action.

The first step in our suggested strategy is to *Set technology goals*. What must the technology do for your organization's e-learning efforts? With broad goals defined, you will probably need to *Form a team*, task force, working group, or (yipes) committee to advise, discuss, and help make decisions. The next two steps usually proceed in parallel. In one step, you define the specific *Categories* of products you need, for example a learning management system, a course authoring tool, and specific media editors. In a parallel step, you set *Policies* for the kinds of companies and products most compatible with your organization and its goals. The next step, *Pick tools*, is repeated for each category of tool you need. Once you pick tools, you must compile a budget and *Get the money* to *Buy* them. Buying tools involves finding the best vendor and negotiating the best deal. The final step, *Implement*, is one that is often forgotten—at least the first time around.

> **Do you really need a strategy?**
>
> The word strategy resonates with undertones of bureaucracy, paperwork, and endless committee meetings. It is natural to question whether you need a technology strategy as such. Before you skip this chapter entirely, take a few minutes to consider whether you need a strategy.
>
> You probably do not need a strategy if you are only purchasing a few copies of a few inexpensive tools. Instead, follow the advice in chapter 20 on how to select individual tools.
>
> If you have an overall strategy for managing the move to e-learning, you may already have a strategy for acquiring needed technology. Just skim this chapter to see if the ideas suggested here can be incorporated into your overall strategy.

This strategy is quite flexible. Take the time to adapt it to your organization and its unique way of doing business. The rest of this chapter goes into detail about each of the steps of this strategy.

SET YOUR TECHNOLOGY GOALS

To set your strategy for acquiring and using technology, you need to conduct some self-analysis. You need to examine your organization's goals and culture and what they imply about the tools and technologies that best suit your organization's capabilities and style of doing business.

Consider organizational goals

In setting your strategy, you must consider your organization's reasons for investing in technology. We recommend you consider three levels: enterprise goals, performance goals, and learning goals. Think of each level as a cascade of ever more specific objectives.

Enterprise goals

The enterprise goals of an organization concern its ability to carry out its chartered mission. These goals are often expressed in monetary terms but not necessarily as profit. Even public institutions and nonprofit organizations have business goals though they may call them "economic goals" or "institutional objectives." Here are some examples of business goals.

▶ Increase profit from sales by 20% over the next quarter

▶ Increase student enrollment by 30% without any new construction

▶ Integrate employees of a newly acquired subsidiary into the overall enterprise

Business goals are the ultimate reason for acquiring technology. They tell you whether the tools are an investment, an asset, or an expense.

Performance goals

Performance goals state who must do what to achieve the enterprise goals. Performance goals generally specify actions. These actions may require learning and technology. Examples of performance goals include:

▶ Double sales of high-margin products by the end of the next quarter

▶ Increase enrollment in online degree programs to 4000 students

▶ Achieve transfer of loyalty by employees of acquired subsidiaries to the new parent organization

Performance goals may be accomplished by learning—hence the need for e-learning technology—or by other means. You can better justify technology by showing how it contributes in multiple ways to accomplishing performance goals.

Learning goals

Learning goals specify who must learn what to accomplish the performance goals. Examples of learning goals include:

▶ Sales representatives will be able to convince customers to switch to high-margin products

▶ Students in online degree programs will learn as effectively as those in conventional programs

▶ Employees from subsidiaries will subscribe to values of the parent organization and feel full membership in it

Learning goals are the most direct impetus for e-learning technology; however, they alone are not always sufficient to justify such large purchases.

Goals are often vague and open-ended. To guide technology purchases, goals must be translated into more specific strategies, policies, and requirements. The translation may be difficult and inexact, but never let your decision-making process stray from the goals behind it.

Consider organizational culture

If you think organizational goals are vague and hard to pin down, try scouting out your organization's culture. Culture is seldom written down. Culture is not found in the grand pronouncements about treasuring diversity found in annual reports or on yellowing posters peeling off cafeteria walls. It is in the assumptions, biases, and predilections that subtly guide day-to-day decisions throughout the organization. Culture is not something stated by the CEO on CNBC or in the *Wall Street Journal*. Culture concerns the unconscious values as actually practiced by everybody in the organization.

These values affect how the organization does business and how it best uses technology. What are some of these values that make up an organizational culture?

▶ **Mission**. How does the organization see its role? Although universities, law firms, and telecoms have a common economic basis, they define their missions very differently. Does you organization aim for social good, for profit, for development of people, or for advancement of technology? An organization whose mission is social good may want to consider the social effects of its purchasing decisions, whereas a for-profit organization may want the best product at the best price.

▶ **Obligations to stakeholders**. What does the organization believe it owes its owners, employees, customers, partners, and community? An organization that values internal talent may want to bring technology in-house to upgrade skills of employees. A public university sensitive to the concerns of taxpayers may seek the most economical solution it can find.

▶ **Skills valued**. What kinds of expertise does the organization treasure? What skills lead to rapid promotion and inclusion in decision-making? What are the skills that got top executives where they are today? Your choices of technology and how it is deployed must be compatible with the skills possessed and valued by the organization. For example, an organization that views IT as core skills will be more receptive to bringing technology in-house. An organization that values general business management skills may prefer to supervise external contractors and consultants.

▶ **Self-reliance**. Is the organization a do-it-yourself or farm-it-out organization? Bill once worked for a computer company that had its own trucking, rental car, and executive housing departments. We have worked for other companies with a skeleton staff of managers who subcontract everything.

▶ **Secrecy**. Does the culture encourage sharing knowledge, or does it enforce a need-to-know policy? Does the organization feel obligated to protect secret, confidential, or proprietary information? Medical facilities, military installations, legal firms, and research laboratories may demand technologies with proven security features. More open organizations may require easy-to-use collaboration tools.

▶ **Innovation**. Does the organization want to be seen as an innovator? Does it reward risk-takers and tolerate eccentric behavior? Is creativity more important than efficiency? Or would the organization rather be perceived as stable and dependable? Innovative organizations are more likely to welcome risky new technology.

▶ **Growth**. Does the organization want to grow rapidly in size? Or would it rather grow slowly? Does its reputation matter more than short-term financial results? Will the organization's ability to acquire and digest new technology limit its growth? Or can technology be used to remove limits to its growth?

Harvard University, IBM, the government of Malaysia, Microsoft, the Houston Independent School District, Hewlett Packard, and the Vatican all have distinct organizational cultures and values that govern their purchasing decisions. Your organization has its own culture, and that culture should be reflected in your strategy for acquiring e-learning technology.

Know what you want to do

Before you proceed, you must know exactly what you are trying to accomplish. A clearly worded statement of objectives will tell you what technical features to look for in tools and technologies.

This statement of objectives should take into account your enterprise, performance, and learning goals as well as your process for acquiring e-learning tools. (See chapters 20 and 21.)

To help you arrive at your objectives, ask yourself:

▶ Do you want to produce a standard type of e-learning, such as instructor-led e-learning, learner-led e-learning? Or, will your solution span several categories or perhaps establish a new category altogether?

▶ How broad are your goals? Are you acquiring tools for a single, carefully circumscribed project? Or does your charter extend to all the e-learning within the organization or beyond to encompass online documentation, Web-based job aids, knowledge management, and e-commerce?

▶ What media do you need? Is displayed text enough? Can you get by with crude line drawings? Do you need sound, music, and voice? How about moving pictures provided by animation or video segments? What level of quality do you require for these media? For example, is computer-synthesized voice sufficient? If you require recorded voice, must it be high-fidelity or is AM-broadcast quality good enough?

▶ Must the learning product be embedded in, packaged with, or displayed alongside some other software or information system?

▶ How experienced are your learners? Do they already know how to operate the computer and its operating system? Have they taken e-learning before? Have they used online collaboration systems? How much training will they need?

▶ Is the purpose of your e-learning to increase long-term knowledge or just to answer immediate questions?

▶ How much time do you have for the whole project?

▶ What is your overall budget? How much have you allocated for technology? Even if you do not have a formal budget yet, can you estimate the range of money you could spend?

▶ Are you creating a prototype or the finished product?

▶ How much content will courses contain? How broad and deep are your educational goals?

▶ Is what you are teaching primarily factual knowledge, technical skills, soft skills, psychomotor skills, attitudes, or some mixture of these different forms?

Answers to questions like these will help you express your goals in a form that can guide your decisions.

FORM A TEAM

If your title is chief learning czar, if you own the majority of stock in your organization, or if you have unbreakable tenure, you may not feel you need a team to help you select and implement technologies. It may be more efficient for one person to make the decisions, but other people do have good ideas and getting a bit of consensus never hurts. And teamwork can be fun.

So who do you need on your team, working group, strike force, or SWAT (Special Wizards Acquiring Technology) team? Here is a recommendation for the makeup of such a team.

At the top is the team leader who is responsible for making decisions. We nominate you. If you choose not to accept this position, please see that it is filled by someone with both technical knowledge and people skills.

Also on the team are a close group of people who may recommend and ratify decisions. They may even think they make the decisions. They suggest, recommend, discuss, debate, deliberate, and consider each decision from many different perspectives. Within this group we recommend representative learners, instructors, instructional designers, and information technologists. These representatives should have the authority and experience to speak for their respective groups. You may want to add representatives of a few more groups to meet the special needs of your organization.

A third group of team members includes those who advise on decisions. Their involvement may be short-term or limited to specific decisions. In this area are specialists in purchasing, accounting, and finance. You may want to call on peers within your organization or in other organizations. You will certainly want to keep executives informed and seek their advice on issues of organizational policy. For some special issues, you may need to seek the advice of outside consultants or trusted vendors. And don't forget the informal advice of friends, parents, and lovers.

The team should be dynamic and flexible. You know your organization and your mission. Pick a team that works.

IDENTIFY NEEDED CATEGORIES OF TOOLS

You may need tools from several different categories. One of your strategic decisions will be to narrow your list of needed tool categories to just a few.

Identify capabilities needed to carry out your designs

To pick tools wisely, design your e-learning before you pick the tools to build it. First, design some example courses or modules of the type you want to create. Just specify them on paper. Second, list the capabilities you require for constructing and deploying them. Third, map your required capabilities to tools that can provide these capabilities.

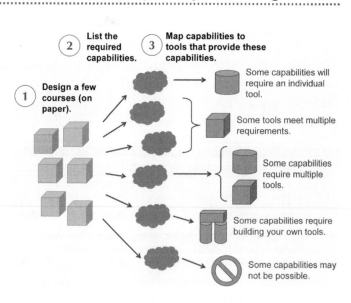

In a perfect world, all your capabilities could be met by one tool. In putting together your real-world toolkit, realize that some tools can meet multiple requirements, and some capabilities will require multiple tools. Some capabilities will require building your own tools or at least creatively combining multiple tools. And, some capabilities may not be possible yet. Your challenge is to put together the best set of tools your can, realizing that the perfect tools may not exist.

By designing first, you ensure that you pick tools that provide as many of the needed capabilities as possible. If you pick tools before you know what capabilities you need, you may later have to scale down your project to fit the capabilities of tools you have already purchased.

Select categories of tools

There are many categories of tools—far more than you are likely to need on a single project. Early in your project, you should identify the specific categories of tools you will need.

To identify categories of needed tools, first determine the role for which you need tools. Using the tools framework, you can spot areas where you need tools and areas that you can leave to others.

Here is an example of some of the kinds of organizations that require e-learning technology and the categories they need.

What roles do you play and what are your areas of responsibility in this framework? Knowing your role will help you pick the categories of tools you need.

Example: Corporate training department

Suppose you manage a corporate training department charged with designing, developing, and offering 50 asynchronous, learner-led online courses. To carry out this role, you will obviously need tools to create and offer courses, lessons, and pages.

What about the other areas on the framework? Because you are offering individual courses, not programs or curricula, you can forego tools at the curriculum level. You may choose to subcontract the creation and offering of media, especially audio and video. You may also opt to leave the choice of tools for accessing your courses to learners. If that is the case, you will have to design your courses so they work with popular browsers and media players and make your requirements clear.

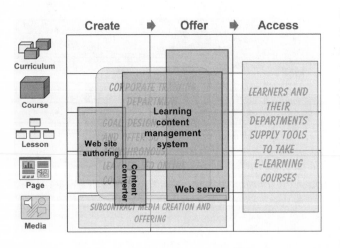

So, how do you pick tools to meet your role? You can start by considering the tools that overlap the tasks and levels that make up your role. One obvious candidate is an LCMS, mainly because it covers much of your area of responsibility.

Of course the LCMS may in turn require a Web server. And, you may want to enrich the content it can provide by including Web site authoring tools to create pages with better formatting and more interactivity than provided by templates in the LCMS. If you wish to include existing documents in your courses, you may need some conversion tools.

By identifying the main categories needed for your specific tasks and levels, you narrow your search and focus your efforts.

SET POLICIES

A strategy manifests itself as policies that govern tactical decisions. In this section we list five mostly independent policies to govern your choices of technology.

Policies are not yes/no binary rules. They are better represented as a scale with two extremes and choices in between. Your policy need not be a single point on the scale. It can be a smear along it. Policies suggest preferences but do not make decisions. They suggest which products to consider first and who gets the benefit of the doubt. Policies can be real tiebreakers. Mainly they keep you grounded in the goals behind your effort.

Let's look at each of these policies, the choices they offer, and how the choices affect your selection of tools and technologies.

Buy or build?

Should you buy tools or build your own? Many prefer to buy a tool in a colorful, shrink-wrapped box and have it do everything they need. Sometimes, alas, one tool can't do everything you need. And there are reasons for building some of your own tools. Let's take a look at when to buy and when to build.

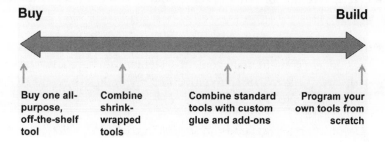

Starting on the Buy end of the scale, you are seeking one all-purpose tool. On the Build end of the scale, you are programming your own tools from scratch. The choice of whether to buy or build a tool is not a choice of one or the other of these extremes, though. You have choices in between.

Rather than seek tools that provide all the needed capabilities, a less extreme position might be to combine smaller, readily available tools. For example, instead of purchasing an LCMS or virtual classroom with built-in project management tools, you could opt to do project management with corporate tools like Microsoft Excel or Project.

The advantages at the Buy end of the scale are:

▶ **Convenience**. Buying tools is more convenient, and the resulting toolset is likely to be consistent.

▶ **Speed**. If you are in a hurry to get started, buying a tool is the better approach because you can open the box and go to work without having to design, build, and debug your own tools.

▶ **Ease of use**. Fewer technical skills are required to operate tools someone else developed. More third-party training and information is available.

Moving closer the Build end of the scale, you might consider combining standard tools and adding some custom programming or scripting to enhance them and make them work better together.

The advantages at the Build end of the scale are:

▶ **Control**. Building your own tools gives you more control over what they do and how they work.

▶ **Innovation**. Building your own tools allows more innovation and flexibility in crafting solutions for learners.

▶ **Revenue**. You can resell tools you build to others, providing a secondary source of revenue. In fact, several tool vendors started out by reselling tools they developed for internal projects.

Look at systems your organization is using already, such as human resource management systems or content management systems. Are there any snap-ins, add-ons, or accessories available to extend the functionality of these systems to meet your needs?

Your buy-versus-build choice depends on several factors. One is the level of technical skills in your organization. Building tools takes considerable skill in writing programs and scripts, configuring software packages, and managing the process of integrating components.

A second factor affecting your approach is your organization's focus. Are you focused on means or ends? If your interest is just the ends of making knowledge more widely available, you want to focus all your efforts on creating effective content, not on building tools. On the other hand, if you are concerned with implementing the most effective processes, regardless of content, then you should focus on building new tools and developing new technologies.

Big name or startup?

Should you go with big-name tools? Big-name tools are certainly the best known. They are the ones everyone compares themselves to. But are they the best choice for you? Let's look at the advantages and disadvantages of big-name products. Again, this is not an either-or choice. There are positions all along the scale.

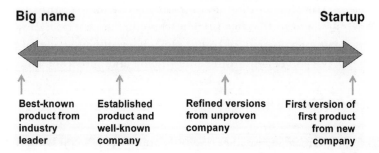

There are certain advantages as you move toward the Big-name end of the scale, such as:

▶ **Track record**. From this historical trail, you can see whether the product has been updated regularly. Has the product been reliable? Have bugs been fixed quickly? Has the product evolved to take advantage of changes in the market and in technology?

▶ **Financial information**. Big-name products tend to come from public companies, for which considerable information is available to help you gauge their future prospects. You can tell whether they are making money and whether they are likely to have the funds to continue to improve their product.

▶ **Training and consulting**. Well-established products are more likely to have third-party training, consulting, books, and contractors available to assist you

As you move to the Startup end of the scale, there are other advantages, such as:

▶ **Innovation**. A startup is not limited by the need to avoid radical changes that might confuse their existing customers. They do not have an extensive "installed base" to cause them to defend their ways of doing things rather than improve them.

▶ **Sensitivity**. Startups can more easily respond to the needs of a small number of users. A small company is likely to be more willing to listen to smaller organizations and to craft solutions for them.

▶ **Pricing**. Startups may have more flexible pricing models aimed at smaller companies. Because they are trying to build their client base, start-ups may be more willing to work with you to arrive at a mutually advantageous agreement.

You may be able to garner benefits from both sides of the scale if you deal with small but established companies, or if you work with a start-up whose tools are mature. For instance, if you do business with an established but less well-known company, you have a track record to evaluate. And the company may be more competitive and perhaps able to offer a more attractive pricing schedule than the best-known company. If you wait for a version 2.0 from a start-up company, you gain more stability in the tool but still benefit from better pricing and individual attention.

Old or new technology?

How far in the vanguard of technology do you want to be? Do you want to use the hottest new tool with the latest and greatest technology, or would you rather stick with tried and true tools based on refined technologies? To help you decide, imagine a scale running from pre-Internet technology on the left to bleeding-edge technology on the right. In the middle is a zone of established Internet technology.

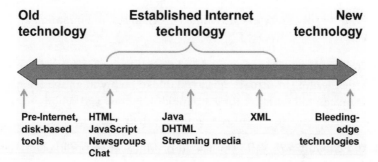

On the left, under pre-Internet technology are disk-based tools from the days before computers were connected. On the left side of established Internet technologies zone are early technologies like HTML, JavaScript, Internet newsgroups, and chat. In the middle of this zone are technologies such as Java, Dynamic HTML, and streaming media. On the right side are the more advanced Internet technologies like Extensible Markup Language (XML). The bleeding-edge end is represented by whatever is hot today.

Where should your organization and your project be on this scale? Let's start with old technology at the left of the scale and look at the advantages.

▶ **Stability and reliability**. Older tools are well developed. They have gone through many version numbers; therefore, most of the bugs and problems have been sorted out—with any luck. The underlying technology they use is stable and well documented.

▶ **Support for existing content**. If you have large amounts of existing content encoded with older tools, you cannot move too far ahead of that legacy content.

▶ **Ease of use**. Established and highly refined tools make creating content easier. These tools have had more time to perfect the user interface and implement feedback from users. And users are more knowledgeable about the technologies they are based on.

There are other advantages if you choose new technology.

▶ **Performance**. Tools supporting new technologies provide higher performance. That is, they are faster and more efficient. If you need high performance to maintain your competitive position in the marketplace—whether it is internal or external—then you should consider tools based on new technologies.

▶ **Chance to start over**. Tools at the new-technology end of the scale do not actively support older technologies to sustain their existing client base. If you adopt tools that use new technologies, you have a chance to rethink your mission, jettison that old content, and make a fresh start.

▶ **Snob appeal**. If your organization values being the first on the block to implement a new technology, then the right end of the scale is where you want to be.

To decide your position on this scale, consider carefully your degree of technical expertise and that of your learners. The higher the levels of technical expertise, the more advanced the technology you can use. Also remember that the scale itself is moving. What is considered advanced today will be ho-hum tomorrow. You may want to aim a bit ahead of your current preferences.

Own or rent?

Do you want to own or rent your e-learning technology? In the United States, businesses and individuals are increasingly opting to lease rather than own automobiles. Some businesses lease almost all their assets, including office buildings, warehouses, manufacturing machinery, and office computers. This trend is extending to software as well. Many vendors of server-based software now offer both a product, which you install on your own hardware, and a service, which they host on their own servers and make available to you over the Web.

19

Strategies for picking technologies

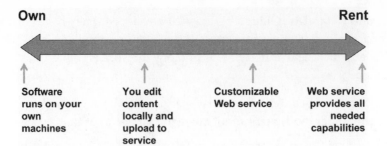

On the left of the scale, you fully own the technology. The software runs on machines you own and that are installed on your premises. At the rent end of the spectrum, you own nothing. You contract with a Web-hosted service. The software runs on their machines. You access it over the Web.

Legally speaking you may not "own" the software you buy. You merely license it. Remember that dialog box that required you to agree to the terms and conditions of the license? Next time read it and you will most likely discover that you merely have a license to use the software. But let's not be pedantic. When we say "own" we mean you control its use inside your organization.

These are the extremes, but there are some compromises in between. Left of center, you may edit content locally and then upload it to the service. Here you own the tools for authoring content but not those for offering it. Another compromise to the right of center is a customizable Web service. Most hosted products let customers adjust the look and feel of the service to match corporate identity standards. Others let customers adjust basic features of the service.

Owning your own technology is an investment in your organization's infrastructure. Owning tools gives you:

▶ **More control**. You can customize, configure, enhance, tweak, and accessorize them.

▶ **Lower long-term costs**. If you are efficient at managing IT, owning may be less expensive over the long term.

▶ **Improved integration**. Bringing the technology in-house may be essential for tools that must connect to existing corporate information systems.

Renting, on the other hand, has advantages like:

▶ **Quicker ramp-up**. Because the Web service is already up and running, you can generally get started quicker. You do not have to install, test, or maintain the tool.

▶ **Lower initial investment**. Renting requires less up-front investment of time and money. And, because you pay for it over time, it requires a lower initial investment of cash. Additionally, it may require less investment of your staff's time to acquire the expertise necessary to set up and maintain the software on your own machines.

▶ **Less technical expertise**. Renting makes sense if IT is not a core activity in your organization or if you are not ready to commit to a particular set of tools.

So, should you own or rent your technology? Consider how much technology you want on your premises and what you want to manage directly. Also, think about whether you prefer to pay for technology as one up-front cost or as monthly payments?

Proprietary or open tools?

One important strategic issue is whether to prefer proprietary or open tools. Proprietary tools are ones that use private file formats and thus cannot easily be combined with tools from other companies. Proprietary tools or toolsets try to do everything you need so you don't need other tools.

No issue evokes more emotion, passion, or silliness than the issue of proprietary or open tools. This policy is only slightly technical and is mostly about philosophy and political alliances.

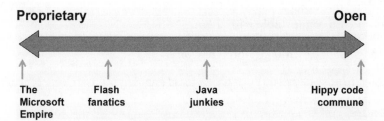

Along this scale you find clumps of interoperable products and compatible technologies. At the proprietary extreme, most people put Microsoft. (Critics and MS-phobes call it The Evil Empire.) Microsoft's operating systems and office suite have achieved dominance in their markets. This dominance has spawned numerous e-learning products that work only on Microsoft operating systems or with Microsoft databases.

Next along the scale, still toward the proprietary end, come products based on Macromedia's Flash animation tool. Flash fanatics prefer to do everything in Flash, eschewing HTML, browsers, and other technologies. Because Flash can be made to run on most common operating systems, its use is not as limiting as the reliance on a single product might imply.

Next along the scale, toward the open end, are tools based on Sun Microsystems's Java programming language. Tools created in Java run on most popular operating systems, at least in theory. Around the basic Java language has sprung an industry supplying components and development tools.

On the open end of the spectrum is what is called the Hippy Code Commune. Outwardly fueled by altruism, this cluster of developers offers open-source tools based entirely on open industry standards. Open source tools come with the underlying source code, which buyers can modify to adapt the tool to their purposes. Because these tools use documented, open file formats, they can be combined with tools from other vendors that use the same file formats.

So, where do you fit on this political spectrum? The proprietary approach offers:

▶ **Simplicity** to those who can accomplish their mission with proprietary tools.

▶ **Comprehensiveness**. Proprietary tools tend to be complete and require less custom programming than open tools.

▶ **Support**. Proprietary tools are generally well documented and supported. If something goes wrong, you know who to blame.

▶ **Trust**. Your organization may trust products from Microsoft and Macromedia. Users within your organization have learned the quirks of these companies and products and are comfortable with them.

Open tools have their advantages too. They offer:

▶ **Broad operating system support**. Open tools enable you to deliver learning on more operating systems and devices.

▶ **Low cost**. Some open source tools are available for free or at a low cost relative to their proprietary counterparts.

▶ **More alternatives**. If one open-source tool does not work, then maybe another will. Or, an open-source programmer may currently be working on the enhancement you need.

▶ **Distrust of large corporations**. You will find a like-minded community among open-source tools users and developers.

Of all the strategic policies, this one is most likely to be set on an organization-wide level. Your IT department may have already standardized on Java-based or Microsoft-compatible tools.

Document your policies

Once you have made your policy decisions, take a few more steps and put them in a format that others can read and understand them. You can start by ticking off the proper position of your organization or project on these scales.

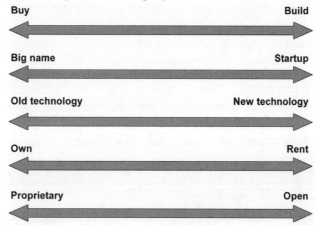

Next, document the reasons for your policies. Relate your decisions back to organizational goals and values. Explain how these policies will help pick tools to accomplish the goals of your project and support your organization's overall mission.

Now, get the policies ratified by your management. Present the policies and ask for concurrence by the executives who will later approve your purchase recommendations. By getting commitment to your policies, you complete part of the approval process in advance.

Finally, promulgate your policies. Make sure everyone involved in the process of picking tools understands them and the reasons behind them.

PICK TOOLS

Once you have identified the categories of tools you need and settled on policies for acquiring them, you are ready to actually pick tools in each of the categories. This process usually involves four main steps:

1. List the requirements for each tool.

2. Identify candidate products that may meet these requirements.

3. Evaluate the candidates against your requirements.

4. Select the best candidate.

The process of picking specific products is the subject of chapter 20.

GET MONEY

Obtaining the funds to purchase tools and technologies requires putting together a budget. Your budget must estimate costs and justify them in terms of enterprise goals you identified.

Estimate costs

Here is an example of a budget. There is nothing at all remarkable about it. It simply tallies the costs of various tools and spreads them out (amortizes them) over their useful lives to arrive at annual costs. Some organizations prefer to see lump-sum costs. Find out the preferred method for your organization.

Notice that the budget rounds off numbers. This signals the reader that these figures are just estimates.

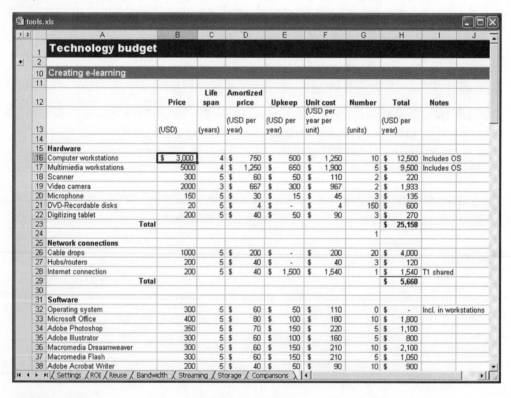

This spreadsheet covers costs for creating, offering, and accessing e-learning. It probably won't fit your situation exactly, but it may help you get started. It is at horton.com/tools.

Don't forget costs beyond initial purchase price. These include:

▶ Maintenance

▶ Upgrades

▶ Training users

Justify costs

To actually get the money in your budget, you must justify the costs to your organization. Getting money is a mixture of rational presentation of your case and organizational cunning. We'll help with the first part.

Show the return-on-investment

Most organizations require some financial calculation to show the financial benefit of an investment. One of the most common ways of calculating such a benefit is as a return on investment (ROI). It is simply the net benefit divided by the costs.

tools.xls			
	A	B	C
11			
12	ROI of capital expenditure		
13			
14	**Benefits**		
15			
16	Productivity after training	110	units per person per year
17	- Productivity before training	100	units per person per year
18	= Productivity improvement	10	units per person per year
19			
20	x Value of productivity unit	$ 50	USD per unit
21	= Value of productivity increase	$ 500	USD per person per year
22			
23	x Number of persons trained	1000	learners
24	= Total benefits	$ **500,000**	USD per year
25			
26			
27	**Costs**		
28			
29	Purchase price	$ 500,000	USD
30	+ Setup and customization	$ 250,000	USD
31	= Total upfront costs	$ 750,000	USD
32			
33	÷ Life span	4	years
34			
35	= Amortized upfront costs	$ 187,500	USD per year
36			
37	+ Operating Costs	$ 50,000	USD per year
38			
39	= Total annual costs	$ 237,500	USD per year
40			
41			
42	**Net benefit**	$ 262,500	USD per year
43			
44	**Return on investment**	111%	
45			

Intro / Settings \ **ROI** / Reuse / Bandwidth

Here is an example from the spreadsheet at horton.com/tools, which shows the form of such a calculation. The formula used in your organization may vary, so why not take a stroll over to your finance or accounting department and ask how they recommend you calculate ROI.

Show contribution to approved goals

Another way to justify your purchase is to show that it furthers already accepted organizational goals.

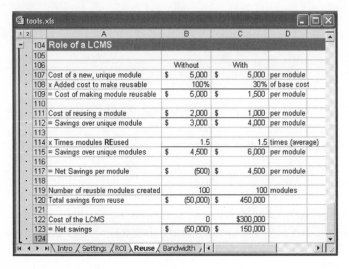

This example, which is available at horton.com/tools, shows the contribution of an LCMS in an organization's strategy to reuse learning materials. It compares the net savings of implementing a strategy of creating courses from reusable modules with and without an LCMS. In this example, the strategy pays off with an LCMS but not without one. (Different assumptions lead to different conclusions. Experiment with the spreadsheet and see for yourself.)

Brainstorm other benefits

Take a few minutes to list other potential benefits of acquiring the technology you propose. Can the tools be used for other organizational purposes? For example, an online meeting system intended for instructor-led e-learning could be used for other types of meetings and collaboration as well. Will the technology have valuable side effects, such as improving the information technology skills of staff? Think of as many benefits as you can and list them in your budget.

BUY

Once you have selected a specific product and obtained the funding, you need to actually buy the product. This step sounds simple, but there are still a few issues to consider.

Get help

Two members of your technology team will be especially helpful during this phase:

Who	What they can do to help you
Legal department	Write and review contracts and service agreements.
Purchasing department	Identify vendors, negotiate the purchase, and arrange payment.

Shop

Shopping is not just buying. Shopping is also looking, comparing, and evaluating alternatives. It is an education in itself. It can also be time-consuming and frustrating. Even if you yield to the temptation of turning it over to your purchasing department, stay involved and informed.

Get reliable data

First of all, get reliable data on which to base your decisions. Invite advice from your IT department and vendors, and consult product reviews.

▶ **Your IT department**. Although they may not be familiar with your specific e-learning needs, your information technologists know computers and computer hardware. Explain your needs as clearly as you can. Ask them for recommendations. Perhaps they have standards for what computers can be purchased or what databases can be used. Learn what the standards are. The IT department may even have repair data on certain brands that can help you judge potential reliability.

▶ **Vendors**. Consult potential vendors' Web sites to nail down specifications, warranties, and other details. Spend some time checking their technical support areas.

▶ **Product reviews**. Frequently, computer hardware magazines carry reviews and product comparisons of new computer hardware and software. Some of these magazines conduct their own performance tests and rate models by how well they performed on these tests. These magazines may also rate other factors, such as customer support and warranty coverage. These reviews sometimes suggest other vendors to investigate—ones you may not have considered. Finally, if you read the reviews carefully, you may pick up hints on the reputation of various vendors. Some online review sites include:

  ▪ zdnet.com

  ▪ computers.cnet.com

  ▪ pcmag.com

Get the best price

Once you have decided what specific product you want, it is time to find the best price—not before. You cannot compare prices unless the products you are comparing are the same. Here are some suggestions for finding the best price.

▶ **Vendor's sales representative**. For simple products, the sales rep for the vendor may not offer the best price. But for a complex system or for a negotiated deal, the sales rep may be able to structure a price, billing, and payment plan that reduces your overall costs and fits your cash flow constraints. Negotiate, negotiate, negotiate. More on that later.

▶ **Online retailers**. Go to several retailers' Web sites and search for the specific product. Use the exact product name or manufacturer's part number. Verify that the item listed has the correct specifications. Compare prices. Be sure to include any shipping charges.

  If you are buying more than one unit, call the online retailer and ask for the business sales division. Yes, all good online retailers take orders over the telephone. You may get a more favorable price or better shipping terms if you are purchasing more than one unit. If you have not purchased anything from the online retailer before, be sure to check them out. Sites like bizrate.com and www.bbbonline.com rate online retailers.

▶ **Vendors' Web sites**. Go to the vendor's Web site and look for the online store. In some cases, the vendor-direct price may be cheaper. Or shipping may be free. Or you may get an extended warranty bonus for ordering directly from the vendor. Most major software vendors sell from their Web site.

  If you have specialized hardware needs, you may be able to order a semi-customized computer to meet those needs. You can specify the desired processor, memory, disk space, video card, and other components. Sites from which you can order semi-customized computers include hp.com, dell.com, ibm.com, sony.com, and others.

▶ **"Best price" shopping sites**. Some Web sites advertise that they can find the best price on anything. Go ahead, give them a try. If you do find a truly low price, be sure to do some research on the vendor if you haven't done business with them before. Some comparison sites include:

  ▪ pricegrabber.com

  ▪ zdnet.com/computershopper

  ▪ cnet.com

  ▪ pricespy.com

▶ **Local computer superstore**. Check your local computer store if you have one nearby. Many popular brands of computer hardware and software may be similarly priced, whether from a retail store or from an online retailer. You may prefer to examine the computer before buying it. However, the savings in shipping will probably be offset by sales tax.

Consider other ways to buy

Here are a few additional ways you might choose to purchase hardware and software for those taking e-learning and those authoring it.

▶ **Custom builders**. If you want the most computer power for the least amount of money, then a custom builder is for you. You can probably find one near where you live or work. They specialize in combining brand-name, off-the-shelf components into any configuration you desire. You get everything you want and nothing you don't. Remember, you may need to negotiate details like warranty and a service contract.

▶ **System integrators**. System integrators specialize in combining all the pieces of a complex, enterprise-wide e-learning solution. They have expertise in workstations, servers, software, and networks—all the elements that must work together seamlessly to create a robust system. System integrators are best for big projects, and the big-name firms may be best qualified for very large projects. Some well known systems integrators include IBM (ibm.com) and EDS (eds.com).

Negotiate your best deal

If you are buying more than a few of the same item or if the total price is high, say over $5000 USD, negotiate with the seller to get the best deal you can.

▶ **Start with the price**. Will the seller give you a discount? Will they give you their deluxe package for the price of their standard package? Will they adjust billing and payment to reduce interest costs?

▶ **Negotiate the terms of the license**. The license for using software can depend on the total number of people who might ever use the tool, the number of concurrent users, the number of machines the tool is installed on, or the number of sites or workgroups in which the tool is used. Some licenses require annual renewal—for a fee. Make sure you understand the terms of the license and negotiate a license that minimizes the cost to you.

▶ **Ask for free upgrades** or at least a discount on future versions of the tool. Upgrades may be sold as a subscription service or piecemeal as released.

► **Request more free goodies**. Will the seller throw in items that normally cost extra? Ask for paper documentation, extra templates, clip art and component media, unlimited phone support, online and on-site training, and access to special resources for developers.

IMPLEMENT

Implementation does not begin after you purchase the product. It begins at the very beginning and should permeate your planning process. Plan ahead or plan to fail. Implementation involves working with all the participants in your e-learning effort: your IT department, producers, and learners.

Involve Information Technology early

At the beginning of your project, talk with the Information Technology department to determine the capabilities of your current hardware and network infrastructure. Elicit their help by showing your interest in topics near and dear to information technologists' hearts. Talk to them about:

► Available bandwidth on the network

► Whether there are existing servers you can use

► Whether there are any restrictions on the types of files you can use or databases you can employ

► What precautions to take to avoid infection by computer viruses, worms, or Trojan horses

If IT is a willing participant, they may ease your workload by helping you set up and test your hardware and software. They may even be willing to help you integrate your purchases with existing enterprise systems.

If you don't have an IT department, play the role yourself. Hire a consultant to train you and help you get started.

Include course authors and developers

Implementation goes more smoothly if authors and developers are included in the selection process for the tools they will have to use. Involvement leads to a feeling of ownership in the decision. But don't stop there: Ensure success by providing training and support for the new tools. Many vendors provide training and consulting as part of the purchase price or licensing fee. Make training a negotiating point with potential vendors.

Help learners start right

Don't forget learners. For many, e-learning is new and somewhat bewildering. If their first experience with e-learning is disappointing, they may be unwilling to try it again. So, design your e-learning to minimize frustration. Test it with real learners. Refine your design as necessary. Then, build in online support that solves problems your design cannot solve.

Here are some guidelines to help you avoid common support problems.

▶ **Limit new technology**. Carefully analyze your learners. What technologies do they use in their jobs or at home? How much more can you ask them to learn? For instance, if learners have used only e-mail, incorporating videoconferencing is too large a leap. On the other hand, you could reasonably ask them to learn to use a discussion forum.

▶ **Minimize separate components**. Reduce the number of plug-ins, ActiveX controls, document viewers, and media players that learners must download, install, and learn to operate. If possible, find media player that can play most of the media you plan to use.

▶ **Provide Help** within the course interface for common actions. E-learning is software. Plan to provide the same kind of online Help you would find in other software programs. And make sure your Help helps.

▶ **Simplify common actions**. Avoid making learners start up and use auxiliary programs. The more programs learners have to use the more opportunities there are for problems, disappointment, and the inevitable calls to the Help desk. For instance, embed the interfaces for chat, discussion, and e-mail directly within the course window.

▶ **Provide ongoing support**. Set up a discussion forum with threads for common problem areas. Make sure that the forum is monitored and questions and problems are handled quickly and completely. If your technology and staff allow, provide chat or instant messaging for immediate problems learners may encounter. If neither of these options is possible, at least provide a clearly visible e-mail link. Promise a 24-hour turnaround for questions—and keep that promise. Let learners test their computer setup, and help them obtain any missing software. Create a single source of support for your e-learning.

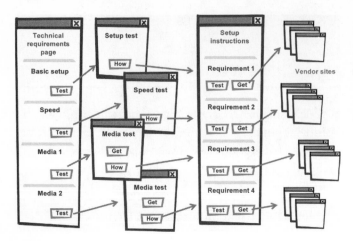

This diagram shows the structure for online support aimed at getting new e-learners started. Learners can test their basic setup—such as operating system, browser version, display size, and connection speed. If they fail any test, learners are sent to a page that explains the problem and provides a link to the vendor's site to get updated software or additional information.

What now?

Applying the ideas of this chapter to craft an effective strategy for acquiring the tools and technologies you need for e-learning is complex. So, let us offer a few suggestions to help you use what you just read.

If	Then
Your organization does not have an overall e-learning strategy	Develop an overall e-learning strategy first. Make sure it incorporates the ideas in this chapter, but don't let your e-learning strategy imply that technology is all you need.
Your organization has an e-learning strategy but it says nothing about how to acquire tools and technologies	Graft the technology strategy suggested here onto your overall e-learning strategy, making adjustments to avoid duplication and fill gaps.
Your organization has a strategy for acquiring technology	Use this chapter as a checklist to see how you can improve your existing technology strategy. Competing strategies seldom succeed.
You'd really like a strategy but you've got to buy a tool next week	Put this chapter aside for now and speed read chapter 20 on picking tools. Come back here for the sections on shopping and negotiating.

Now that you've developed a strategy based on enterprise, performance, and learning goals, we turn our attention in chapter 20 to the four main steps you need to take when selecting tools and technologies. In chapter 21, we cover general criteria for picking tools.

20 Picking tools

No matter how much you know about tools, you can still go astray unless you use an objective, systematic process to pick tools that meet your needs. Let's look at such a process and how to avoid the common mistakes people make in picking tools.

STEPS IN SELECTING PRODUCTS

There is no algorithm or recipe that can guarantee success in selecting tools. Nevertheless, an orderly, systematic process can eliminate many of the pitfalls of a purely subjective choice made on incomplete information. Use the following steps as a model for your own selection process.

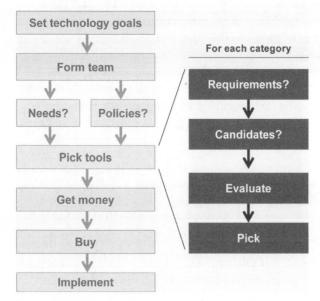

1. List and rank your requirements.

2. Identify candidate products.

3. Evaluate the candidate products.

4. Pick an individual product.

RECRUIT OTHERS TO HELP YOU

Picking tools and technologies is a difficult, frustrating, and risky endeavor. If you don't yet feel confident about making these decisions, seek the help of others. Remain in charge, but seek knowledgeable, objective advice.

Throughout the process of picking tools you should give careful thought to crucial business, legal, and financial issues. Even at this early stage in the selection process, it is not too early to sit down with your legal and purchasing departments to discuss what kind of deal you can make with a vendor. In particular, decide what licensing fee you can afford to pay. Some vendors charge a single up-front fee while others demand a fee for each user. The fee can be a few dollars or hundreds of dollars. A per-use fee may require you to track distribution of your learning products and reveal sales figures to an outside company.

For help putting together your budget and evaluating the financial health of prospective vendors, turn to your accounting and finance departments. Balance sheets are their native language and cash flow their dialect. If numbers make your eyes glaze over, consult people who love numbers.

You must be able to describe your needs in terms a tool vendor can understand. Unfortunately, not all vendors are customer-friendly. Few understand the difficulty of teaching complex technical or business information. None understand your job and exactly what that job requires. If you don't know a proximity operator from a phone operator and a relational database sounds like a place to list your aunts and uncles, get help from someone who speaks the lingo. Don't let your justified dislike of computer jargon lead you to buy an inadequate product. If the vendors do not speak your language, you must speak theirs.

Rely on your organization's IT department. Information technologists may not know the specifics of e-learning or knowledge management, but they do understand computers and networking. They are also familiar with how computers and networks are currently used in your organization.

You can hire an independent consultant to advise you. Make sure the consultant is truly independent and unbiased, without a stake in any particular product or technology.

Another option is to hire a systems integrator to select tools for you, integrate them into a coherent package, and train you on its use. Some systems integrators can develop content for you as well.

So if you are not comfortable making decisions on tools, get help. There are others who, for a fee perhaps, are willing to assist you.

LIST AND RANK REQUIRED CAPABILITIES

With your roles clearly in mind, your can compile a complete list of required capabilities. Start by designing—on paper, at least—a few typical courses.

List needed capabilities

List the kinds of learning experiences that are necessary to accomplish your learning goals. For these learning experiences, ask questions such as:

▶ What activities will learners engage in? Will they read and write text, listen to speeches, watch presentations and demonstrations, conduct experiments, practice manual activities, design objects, or plan projects?

▶ What media are needed to create the learning experiences—text, graphics, sound, voice, music, animation, video, or combinations of these?

▶ Will learners work alone or with cohorts? How many cohorts? Will they be teamed in pairs, small teams, or large groups?

▶ By what means do learners need to collaborate? Is typing text adequate or should they hear each others' voices and see each others' faces? Do they need to share and work together on documents and other displays?

 Here's a quick way to compile a checklist of potential capabilities. For each category of tool you need, get data sheets and brochures from the vendors' Web sites. Consolidate the various bullet lists of features. Edit the list to remove duplicate items, delete unnecessary features, and express capabilities in consistent, vendor-neutral terminology. Then scan the list for missing capabilities critical for your project.

▶ With whom and what will learners interact? With the learning software, with an instructor or facilitator, with fellow learners, with animated characters, or with outside experts? How often will they interact? What form will the interaction take?

▶ Who will author and lead these learning experiences? What technologies are these people comfortable with?

▶ How will learning experiences be sequenced or organized? Will all learners go through all experiences in the same order? Or will each learner have a custom path? Who will decide that path?

▶ How will learning be measured? What kinds of tests, practices, and projects can help learners demonstrate and measure their mastery of the subject matter? Will humans or machines evaluate learners' performance?

▶ Where are the learners? Are they all in one office, one time zone, one country, or are they all over the globe? Do they speak the same language?

Answers to these questions will help you think of the features you need. Don't forget the general criteria listed in chapter 21.

Rank these desired capabilities

Not all the capabilities of a tool are equally valuable. Some are essential, some are cool, and others you could care less about. To keep your evaluation process objective, assign a priority to each desired capability. Clearly distinguish essential features.

Category	Ranking
Not needed	0
Nice to have	1
Convenient	2
Valuable	4
Very important	8
Must have	*

There are several ways to assign such priorities. The most common way is to rank the items on a numerical scale such as this one.

* Treat must-have features differently. Red-flag products that lack must-have features. If the must-have features cannot be provided in some way, reject the product regardless of its numeric rating.

A second way to prioritize features is to rank them by how much you would pay to have the feature included in the product.

This spreadsheet shows a third way. Here each criterion is assigned two point values. The maximum point value is the highest number of points a product can score for a given criterion; it provides a means for weighting each factor. For example, a criterion with a maximum of 30 points can contribute three times as much to the final score as one with a maximum of 10 points.

Criteria	Max points	Min required
High-fidelity WYSIWYG construction of pages without having to know HTML.	30	20
Ability to edit in HTML. Automated code checking and command completion.	10	4
Roundtrip HTML. Editing in WYSIWYG mode does not undo hand-crafted HTML.	20	15

Weight or importance of this criterion

Minimum acceptable level. Scores below this level disqualify the product.

The second point value is the minimum points required for the product to remain under consideration. If the product scores less than this minimum on any criterion, it is eliminated from consideration. For criteria that absolutely must be met, this value is the same as the maximum points. A perfect score is required. For a completely optional feature, the minimum may be zero.

COMPILE A LIST OF CANDIDATES

Hundreds of products are available to author and deliver e-learning, Web pages, multimedia, and online documents. New products and new versions of existing products appear daily.

Search available sources

To compile a current list of candidate products, consult various sources of information including magazines, newsletters, conferences, expos, Web sites, and newsgroups.

Magazines and newsletters

For up-to-date information, look at the feature articles, product reviews, buyers' guides, and advertisements in magazines and newsletters such as these:

Magazine	Web address
Training & Development	astd.org
e-learning Magazine	elearningmag.com
CLO magazine	clomedia.com
CIO Insight	cioinsight.com
PC Magazine	pcmag.com
Training Magazine	trainingmag.com
OnLine Learning News	vnulearning.com

Conferences and expos

If you want to see demonstrations of products and talk to product representatives, consider attending a conference of e-learning practitioners. Most such conferences have an accompanying expo where exhibitors demonstrate their products and answer questions. Here are some conferences to sprinkle over your calendar.

Conference	Web address
ASTD International Conference and Exhibition	astd.org
Distance Teaching & Learning	uwex.edu/disted/conference
E-learning Guild Conference	elearningguild.com
Online Learning Conference and Expo	onlinelearningconference.com
TechKnowledge	astd.org
TechLearn	www.techlearn.net

Web sites

The following Web sites frequently contain reports and other information about tools for e-learning:

▶ horton.com/tools

▶ brandon-hall.com

▶ designingwbt.com

▶ www.learningcircuits.org

▶ www.masie.com

▶ tmreview.com

▶ www.trainingsupersite.com

Newsgroups and discussion forums

Internet newsgroups and Web discussion forums frequently discuss tools and technologies for e-learning. Visit one of these locations in search of answers to your questions.

▶ astd.org/virtual_community/interact

▶ news:alt.training.technology

▶ news:alt.education.distance

Gather information

Once you have identified candidate products, the next step is to gather information about them.

Ask the vendor

Don't be shy about asking questions of the vendor. If the vendor is reluctant to answer questions before the sale, just think about what getting technical support will be like after the sale when you are trying to operate or install the product.

Ask embarrassing questions such as "What happens to me if you go out of business?" or "How hard is it to get my content out of your system and into your competitor's system?"

Allow the vendors some latitude in how they answer the questions. There are many ways to provide a needed capability. The best solution may not be the one that answers the question most directly, but it should clearly meet your needs. Often vendors cannot give precise answers to your questions. When their answer is "Well, it depends," they should be able to explain what it depends on.

Play fair. Most vendors are honest and want to be helpful, but even good vendors sometimes have a sub-par representative, and even good representatives have bad days or suffer from brain fade. Don't dangle the prospect of your business in front of their noses just to watch them drool. Vendors have feelings, too. Also, don't exaggerate the size of your potential purchase.

Ask existing users

People who are already using the product can provide excellent information about the product. Ask vendors for such reference accounts. They are less biased than vendors, and their concerns are similar to yours.

Questions to ask existing users include:

▶ How long have you used the product?

▶ How many people use it?

▶ What other products did you consider?

▶ Why did you pick this one?

▶ How helpful is the vendor's documentation, training, customer support?

▶ How long did it take you to learn the product?

▶ How productive are you using the product?

▸ If you could do it over again, would you pick this product?

▸ Has the vendor kept promises to improve the product?

▸ Were enhancements delivered on schedule?

If possible, get reference accounts for deals that went sour. Did the account feel they were treated fairly? Honestly?

Check the vendor's and product's reputation

Consult message boards, discussion forums, and newsgroups for scuttlebutt about the product and its producer. Follow up to filter out malicious gossip ("I heard they're owned by aliens."), messages planted by competitors ("They don't meet the Toponix 232.4/b standards."), or ravings of paranoid customers ("Their software spies on you."). All in all, are comments generally positive regarding the product's capabilities and the vendor's integrity?

Consult other sources

Dig deeper. Rely on additional sources to round out your picture of the product. Gather additional information from these sources:

 Search the Web for product reviews and comparisons. Check the date and source to make sure you are getting unbiased and current information.

▸ Competitors of the vendors you are considering

▸ Brochures and data sheets

▸ Manuals and other forms of documentation

▸ Reviews and feature articles in trade magazines

EVALUATE PRODUCTS

By now you have gathered much information and identified several candidate products. Now you must begin narrowing your choices.

Rate products

The first phase in narrowing choices is to select a handful of products for closer scrutiny. Rank the products according to your list of desired features and select the best two or three finalists.

Criteria	Max points	Min required	Front Page Points	OK	Dream-weaver Points	OK	Go Live Points	OK	Net Objects Points	OK	Hot Dog Points	OK
Product comparisons												
Category Website authoring tool												
High-fidelity WYSIWYG construction of pages without having to know HTML.	30	20	25		20		20		20		10	*
Ability to edit in HTML. Automated code checking and command completion.	10	4	8		7		4		5		8	
Roundtrip HTML. Editing in WYSIWYG mode does not undo hand-crafted HTML.		15	16		18		15		16		18	
Tools to construct navigation schemes without manually linking individual pages.	10	0	5		5		5		8		2	
Ability to create and reuse templates for pages.	20	10	15		15		10		18		5	*
Ability to create and reuse customized tables, lists, and other components on pages.	20	10	12		15		10		12		5	*
Produces pages that display correctly in last two versions of IE and Netscape browsers.	30	25	20	*	25		25		25		25	
Ability to create and edit cascading style sheets and to attach them to pages.	20	10	15		15		15		12		10	
Ability to visually design a sight with placeholder pages.	10	0	5		7		5		8		2	
Check-in and check-out feature to prevent simultaneous editing of the same page.	10	0	5		7		5		7		0	
Versions for both Windows XP and Macintosh OS X operating systems.	20	20	10	*	20		20		10	*	10	*
Easy to learn for users of Microsoft PowerPoint and Word	10	4	8		5		5		4		2	*
Totals			0	*	159		139		0	*	0	*

Intro / Settings / ROI / Reuse / Bandwidth / Streaming / Storage / Com

This spreadsheet shows a simple ranking of Web site authoring tools for a particular project. Note that asterisks flag categories where the product fell below a specified minimum, yielding final scores of zero. That does not mean that these products might not be right for you, just that they lacked a capability crucial to this particular project.

This spreadsheet is available at horton.com/tools.

20

Picking tools

Test finalists

The next step is to try a small, simple project with each product to gain some hands-on experience with the product.

Select a typical module of the e-learning you must produce. This might be a 10-20 minute lesson. Do the same project with each candidate product. Use your normal staff and carefully record both objective results (time taken, assistance required, and errors) and subjective reactions. Some questions to ask include:

▶ Does the product meet all the basic requirements?

▶ How long did it take to get the product installed and running?

▶ Was the documentation for the product complete and accurate?

▶ Was provided training sufficient?

▶ Can you get answers to your questions from the documentation? From the customer support hotline?

After testing a small project, review the results and identify the best two or three candidate products. These are your finalists.

Now do a full-sized project with each product. One way to do this test is to reuse the same lesson or other module throughout the test. Before you dismiss this suggestion as an extravagant waste of resources, consider the costs of failing on your first real project and paying the price for picking the second-best product. The total may be considerable indeed.

In this test, pay special attention to the ease of use for authors and users. Important questions include:

▶ How much time was required to perform the project? Distinguish time spent learning the tool from time spent using it.

▶ Was the product reliable and predictable?

▶ Did the productivity of authors continue to improve throughout the test or did it plateau? To what extent did authors master the product and use its advanced features?

▶ How easy is it to revise the document? To maintain multiple versions of a document?

▶ Do authors enjoy using the product? Is using it fun or drudgery?

PICK A PRODUCT

If one product meets your basic requirements and is clearly superior to other products, then proceed to purchase it. Making a purchase may be as simple as phoning your local computer store, or it may require having your legal department draw up a contract and your purchasing department negotiate the best terms.

If two or more products are close in your evaluation, you can evaluate further or just toss a coin. Decision-making is never perfect. A clear, timely decision may be better than another decimal point of analysis.

Not even a perfect product can succeed unless its benefits are visible and understandable by those who must purchase and use it. Announce your choice and communicate the reasons for it to all those affected, especially the authors who must use the product.

Keep good records; because by the time you get the project done, tools that "would have been better" will be available—and you may be called on to justify your decision.

Whew! That was a lot of work. Congratulate yourself. Your hard work will increase the productivity of authors and lower the blood pressure of learners. Thank your peers, your management, and your staff for their help.

Never get fooled again!

Two simple words will ensure that you are never confused, misled, or bamboozled by a vendor of technology. Here they are in action:

Vendor: It's got electrophonic, hypermedial, virtual reality with internetworked asynchronous refraction and a dual-ported carburetor.

You: So what?

Vendor: It's got 42 gigabytes of RAM, on-board NSA-compliant encryption, 802.11c wireless port, 6 GHz processor, 48-bit audio interface, and a plug-in for three joysticks.

You: So what?

Vendor: It's fast, real fast. And, it makes a cute sound when it starts up. And, the buttons all have rounded edges. And it'll keep your office real warm.

You: So what?

Vendor: Well, you could say you're the first person to own one and I'd get a 20% commission.

At the end of such an interrogation, you either understand what the product offers you or you are prepared to move on to another vendor. Because repeatedly chirping, "So what?" can become monotonous and because you want to be polite, you may prefer to phrase your questions along these lines:

> And how does that capability apply to my project?
>
> How do I explain that feature to my CEO who knows nothing about technology?
>
> I must not have had my coffee this morning. Could you explain how that feature benefits me on my project?
>
> And that's a good thing?

The important point is not the form of the question but that you persist until you can see how each technical feature helps you accomplish your objectives.

WHAT IF NO PRODUCT MEETS YOUR REQUIREMENTS?

What do you do if at the end of your selection process, no product seems to meet your requirements? Before rejecting your best candidate because it lacks a few "must-have" capabilities, consider all your alternatives.

Wait for needed features

If you identify a product that almost meets your requirements, you may decide to wait until the missing capabilities are added. If the vendor has committed in writing to add the features in a forthcoming version and you can depend on the vendor to produce that version on time, you may decide to wait. You can use the time to train your authors on the basic features of the current version and prepare to install the new version when it is released.

If the wait is longer than a couple of months, you should consider whether your choice is still the best. Perhaps other products have been developed or have added new features. Review your decision every few months.

Consider other products.

As you proceed, your knowledge will grow and you may find your basic criteria were premature. If your initial evaluation seems shaky, drop back a few steps or start over.

However, avoid "chasing the rainbow." The ideal product may not be available when you need it. To make any progress, you may have to adapt to an inconvenient, awkward product or combine several products. Remember that bright people using a poor tool will outperform dull people with the best tools.

Lower your standards

Do you really, really need all the capabilities you listed as requirements? Are a few of your must-have features merely nice-to-have? Can you go ahead and launch your project without all the capabilities you listed?

Take some time off. Go on vacation. Go see a movie. Come back to your list with fresh eyes, and honestly review your rankings of criteria.

Fix the product

Consider whether you can add the missing must-have features. Here is a list of alternatives from technically simple to complex.

▶ **Find a workaround**. Check with existing users. Contact user groups and computer bulletin boards.

▶ **Have the vendor add them for you**. Get a commitment in writing stating when the new feature will be added and what it will cost you.

▶ **Buy an add-on product**. Many popular authoring tools can be extended with off-the-shelf options and external programs.

▶ **Write a script or macro**. Products that come with built-in programming languages are relatively easy to extend. However, features added by scripts may run slower than those native to the product.

▶ **Write an external program module**. Using a high-level language, you can write an external program that provides more capabilities for the authoring system. Although programming skills and tools are required, the result is fast and compact. And you can sell your module to others.

▶ **Modify the program directly**. Some vendors, for a price, will give you a copy of the source code for their product and let you make any changes you want. Of course, once you change it, you're stuck maintaining it.

Cancel the project

After examining all the available products and considering other options, you may conclude that no product meets your need or even that e-learning is not the best way to accomplish your goals. Never forget that your goal is to further learning, not to generate computer screens.

COMMON BLUNDERS IN PICKING TOOLS

As consultants, we are often called in after clients have blundered in picking tools. The reasons for their choices are often logical and perfectly understandable, but nonetheless wrong. Let's look at some common blunders people make when purchasing tools.

Often people purchase tools without considering the needs and capabilities of those who develop and those who consume learning products. Some tools require advanced technical skills, precise eye-hand coordination, or artistic skills.

Another problem occurs when tools dictate design. Often teams will purchase a tool and then design their e-learning to fit what the tool does well—rather than what learners really need. Many teams settle for the default settings in tools, further constraining their designs.

A related problem comes from picking a tool before deciding on standards and other requirements such as file formats, compatibility with existing corporate databases, or regulatory requirements.

Many tools are bought based on a bulleted list of features on a data sheet with scant consideration of the service required from the vendor after the sale. If you have a problem, does the vendor answer the phone on the first ring? What happens at 2 AM on a Sunday just before your most critical deadline?

 Only the emotionally deficient want a "personal relationship" with a vendor. If you want a personal relationship, spend more time with your mom, dad, or spouse. If you are lonely, get a friend or a dog. What you want from a vendor is capable products and reliable service. That's all.

Many teams defensively preserve their investment in outdated tools and skills. They stick with tools and technologies because converting materials and retraining staff would be expensive and difficult, even though the efficiency of the right approach might more than make up for the cost of converting.

Many teams rely on proprietary and platform-specific file formats. But platforms can change, and proprietary products can fade.

HOW MUCH DILIGENCE IS DUE?

You have an obligation to exercise due diligence in picking tools. That's *due* diligence, but not *excessive* or *obsessive* diligence. A three-month study by a committee of ten to consider buying two copies of Dreamweaver is excessive.

So what is reasonable? Here are some rough but reasonable rules.

- ▶ Number of criteria = 1 for each $1000 USD of costs
- ▶ Pages of detail = 1 for each $5000 of costs
- ▶ Number of people interviewed = 1 per $5000 of costs
- ▶ Cost of selection process = 5% to 10% of costs

So, if you are planning to buy tools costing about $100,000, you should expect to define 100 criteria, specify 20 pages of detail, interview 20 people, and spend $5,000 to $10,000 in the selection process.

These are only guidelines. If you are in a trusting organization where time is more important than money, spend less on selection. If you are in a paranoid organization with lots of people ready to cast blame and point fingers, spend more.

WHAT NOW?

Picking tools is as much a skill as a process. It takes practice to become quick, reliable, and comfortable picking tools. Here are some recommendations to get you started.

① Start with your less expensive tools and ones where a less-than-ideal choice does not endanger your whole department.

② Develop your abilities to identify requirements, scout out candidate tools, evaluate them, and render your decision.

③ Catalog reliable sources of information and knowledgeable evaluators.

④ Hone your spreadsheets and create templates for documenting your process.

⑤ Win the confidence of your management and the respect of vendors as you work your way up to choices for those budget gobbling, bet-the-farm systems.

In developing your tool-picking skills, you may find the general criteria in the next chapter helpful in filtering and evaluating candidate products.

21 General criteria for picking tools

Buyers have suffered more from the questions they forgot to ask than from the incomplete and inaccurate answers of vendors. This chapter suggests some general questions you should ask for almost all tools. These questions cover criteria that apply broadly to most vendors and tools. They are especially important for expensive, complex server-based tools. No checklist of desirable characteristics or features can guarantee success. No list of criteria is ever complete, but the ones here should increase your odds of success.

These general criteria further articulate your strategy and policies. When combined with specific criteria for each category of tools, they provide an initial shopping list of needed capabilities.

The criteria in this chapter fall into two groups: those for picking a vendor and those for picking a product.

VENDOR CRITERIA

Buying a tool requires a relationship with its vendor. That relationship may be relatively minor for procuring a small, inexpensive tool. But for a tool that is crucial to your project or that consumes much of your budget, the relationship with your vendor is critical for success. Before purchasing such a tool, you should examine the vendor just as if you were investing in the company, because in a way that is just what you are doing. Here are some criteria for considering vendors on whose products you will depend.

Is the vendor customer-oriented?

Does the company understand the needs of your kind of organization? Is the vendor focused on corporate training, higher education, or K-12? Does the vendor understand your needs and value your concerns? Some target only Fortune 100 firms or large universities. Getting their undivided attention can be a problem if you are a small organization or a single department within a large organization.

Does the company make satisfying its customers a top priority? Is the company loyal to its customers? Does it have a history of supporting its legacy products and their users? Does it continue support of products produced by companies it has purchased? When it discontinues a product, does it give customers financial and technical assistance to upgrade to newer products?

Is the company financially healthy?

Is the vendor financially healthy? Is the company consistently profitable, or is it desperately seeking funding just to survive? A financially healthy company has the assets to develop, market, and support its products. It will grow continuously and smoothly rather than undergo disrupting contractions and reorganizations.

How can you gauge the financial health of a company? If the company is publicly traded, you have insight into its financial workings.

Ask financial professionals

Whatever you do, talk to financial professionals. They have the background knowledge and speak the lingo. Balance sheets are their native tongue. Consult experts in your finance or accounting departments. Have your stockbroker look over the company's financial records. As you talk to financial professionals, discuss the issues that follow.

Consult financial records

For public companies in the United States, examine their Form 10-K (annual) and 10-Q (quarterly) filings to the U.S. Securities and Exchange Commission. You can download these documents from the Electronic Data Gathering, Analysis, and Retrieval (EDGAR) database at www.sec.gov/edgar.shtml. Or you can get them from the vendor's Web site. Such information usually resides in the Investor Relations section. It is a ponderous and imposing document that looks something like the 10-K shown.

Do not be daunted by the arcane language. Peruse its balance sheets and income statements. Look at the footnotes and details. Watch for trends. Do you see a stable, profitable business steaming confidently toward greatness—or one drifting toward the shoals of insolvency? Ask yourself whether you would invest your savings in this company. If your answer is no, then you should question investing your e-learning project's future there.

While looking over the financial records, you may want to search for some specific measures of success or failure. Here are some of the ones Bill likes to look for.

▶ **Hype ratio**. Spending on marketing and sales divided by spending on R&D. A hype ratio greater than two indicates that a company is spending twice as much promoting its current products as it is developing new products. Not good. On the other hand, a hype ratio of less than one may indicate that a company is not adequately promoting itself.

▶ **Countdown to doomsday**. If the company is losing money, how long can the company pay losses from cash reserves? To calculate the time before the company runs out of funding, divide its cash on hand and short-term investments by its rate of losing money.

▶ **Icebergs**. Is the company facing lawsuits, scandals, or some impropriety that could sink the company? Does the company's auditor use questionable means for calculating value? Check the footnotes of financial reports and get reports by independent financial analysts. Check Web sites like MSN Money (moneycentral.msn.com), CNNmoney (money.cnn.com), or Hoover's Online (hoovers.com).

▶ **Bloopers**. Unusual events can throw a balance sheet for a temporary loss. These can be settlements of lawsuits or restructuring charges for digesting an acquisition. One-time events are nothing to panic over if the company shows strength in dealing with setbacks.

- ▶ **Endangered product lines**. If the report shows the relative contributions of various product lines, take a close look at the results for the products you plan to purchase. If these products are declining in profitability, is the vendor likely to discontinue them soon or cut back on development and support?

For perspective in gauging these measures, compare the results of similar companies.

Track the stock price

Does the stock market value the company and its prospects? Has the stock price grown steadily even during periods of market decline? What is its price-earnings ratio? A company with a high price-earnings ratio is valued beyond its current financial results because investors think it will grow—or that other investors will believe so in the future.

If the stock has recently dropped, find out why. If the drop was because the company missed its quarterly projections by 2%, that is one thing. If it is because the patent on its main product was declared invalid, that is quite another thing. Be sure to compare similar companies in the same market.

What about privately held companies?

Getting financial information for small, privately held companies can be more difficult. First, check the vendor's credit rating through organizations such as Dun & Bradstreet (dnb.com). Your purchasing department can help obtain credit ratings for you. Second, ask the vendor for a summary of their recent financial data. Be prepared for reluctance and be willing to sign a nondisclosure or confidentiality agreement. Another possibility is Hoover's Online (hoovers.com). Some information is free of charge. You can access more by subscribing. A subscription costs less than $200 a year. Using Hoover's Online, you can compare firms against their major competitors.

Is the company professionally managed?

Is the company managed by a team of competent business managers with experience managing that type of company? Or are the top executives primarily technical wizards with a good idea that caught on? Is the business their primary focus, or is this venture a sideline for them? Are the managers college professors, who when the crunch occurs, may opt for tenure rather than commit to 80-hour weeks resurrecting the company?

Ideally managers should combine proven business management skills with technical knowledge of the company's market and product lines. And they should have a passion to see the company and its products succeed.

Who owns the company?

Is the company owned by the founder, who is also the president, CEO, and chairman of the board? Is it tightly held by a small group of founders? Does the majority of ownership rest with a venture capitalist? Or is it broadly owned by a diverse mix of institutional and individual investors? Is it a small subsidiary of a massive conglomerate?

Ownership affects the goals and decision-making processes of the company. It also affects the relationship with your organization. What kind of ownership makes the company a solid business partner?

Has the company proven itself?

Does the company have a reputation of delivering on its promises? Does the company have a base of satisfied customers? Has the company consistently released bug-free versions of its products on time? Or is it only selling vaporware and promises?

TOOLS CRITERIA

As you begin preparing a list of capabilities your tools must provide, start with the general criteria listed here. These include criteria that apply to a wide variety of tools. Such general criteria are especially helpful in your initial screening of products.

Not all of these criteria apply to all products. Some, for example, apply mainly to server-based products. Some criteria depend on your strategy and may be included or not as appropriate.

Ease of use

A tool is easy to use if new users can install it, learn it, and operate it quickly, confidently, and reliably. With an easy-to-use product, users can employ its full range of features and obtain help when they need it.

 A lot of products are easy to use because they don't do much. Get a capable tool and invest in the training needed to make it easy to use.

Installation

Installation should be a simple, reliable process. Here are some issues to investigate.

▶ **One-click operation**. The installation should be as simple as pressing a button. The options most needed by most users should be automatically selected. Advanced users should be able to easily change and add to these preset selections.

▶ **Easy uninstall process**. The tool should also make it easy for the user to remove all components installed and to set the computer's configuration back the way it was before the installation. The tool should also log all components installed and the directories into which they were placed.

▶ **System safety**. The installation process should never overwrite newer components without asking permission. Nor should the process change users' system configurations without warning them.

User interface

The user interface of the tool should follow standard conventions, especially for operating system functions like selecting files and displaying directories. All text should be legible and all buttons labeled with tool tips that clarify their function.

Documentation

The tool should provide complete documentation for all roles (learner, instructor, administrator, instructional designer, and programmer) and levels of user (beginner, intermediate, advanced). Ask tough questions. Does the tool provide context-sensitive online Help on all features of program operation? Does the documentation go beyond mechanical use of the product to provide instructions on good design and technique? Does it provide good examples and models?

Support

Does the vendor provide free, 24-hours-a-day, 7-days-a-week phone, e-mail, and discussion forum support? Does the tool provide complete support information, such as:

▶ Support contact

▶ Sales contact

▶ Technical contact

▶ Address

▶ Phone

▶ Fax

▶ E-mail

▶ Web site

Third-party support

What independent support services are available to help you learn and use the product? Are consultants and contractors available to advise you and work in the product? Are there Internet newsgroups, discussion forums, and other online support services? Are third-party books and training available on the product?

Reliability

The tool must be stable and not freeze the learner's computer, crash the browser, or overwhelm the server. When problems do occur, disruption should be minimal, and information should be provided to help overcome the problem and prevent its recurrence.

Clear error messages

Does the tool report errors in simple but complete language? Or are they cryptic codes that read like lottery ticket numbers? Do error messages suggest a remedy? Or do they blame the user? Is there documentation that explains error messages? Or must users call a psychic?

Problem-reporting mechanism

The tool should provide a simple, standard way for reporting problems. It should have a standard problem-reporting screen that is friendly looking and easy for the user to fill out. The mechanism should automatically record what the user was doing when the problem occurred. When specific remedies are not practical, the tool should help users diagnose and correct problems.

Logging server activities

Server-based tools should log all activity, including errors. The following items should be logged for the server or software itself:

 To humble a system vendor, ask to see their tool's error log.

▶ Start up and shutdown

▶ Problems with database integrity

▶ Problems with the tool itself

- ▶ Problems with attempted access, such as a missing piece of information or bad command
- ▶ Execution of successful commands
- ▶ Debugging information

This log should display in a standard, easily understood format. The tool should be able to generate reports summarizing data from the log. Furthermore, the log should be secure.

Reliability of hosted solutions

If the tool is hosted by an external vendor, ask how fast and reliable the hosting system is.

- ▶ **Capacity**. How many machines does the vendor have? How fast are they? How much data can they hold?

- ▶ **Redundancy**. Do their systems feature a session failover capability that lets users continue when the specific machine they are connected to fails?

- ▶ **Backups**. What are their backup and archiving procedures? Where are backups stored?

- ▶ **Databases**. What database do they use? Running on how many servers?

- ▶ **Network**. What network bandwidth do they have? What network redundancy do they have?

- ▶ **Statistics**. Ask the vendor for statistics on downtime and outages.

Efficiency

Efficiency makes the best use of users' efforts and time. Efficient tools do not waste keystrokes, mouse clicks, thoughts, time, or motion. Look for efficiency features such as:

- ▶ **Keyboard shortcuts** so users do not have to use the mouse to select menu commands for common actions.

- ▶ **Macro language** so users can write scripts to automate repeated operations. Better still, some tools include a macro recorder that lets users record a series of actions and play it back as many times as needed.

- ▶ **Operations on multiple objects**. Users can change multiple items by selecting all of them and then specifying the changes once.

▶ **Defaults and templates**. The tool should include intelligent defaults and templates for everything including the course home page.

▶ **Import and check in**. Users can easily register large numbers of components with the system in one operation. And the system keeps track of the components to ensure that two or more users do not make changes to the same file at the same time.

Flexibility of pricing

Tools range in price from free to more than a million dollars in cost. And the lowest cost is not always the best value. You must ask whether the vendor's pricing structure fits your way of doing business, especially if the cost of your solution is a primary factor in its success.

Is the pricing and licensing model simple? Are costs reasonable and predictable? What mixture of pricing models does the license require?

▶ One-time fee

▶ Annual fee

▶ Per-user fee

▶ Per-use fee

Hidden costs such as maintenance, customization, and operational inefficiencies can far exceed the purchase price. Find out which features are standard, which cost extra, and which would require custom development.

 Watch out. Per-use and per-user fees can accumulate as your efforts grow. Get out your spreadsheets and see what the costs will be under all likely scenarios.

If the tool has an intricate licensing scheme, make sure that the tool helps you automatically track and allocate licenses. Such a tool should allocate user licenses across the network, notify the administrator when limits are reached or are near, and enforce the limit, giving users a polite message.

Availability as a hosted solution

Do you have to install the product on your own machines or is it available as a Web-based service? Such offerings are sometimes called a Web hosting, application hosting, or application service provider (ASP). The service may be provided directly by the vendor of the tool or by a third-party hosting service.

Minimal dependencies

Products seldom work entirely alone. They require certain computer hardware and software. Always read the list of requirements for a product. A low-price product that requires you to replace a large number of computers is more expensive than a higher-priced product that runs on the machines you already have.

Ask what processor, memory, disk space, operating system, screen size, sound card, and network speed and other computer resources the product requires. Compare these requirements to what you already have. Factor in the costs of any upgrades necessary to run the product.

Don't just read the requirements in the vendor's data sheet—test them! Verify how well the tool runs on the systems you already have and that there are no incompatibilities with other required software.

Also ask about other products the product requires. The product you want may in turn require a separate core product or a specific Web server, server operating system, and hardware. An individual component may be a loss leader to sell hardware or Web servers. Compute the whole cost of the product and its required entourage.

Security

Security is especially important to protect data from malicious or accidental damage or misuse. An authoring tool may need to ensure that multiple authors do not overwrite each other's contributions and that only authorized changes are made. An LMS must maintain the confidentiality of information about learners and secure proprietary content. Ask how the tool implements the security required for:

▶ E-commerce and billing

▶ Private or confidential content

▶ Learner information, especially grades

▶ Personnel records

▶ Medical records

▶ Government secrets

▶ Trade secrets

Here are some additional criteria to use in evaluating the security of an e-learning tool.

Security protocols

If potentially sensitive and private information is likely to be accessed or distributed, the tool should incorporate standard security features and protocols, such as:

▶ Secure Sockets Layer (SSL) for login procedures and encryption of critical data

▶ HTTPS for Web pages displaying or transmitting sensitive data

Other security protocols are possible so be sure to ask "How do I know my content is secure while in transit?"

Encryption

Encryption encodes data in a form that only someone with a decoding key can unscramble. Consider encryption for especially sensitive data stored in a system and for data as it travels over the network, especially if it goes outside your organization. Tools should offer the option of 128-bit encryption of secret, proprietary, or sensitive information.

Password policies

Passwords are the most basic form of security and authentication. They attempt to control who has access to data. Tools commonly provide password protection of all courses, events, and resources.

Password policies may require learners to pick hard-to-guess passwords and to change them often. Ask what kind of password policies administrators can require.

Make sure that your tools can connect to authentication and security features built into operating systems and network servers so that authors and learners do not have to log in multiple times, or remember several different passwords.

Copyright protection

Does the tool provide a mechanism for requesting, recording, and documenting copyright permissions? Does it require a copyright permission or an override before including any external content? Does the tool support digital rights management (DRM) software? Does the tool automatically insert a copyright notice into the media file or its metadata? Just as you take care to obtain and assign copyright to your written content, so should you take the same degree of care with your media components.

Security model

A security model says who can take what actions with what data in the system. Look for a tool that provides a rich mixture of roles, privileges, and objects.

Are roles and objects ones that your users will recognize? Do they correspond to the job responsibilities of individuals? Can privileges be assigned using plain language rather than cryptic codes? Can administrators define any combination of the following?

Roles (People)	Privileges (What they can do)	Objects (What they can create or change)
Author or developer	Create or write	Course content
Learner	View or play	User names
Administrator	Edit	Passwords
Instructor, facilitator, teacher	Delete	Grades
Supervisor, sponsor, or parent of the learner	Post or distribute	Profiles and biographies
		Courses
		Individual topics or pages
		Discussion and e-mail messages.
		Announcements
		Individual columns or fields in reports

Firewall compatibility

Can the tool work across firewalls? Does it transport media commonly blocked by firewalls? Do firewalls slow it down? Does it rely on technologies such as Java or Flash, which some companies may block? Can the tool distinguish between a valid Java application and a Java virus?

Openness

What if your relationship with the tool or its vendor does not work out? How much will it cost to get your material out of the tool and into its replacement? Tools that lock your content away in proprietary file formats or databases can seem like a black hole.

Open tools are interchangeable. An open tool can be replaced with another tool from another vendor. Open tools can be reprogrammed and interconnected. Buyers can add to their open system and combine open tools with other open tools. Open tools are an essential part of an open strategy (chapter 19).

 Do not confuse openness with extensibility. Openness concerns the tool's ability to serve as a component in a larger system. Extensibility concerns adaptability within a single tool.

There are several aspects of openness and several capabilities to look for in such products.

Operating system availability

You mean Windows and Mac, right? Not quite. Consider all the operating systems the product will need to run on in the foreseeable future. For example:

▶ Windows NT, 98, 2000, XP

▶ Macintosh OS 9 and OS X

▶ Linux

▶ Palm OS

▶ Pocket PC

One strategy used by some vendors to make their tools run on multiple operating systems is to develop them in the Java programming language—Java 2 Enterprise Edition (J2EE), more specifically.

Browser compatibility

Does the tool work with recent versions of Netscape and Internet Explorer browsers? See chapter 6 for some of the issues of browser compatibility as well as a list of additional browsers.

Standards compliance

Does the tool support industry standards for interoperability? Support for standards makes it easier for you to combine separate tools, buy and integrate separately developed content, and to sell

 By the time a standard is agreed upon, it is obsolete. Many standards are already a generation or two out of date.

your own content. Examples include AICC, IMS, and SCORM specifications for packaging, metadata, and communications (see chapter 22).

Open protocols

Protocols are communications standards whereby one open tool exchanges data with another. Open protocols include familiar standards such as HTTP and FTP as well as more esoteric ones such as HTTP AICC Communication Protocol (HACP), Simple Object Access Protocol (SOAP), and telecommunications standards such as H.323 or T.120. Tools that use open protocols allow server and client components from different vendors.

Programmatic interface

Open tools often provide a programmatic interface, either through an application programming interface (API) or a macro language. This interface means that its operations can be automated from the internal macro language or a common programming language such as Java Script, Java, or Visual Basic. Through a programmatic interface, a clever programmer can make incompatible proprietary tools fly in formation and even do a bit of a tango.

Interchangeable databases

Proprietary Tool A stores its data only in an Oracle 9i database while Proprietary Tool B insists on SQL Server. Neither tool documents the internal organization of its database. Swapping Tool A for Tool B is a major corporate effort.

Open tools, on the other hand, tend to allow a choice of database. Open tools support standard programming interfaces, such as Open Database Connectivity (ODBC) or Java Database Connectivity (JDBC), so programs can pluck data from one brand of database and deposit it safely in another.

Open file formats

Open tools can read and write data in standard, well documented file formats instead of secret proprietary formats. Open formats include Internet standards, such as HTML, GIF, JPEG, MPEG, and MP3.

Exporting content

An open tool can export all finished and raw content in a form that can be imported into another comparable tool, thereby avoiding the black hole effect.

Open tools either export content in an open file format or as XML with a well-documented schema or document type definition (DTD) that completely explains the format of the XML. For more on XML, see chapter 23.

Extensibility

How easy is it to extend and customize the product? Can you write macros or scripts to automate complex sequences of actions? Can you create toolbars to make using the tool more efficient? Can you design templates for components that do not change? If the tool does 85% of what you want, can you complete the extra 15%? Here are some criteria to help you determine the extensibility of a tool.

Source code availability

Can you modify the underlying code of the product to customize it to your needs? Or is the code in uneditable, compiled modules that you must take as is? Is the code offered under an open source license that allows you to make changes but requires you to make them available to other users of the tool as well?

Documentation

Are the architecture and operations of the tool revealed in enough detail and clarity for you to make changes? Look for:

▶ **A general schematic-level diagram** showing how all the pieces fit and work together

▶ **Explanation of the database** tables and fields listing their function, format, and relationships

▶ **Annotations in source code** explaining functions and their internal workings

Customizable

Developers often want to customize the look and feel of the interface to suit corporate styles or other goals. Developers or learners should be able to define unique skins.

At a minimum, the tool should offer predefined, coordinated color schemes, font sets, graphics, and layouts. Each scheme should have a library of possible accent graphics. The author should be able to pick from these available alternatives.

Does the tool let administrators and authors:

Change	By
Buttons and icons	Replacing icons or editing them
Frame arrangement and size	Editing frame template

Change	By
Arrangement of standard items in the window	Editing template files and placeholders
Headers and footers	Editing template files and placeholders
Interface text	Editing forms ad templates

In addition, can developers extend the product and customize its user interface through:

▸ Macros or a built-in programming language

▸ Custom menus

▸ Custom templates

▸ The application programming interface (API)

Accessibility

An accessible tool is one that can be used by those with common disabilities, such as less-than-perfect vision, hearing, or movement control. It is also a tool that simplifies the process of creating accessible content.

Accessible tools do not rely on one sensory modality or provide only one way of performing actions. In addition, accessible tools work with accessibility aids built into the operating system as well as with common screen readers.

A tool complies or enables compliance with the W3C Web Accessibility Initiative recommendations and Section 508 of the U.S. Rehabilitation Act of 1998 (chapter 22) if, when used with accessibility aids, it provides capabilities such as:

▸ Keyboard shortcuts

▸ Enlargement of portions of the screen

▸ High-contrast display

▸ Shifting colors to avoid color blindness problems

▸ Audio cues for system actions

▸ Text-to-speech synthesis

▸ Voice-recognition for selecting commands and entering text

▸ Text equivalents for every non-text element

Visit the W3C Web site for a complete checklist (w3.org/TR/WCAG10/full-checklist.html).

Scalability

If you plan to grow your e-learning efforts, perhaps starting with a few courses by a small department and eventually expanding to cover not just your entire enterprise but its network of customers, suppliers, and partners as well—then you better buy a scalable system.

In marketing, the term scalable is often used as a fancy way of saying, "We don't crash when you load in a lot of data." What it should mean is that the tool is economical at the smallest number of users or amount of content you need to manage and the tool remains responsive and reliable with the largest number.

Ask this tough question: "At the maximum advertised size, what response time and downtime should I expect from your tool running on the minimum machine you specify?"

Scalability is not just a technical issue. The tool must be offered with a flexible pricing structure that makes it affordable for small and large numbers of users.

Localization

If you're authoring and delivering training internationally, it is important that your tools are localized to the language and culture of their users.

Does the tool work globally? Is the interface available in all the languages you need? Has all the text, including button labels, ALT (alternative) text, tool tips, and Help files been translated to the target language? Are instructions for learners, course authors, and administrators available in all needed languages?

Can the customer select the language at the time the system is set up? Can different users see the interface in different languages from the same server?

Can the tool create and offer content in all necessary languages? Does it support Isocode and other double-byte fonts necessary to display text for Asian languages?

Remote administration

Can the tool be operated and administered from anywhere with just a browser? Are all features available in a Web-based console? Can all operations be performed from a browser anywhere on the network, without having to install a separate

 This criterion applies to server-based components. It would not apply, for example, to a local media editor.

authoring or administrative application? Does remote administration require a plug-in, Java applet, ActiveX control, or some other component that runs locally on the administrator's computer?

Corporate systems integration

Organizations may have established standards and preferences for technologies and tools. They may have systems in place. If your e-learning tools and technologies must fit into an existing infrastructure, your choices need to be compatible with:

▶ Standard operating systems, such as Widows XP.

▶ Databases such as Oracle 9i or SQL Server.

▶ Web browsers, such as a specific version of Netscape or Internet Explorer.

▶ Corporate information and security systems, such as Microsoft Active Directory for a single login to all systems.

▶ Network and Internet servers, such as Microsoft Windows 2000 Server.

▶ Suites of desktop programs, such as Microsoft Office. For example, some learning management systems can enter training schedules directly into employees' personal calendars in Microsoft Outlook.

▶ Corporate information systems, such as an enterprise resources planning (ERP), human resources information system (HRIS), customer relationship planning (CRM) system.

 If vendors claim their product integrates with other systems, be sure to ask exactly what data items the systems exchange and how they handle inconsistencies in formatting.

In addition, organizations may have a philosophy of supporting open systems or they may prefer to standardize on the products of one vendor as much as possible. Early on, uncover the standards and preferences of your IT department. (See chapter 19.)

Vendor services

Are you buying just software with no support, or does the package include hardware, implementation, training, and consulting? Some services you may want include:

▶ Course and content development

▶ Customization and extension of their product

▶ Development of custom templates

▶ Management consulting

▶ System configuration and setup

▶ Hosting

▶ Technical support

▶ Training

▶ Marketing of courses and learning objects

WHAT NOW?

You will apply the criteria listed in this chapter when you get ready to evaluate a product or vendor. To make them effective, follow these guidelines.

1 Decide which of these criteria apply to the type of tool you are picking.

2 Combine these general criteria with more specific ones found in the chapter covering the type of tool you are picking.

3 Assign priorities for these criteria that reflect your organization's needs.

Evolution, trends, and big ideas

Advances in the technological infrastructure behind tools are transforming e-learning. These changes are as much social as technical. They are discussed in the three chapters of this section.

▶ **Standards for e-learning** explains both established and emerging standards to guide you in creating high-quality reusable chunks of learning, sometimes called learning objects (chapter 22).

▶ **What the L is XML** explains Extensible Markup Language and shows how it is the logical successor to HTML as well as the *lingua franca* of data exchange. Though you may never see XML directly, it will be at the core of many of the e-learning tools you use (chapter 23).

▶ **Trends in technology and learning** surveys the advances in information technology that make e-learning possible and shows how continuing advances will enable learning to evolve in new and productive directions (chapter 24).

22 Standards for e-learning

Standards for e-learning are bursting forth from committees, infiltrating sales brochures, blossoming on shrink-wrapped boxes of authoring tools, and popping up on purchasing requests for courseware.

WHAT'S ALL THE FUSS ABOUT STANDARDS?

In an ideal world, the people who design, build, administer, sell, and take e-learning would never notice the standards underlying e-learning any more than they notice the standards for the light bulbs that illuminate the rooms where they work, the power plugs for their computers, and the coins in their pockets. As the heads of e-learning standards bodies have repeatedly said, standards are written for toolmakers, not for designers, developers, and purchasers of e-learning content. So why do you need to understand standards?

Do I need to understand standards?

You need to understand these emerging e-learning standards and specifications if you are:

▶ Responding to a request for proposals that requires SCORM compliance. The RFP doesn't elaborate, and the issuing authority doesn't seem to know either.

▶ Developing training for a U.S. federal agency. Somebody mentions, "Don't they require Section 508 compliance?"

▶ Planning to reuse content extensively. You have heard that standards will help but are not sure which standards the tools should implement.

▶ Working for a boss that believes that standards are the answer for everything but can't say why.

▶ Dealing with concerns that standards will crush your staff's creativity.

▶ Managing hundreds of courses that were developed to earlier versions of standards. Now you are wondering if you should update the courses.

Even if you have no immediate requirement for standards, you can learn a lot by reading, or perhaps, skimming them to see how many bright and influential people view the architecture of e-learning.

Many who require or claim to meet standards are doing so because they want to be "with it," or because they are trying to add more buzzwords to marketing brochures. You need a solid reason to use standards.

Do I need a standards strategy?

This chapter will help you decide when and how to integrate standards into your e-learning. Along the way it will also help you develop a standards strategy that helps you answer questions such as:

▶ **Which standards apply to your project or your role**? Which can add value to the finished product? Which can make your workflow more efficient? Which will allow you to reuse components?

▶ **How will you incorporate standards into your work**? Will you purchase tools that follow standards or make following standards easier? Will you build standards into the templates and scripts you use in constructing content? Will you require standards compliance in your request for proposals from vendors?

▶ **Which standards will you follow first**? Which aspects of these standards will you follow?

▶ **To whom can you turn for advice on standards**? Who can guarantee compliance?

THE PROMISE OF E-LEARNING STANDARDS

To understand the frenzy over e-learning standards, you need to understand the underlying problems that are fueling the development of these standards. Learners cannot easily find the courses they need. Course authors find it difficult to combine content and tools from different vendors. Course administrators cannot move courses, each with hundreds of files, from management system to management system. Learners with common disabilities cannot take the courses they need Custom-developed courses may only communicate with the systems on which they were developed.

Standards organizations are addressing these problems in several ways. They are developing standards that promote building e-learning from reusable parts and that help reduce dependence on individual vendors and products.

Build from reusable parts

One of the explicit goals of standards is to allow the reuse of content at all levels—not just whole courses and online books, but smaller units as well. The concept of building from reusable parts works like this:

A curriculum is assembled from reusable courses, which are assembled from reusable lessons, which are made of reusable pages, containing reusable media elements.

These units are called *reusable learning objects*. They are also called *knowledge objects* and *sharable content objects*. Course authors can reuse these objects for different purposes in different projects. They can reuse entire courses or books; their lessons or chapters; their individual pages, topics, or displays; and even their media components.

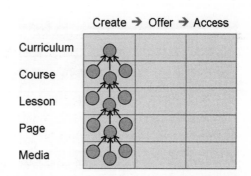

That means course authors do not need to develop all the content for a particular project. Objects, once perfected, can be reused on several projects. Here's how this modular approach can work:

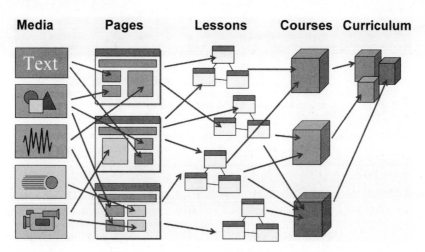

At the top level you may assemble a *curriculum* from reusable courses. To create *courses*, you shop for proven lessons. Effective lessons may contribute to multiple courses. To create the *lessons*, you combine existing pages. Relevant, well-crafted pages may appear in multiple lessons. *Pages*, likewise, may incorporate existing lower-level media components. These *media components* may consist of reusable boilerplate text, standard graphics, narration segments, animations, and video clips.

Even though you may develop original content, the costs are lower because that original content can be reused in subsequent projects.

Reduce dependence on individual products and vendors

Whenever you buy courses or license a tool, you should consider your exit strategy. Call it due diligence or risk management, but you need to think about what you will do if a vendor goes broke or if a better product comes along. Standards promise to make it easy to migrate to a better tool, course, or vendor.

The holy grail of standards is interoperability—interoperability among authoring tools, content, and management systems. Here's what we mean by true interoperability.

Let's examine this diagram starting at the right side with the producers. *Producers*, in this context, are the people and organizations that produce learning products. Imagine that we have a couple of producers, Producer A and Producer B. Each producer uses certain

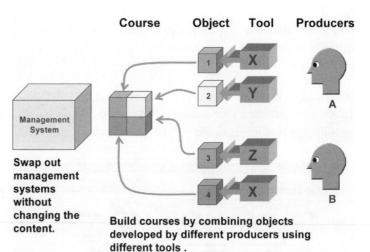

Swap out management systems without changing the content.

Build courses by combining objects developed by different producers using different tools .

tools to produce learning *objects*, that is, self-contained, reusable modules of education or training. Tools are things like Dreamweaver, ToolBook, Trainersoft, or Authorware. Suppose that Producer A uses Tool X to produce Object 1 and Tool Y to produce Object 2. Producer B then uses Tool Z to produce Object 3 and Tool X to produce Object 4.

In this brave new world of interoperability, the learning management system can assemble a course by integrating these separate objects developed by different producers using different tools.

Furthermore, you can replace the learning management system with another of comparable capabilities, without having to redevelop or reassemble our course.

Interoperability allows you to pick the best producers, tools, content, and management systems—and to swap out any of them without having to redo any others. How would such true interoperability improve your operations?

 The metaphor of the Holy Grail is apropos. Knights questing for the Holy Grail never found it and most of them ended up dead.

WHAT EXACTLY ARE STANDARDS?

Much of the difficulty of implementing e-learning standards has nothing to do with e-learning but everything to do with the nature and perception of standards in general. The word standard takes on different meanings for different people.

Standards vs. specifications vs. guidelines

So, what is a standard? That is one of those philosophical questions like "If a tree falls in the forest and no one is there to hear it, does it make a sound?" The answer to that question is still being debated.

A similar question about standards might be, "If a standard is written and nobody follows it, is it really a standard?" The answer to this one is no. The reason is that a written specification is not a standard. Specifications, guidelines, and recommendations are not standards unless large

 But, how many people must follow a specification for it to become a standard? One? Two? Ten thousand? Ten percent of a profession? One hundred percent?

numbers of people follow them. Using that definition, much of what we call e-learning standards today are really just specifications aiming to become standards.

Standards are not guarantees

Compliance with a standard does not guarantee achievement of the goal behind the standard. ISO9000 certification does not guarantee that a factory will not consistently manufacture useless or dangerous products any more than a high score on the Scholastic Aptitude Test guarantees a student will not flunk out of college. As the issuers of these standards point out, all a standard can do is to provide reliable information upon which to base decisions. A standard may put the odds in your favor but it cannot guarantee success.

Different kinds of standards

The term standard is used to describe several methods by which conformity and consistency are achieved. These different types of standards vary in the source of their authority and their degree of influence. Here we discuss three main types of standards: accredited, de facto, and internal.

Accredited standards

Accredited standards are based on written laws, government regulations, or specifications issued by professional organizations. Such standards are sometimes called *de jure* (Latin for "in law") standards. They require a complete and unambiguous written specification, the authority of an authenticating organization, and a certification process whereby compliance with the standard can be verified. Examples of accredited standards include the ISO 9000 process and documentation standards; the TCP/IP standard that governs exchange of data over Internet connections; and electrical codes for wiring in homes and office buildings. Some people reserve the word standard for accredited standards.

De facto standards

The term *de facto* is Latin for "in fact" and is used to describe conventional standards that are widely followed, though they lack regulatory authority. De facto standards evolve when a large number of people use the same product, for example Microsoft Word or Adobe Acrobat. De facto standards also occur when groups of people more or less follow the same set of rules. Adherence to such conventional standards comes about because the standard way of doing things is significantly more effective, less costly, quicker, or more convenient. Examples include human languages, the physical structure of books, and the placement of buttonholes.

Internal standards

Internal standards are the rules proposed and followed by a specific team. On a multimedia development project, you may find standards for color usage, screen layout, terminology, and styles of interactivity. Such internal standards usually aim at achieving consistency of results and efficiency of production.

So what do I do?

You cannot force everyone to use the word standard for one narrow meaning. You have to cope with the linguistic noise. You can, however, ensure that you are clear in your communications about standards by:

▶ Stating clearly what you consider a standard to be in speaking and writing

▶ Questioning others until you understand what they mean by the term

Consistency and context go a long way in communicating clearly about standards.

E-LEARNING STANDARDS

Now we are ready to talk about four types of emerging standards for e-learning. For each, we will discuss what they specify, which organizations issue the standards, and how you can make your e-learning comply with them.

Components and standards

Let's look at the main types of standards and how they enable the interchange of components in a learning system. On one side are the consumers of e-learning and on the other, the producers of e-learning content.

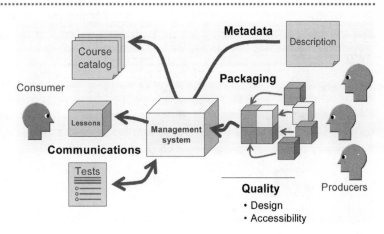

Producers create individual modules or learning objects which must be integrated into a unified course. Standards that allow the assembly of courses authored in different tools by different producers into integrated modules are called *packaging standards*. These same standards enable a management system to import and organize all the components of the course.

A second group of standards is necessary so that management systems can launch individual lessons and other components and can administer tests and other assessments. These standards are called *communications standards*, and they specify how the consumer and the management system exchange information.

 We are using the term management system to encompass LMSs, LCMSs, and other content management systems.

A third group of standards specifies how producers can prepare descriptions of their courses and other modules so that the management system can compile catalogs of available learning content. These standards are called *metadata standards*.

A fourth group of standards concerns the quality of modules and courses. These quality standards govern overall course and module design as well as accessibility by those with disabilities.

Though somewhat independent, these four types of standards all contribute to the goal of combining of high-quality components to create richer, more effective learning solutions.

Standards organizations

Who are the players in the drama of standards? Standards groups work in several areas: e-learning technology, e-learning quality, underlying technology, and an accreditation pipeline.

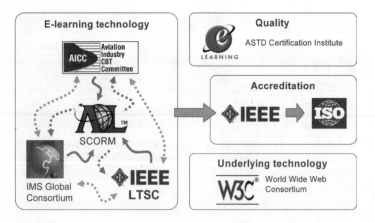

Within the area of e-learning technology, four main groups are active in proposing standards. Each group is greatly influenced by the others. Much of the effort of all these groups has gone into tweaking and tinkering with standards authored by other groups or the modifications made by other groups.

The oldest among these is the Aviation Industry CBT Committee, or AICC for short. Though originally formed to serve airframe manufacturers, suppliers, and buyers, the AICC has expanded its base to include many other groups producing and using e-learning content. Other organizations actively proposing standards are the IEEE's Learning Technology Standards Committee and the IMS Global Consortium.

The fourth member of this elite club is the Advanced Distributed Learning (ADL) group's Sharable Content Object Reference Model (SCORM) project. SCORM does not directly author standards but pledges to adopt and make practical the best standards put forth by the other groups. However, SCORM has done some serious arm- twisting to inspire the changes it desired.

Eventually, to achieve authority, standards must be submitted to an organization with the authority to accredit and promulgate them. The first stop along this route for most standards is the IEEE. Eventually, standards may become ISO standards.

 By the way, IEEE is always pronounced "eye-triple-E" and never "eye-E-E-E." It stands for the Institute of Electrical and Electronics Engineers, but no one ever calls it that. Don't embarrass yourself by doing so.

Two additional types of standards efforts are worth noting. One area covers quality and is typified by the ASTD Certification Institute's E-learning Courseware Certification program, which evaluates not the technology of e-learning but the quality of its content. The other area of standards is that of underlying technologies such as HTML and XML, which are governed by the World Wide Web Consortium (W3C). The W3C also promotes standards for accessibility of Web content.

There are dozens more standards organizations, but the ones discussed here are the most influential and the ones whose names find their way into bulleted lists of product features and requests for proposals. For a more complete list of standards groups, go to horton.com/tools.

PACKAGING STANDARDS

Packaging standards prescribe ways to bundle separate objects, to protect them, and to transport them—much like the standard egg carton that get eggs from the grocery store to your refrigerator shelf.

Packaging standards for e-learning specify how to bundle the separate files that make up a lesson, course, or other unit of content. They are necessary to ensure that all the hundreds or thousands of files are included and installed in the right location.

What does a packaging standard provide?

Packaging standards for e-learning content provide:

▶ A way to specify or catalog the content of a course or other unit of learning content. The package includes the course definition, HTML files, images, multimedia, style sheets, and everything else down to the smallest icon.

▶ An organizational scheme for a module or course so that it can be imported into a management system and the management system can display a menu for the course and launch components chosen by the learner.

▶ Some techniques to move courses and modules from one management system to another, without having to re-catalog or reorganize their parts.

▶ A method to bundle all the separate files and Web addresses into a single file for easy transport.

Packaging standards do just what their name implies. They make it easy to bundle all the components of an e-learning product into an easily managed unit.

What packaging standards?

What packaging standards are available? Several similar packaging standards have evolved.

Aviation Industry CBT Committee	Making courses interchangeable under the AICC standard requires a number of files, depending on the level of complexity. These include the course description file, assignable units files, descriptor files, course structure files, prerequisites files, completion requirements files, and objective relationships files. This standard can designate complex flows through content. However, many developers complain that this standard is hard to implement and that it does not encourage reuse of already-defined lower-level modules.
IMS Global Consortium	In contrast, the IMS Content and Packaging specification is simpler and more constrained. It is easier to implement, but only hierarchical courses are possible in the current version (1.1.2) of this standard. Microsoft's LRN Toolkit implements this standard (microsoft.com).
SCORM	SCORM, in Version 1.2, adopted the IMS Content and Packaging Standard virtually intact. SCORM 1.3 promises to let designers sequence models by prerequisites.

For future projects, you will probably want to implement the SCORM specification, although you may encounter earlier implementation of AICC and IMS versions.

IMS Content and Packaging Standard

Both SCORM and IMS use the IMS Content and Packaging specification, as does the Microsoft LRN Toolkit (microsoft.com/elearn). Let's take a closer look at it.

The core of the Content and Packaging specification is a manifest or packing slip for the package. This manifest must be named *imsmanifest.xml*. As its extension indicates, this manifest follows the rules of XML for internal structure and formatting.

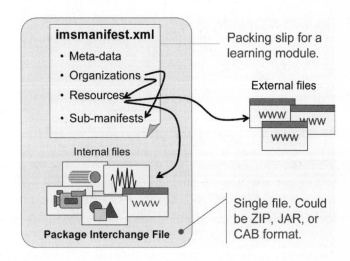

Within this file are four main sections:

▶ The *Meta-data* section records specific information about the module.

▶ The *Organizations* section is the actual inventory of content. It is essentially a table of contents for the module. It refers to specific resource descriptions and to sub-manifests, each of which is further detailed in its own section.

▶ The resource descriptions occupy the third section of the manifest, called *Resources*. These descriptions point to local files that are included in the package and to external files (i.e., Web addresses) on the Internet.

▶ *Sub-manifests* completely describe included packages. Each sub-manifest has the same Meta-data, Organizations, Resources, and Sub-manifests sections as the main manifest. Manifests can thus include sub-manifests which include further sub-manifests.

This process of inclusion allows assembly of courses and other high-level components from individual lessons, topics, and other lower-level learning objects.

The specification also provides techniques to wrap the manifest and files up into one physical package. The recommended file formats for consolidating separate files are as a PKZIP (ZIP) file, a Java archive (JAR), or a cabinet (CAB) file. This method of implementing a standard in a particular technology is called a *binding* and is not a core part of the standard.

Help meeting packaging standards

Handcrafting the Content and Packaging manifest is a time-consuming and error-prone process. Fortunately tools exist to help with the task. Here are some free tools for creating a package manifest.

LRN Toolkit

By Microsoft   microsoft.com/elearn

Microsoft provides several tools for implementing the IMS Content and Packaging specification and for displaying IMS packages. Microsoft calls its toolkit LRN, which is pronounced "learn" and stands for Learning Resource iNterchange. Within this toolkit are three tools helpful in constructing IMS packages. The LRN Editor can be used to create and modify package manifests. The LRN Validator tests a manifest for compliance with the IMS specification and XML structuring rules. The LRN Converter for FrontPage lets authors use FrontPage to assemble their module as a Web site and then run the converter to generate the corresponding IMS manifest.

Manifest Maker for ADL SCORM

By Macromedia   macromedia.com

Macromedia provides access to dozens of extensions to their Dreamweaver tool on their Dreamweaver exchange. Some of these extensions are provided by Macromedia and some by third parties. There you will find the Manifest Maker for ADL SCORM by Tom King. This extension enables Dreamweaver to create a manifest for a course authored in Dreamweaver

Some LMSs and LCMSs provide commands for packaging courses for exchange with other learning management systems. Look for an "Export as IMS package" command or some similar command.

COMMUNICATIONS STANDARDS

Communications standards define a language whereby people or things can communicate. A tangible example of a communications standard is a dictionary that defines the common meanings of words in a language.

In e-learning, communications standards define a language whereby the management system can start up modules and communicate with them.

In this segment, we will consider what the management system and modules need to communicate, what communications standards have been proposed, how they work, and what must be done to comply with them.

What does a communications standard provide?

What do the management system and learning object need to communicate? What could they possible have to say to one another? Here are some topics of a possible conversation.

▶ The management system needs to know whenever an object starts up.

▶ The object asks the name of the learner so it can personalize responses.

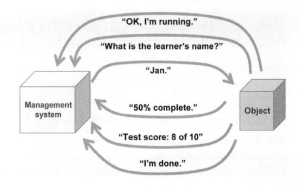

▶ The object reports back to the management system how much of the object the learner has completed.

▶ The management system needs to record the scores.

▶ Finally, the management system needs to know when the learner has completed and closed an object.

Keep in mind that none of these communications are new. You never noticed them in traditional computer-based training (CBT) modules because the communication was within a single integrated piece of software running on a single machine, rather than among distributed components running across a network.

A communications standard typically specifies two things: a protocol and a data model. The protocol specifies rules for how the management system and module send messages back and forth. The data model defines a vocabulary of things they can talk about, such as test scores and the names of learners.

Which communications standards?

Which communications specifications and standards do you need to be aware of? Two main organizations have proposed communications standards that have been implemented in learning management systems.

Aviation Industry CBT Committee	AICC has two related standards, called AICC Guidelines and Recommendations (AGRs). AGR006 covers computer-managed instruction in general. It applies to disk-based, mainframe-based, and Web-based learning. AGR010 specifically addresses Web-based computer-managed instruction. It is a short specification that refers to AGR006 for most of its content.
SCORM	ADL's SCORM specification includes a Runtime Environment (RTE) specification that covers communication between learning management systems and sharable content objects, which is SCORM's terms for a module. SCORM incorporates the latest AICC specifications.

Help meeting AICC (AGR-010) requirements

Some LMSs and other management systems let content developers use AICC communications standards to swap information with the management system. How can you incorporate AICC communication, namely AGR-010 for Web-based CMI, into your content? Tool vendors are offering help in building content that can communicate with management systems.

The Knowledge Track feature built into CourseBuilder interactions in Dreamweaver (macromedia.com) lets course authors add tests and other interactions to the course and has them report scores back to an AICC-compliant management system. The course author just clicks a checkbox on a dialog and Dreamweaver adds the necessary frames and scripting.

Similar features are available in ToolBook (click2learn.com), Trainersoft Professional (trainersoft.com), Macromedia Flash (macromedia.com), and other tools so they can communicate with AICC-compliant systems.

SCORM Runtime Environment

The SCORM Runtime Environment specifies a protocol and data model for communication between learning objects and management systems. In common implementations, course authors make their HTML pages communicate with a management system by using JavaScript functions defined in a file typically called APIWrapper.js. The behind-the-scenes details are complex, but the basic exchange of information is straightforward.

The SCORM communications standard prescribes a rich language whereby the management system and module can communicate. Here are four of the most important SCORM commands: LMSInitialize, LMSFinish, LMSGetValue, and LMSSetValue. Consider this a phrase-book for the SCORM language.

SCORM phrase: LMSInitialize

One of the first commands a module issues is *LMSInitialize*. It says to the management system, "I'm starting up. Start your clock and begin tracking me."

This command is placed at the beginning of each learning module. For multiple-page modules, the command is placed only at the start of the first page. Some tools automatically put this command on each page by default, so you may have to remove it manually for multi-page modules.

```
<html>
<script language=JavaScript>
LMSInitialize()
…
who =
LMSGetValue("cmi.core.student_name")
…
LMSSetValue("cmi.core.lesson_status",
"completed")
LMSFinish("")
</script>
</html>
```

SCORM phrase: LMSFinish

The SCORM command *LMSFinish* marks the end of a module. It says to the management system, "I'm done. You can stop the clock and cease tracking me."

This command is placed at the end of each learning module. For multi-page modules, the command is placed only at the end of the last page.

Together LMSInitialize and LMSFinish can implement rudimentary tracking. With these two commands, the management system can track which modules the learner visited and how long the learner spent in each module.

 Some vendors of courseware put a single LMSInitialize command at the beginning of their course and an LMSFinish command after the final exam and—rather brazenly—claim SCORM compliance.

SCORM phrase: LMSGetValue

The *LMSGetValue* command enables the module to request information from the management system. For example, LMSGetValue ("cmi.core.student_name") says to the management system, "Who's taking me? Send me the name of the student who launched this module."

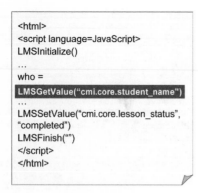

This is just one example of the kind of data LMSGetValue can retrieve from the management system. The part of the command within parentheses determines which item of data the module is requesting. The vocabulary of available items is determined by another part of the standard called the SCORM Runtime Data Model. The model sets the vocabulary that the management system and learning module use to talk to one another.

The LMSGetValue command can be used anywhere within the module between the LMSInitialize and LMSFinish commands and can be issued as many times as necessary within the module.

The data retrieved from the server can be used in displayed messages, in calculations, and in making decisions about how the course should branch and continue.

 Not all management system vendors support all the items in the data model, and some management system vendors define their own nonstandard items.

SCORM phrase: LMSSetValue

A learning module can also send data to the management system with the *LMSSetValue* command.

For example, the command LMSSetValue("cmi.core.lesson_status", "completed") tells the management system that the learner has completed the current module and thus the management system should record the module's status as "completed." The first part within parentheses is the data item the

```
<html>
<script language=JavaScript>
LMSInitialize()
...
who =
LMSGetValue("cmi.core.student_name")
...
LMSSetValue("cmi.core.lesson_status",
"completed")

LMSFinish("")
</script>
</html>
```

management system should set and the second part is the value it should record for this item.

The LMSSetValue command can be used to send a wide variety of data to the management system. The exact items and their formats are determined by another part of the standard called the data model.

SCORM Runtime Data Model

The *SCORM Runtime Data Model* sets the vocabulary that the LMS and learning module use to talk to one another. Items like "cmi.core.student_name" and "cmi.core.lesson_status" are defined items in the vocabulary understood by the LMS and specified in the SCORM Runtime Data Model specification. The AICC standards define an almost identical data model.

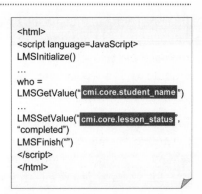

```
<html>
<script language=JavaScript>
LMSInitialize()
...
who =
LMSGetValue("cmi.core.student_name")
...
LMSSetValue("cmi.core.lesson_status",
"completed")
LMSFinish("")
</script>
</html>
```

Note, not all LMS vendors support all the items in the data model and some LMS vendors define their own non-standard items.

Help meeting SCORM communications requirements

Several management system vendors, such as Pathlore (www.pathlore.com) and Integrity (www.ielearning.com) offer a SCORM Runtime Toolkit containing the JavaScript functions and API adapter necessary to add SCORM commands to HTML pages.

An extension for Dreamweaver called the SCORM Runtime Wrapper (macromedia.com) lets authors add basic SCORM commands to their Web pages within Dreamweaver. There are also two similar extensions for Flash.

Test compliance with communications standards

To test the learning object's or management system's compliance with communications standards, download the test suites for each standard and run them on your candidate object, LMS, or LCMS. Get the AICC/CMI Test Suite from aicc.org and the SCORM Conformance Test Suite from adlnet.org. At a minimum, require vendors to show you the test logs that resulted when they ran the test suites against their products.

Keep in mind, these tests do not guarantee that your content and management system will communicate flawlessly. Test the system with actual content.

METADATA STANDARDS

Imagine trying to find a book on a shelf full of books without titles printed on their spines. That's the problem you would face in a world without metadata.

Metadata is data about data. For e-learning, metadata describes courses and other modules. Metadata standards provide ways to describe learning modules so that potential learners and authors can find the module they need.

What is metadata?

Still unclear as to what we mean by metadata? Metadata is nothing mysterious. It is simply informative labeling. Perhaps this example will help.

This handsome fellow is Batu. Batu has a city license and has been vaccinated for Rabies. He also has a phone number, a postal address, and an e-mail address. Around Batu's neck is a collar from which hang several tags. These tags contain that information about Batu. They contain his metadata. Batu would be the same dog without the metadata, but the metadata helps someone identify and appreciate him.

Metadata is pervasive in our daily lives. Perhaps you have consulted the tables of nutritional ingredients on food packages. Or, maybe you have judged a book by its cover, title page, dedication, copyright notice, table of contents, index, or colophon. Have you ever read a movie poster or stayed to read the credits at the end of the movie? If you have done any of these things, you have used metadata.

What does a metadata standard do for us?

Metadata makes e-learning content more useful to buyers, learners, and designers. Metadata provides a way of describing courses, lessons, topics, and media components that is consistent in format and in items recorded. Such descriptions can be compiled into catalogs that can be electronically searched.

Using metadata, sophisticated searches are possible. You are not limited to simple word matches. You could search for all Japanese-language courses about Microsoft Word that are under two hours in length and find just what you want, without having to sort through the Microsoft Word documents in the Japanese language.

Metadata enables management systems to automatically compile catalogs of all the courses, lessons, and other modules they offer. Metadata can also help course authors find content they can license or borrow rather than developing it from scratch.

What metadata standards?

What metadata standards should you consider? Over the years, three metadata specifications have emerged that have at least partial implementation. They include:

▶ IEEE 1484.12 Learning Object Metadata Standard (ieee.org)

▶ IMS Learning Resources Meta-data Specification (imsproject.org)

 Can you really trust standards organizations that cannot standardize on how to spell metadata? IMS, and recently SCORM, spell it meta-hyphen-data while IEEE and most of the rest of the world omit the hyphen.

▶ SCORM Meta-data standards (adlnet.org)

Of the three listed, the IEEE metadata standard is the only one actually accredited with the oomph of a standards body (namely IEEE).

Our favorite metadata items

Metadata standards specify dozens of required and optional items. Some are absolutely necessary, and others are embarrassingly obscure. By way of example, here are some metadata items from the IEEE 1484.12 standard. On the left are the names and numbers of these items and on the right are their values for a particular course.

 Not all metadata items in the standard are mandatory. It is left to the individual organization or community of practice to decide which items are necessary.

1.2 Title	**Introduction to Gantt Charts**
1.3 Language	**en-US** (American English)
1.4 Description	**Overview of using Gantt Charts in business**.
1.5 Keyword	**Gantt chart, project management**
1.7 Structure	**Hierarchical**
1.8 Aggregation Level	**4** (course)
2.1 Version	**1.1**
4.1 Format	**text/html, image/gif, application/x-shockwave**
4.2 Size	**1200000** (bytes)
4.3 Location	**http://www.GanttGroup.com/courses/rgc.htm**
4.4 Requirement	**Browser: Internet Explorer, 4+**
4.7 Duration	**PT3H30M**
6.1 Cost	**no**

The Title records the official name of the course. Language specifies both the language family (en for English) and the variant (US for American English). The Description includes a textual catalog entry for the course, and Keyword records terms under which to list the course in an alphabetical index. Structure records the primary organization of the course: sequential, hierarchical, and so forth. Aggregation Level specifies the size of this unit. A whole course is level 4; a lesson is level 3, and individual topic is level 2. Version records the edition of the course. Format records the file formats used in the course. These are stated as MIME type and subtype. Size is the total size of all the files of the course, expressed in bytes. Location records the Web address where consumers can access the course. Requirement list things such as the browser and operating system required to experience the course. Duration tells how much time is required to take the course. Cost records whether the course charges a fee or is free.

Other items may be important to you, but you get the idea of the type of information recorded in metadata.

Help meeting metadata standards

To be useful, metadata must be collected and formatted typically as XML, not an easy task to do by hand. Fortunately standards bodies and vendors are providing tools to create standards-compliant metadata.

IMS offers a Developer's Toolkit developed by Sun Microsystems. You can download it from imsproject.org. ADL offers the SCORM Metadata Generator, which you can download from adlnet.org. Future tools will greatly simplify the process by automatically inferring items of metadata, rather than requiring manual entry.

Meta-questions on metadata

Although much of the technical work has been done to enable content developers to label their courses, learning objects, assignable units, sharable content objects, and humble bits of clip art, issues remain for you to decide. Let us pose some questions for you to consider before adopting any metadata scheme.

Who writes subjective metadata?

Some metadata items, such as size and location, are objective. The rules are clear and the values are easily verified. There is no incentive to cheat on the objective items of metadata. But what about the subjective ones, such as description and keywords? Whom do we trust to write these items? The vendor of the module? An independent agency?

 How about the movie critic for The New York Times? "Four stars! Boffo performance, literate script, and an unguessable ending."

The temptation to cheat is great. The desire to make a module more attractive to potential buyers and adopters may lead some to fudge a bit on their descriptions or keywords. We are not too long past the time when unscrupulous Web sites repeated the word "sex" over and over in their description to snare unsophisticated search engines working on behalf of porno-seeking Web surfers.

Which subset of metadata?

The IEEE 1484.12 Learning Object Metadata Standard is the mother of several other standards efforts. Several organizations are implementing different subsets of the IEEE scheme. They include:

- ARIADNE (www.ariadne-eu.org)

- CanCore (www.cancore.org)

- HEAL (Health Education Assets Library) (www.healcentral.org)

- MERLOT (merlot.org)

- SCORM (adlnet.org)

You may need to ally your metadata efforts to one or more of these organizations or with a more local effort centered within your profession. You may even need to articulate metadata standards for use just within your own organization.

Whose taxonomy do you use?

A *taxonomy* is a classification scheme that organizes subjects by their relationships and provides a vocabulary for describing these items. Examples are the Dewey Decimal System (oclc.org/dewey) used to number books in U.S. libraries, the Systematized Nomenclature of Medicine (snomed.com), and the Linnean system for classifying living organisms (palaeos.com/systematics).

Obviously taxonomies depend on the subject matter. They also depend on someone's view of how that subject matter is best carved up and the pieces named. Picking a scheme is a major issue for those publishing their content and those searching for content. Many university associations, professional organizations, and other communities of practice are developing their own taxonomies.

How much metadata is enough?

If you plan to publish thousands of modules, you must consider the amount of effort required to write metadata for them. Will you include all optional metadata items or just required items? Will you provide metadata just for high-level modules such as courses or for atomic pieces of media as well? What metadata can be inferred or scooped up automatically?

What is the metadata for mushware?

Some forms of collaborative content have the audacity to include human beings as participants. These aberrant modules raise issues of how to describe the contribution of instructors, facilitators, and learners in collaborative events and how blended learning is described. If a course relies on an instructor, where does the résumé or curriculum vitae of the instructor go?

QUALITY STANDARDS

Quality standards concern the design of courses and modules as well as their accessibility by those with disabilities. Quality standards ensure that e-learning has certain characteristics or was created using certain processes—but they do not guarantee success.

Why do you need quality standards?

Are not standards for e-learning technology sufficient to ensure a free exchange of reusable learning objects? Well, take a look at this object.

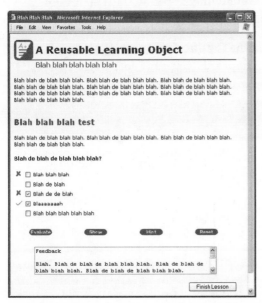

It has content and a test that is automatically scored. It gives feedback and complies with SCORM specifications. But is it a reusable learning object? No. It is not a learning object because nobody can learn anything from it. And, it is not reusable, because it was not usable in the first place. Yet it meets the technical requirements for a reusable learning object. What's missing?

 I've seen worse.

Quality standards ensure that objects are not only reusable but usable in the first place.

Quality standards guide decisions

Quality standards help consumers select products. Quality standards are common in manufacturing, commerce, and even education. Well known quality standards include the *Good Housekeeping* magazine's Seal of Approval, Underwriters Laboratories approvals, and the crash-safety ratings from the Insurance Institute for Highway Safety.

Consider what all of these standards promise—and what they do not promise. They promise that items meeting the standard have achieved some minimal level of performance or were created by a consistent process. They do not guarantee that the items can never fail. To use quality standards, you must understand that they increase the odds of success, but can never ensure success. Quality standards can inform your decisions but should not make them for you.

E-learning design standards

The primary design quality standard for e-learning is the E Learning Courseware Certification Standards from the ASTD E-learning Certification Institute. The Certification Institute certifies that e-learning courses comply with composite standards covering user-interface design, compatibility with standard operating systems and tools, production quality, and instructional design.

Copies of these standards are available from the Certification Institute at astd.org/ecertification. Even if you do not choose to have your e-learning certified, you can use the standards as a checklist for your own quality effort.

Accessibility standards

Accessibility standards concern how to make jobs, buildings, and information technology accessible to those with common disabilities, such as impaired vision or hearing, lack of eye-hand coordination, or reading disabilities. There are no explicit accessibility standards for e-learning alone; however, e-learning falls under accessibility standards for information technology and Web content.

Section 508

The most important accessibility standard for information technology is Section 508 of the U.S. Rehabilitation Act, or more precisely, the 1998 Revision of Section 508 of the Rehabilitation Act of 1973. This law requires that information technology, including e-learning, purchased by U.S. federal agencies must be accessible by those with common disabilities.

Section 508 requires that employees and the public "with disabilities have access to and use of information and data that is comparable to the access and use" by those without disabilities. Lawyers will be arguing about the exact meaning of these words for decades. Meanwhile, several U.S. states and other governments have adopted the provisions of Section 508 as requirements.

Section 508 lists technical standards in several areas of information technology.

§1194.21   Software applications and operating systems

§1194.22   Web-based intranet and internet information and applications

§1194.23   Telecommunication products

§1194.24   Video and multimedia products

§1194.25   Self contained, closed products

§1194.26   Desktop and portable computers

All of these apply to e-learning, but §1194.22 is especially relevant.

For a copy of the Section 508 standards, go to section508.gov. There you will also find links to help interpreting and complying with the standards. You may also find help in the IMS Guidelines for Developing Accessible Learning Applications (imsproject.org).

Section 508 provisions refer to the W3C Web content Accessibility Guidelines, so keep reading.

W3C Web Accessibility Initiative

The World Wide Web Consortium (W3C) has launched a Web Accessibility Initiative. The W3C has published Web Content Accessibility Guidelines. Its goal is to "make all Web content accessible to people with disabilities." This standard will cover all Web-based training directly and disk-based training by analogy. For more on this initiative, go to w3c.org.

OTHER STANDARDS AND REGULATIONS

Packaging, communications, metadata, and quality are the main standards for e-learning, but other important standards are on the way. What other standards are coming? Let's gaze into the crystal ball.

More e-learning standards

Currently the IMS is busy developing specifications for other aspects of interoperability.

▶ **Test questions**. High on their list are standards for test questions. Test questions developed in one LMS, LCMS, or virtual-school systems often cannot be transferred to another system. The IMS Question and Test Interoperability specification seeks to define generic ways of specifying tests that can be realized in many different systems. This and other IMS specifications are available at imsproject.org.

▶ **Enterprise Information Model**. Learning management systems often need to exchange data with other corporate systems. The IMS Enterprise Information Model seeks to define formats for exchanging administrative data among such systems.

▶ **Learner Information Packaging**. Likewise, administrators often spend much time entering information about the learner into multiple learning management systems. The IMS Learner Information Packaging specification attempts to define a common format for information about learners. Descriptions adhering to the specification could then be freely exchanged among systems.

Telecommunications standards

Telecommunications standards make possible the Internet and thereby e learning. A few of these standards are relevant to you if you plan to combine separate tools for collaboration. Among the most important are the following by the International Telecommunications Union (itu.org):

▶ H.323 for Packet-based multimedia communications systems. It promotes compatibility in videoconference transmissions over IP networks

▶ T.120 for Data protocols for multimedia conferencing. It covers the document conferencing and application-sharing portion of online meetings.

Other ITU telecommunications standards may become important on specific projects. If you see a reference to a standard beginning with "T." or "H.", check with the ITU for details.

Media standards

Media standards cover the format of various common forms of media. Most of these standards originate with the World Wide Web Consortium (w3c.org). Here are a few of the W3C standards for media that are common in e-learning.

- ▶ CSS (Cascading Style Sheets) for controlling appearance of HTML and XML pages

- ▶ DOM (Document Object Model) for programming browsers and their pages

- ▶ HTML (Hypertext Markup Language) for creating Web pages

- ▶ HTTP (Hypertext Transfer Protocol) for sending data between servers and browsers

- ▶ MathML (Mathematics Markup Language) for displaying mathematical equations

- ▶ PNG (Portable Network Graphics) for raster graphics

- ▶ SMIL (Synchronized Multimedia Integration Language) for creating multimedia presentations

- ▶ SVG (Scalable Vector Graphics) for images defined as points, lines, and fills

- ▶ XML (Extensible Markup Language) for creating custom markup languages

Additional media standards and their sponsors include the following:

- ▶ GIF (Graphics Interchange Format) standard for raster graphics by CompuServe (compuserve.com)

- ▶ JPEG (Joint Photographic Experts Group) standard for photographs (www.jpeg.org)

- ▶ MPEG (Moving Picture Experts Group) standard for video (mpeg.telecomitalialab.com)

- ▶ vCard standard for electronic business cards (www.imc.org)

- ▶ MIME (Multipurpose Internet Mail Extensions) by the Internet Engineering Task Force (ietf.org) for identifying file formats and sending them in e-mail messages

MAKE STANDARDS WORK FOR YOU

Despite much progress, much remains to be done before standards realize their promise. A common-sense approach to standards is necessary to use them wisely and not be hoodwinked.

Focus on your content

Standards should not become an end unto themselves. If you use them, use them to accomplish your goals for e-learning. Standards provide reusable, modular containers. It is what you put into those containers that determines whether the training content is useful and reusable.

Have an exit strategy

Worry more about getting content out of a tool than getting it into one. Vendors can gain a competitive advantage by making it easy to get material into their system but difficult to move material from their system to a competing system. Check out the export command just as carefully as the import command.

 Standards people speak an interesting dialect that fails to distinguish future and present tense, i.e. between fact and prediction. And if you ask exactly when some provision will be real, they tend to respond with the word "realsoonnnow."

Clarify exactly which standard

When someone claims to meet a standard, ask exactly what standard, guideline, or specification they mean. AICC, for example, defines three levels of complexity. Few vendors fully implement Level 3. Many standards include multiple parts or specifications. For which is compliance claimed? Be sure to ask what version of the standard an item claims to meet. Standards are evolving at Internet speed. Version 1.2 may differ from Version 1.1 of a standard.

Question claims of compliance

Some vendors claim compliance with a standard when they only meet a few of its provisions. Some standards groups define a minimal set of requirements for claiming conformance. However, the minimal requirements may be insufficient for your purposes. Be sure to ask about the degree to which the item meets the standard.

How can a vendor's claim be verified? Does the standards group authenticate or certify compliance? Is this task done by third-party evaluators? Or are the vendor's claims all you have to go on?

You may, alas, have to do your own testing. Check the Web site for standards group to see if they have a test suite that will report on the degree of compliance of your content or of a tool you are considering buying.

When it comes to claims of compliance, *caveat emptor*.

WHAT NOW?

Think about how you will make standards work for you, your project, and your organization. Here is a decision aid to help you.

If	Then
You are developing new courses without a requirement for standards compliance.	**Rationally procrastinate**. If you don't need standards, wait until they mature further. Standards will grow simpler and become more clearly expressed. Better tools to automate compliance will be developed.
	Instead, focus on making your content so effective people will want to reuse it.
You must supply content that complies with specifications or standards.	**Clarify requirements**. Which aspects of which versions of which specifications? Who will verify compliance and how?
	Seek point-and-click tools. Hand-coding is time-consuming and error-prone.

You have legacy content that complies with earlier versions of standards.	**Maintain instructionally effective legacy content**. If you have courseware happily communicating with your LMS, stick with it. Investigate the costs and benefits of recoding content to more recent standards.
You are too busy to track the development of standards.	**Go with SCORM**. It's the latest generation and has the backing of a lot of big buyers like the U.S. Departments of Labor and Defense. It also has wide support in Europe and Japan.
You are buying an LMS, LCMS, or other system that implements standards.	**Do your own testing** of your content with the management system. Use tools such as the test suites from AICC and SCORM to measure compliance. Keep in mind, though, that official procedures do not test every possible combination of variables. Test with content of the type you plan to use.
You want to promote reuse of content.	**Identify what components you can reuse.** Consider what types of standards will help with reuse of these components. Pay attention to packaging and metadata standards. Begin packaging your content and developing metadata for it.
You are considering buying content to run on your own LMS or LCMS.	**Investigate what standards the LMS or LCMS implements**. What packaging and metadata formats can it import? What communications standards does it use to communicate with courses and other modules?

If you feel standards can save you money or give you a competitive advantage, consider appointing a standards team or czar to plan how your organization will bring e-learning standards into play.

Several times in this chapter we mentioned XML. It is one of the important underlying technologies for e-learning tools. XML can help us make e-learning content available in many different forms for many different devices. To learn about XML, continue in the next chapter.

23 What the L is XML?

You may go your entire career—creating, offering, and even taking hundreds of e-learning courses—and never directly see any XML. Yet, without XML, much current e-learning and most future e-learning would not be practical. Though you will probably never need to code anything directly in XML, you will constantly need to understand the role it plays.

WHAT IS XML?

What is XML? Unless you have spent the last five years in hibernation, you have probably heard something about XML. If you are like most people, you are still a bit confused about exactly what XML is and where it may fit in your future.

You probably know that XML stands for Extensible Markup Language. It's not that its developers could not spell *extensible*; it's just that EML didn't have the same ring.

When most people hear about XML, their first reaction is, "Yipes! Not another markup language!" We've struggled with versions of HTML. Some of us even struggled with SGML or its predecessor GML. Why do we need another markup language? Well, despite its name, XML is not really another markup language, certainly not the way that HTML is.

```
<?xml version='1.0'?>
<CourseDescription>
<CourseTitle>Evaluating E-
Learning</CourseTitle>
<Description>
E-learning has racked up a lot of
publicity and some impressive
case studies. But does it work
for your organization? This
presentation will show how you
can evaluate the effectiveness of
e-learning in your organization.
It shows how to implement four
levels of evaluation from simple
reaction through return on
investment. It shows how to fit
evaluation to your business and
learning goals as well as to your
budget and schedule. This
presentation is based on
```

Do-it-yourself HTML

XML is really a scheme for creating tagging (or markup) languages like HTML. In fact you could almost create HTML using XML. We say almost, because XML is stricter in its rules than HTML. XML, for example, requires all opening tags to have a matching closing tag or else be explicitly flagged as both start and finish. In fact, the World Wide Web Consortium has defined a variant of basic HTML that follows XML conventions. It is called XHTML.

The advantage of XML and the excitement over it is that you can use it to create your own HTML. If you don't like using tags <H1>, <H2>, <H3>, and so on for headings, you can define your heading tags as <top_head>, <second_head>, <third_head>, or whatever you want to make them.

Just revising the tags of HTML would hardly justify the excitement about XML. The real use of XML is to define markup languages that let you precisely match the kind of information you deal with and what you want to do with it. Catalog publishers can define tags to identify the price, description, and photograph of products. Dictionary publishers can have tags for terms, definitions, synonyms, and pronunciation. Instructional designers can have tags for objectives, test questions, feedback, and all the other common components of training content.

Universal file format

XML is being used to define file formats for a wide variety of media beyond simple text and numeric data. Here are some of the file formats based on XML that you may encounter in creating e-learning.

SVG	Scalable Vector Graphics for graphics defined as lines and areas.
MathML	Math Markup Language to display mathematical expressions in Web pages and other media.
SMIL	Synchronized Multimedia Integration Language for multimedia presentations.
VoiceXML	To script dialogs using voice and telephone dial tones.
MusicXML	By Recodare (musicxml.com), for publishing music scores.

And why should I care?

Since you will most likely never have to code directly in XML and may never actually see the ugly guts of an XML file, why should you bother learning about XML? Here are some of the reasons that have motivated us to engage in the brain-numbing effort of understanding XML.

▶ **To understand vendors' claims**. Those offering tools are touting their XML support. The sales rep at the expo booth, however, can be forgiven for glazing over when you ask for details on the product's XML support: After all, it was only the 43rd bullet-list item in the data sheet. The sales rep will probably refer you to a white paper on the product's Web site. Said white paper is likely written in gobbledygook that makes ordinary folk suspect it is not too far removed from its XML source. But you, armed with the knowledge in this chapter, can whiz right through it.

▶ **To glue together the separate tools of your plan**. XML has the potential to serve as the *lingua franca* of data, enabling your LCMS to swap learner data with your ERP system, which lobs it back to your virtual-school system.

▶ **To guide the appropriate use of XML**. The uses of XML multiply as you extend from simple e-learning courses to enterprise-spanning knowledge management efforts. All the organization's data is up for grabs as legions of data miners whistle while they work away extracting trends and refining best practices.

▶ **To separate format from content**. If you have to deliver the same content in two formats or 20 formats, XML can help you define the content in a way that puts the content in one file and the format in another. Sure, HTML can do this with style sheets, but the separation is much cleaner in XML.

▶ **To author in XML**. Sometimes it is just easier to type in the text and codes. Because XML does not mix structural and formatting codes, authoring directly in XML is simpler than authoring in HTML.

▶ **So you don't sound dumb**. Everybody's talking about XML. Some of them understand a little about XML. By understanding XML, you can take part in these conversations and, oh so subtly, guide them in the ways you want them to go.

HTML versus XML

XML is a markup language much like HTML. However, XML was designed to describe information. HTML was designed to display information. Unlike HTML tags (<p>, <h1>, and so forth), XML tags are not predefined. The owner or keeper of the information must define a set of tags to describe the different pieces of information. Some other file is needed to "tell" the program displaying the XML (for our purposes, a browser) how the document should appear.

Example of XML

Here is an example of a very small XML file, containing a simple e-mail message.

```
<memo>
<to>Bill</to>
<from>Kit</from>
<subject>Reminder</subject>
<mItem>Don't forget to pack the disk.</mItem>
</memo>
```

This file doesn't do anything. It is just some text wrapped in some made-up tags. It will require further processing before it can be displayed, say in a mail reader or a Web browser. Also, there is some special heading data that's missing from this example.

How XML differs from HTML

If you are familiar with HTML, Hypertext Markup Language, you may have trouble understanding XML at first. Though HTML and XML data look similar, the function of the tags is fundamentally different.

HTML	XML
<p>Washington</p> <h2>Washington</h2> Washington	<us_state>Washington</us_state> <city>Washington</city> <us_president>Washington</us_president>

In HTML we might put different kinds of tags around the word Washington. We might put <p> tags around it to mark it as a paragraph. We might put <h2> tags around it to turn it into a second-order heading. Or we might put <strong> or <b> tags around it to emphasize the word.

The same word in XML might be surrounded by different kinds of tags. We might surround the word Washington with a <us_state> tag to flag it as a state in the United States. Or, we might put <city> tags around it to mark it as a city. Or, to indicate that it represented a president of the United States, we might surround it with <us_president> tags.

The big difference

HTML tags mark the components of a document, such as headings, lists, and paragraphs. Or, they may mark how the content is to be formatted by specifying that it is to be displayed in bold type or in a font of a particular color and type face.

XML specifies what the tagged content means. It announces what the tagged item represents. It does not specify how it should be formatted. Other related components of the whole XML system take care of the format.

Of course, XML could be used the same way as HTML, but that would add no value. The value of XML is that it can label different kinds of information in meaningful ways.

Not just data

Displayed XML files may look like Web pages, and the underlying XML-tagged data files may look like HTML. These similarities mask the fundamental differences that work behind the scenes and give XML its advantages.

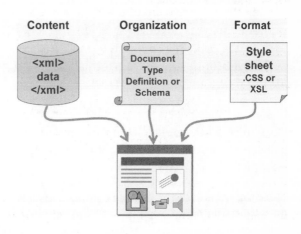

XML is more than XML-tagged data files. It may consist of two additional parts, each providing an additional level of control over how information is organized and formatted.

DTD or schema for structure

Many XML systems will have a Document Type Definition (DTD) or an XML Schema that defines what the XML data file can contain. This DTD or schema specifies what tags the data file can use and relationships among the tags. For example, it might say that a glossary entry must have a term tag and at least one definition tag.

The DTD is a remnant of Standardized General Markup Language (SGML) which preceded HTML. SGML was a highly detailed scheme for defining documents. Its proponents said it was rigorous. Its critics called it obtuse. The DTD was the most complex element of SGML and one of the first things thrown out when HTML was invented.

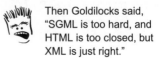

Then Goldilocks said, "SGML is too hard, and HTML is too closed, but XML is just right."

Both the DTD and Schema are optional in some applications. If no DTD or schema is specified, the use of tags in the XML file is not limited other than by basic syntax rules. The DTD may be especially rare as most developers prefer using an XML Schema because it can be written in XML itself and does not require using the DTD's obscure, difficult format.

Style sheet for formatting

The third component of an XML system is a style sheet that specifies how the XML data is to be displayed. Two forms of style sheet are common. The first is the Cascading Style Sheet, which specifies the visual characteristics (font, position, spacing, color, and so on) of the content of each tag. Cascading Style Sheets are supported in current versions of Netscape and IE browsers and can be applied to both XML and HTML. The second type of style sheet is an Extensible Stylesheet Language (XSL) Transformation. A Transformation is a program for converting the XML data file to a new format, such as HTML.

Cascading Style Sheets will probably be replaced by XSL Formatting Objects (XSL-FO), which add page-layout controls and use XML syntax. For now, though, when we talk about style sheets for formatting, we mean Cascading Style Sheets. And when we refer to XSL, we are transforming XML.

The combination of these three components lets us verify the content of an XML data file and display it in a Web browser or other device.

COMMON APPLICATIONS OF XML

XML is a flexible, useful technology. Let's take a look at some of the ways it is being used to store, share, and manipulate the data on which our lives depend. We'll concentrate on ways it is used in and among e-learning tools.

Mainstream tools use XML

XML is making inroads even in established mainstream products. Vendors of these products are making sure their tools can read and sometimes write XML. Some are even adopting XML for the file format the program uses to store its own data. Here are just a few examples of XML features in common desktop and e-learning applications.

Program	What it lets you do with XML
Microsoft Excel and Access	Import and export data in XML files structured as rows and columns of data. Query data in XML data files.
Microsoft Visio	Import and export drawings in XML files consistent with the Visio schema.
Macromedia Dreamweaver	Export data from templates into XML and import XM L data into templates.
Macromedia Flash	Use ActionScript to read and write data in XML files.
Adobe Acrobat	Export form-field data and annotations as XML. Stores metadata about documents in XML.

These are just a few examples. Why not check the online help of your favorite programs to see how they use XML.

Separating data and format

XML can be used in an almost unlimited number of ways. One of the simplest is to combine an XML data file with a fill-in-the-blank template to cleanly separate data from the way it is displayed. Let's see how that might work.

How templates and XML work together

In a tool for authoring Web pages, such as Macromedia Dreamweaver, you can create a template. On this template you create editable

 This is a simple, yet productive, way to begin experimenting with XML.

regions and give them names. Content can be entered into these editable regions but the rest of the page cannot be changed by the author.

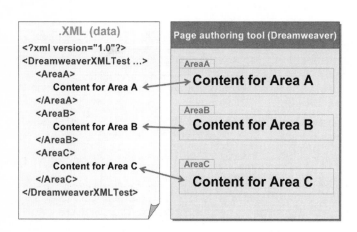

You can link this template to an XML data file. This XML data file would contain tagged regions corresponding to each of the editable regions in the template. For example, the content to go into the area named Area A would be inside <AreaA> tags. The same would be true for other editable areas in the template.

This relationship between template and XML files is a two-way relationship. Data entered into the template could be saved as an XML data file, and data saved in an XML data file could be read into the template.

This division of labor illustrates one of the essential characteristics of XML: Content and format are independent. The XML data file stores the content and the template controls how the content is displayed.

XML in Dreamweaver templates

Let's look at a real example of a template and a related XML file.

We create a template in Dreamweaver. This template contains content that will be the same on all pages and areas for content that will vary. The fixed content consists of the headings "Description" and "Objectives." Editable regions are available for the course title, description, and objectives. Each editable region is indicated by a rectangle with its name on a tab at the upper left.

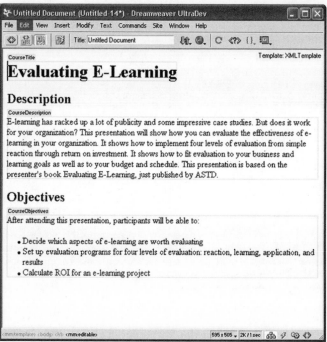

We fill in the template with a real title, description, and objectives. We cannot change the headings or rearrange areas because they are fixed by the template.

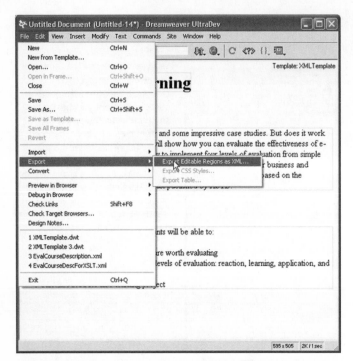

To save the data as XML, we select
File > Export > Export Editable Regions as XML ... and give the file a name.

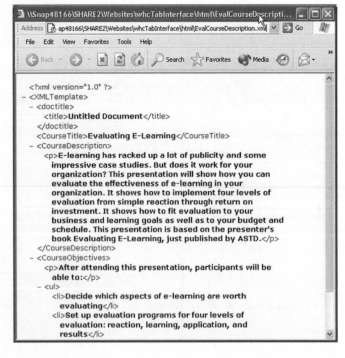

If we open this XML data file, we see that it wraps XML tags around the data we entered. These tags correspond to the names of the editable regions in the template.

To see how we can use this data, we create another template. This one has a different look from the first and it reverses the order of the objectives and description. Note that it still uses the same names for the editable regions as did the original template.

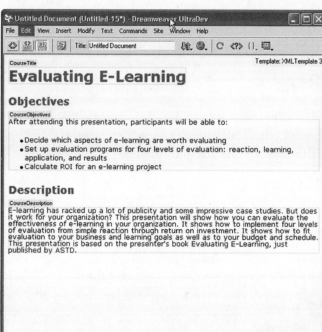

Now we import the XML data file into this template. Notice that the content appears as specified in the template. One XML data file can have two or more distinct looks.

(We pause now while you think of how this feature can save you time and effort.)

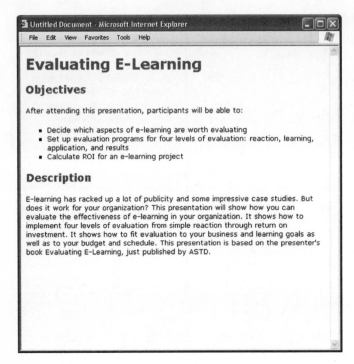

We then save this template as an HTML page and open it in a Web browser to see that it replicates the appearance specified in the template.

To create an HTML page with a different appearance and organization, we just import the XML data into another template and save it as HTML.

Using templates, we could easily maintain information in one file but publish it in several distinctly different formats.

XML generating Web pages

Let's look at a common, simple model of how XML can be used to create Web pages for display in any browser. The core of this application is a piece of software called an *XML parser*. It is a component that reads an XML file and converts it to another form for display in a Web browser.

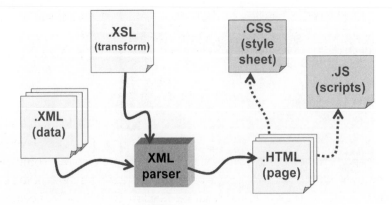

The recipe for how the parser is to transform or reformat the XML data file is found in an Extensible Stylesheet Language (XSL) Transformation.

The XML parser applies the instructions of the XSL file to rewrite the XML as a conventional HTML Web page. Typically that Web page contains links to a Cascading Style Sheet (CSS) that further specifies how its content is to be displayed. The HTML file may also link to a JavaScript (.JS) file that adds interactivity.

 An XSL Transformation is sometimes written as XSL-T or XSLT.

Where and when does this transformation take place? XML parsers are built into Web servers and Web browsers, so the XML could be transformed just about anywhere. The scheme shown in our simple model is most often performed on the server, either on the fly as each page is requested or as a batch process ahead of time to generate all the HTML pages that might be needed.

Reusing knowledge in many ways

How does XML benefit those who produce courses, books, and other knowledge products? Let's look at an example.

Imagine that we need to distribute different pieces of knowledge to different groups of people but want to avoid manually creating and maintaining separate versions. We might start by putting all the knowledge we need to distribute into a big XML file. Let's call it "all.xml." It contains complete knowledge about a complex subject.

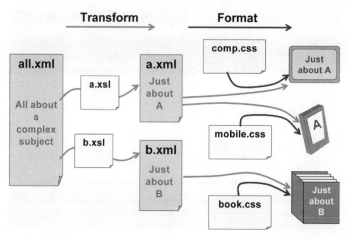

Now, suppose we need to create an online course just about a part of the whole subject. Call this "Part A." To extract the content we need, we might write a Transformation. Call it "a.xsl." It converts or transforms the large file to one containing just the content we need. To format that content for online display, we can then create a style sheet called "comp.css" that could be used for any content we want to display on the computer. The combination of the extracted content and the style sheet give us just what we need in the format we need.

Whew! That was a lot of work. We could have done this quicker by just writing the information we needed in HTML. But, suppose we now need knowledge about B delivered as a paper book. We could again write a Transformation (b.xsl) to pull out just the information we need. Then we could write a style sheet (book.css) to format it for printing. Do you see the advantage? We are not maintaining duplicate copies of the original content.

Now, suppose we need to display the first subset on a portable device, such as a Palm Pilot. This time, all we have to do is write a new style sheet (mobile.css).

The secret to this labor-saving scheme is a two-part process of first transforming the original XML to get just the part we need and then attaching a style sheet to format it for the target medium.

Connecting separate tools and data repositories

On a complex project, you may need to move information through a chain of different tools, databases, and repositories—each with its own private file format. If some of those tools can export their data into an XML dialect, your job is much easier.

Let's look at how XML can play a role in synchronizing two databases that store overlapping data items. Suppose Database A stores the names of employees in an organization that uses a virtual-school system whose Database B stores names of students enrolled in classes. Obviously you want to keep the names consistent.

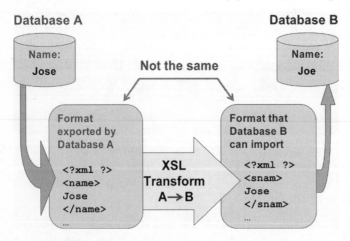

Database A

Name:
Jose

Not the same

Format exported by Database A

```
<?xml ?>
<name>
Jose
</name>
...
```

XSL Transform A→B

Database B

Name:
Joe

Format that Database B can import

```
<?xml ?>
<snam>
Jose
</snam>
...
```

Knowing the structure of the XML emitted by Database A and the format that Database B understands, we can create an XSL Transformation to rewrite the data in Database A in the format Database B understands.

Suppose a new employee says, hey, "My name is not Joe, it's José." Changing the name in Database A is simple enough, but how do we make sure the same change is made in Database B, which is run by a completely different department?

Well, we could export the changes from Database A and import them into Database B, right? Unfortunately the format exported by Database A is not the same format that Database B can import. Are we out of luck? Not if Database A can export into XML.

If only a few data items a month need synchronizing between the two databases, it would not be worthwhile to automate the process as suggested here. However, if many items overlap the databases or the data changes frequently, such a conversion process can reduce labor and errors.

In fact, the process of synchronizing two databases can be made into a Web service whereby one database periodically sends a message to the other saying, "Got any updates for me?" and the other either says "No" or sends the revised data in XML format for transformation and updating of the out-of-date data.

When we spoke of XML as the *lingua franca* of data, we were talking about databases too.

EXTENSIBLE STYLESHEET LANGUAGE TRANSFORMATION

The Extensible Stylesheet Language provides the means to transform and format data stored in XML. The XSL Transformation makes it possible to output different versions and forms of information using the same input content. Some possible results include:

To create this	Use XSLT to transform XML into:
Web pages	HTML
Mobile phone displays	WML (Wireless Markup Language)
Paper documents	RTF or PostScript
Electronic books	Acrobat PDF
Synthesized speech	Java Speech Markup Language, SpeechML, or TalkML
Input for a database	Comma-separated values, tab-delimited values, or an XML format that the database can understand

How XSL transforms XML

How does XSL transform XML? And what exactly is XSL? Simply put, an XSL Transformation is a computer program for converting an XML data file to a new format. Let's step through an example.

```
<?xml version='1.0'?>
<CourseDescription>
<CourseTitle>Evaluating E-learning</CourseTitle>
<Description>
E-learning has racked up a lot of publicity and
some impressive case studies. But does it work for
your organization? This presentation will show how
you can evaluate the effectiveness of e-learning in
your organization. It shows how to implement four
levels of evaluation from simple reaction through
return on investment. It shows how to fit
evaluation to your business and learning goals as
well as to your budget and schedule. This
presentation is based on Evaluating E-learning,
just published by ASTD.
</Description>
<Objectives>
<ObjectivesIntro>
After attending this presentation, participants
will be able to:
</ObjectivesIntro>
<ObjectiveList>
<Objective>
Decide which aspects of e-learning are worth
evaluating
</Objective>
<Objective>
Set up evaluation programs for four levels of
evaluation:
reaction, learning, application, and results
</Objective>
<Objective>Calculate ROI for an e-learning
project</Objective>
</ObjectiveList>
</Objectives>
</CourseDescription>
```

XML data

The first component is the XML data file we want to transform and display. This example contains a description of a course.

```
<?xml version='1.0'?>
<xsl:stylesheet xmlns:xsl='uri:xsl'>
<xsl:template match='/'>
<html><body>
<xsl:for-each select='CourseDescription'>
<h1><xsl:value-of select='CourseTitle'/></h1>
<h2>About this course</h2>
<p><xsl:value-of select='Description' /></p>
<h2>Objectives of the course</h2>
<p><xsl:value-of
select='Objectives/ObjectivesIntro' /></p>
<ul>
<xsl:for-each
select='Objectives/ObjectiveList/Objective'>
<li><xsl:value-of select='.' /></li>
</xsl:for-each>
</ul>
</xsl:for-each>
</body></html>
</xsl:template>
</xsl:stylesheet>
```

XSL Transformation

The XSL Transformation is the recipe for converting the XML data file. It contains commands to select parts of the XML data file and to rewrite them. In this case, it rewrites them as plain old HTML.

```
<html><body>
<h1>Evaluating E-learning</h1>
<h2>About this course</h2>
<p>E-learning has racked up a lot of publicity and
some impressive case studies. But does it work for
your organization? This presentation will show how
you can evaluate the effectiveness of e-learning in
your organization. It shows how to implement four
levels of evaluation from simple reaction through
return on investment. It shows how to fit
evaluation to your business and learning goals as
well as to your budget and schedule. This
presentation is based on Evaluating E-learning,
just published by ASTD.</p>
<h2>Objectives of the course</h2>
<p>After attending this presentation, participants
will be able to:</p>
<ul>
<li>Decide which aspects of e-learning are worth
evaluating</li>
<li>Set up evaluation programs for four levels of
evaluation:
reaction, learning, application, and results</li>
<li>Calculate ROI for an e-learning project</li>
</ul>
</body></html>
```

Transformed XML

The XSL Transformation rewrites the XML as this HTML. If you are familiar with HTML, you can see how it has surrounded blocks of text with common HTML tags.

23

What the L is XML

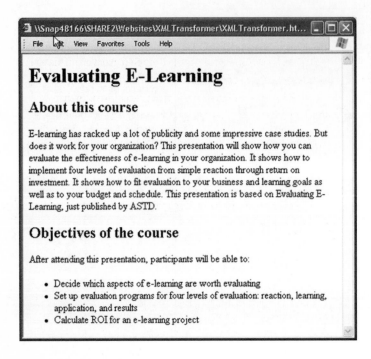

Resulting Web page

If we display the transformed XML, the result looks like a plain and simple Web page.

There is, of course, no limitation on how the Transformation formats the page. That depends entirely on how you write the XSL Transformation.

What XSL does with XML

XSL is a programming language, but it does not look like Visual Basic, C++, or JavaScript. It is a special-purpose language. It is designed to convert XML data from one form to another. It contains commands to:

▶ Select content from the file, for example, just the courses that meet certain criteria

▶ Reorganize the content, perhaps putting it in alphabetical order by title

▶ Format it using HTML or CSS

XSL lets us make XML data available in almost any format, to almost any computer program, and on most devices.

BROWSERS UNDERSTAND XML (SORT OF)

If you want to start experimenting with XML or delivering XML to your learners, you may not have far to go. Modern Web browsers can read XML data directly. There are two approaches that can be used to have a Web browser display XML data. One approach formats the XML directly. The other transforms the XML to HTML.

Using a CSS to format XML

Browsers can use a CSS to format an XML data file directly. In this approach, the XML file contains a link to a CSS file that defines the format to use for each XML tag in the data file. When the XML data file is read into Internet Explorer 5 and later, or into Netscape 6.2 and later, the browser displays the XML as specified in the style sheet.

Using the browser to format XML is thus as simple as opening the XML file. Here's an example of an XML data file.

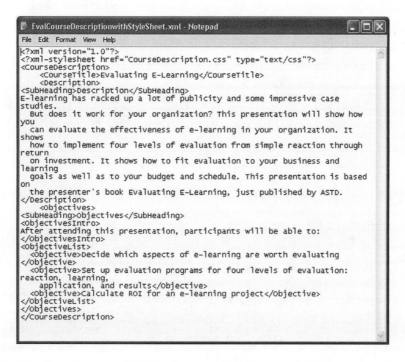

```
EvalCourseDescriptionwithStyleSheet.xml - Notepad
File  Edit  Format  View  Help
<?xml version="1.0"?>
<?xml-stylesheet href="CourseDescription.css" type="text/css"?>
<CourseDescription>
      <CourseTitle>Evaluating E-Learning</CourseTitle>
      <Description>
<SubHeading>Description</SubHeading>
E-learning has racked up a lot of publicity and some impressive case
studies.
   But does it work for your organization? This presentation will show how
you
   can evaluate the effectiveness of e-learning in your organization. It
shows
   how to implement four levels of evaluation from simple reaction through
return
   on investment. It shows how to fit evaluation to your business and
learning
   goals as well as to your budget and schedule. This presentation is based
on
   the presenter's book Evaluating E-Learning, just published by ASTD.
</Description>
      <Objectives>
<SubHeading>Objectives</SubHeading>
<ObjectivesIntro>
After attending this presentation, participants will be able to:
</ObjectivesIntro>
<ObjectiveList>
   <Objective>Decide which aspects of e-learning are worth evaluating
</Objective>
   <Objective>Set up evaluation programs for four levels of evaluation:
reaction, learning,
      application, and results</Objective>
   <Objective>Calculate ROI for an e-learning project</Objective>
</ObjectiveList>
</Objectives>
</CourseDescription>
```

The XML data file refers to a CSS file that specifies how each XML tag is to be formatted. This is done on the second line of the file.

```
<?xml-stylesheet href="CourseDescription.css" type="text/css"?>
```

Opening the file in Internet Explorer 6 or Netscape 6.2 displays the file as specified in the style sheet.

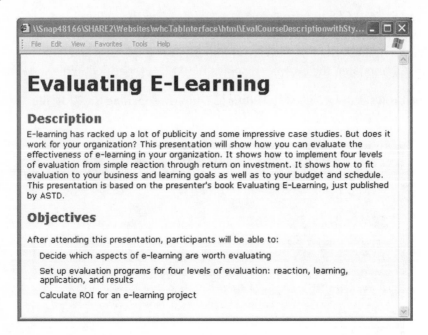

Transforming XML with XSL

Instead of displaying an XML file as directed by a CSS file, the browser could transform the XML into the browser's native language, HTML, and display that HTML. In this case, the XML data file would contain a link to an XSL Transformation file. To transform this XML, the browser must contain an XML parser, such as the one built into Internet Explorer Version 5 and later. The browser reads the XML data, finds the XSL Transformation file, and converts the XML into HTML which it then displays directly.

 Another way to transform XML is to write a program that manipulates its document object model. If you are a programmer you know what I mean.

Let's look at an example of the browser transforming XML. We start with an XML file containing a description of a course.

The second line of the XML data file refers to an XSL Transformation file.

```
<?xml-stylesheet type="text/xsl" href="XMLCourseDescToHTML.xsl"?>
```

When we open this XML file in Internet Explorer 6, it finds the XSL Transformation file, applies it, and—voilà!—displays the results as a conventional Web page.

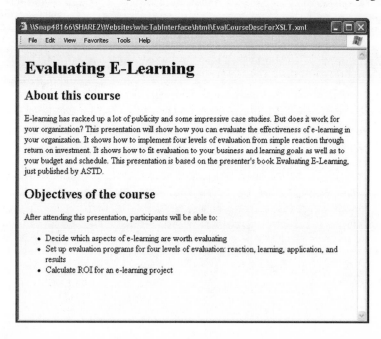

The ability of the browser to transform XML can help offload that task from already overloaded servers.

TOOLS FOR XML

If you have special needs not met by off-the-shelf e-learning tools or if you are especially ambitious, you may want to consider tools expressly for creating XML documents and data files and tools for building sophisticated XML-based applications.

Tools for creating XML documents

XML documents and data files are complex. They require the ability to enter text, wrap chunks of text in tags, and rearrange chunks without breaking delicate dependencies among tags. They also require capabilities to create a Document Type Definition or XML Schema, to define relationships among tagged components and to create a style sheet to format the components.

Tools for creating and editing XML documents include the following:

Product	Vendor	Web address	Cost
FrameMaker	Adobe	www.adobe.com	About $800 USD
XMetaL	Corel	corel.com	About $500 USD
Epic Editor	Arbortext	www.arbortext.com	About $700 USD

Keep in mind that such tools are designed primarily for producing complex paper and online documents and lack many of the features needed for richly interactive e-learning. They may be attractive, though, to those who need to produce both documentation and training from a single source and those embarking on an enterprise knowledge-management effort.

Tools for developing XML applications

Developing complex XML applications requires sophisticated software to plan, create, test, refine, and deploy XML solutions. Suites of tools for developing XML applications are available from several sources.

One such toolkit is Visual Studio .NET by Microsoft (microsoft.com). It contains programming languages, XML editors, database-to-XML interfaces, and other tools for designing Web services and other XML applications. Similar tools are available from Oracle (oracle.com) and Sun Microsystems (sun.com).

In picking a toolkit for developing XML applications, keep the following in mind. First, how much programming is required? Do you have professional programmers on staff that can do the programming? Some tools require more programming than others.

Before you purchase any tools, make sure they comply with corporate IT policies concerning databases and servers. A company that has standardized on Oracle databases may not welcome Microsoft tools.

WHAT NOW?

This chapter was primarily a briefing to give you background knowledge on the wave of the future: XML. We conclude with some recommendations if you want to learn more about XML.

▶ Investigate the XML features in the tools you use already. Can they export and import content as XML data?

▶ If you have Dreamweaver and Internet Explorer, replicate the example in this chapter. Get your hands dirty. Remember your first HTML page?

▶ Visit the Web site of the World Wide Web Consortium (w3c.org) to see the many applications of XML and to check on its development.

▶ Continue reading and learning. Try www.w3schools.com, xml.com, or troll around on amazon.com.

24 Trends in technology and learning

Technological changes are reshaping the landscape of learning and knowledge. Some of these changes are firmly underway and have momentum. Others are a bit more speculative. These trends are affecting how we all provide learning and offer knowledge. In a broader sense, they are transforming society.

Technological advances challenge us to plan for and guide their influence on education and knowledge management. To meet that challenge, you must be prepared to answer these questions.

▶ **What do you need to monitor**? How can you get reliable and timely information about technologies and discern their implications on what you do?

▶ **When must you act**? What are the indicators that signal when a technology is mature and practical enough for you to incorporate it into your activities?

This chapter points out trends in technology that you should monitor and helps you see how they may apply to your e-learning efforts.

TRENDS AND ADVANCES

Let's look at some of these technological trends and what they mean for e-learning and knowledge management.

We divide these trends into three areas. The first area is fundamental, underlying technologies. The second area is technological trends that rely on these fundamental technologies. The third area deals with learning trends based on these technological trends.

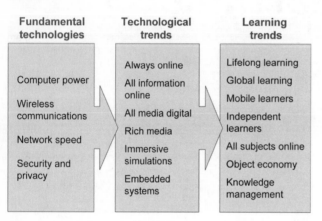

Fundamental technologies	Technological trends	Learning trends
Computer power	Always online	Lifelong learning
Wireless communications	All information online	Global learning
Network speed	All media digital	Mobile learners
Security and privacy	Rich media	Independent learners
	Immersive simulations	All subjects online
	Embedded systems	Object economy
		Knowledge management

As we examine these trends, keep in mind that technologies are not separate from social trends. Technology enables social trends to develop and is, in turn, inspired and driven by them.

FUNDAMENTAL TECHNOLOGIES

Multimedia, the Internet, the Web, online information, and hence e-learning—they are all dependent on basic computer and network technologies. Advances in these basic technologies make e-learning more powerful and less expensive.

Computer power

Today's computers run eight times faster, have eight times more memory, sport disks 32 times larger, communicate three times faster, and cost 40% less than computers of just five years ago. Today's Palm Pilots and Pocket PCs provide more computing power and memory than laptop computers did only a few years ago. And, laptops today have the capabilities of workstations from a few years ago. What does this mean for computer buyers and those of use who develop e-learning to run on these computers?

Decades of increases in processor speed, memory speed and density, disk capacity and speed, display size, and color fidelity ensure that it is almost impossible to buy a new computer that is not capable of delivering e-learning. E-learning solutions that were impossible a few years ago are mainstream today.

As more and more e-learning–capable computers make their way into use, e-learning becomes practical for more of the world's population.

Network speed

Connection speeds available in offices and homes are increasing steadily. Today's home user connects to the Internet at speeds greater than those available in many offices. Offices are upgrading to Gigabit Ethernet, and universities are connecting by Internet 2 connections.

 As I write this, I am listening to an Internet radio station, after just seeing an ad for full-screen movies available over the Internet.

 And, more video talking heads.

Faster network speeds mean more use of rich media. E-learning can employ larger graphics, higher-quality audio, visually rich and responsive simulations, and more natural collaboration.

 Internet2 is important, but not as important as the local connections that funnel users to high-speed conduits. I recently spoke on a panel, one of whose members spoke via an Internet2 link. Unfortunately, the decoder box only worked at 384 Kbps—like using the Space Shuttle to send a letter

Wireless communications

Cell phones have freed managers and other knowledge workers from their desks. More and more work is done in the field, on the move, and at the source. Wireless data communications, either through cell phone modems or direct wireless connections, mean that now people can learn and access online learning and information from just about anywhere.

The speed and availability of wireless connections continues to increase as the price of wireless devices and usage fees drop. Standards for wireless connections are being adopted and products are proliferating. These include connections to local devices (Bluetooth) as well as to data networks (WiFi, 802.11a, and 802.11g.

These trends are leading to expectations of anything any time. Learners expect to learn while mobile. Advances in wireless technologies are lowering "cable drop" costs for connecting people within schools and offices. However, wireless links are not as fast as wired links. (See chapter 5 for relative speeds.) If you go wireless, you will need to monitor the wireless speed penalty to ensure that e-learning can be delivered where it is needed.

Security and privacy

As more and more data is stored on networks, concerns of security and privacy have led to research and development aimed at protecting that data and its owners. Areas of interest to e-learning developers include:

▶ **Encryption** to protect privacy of student data stored on public servers and transmitted over the network

▶ **Biometric identification** to identify remote learners, especially when taking tests

▶ **Digital signatures** to ensure the authenticity of learning materials

▶ **Digital watermarks**, such as those possible in Photoshop, to make it hard to disguise ownership of material

▶ **Digital rights management** to prevent unauthorized copying of materials and to support development of markets for e-learning content

Many are concerned that new technologies will reduce unauthorized use of material that is common in classroom settings today. "What, you mean I can't include that Dilbert cartoon in my e-learning?"

TECHNOLOGICAL TRENDS

Fundamental technological developments have led to technological trends. Several of these trends are especially important for the future development of e-learning.

Always online

Soon people will be always online. Plummeting costs for network equipment and telecom rates are putting continuous connectivity within range for many.

Today near-continuous connectivity is possible, and the gaps are closing. Starbuck's coffee shops are installing WiFi networks so patrons can connect their Palm Pilots and Pocket PCs as they quaff double espressos. Boeing has announced that on aircraft of the future being on board will also mean being online.

With the ability to look up information at any time, there is less need for learners to possess personal copies of reference information—in textbooks or on CD-ROMs.

Learning events will become more spontaneous. As more people are online more hours, online meetings, and collaborative activities will be easier to schedule. Just-in-time training will become the norm.

Network dependency may, however, be a real danger. Expectations may get out of hand. Students may expect their teachers to respond to questions at any hour of the day. Institutions will be required to provide 24/7 learning support, as does SkillSoft (skillsoft.com).

All information online

You used to go to the library. Today, the library comes to you. A growing proportion of recent human knowledge is now available over the Internet. Increasingly people, especially young ones, expect to find everything online.

The Web offers the equivalent of over two trillion pages on the Web. If they were printed out, the stack of pages would reach 100,000 kilometers into space. If the pages were laid end to end, they would stretch out to the orbit of Mars, back past earth to the orbit of Venus, and back to earth, with enough left over to go to the moon and back 50 times.

With digital libraries and online databases offering trillions of pages of information online, what's left to teach? And how does learning occur in a world when all the information and education a worker needs is just a mouse click away? Some have suggested that the basic nature of learning has changed (or will):

> The verb to *know* used to mean having information stored in one's memory. It now means the process of having access to information and knowing how to use it.
>
> —Herbert Simon, Nobel Laureate

Education is now more about teaching high-level skills such as research, judgment, and synthesis. Memorization and recall are becoming less important. An essential part of instructional design is locating reliable, complete, permanent online sources for the information component of a course. Database programming skills are becoming necessary for even modest e-learning projects. Online librarians and search agents are serving as learning coaches and mentors.

All media digital

Today almost all data and all media are created directly in digital form or can easily be converted to digital form. The economic consequences are vast. Bits are bits. The dream of the Universal Turing Machine that can manipulate any kind of data, image, or signal has been realized. With digital media, there is no longer a need to separate circuitry for audio, video, radio, telephony, photography, and other media. Programmable signal processors let you mix and match media with abandon. The result is a convergence of broadcast TV, cable TV, radio, and Internet. This convergence means you need fewer separate devices. You now expect a single device that can conduct a phone call, record dictation, play music and movies, calculate a tip, …or teach you how to do any of these things.

The emergence of the HDTV video standard means that television becomes a potential medium for e-learning—unlike the clunky WebTV that played on earlier generation television.

The creation of media has become almost easy. More people have digital voice recorders, voice-recognition software, digital cameras, and digital video cameras. A cornucopia of raw media sprawls before us. As a result, capture of media is less of a problem, but the editing of media by amateurs is a greater problem.

 Remember the ransom-note typography common when Macintosh computers first gave writers access to 27 fonts? Everybody had to use every font in every document!

 What was the first commercially successful use of photography, videocassette recorders, and the Internet? Yep, pornography. I'm sure there's an implication for e-learning there somewhere.

In picking e-learning tools and technologies, you should invest in technologies subsidized by entertainment and other uses. Writeable CDs (CD-R) now retail for 7 cents in bulk—not because of their use for e-learning but because of their use copying music.

Rich media

Computers and networks now have the speed and storage capacity to handle media beyond static text and graphics. Several forms of rich media offer the potential to make learning more effective.

Audio

Advances in network speed and voice-over IP (VoIP) are making audio more reliable and pleasant. More computers now come with sound input and output capabilities, and microphone-earphone headsets are now commonplace.

Sound can take a larger role in e-learning. People do not have to read long passages of text. They can carry on conversations naturally, rather than having to type in text.

The ready availability of sound can help those with limited vision, reading difficulties, tired eyes, or a migraine headache. In addition, sound capability makes learning available to those whose eyes are needed for other tasks like driving or operating a piece of equipment that provides instruction.

Higher-quality audio lets you use the tone and timbre of voice to convey subtle emotion. You can better inspire, warn, and motivate others. Surround sound can also provide ambiance and directionality for immersive simulations.

Video

Increasing network speed will enable wider use of video for presentations and collaboration. Video windows can be large enough to actually demonstrate complex tasks involving three- Yeah, more ego-fueled talking heads. Can hardly wait. dimensional objects and fluid movements. Video conferencing will become more common for collaboration.

Voice recognition

Voice recognition converts spoken words to text. It can be used to dictate an e-mail message and to command the computer to send the message. It enables those who cannot type quickly and accurately to see their words appear as text on the computer screen. Voice recognition will prove a boon to those whose disabilities make it hard to type or manipulate the mouse.

For e-learning, voice recognition can enable hands-off learning. Learners who cannot type quickly will not be penalized on tests and other activities. It will also assist those who learn verbally.

24

Trends in technology and learning

Force feedback

Force or *haptic* feedback lets the user feel forces through a device attached to the computer. For example, in Microsoft Flight Simulator, a pilot can feel tar strips in the runway and the chatter of spoilers through the control yoke or stick.

You can probably imagine applications for force feedback to teach the delicate manual skills needed by surgeons, dentists, and bomb-disposal technicians. Force feedback can also be used in Can haptic feedback be used for corporal punishment? conceptual realms, for example, to let learners experience the strength of forces within a simulated atom or in the airflow around a Formula 1 race car.

Telepresence

Telepresence is the ability to project human dexterity and perception. Two-way video links and remote-controlled robots now enable human beings to perform intricate tasks in places they have never been. Surgeons operate on a patient across an ocean. Controllers steer a robot on a remote planet. Ground-based "pilots" guide a spy plane through enemy radar.

Telepresence has implications for the availability of specialists and the performance of hazardous work—like teaching. Telepresence could provide direct training in psychomotor skills and lead to new forms of apprenticeship and mentoring.

Immersive simulations

Simulators that surround the subject with all the sights, sounds, and sensations of a real environment have become so sophisticated that participants in such simulations have to struggle to point out differences from the real environment. Aircraft simulators allow pilots to obtain decades of experience handling emergencies, all through simulations.

The technologies for such simulations have heretofore been too expensive for widespread use, but advances in virtual-reality displays and a better understanding of the characteristics of authentic simulations now make highly involving simulations practical for wider use. Computers can display dynamic virtual-reality worlds. Faster networks enable distributed simulations à la network gaming.

Immersive simulations will have profound applications in emergency training for medical doctors, nurses, pilots, police, and soldiers, where being able to function in a complex, dynamic, chaotic environment is the lesson being taught.

Such simulations will be valuable in teaching sales, speaking, leadership, and other interpersonal skills. Imagine social simulations like the game "The Sims" (thesims.com) but with learners participating in real time.

Data caves that surround the learner with responsive displays on walls and ceiling will make immersion nearly total. Can smell and taste be far behind?

Embedded systems

Computers are finding their ways into airplanes, telephones, vending machines, automobiles, refrigerators, TVs, stereo systems, and even your clothing. The proliferation of embedded computer systems means that you are never far from a computer. Such embedded systems offer opportunities to deliver e-learning and require e-learning to keep them working.

As e-learning platforms, embedded computers will be idiosyncratic at best. E-learning must fit to their display capabilities and environments. Instead of listening to language-learning audiocassettes as you drive home from work, you may learn using the audio and voice recognition capabilities of your car's onboard computer.

Wearable computers are computer systems embedded in your clothes (www.media.mit.edu/wearables). By wearing your computers, you ensure they are with you always. Such computers can deliver training in the workplace to those whose hands are otherwise occupied.

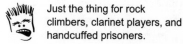 Just the thing for rock climbers, clarinet players, and handcuffed prisoners.

Embedded computers can provide embedded learning. A kitchen range could show you how to prepare dishes, warn of hazards of uncooked meats, and ask the refrigerator for suggested dinner dishes. Systems with embedded computers will be too complex for a simple instruction pamphlet to suffice. Devices with embedded computers will need to teach users how to set up, program, diagnose, and repair these devices.

LEARNING TRENDS

Learning trends are movements motivated by the desire for better learning but sparked, extended, sustained, aided, and abetted by technological advances. Some of these trends go back hundreds of years and others are more recent than e-learning. Let's look at some of these learning trends to see how technological advances are changing the ways people learn.

Lifelong learning

No doubt, pre-adult learning will still be the most intense, dedicated period of learning in our lives, but lifelong adult learning will be equally important for a fulfilling life.

As adult learning theorists and practitioners, such as Malcolm Knowles (nlu.nl.edu/ace/Resources/Knowles.html), have frequently pointed out, adults learn differently from children. Adults have their own reasons for learning. They already have busy lives and rich networks of social interaction. They already know a great deal. E-learning would seem ideal for lifelong learning.

But, to work for lifelong learning, e-learning must be designed for that purpose. It must work for all ages, not just 20-year-old traditional university students. It must work for those with less-than-perfect eyesight, hearing, and motor control. Developers must consider accessibility standards (chapter 22). E-learning must also work for those with various levels of technical exposure and interest.

The use of e-learning raises some important social and economic issues for us to ponder.

- **Who provides lifelong learning**? Universities, e-learning companies, professional associations, corporations?

- **Who pays for continuing education of adult professional and skilled workers**? Do individuals pay or do their employers pay? Will your alma mater give a discount? Can you buy re-education insurance?

- **How will the role of the university change**? As lifelong learning grows in importance, will the undergraduate university's role become more one of social integration and preparation for lifelong learning?

Lifelong learning will entail more changes than just when learning occurs and it will require more than technology. Lifelong learning requires redefining education as an inalienable part of life.

Global learning

Next time you type a Web address beginning www, think about what those first two w's mean (world-wide): Internet and Web technologies ignore time zones, border fences, and customs agents. As a result, e-learning markets and jurisdictions are global. Even local institutions are global when they go online.

Subjects that are uneconomical to teach on a local scale become practical or even profitable when offered to a planet full of potential learners. More than 1.5 billion people speak English either as a first or second language. Translate to a few more languages and you can reach another billion or so.

If the market for e-learning is global, so too is the competition. Only truly world-class e-learning will be competitive. For global learning, *world-class* does not mean combining French cinematic techniques with Hollywood-style special effects. It does mean creating highly effective content. It also means using simple language and media that can be understood by second-language learners and can be localized readily.

Global learning requires that you take a global perspective to all e-learning efforts. You must give more thought to localization when purchasing tools or creating content. You must create learning experiences that work across 24 time zones and are understandable by all cultures.

For learners, the globalization of learning makes learning more, well, worldly. Learners from the smallest hamlet can routinely interact with people of different cultures and backgrounds.

Mobile learners

Mobile data links, ubiquitous networks, and dense storage media are making it possible to learn anywhere: in the home office, at field offices, in the field, in shopping mall, or in transit.

Mobility offers more opportunities for learning. Adults can squeeze learning into hectic work schedules and family duties. Motivated learners can take a quick lesson while waiting for a child's soccer practice to end or while standing in line at the grocery store. Mobile learning lets students fit in a little learning between parties and pizza runs.

Mobility benefits teachers too. Working professionals can more easily teach online. We, Kit and Bill, have taught courses online when in Stockholm on business or in Hawaii attending a conference. Many retired professionals teach from their vacation homes, supplementing their income while sharing lifelong expertise that would otherwise be lost.

Mobile learning will impose its own requirements on designers and producers. Mobile learning must compete with other uses of the learner's time and must instruct effectively in noisy, distracting environments. And, learning content must fit the small screens and adapt to wireless connection speeds.

Modules of learning designed for mobile learners must be short, focused, and highly engaging. They must make points quickly and provide closure. A new design criterion, interruptability, will enter the designer's lexicon.

Independent learners

Most learning has always been independent but not most formal education. Now e-learning is emancipating learners who want formal education—on their own terms.

Although no one disputes the contribution of teachers and fellow learners, formal learning has been possible by learners working independently since Sir Isaac Pittman began teaching shorthand by postal correspondence in 1840. Independent learners have long been ignored by classroom I prefer the term *non-institutional learner* because what we are really talking about are people who prefer to learn without the loving embrace of a school or corporate training department.

instructors and professors who prefer to believe that they are necessary for learning. Independent learners have been spurned by institutions that want to apply cost-effective batch-manufacturing techniques to education.

Learning independence may be in the nature of a person or it may result from special needs, such as achieving certification by a certain date while not being able to take time off from travel and other job duties to learn with cohorts. Though truly independent learners will probably never be a majority, they are a crucial segment of learners. And independent learners, because they learn for their own reasons, are more likely to apply what they learn.

E-learning for independent learners must provide tools and techniques that let learners learn what they want to learn, when they want to learn, and in the way they want to learn. Independent learning requires:

▶ **Simple, reliable tools**. Independent learners need to be able to take e-learning on their own, without the support of an IT department.

▶ **Tools for individuals and small groups**. Independent learners must be able to spontaneously create and engage in learning events.

▶ **Independent certification of learning**. Independent learners crave valid assessments that are independent of how learning was accomplished. Educational institutions and professional organizations can assist independent learners by helping them document their learning and obtain credentials attesting to their knowledge and skills.

Independent learning presages the era of consumer control of e-learning. Until now, most of the decisions about the form and content of e-learning were made by those who knew best, that is, the producers of e-learning. That was appropriate. Only the producers knew what the technology could do.

Independent learners will revolutionize e-learning. They will provide creators of tools and learning content with complete, detailed specifications of what they want. They will report a million bugs and make a billion informed suggestions. Economics will be guided by what people want and are willing to pay for rather than what someone convinced a venture capitalist would sell.

All subjects available online

Richer media, immersive simulations, and more natural collaboration mechanisms make it possible to use e-learning for almost all subjects.

Originally e-learning was used almost exclusively for information technology training of IT personnel. The subject matter was specific, and learners had the technical skills to handle the crude technology. Since then, e-learning has evolved to teach softer skills, such as leadership, interpersonal communication, and anger management to non-technical learners. Even psychomotor skills may soon yield to e-learning's advances.

As more subjects can be learned online, you can expect to see changes in strategies employed by corporate training departments and school administrators. More and more of the blend of online and classroom learning will be online. Gradually, online will become the default place to look and will become the mental model for learning. No longer will potential learners have to think, "Is it available online?" They will just search for it.

And, you can expect to see e-learning more widely used in areas that have traditionally resisted technology-based learning: home schooling, training for manual trades, and leisure learning.

Relieved of the burden of tasks better performed by online learning, the classroom will be free to evolve in ways that take advantage of its intimacy and immediacy. Classroom learning may become a perquisite and a luxury. Online will be the baseline. The classroom may soon seem exotic.

Object economy

Many predict that we are heading toward a learning-object economy in which people design, build, market, buy, combine, and deploy reusable modules of e-learning content. It is hard to argue with the economy of building most of your course from content you can license for a low fee.

Realizing this vision will require advances in technology and business practices. Some of these requirements are:

▶ **Standards for interoperability** (chapter 22). These will include standard ways of packaging modules, labeling them, and communicating among them.

▶ **Further standards** for classes of interchangeable objects, say, within a single subject area or curriculum.

▶ **LCMSs and other tools** for creating complete, coherent, self-contained learning objects and assembling them to form lessons and courses.

▶ **Independent certification** of the effectiveness of learning objects, à la Merlot's peer review process merlot.org/home/PeerReview.po).

▶ **Economic scheme** to compensate contributors, for example, royalty payments to reward the creation of high-quality reusable modules and a sophisticated distributed e-commerce network to route payments to the right organizations and individuals

▶ **Market mechanism**, à la eBay (ebay.com), whereby buyers and sellers can swap objects for money.

This object economy will define new job positions such as the *object architect* who designs effective reusable learning components, the *object builder* who uses multimedia tools to create objects to meet specifications, the *object wrangler* who herds together related objects to form a course, and the *personal learning object shopper* who assembles learning objects to create individual programs of learning.

Knowledge management

Despite grandiose pretensions, knowledge management is nothing more than simple attempts to do for groups of people what education does for individuals. At William Horton Consulting, we define knowledge management as: "Ways groups of people make themselves collectively smarter."

Let's dissect that definition for a moment:

Ways	Notice we did not say "technologies" or "electronic means." Knowledge management will use many of the same tools and technologies as e-learning but at the level at which knowledge management operates, you should not expect to do everything electronically.
groups of people	Groups of people could be the individuals in a department, all the employees of a corporation, the faculty of a university, the entire supply-chain for a product line, the citizens of a country, or the population of Planet Earth. This definition is scalable, so handling entire galaxies should not prove a problem.
make themselves	Knowledge management is not something imposed from outside the group. It is not injected by hit-and-run consultants who leave little more than cute slogans on pencils and coffee mugs. It involves changes in internal decision-making skills and processes as well as changes of attitudes and underlying assumptions.
collectively	Education and training help individuals increase their skills, creativity, and knowledge. Knowledge management is more concerned with the same things but at the level of the group as a whole. The skills of a group represent its capabilities. Creativity, for instance, might be measured by a research lab's rate of new patents. The knowledge of the group would include not just what is in the heads of individuals, but what is in corporate libraries and databases.
smarter	Smarter people make better decisions. Smarter groups do, too. Having skills, creativity, and knowledge is not enough if the group does not apply those to making wise decisions. In knowledge management, application is the payoff.

Many of the same technologies and processes of e-learning can contribute directly to knowledge management. In fact, the availability of e-learning raises organizational IQ at least 20 points.

Tools and skills for creating e-learning can be used to create a wide range of knowledge products to further knowledge management. Informational Web sites, online databases, and online help files make knowledge available to whole groups. Tools for capturing presentations by instructors and subject matter experts add to what the organization knows.

24

Trends in technology and learning

Collaboration tools used in e-learning can be used to stimulate the organizational nervous system. Decision-making can draw on more viewpoints and vigorous discussion. Archived chat sessions and online discussions can be data-mined for insights and best practices. Better still, familiarity with online collaboration mechanisms can build a culture of sharing that includes everyone in the group—even those friendly foreigners in that tiny office eight time zones away.

NOT THE END

This is not the end. While you were reading this chapter, technologies advanced. New products were introduced, companies merged, and somebody filed a patent for the next great thing. Whatever your choices of technology and tools, they can only be temporary choices. Continue to monitor developments and be prepared to adopt better tools and technologies as they are ready for you.

We are only a few seconds past midnight at the first day of the e-learning era. And— this is only the first edition of this book.

Good
luck!   Bye!   Do great
                  things!

Appendix A

Bits, bytes, Ks, and other measures of digital data

Throughout e-learning technology you will encounter expressions of amounts of data, speeds, and frequencies, all delivered in a mixture of Latin, Greek, and technospeak. Misunderstanding these units can cause more than embarrassment, as these terms show up in specifications and contracts. Writing giga when you mean mega, or bit when you mean byte, can have serious consequences. Let's consider what all these terms are about and how to use them accurately.

BITS AND BYTES

Bits are the beginning, the root, the atom. A bit is the smallest unit of digital data. The word bit is a contraction of "binary digit." The word binary refers to the fact that a bit can have only two possible values: 1 or 0.

A bit is quite simple. Answers are yes or no, colors black or white, and uncertainty limited to heads or tails. There are no colors or shades of gray in bitdom. The whole of mathematics involves counting up to one.

Now a bit wouldn't be useful if was the only possible unit of data.

Next up the food chain is the byte. A byte is eight bits. But here's where the math gets interesting, because a byte is not just eight times more powerful than a bit. A byte can represent up to 256 different things—colors, numbers, letters of the alphabet, and so on.

KILO, MEGA, AND GIGA

Individual bits and bytes are interesting, but in e-learning, we have to think big. So we use some prefixes to refer to large numbers of bits and bytes. For example, we might refer to a computer file as being so many kilobytes in size. How big is a kilobyte? Well a kilometer is 1000 meters and a kilogram is 1000 grams, so a kilobyte must be 1000 bytes. Well, almost. Actually a kilobyte is 1024 bytes. The extra 24 are a gift of binary math and hasn't really mattered much since the era when a computer with 16 kilobytes of memory was the biggest and best you could get.

OK, a kilobyte is a bit over 1,000 bytes. But how big is that. Well a kilobyte could hold an e-mail message about 180 words long.

Once you understand kilo, mega and giga are easy. Mega means million and giga billion. So a megabyte is a 1,000 kilobytes or a million bytes. A gigabyte is 1,000 megabytes or 1 million kilobytes or 1 billion bytes.

These prefixes can apply to bits as well as bytes. Most quantities of data are stated in bytes. You might see an advertisement for a 156- megabyte memory module or a 100-gigabyte disk drive.

To recap:

▶ 1 gigabyte = 1 billion bytes

▶ 1 megabyte = 1 million bytes

▶ 1 kilobyte = 1 thousand bytes

KS, MBS, GBS, AND OTHER ABBREVIATIONS

Why waste 8 bytes writing megabyte, when you could get by with a 2-bit abbreviation like MB? By and large, the abbreviations of these units are simple and logical. We use K for kilo, M for mega, and G for giga. The difference between bits and bytes is indicated by B for bytes and b for bits. Bytes are bigger than bits so the capital letter makes sense. So here's what we have:

10 KB = 10 kilobytes	10 Kb = 10 kilobits
10 MB = 10 megabytes	10 Mb = 10 megabits
10 GB = 10 gigabytes	10 Gb = 10 gigabits

Now, while these abbreviations are technically correct, there are some idiomatic variations in common practice. The abbreviation for kilobyte is most commonly written as just K. In some parts of world, the natives have the peculiar habit of using a small k for the prefix kilo. So:

$$1 \text{ GB} = 1000 \text{ MB} = 1 \text{ million K} = 1 \text{ billion bytes}$$

So how big are these units? Here are some typical sizes of data you may be familiar with:

CD-ROM	650 MB
DVD movie	4.2 GB
MP3 pop song	4 MB
Text of a 300-page novel	900 K

SPEED READING WITH KBPS, MBPS, AND GBPS

Communication speeds are usually stated as so many bits (not bytes) per second. A common modem speed is 56.6 kilobits per second. This is abbreviated 56.6 Kbps. The K stands for kilo, b for bits, and ps for per second. So:

▶ 10 Kbps = 10 kilobits per second

▶ 10 Mbps = 10 megabits per second

▶ 10 Gbps = 10 gigabits per second

How fast are these units? Let's say you want to download a 4 MB pop song in MP3 format. Here's how long it would take at some representative communication speeds:

Speed	Time
56.6 Kbps	9 minutes
1 Mbps	32 seconds
1 Gbps	0.03 seconds

HERTZ AND GOING AROUND IN CYCLES

Frequencies are commonly expressed in the number of cycles that occur per second. Cycles per second would seem a logical term for such things, but instead we use hertz to honor Heinrich Rudolf Hertz, the 19th Century German physicist. If the connection to a physicist seems vague, consider that radio frequencies were being stated in megahertz and gigahertz long before we began using these units to describe the speed of computer processors.

The unit hertz is abbreviated as Hz and frequently merges with our trio of prefixes kilo, mega, and giga.

100 MHz = 100 megahertz = 100 million cycles per second

10 GHz = 10 gigahertz = 10 billion cycles per second

A measure of frequency might seem an odd unit for measuring the speed of a computer processor until you remember that processors carry out instructions in cycles, kind of like a blacksmith's bellows or the piston engine in an automobile.

Appendix B File formats for e-learning

Throughout *E-learning Tools and Technologies*, we have referred to many different file formats. And in several places we promised you a list of those formats. Well, here it is.

It is not a comprehensive, all-inclusive catalog of all possible file formats. Instead, it is a listing of those formats you are most likely to encounter as you design and develop your e-learning project.

Name	Extensions	Description	For more information
Active Server Pages	.asp	Pages containing scripts usually written in VBScript or JavaScript that are processed by a Web server. Used to provide interactive Web content and to build database-driven Web applications. MIME type: text/asp.	microsoft.com
Adobe Illustrator	.ai	Native file format for vector graphics created in the Adobe illustrator drawing program. MIME type: application/postscript.	www.adobe.com
Advanced Streaming Format	.asf	Microsoft video format optimized for Web delivery using a streaming media server. MIME type: video/x-ms-asf.	microsoft.com
Audio	.au, .snd	Early sound format popular on Sun, Dec, NEXT, and other UNIX systems. Not optimized for Web delivery. MIME type: audio/basic.	sun.com

Name	Extensions	Description	For more information
Audio Interchange File Format	.aif, .aiff	Standard audio file format for Macintosh operating systems. Not optimized for Web delivery. MIME types: audio/aiff, audio/x-aiff.	apple.com
Audio Video Interleave	.avi	Standard video format for Windows operating systems. Not optimized for Web delivery. MIME types: video/avi, video/msvideo, video/x-msvideo.	microsoft.com
Authorware Macintosh	.a4m, .a3m	Native file format for multimedia created in Macromedia Authorware for Macintosh operating systems.	macromedia.com
Authorware Shockwave	.aam	Authorware multimedia and e-learning files optimized for Web delivery using Macromedia's Shockwave technology. MIME type: application/x-authorware-map.	macromedia.com
Authorware Windows file	.a5w, .a4w, .a3w	Native file format for multimedia created in Macromedia Authorware for Windows operating systems.	macromedia.com
AutoCAD Drawing	.dwg	Native file format for 2-D and 3-D design drawings created in AutoCAD. MIME types: image/x-dwg, image/vnd.dwg.	www.autodesk.com
Bitmap	.bmp	Common format for bitmap graphics on Windows operating systems. MIME types: image/bmp, image/x-windows-bmp.	microsoft.com
Cabinet	.cab	Common format for compressing groups of files. Used primarily for distribution of software on Windows operating systems.	microsoft.com
Canvas	.cnv	Native format for vector and bitmap graphics, page layouts, animations, and presentations created in the Deneba Canvas drawing program.	deneba.com
Cascading Style Sheet	.css	File used to specify styles that can be applied to related HTML and XML files. MIME type: text/css.	w3c.org

Name	Extensions	Description	For more information
Compiled Help	.chm	Windows Help files in HTML format that have been compiled into a single file containing the separate HTML pages and graphics.	microsoft.com
Corel Metafile	.cmf	Native file format for vector graphics, bitmap graphics, page layouts, and animations created in CorelDraw.	www.corel.com
Corel Presentation Exchange	.cmx	Proprietary format for vector graphics from Corel. Used for exchanging graphics among other programs. Some clip-art libraries are in CMX format.	www.corel.com
Director	.dir	Native file format for multimedia created with the Macromedia Director program.	macromedia.com
Director Shockwave	.dcr	Director multimedia files optimized for Web delivery using Macromedia's Shockwave technology. MIME type: application/x-director.	macromedia.com
Encapsulated Postscript File	.eps	Common file format for vector graphics based on the Adobe PostScript printing language. MIME type: application/postscript.	www.adobe.com
Enhanced Windows Metafile	.emf	Common format for files that mix vector and bitmap graphics. Used mainly on Windows operating systems.	microsoft.com
Excel Spreadsheet	.xls	Native file format for spreadsheet data created in the Microsoft Excel program. MIME types: application/excel, application/x-excel, application/vnd.ms-excel, application/x-ms-excel.	microsoft.com
eXtensible Markup Language	.xml	Format for a family of markup languages. MIME type: text/xml.	w3c.org
Extensible Stylesheet Language	.xsl	Language used to specify the formatting of XML documents. Main use is to create transforms (XSLT) to select, organize, and format XML data. MIME type: text/xsl.	w3c.org
Flash	.fla	Native format for multimedia created in the Macromedia Flash program.	macromedia.com

Name	Extensions	Description	For more information
Flash Shockwave	.swf	Flash multimedia files optimized for Web delivery using Macromedia's Shockwave technology. Does not require a media server for Web delivery. MIME type: application/x-shockwave-flash.	macromedia.com
FreeHand	.fh5, .fh6, .fh7, .fh8, .fh9, .fh10	Native file format for vector graphics created in the Macromedia FreeHand drawing program.	macromedia.com
Graphics Image Format	.gif	Common format for bitmap images used in Web pages. Can contain up to 256 colors, be animated, and have transparent areas. MIME type: image/gif.	www.compuserve.com
Hypertext Markup Language	.htm, .html	Common file format for Web pages. Uses markup tags to designate structure and formatting as well as links to other files and embedded media. MIME type: text/html.	w3c.org
Java Archive	.jar	Compressed file format for Java applications and applets.	sun.com
Java Class	.class	Program or module written in the Java programming language and compiled into byte-code. MIME types: application/java, application/java-byte-code, application/java-class.	sun.com
JavaScript	.js	Scripts written in the JavaScript language that can be referenced by other files such as HTML and ASP files. MIME type: application./x-javascript.	netscape.com
JavaServer Pages	.jsp	Pages containing scripts written in a Java-like syntax that are processed by components on a Web server. Used to provide interactive Web content and to build database-driven Web applications like an LMS. MIME type: text/jsp.	sun.com
Joint Photographic Experts Group	.jpg, .jpeg	Common format for bitmap images, typically photographs. Images may be highly compressed with some loss of quality. Used in Web pages. MIME type: image/jpeg.	www.jpeg.org

Name	Extensions	Description	For more information
Microsoft Word Document	.doc	Native file format for documents created in Microsoft Word. MIME type: application/msword.	microsoft.com
Motion Picture Experts Group	.mpg, .mpeg	Widely-used video format. Optimized for Web delivery using a media server. Video may be highly compressed while maintaining good quality. MIME type: video/mpeg.	mpeg.telecomitalialab.com
MP3	.mp3	Highly compressed format for audio. Popular for music files exchanged over the Web. Requires a media server for Web delivery. MIME types: audio/mpeg3, audio/x-mpeg3, video/mpeg, video/x-mpeg.	mpeg.telecomitalialab.com
Musical Instrument Digital Interface	.mid, .midi	Common music format that stores definitions of notes rather than actual sound waves. MIME types: audio/midi, audio/x-mid, audio/x-midi.	www.midi.org
Paint Shop Pro	.pcx	Native file format for vector and bitmap graphics created in the Paint Shop Pro drawing program. MIME type: image/x-pcx.	www.jasc.com
Perl	.pl	Script files written in the Perl programming language. Popular on Linux and other UNIX systems. MIME type: text/s-script.perl.	www.perl.org
Photoshop	.psd	Native file format for bitmap graphics created in the Adobe Photoshop image-editing program.	www.adobe.com
PHP Hypertext Preprocessor	.php	PHP is a general-purpose scripting language that is used for Web development and can be embedded into HTML pages. It commonly runs on Web servers that have PHP services installed, such as Apache.	www.php.net
PICT	.pct, .pict	Standard format for bitmap and vector graphics on Macintosh operating systems. MIME types: image/pict, image/x-pict.	apple.com

Name	Extensions	Description	For more information
Portable Document Format	.pdf	Common format used for making precisely formatted versions of any document that can be printed. Can contain menus, links, and multimedia. Can be optimized for Web delivery. MIME type: application/pdf.	www.adobe.com
Portable Network Graphic	.png	Bitmap graphics format optimized for Web delivery. Designed to replace the proprietary GIF format. Supports 16-bit grayscale, 48-bit color, as well as an alpha channel for transparency. MIME type: image/png.	www.libpng.org/pub/png
PostScript print file	.ps	File containing graphics and text ready for printing on a PostScript printer. MIME type: application/postscript.	www.adobe.com
PowerPoint Presentation	.ppt, .pps	Native file format for Microsoft PowerPoint slide presentations containing text, graphics, animations, and other media. Can be optimized for Web delivery. MIME types: application/powerpoint, application/x-mspowerpoint, application/vnd.ms-powerpoint.	microsoft.com
QuickTime	.mov, .qt	General-purpose format for video, sound, music, and text captions. Can be optimized for the Web and delivered using a media server. MIME type: video/quicktime.	apple.com
RealAudio	.ra	Common audio format encoded using Real Network's compression algorithm. Optimized for Web delivery using a media server. MIME type: audio/x-pn-realaudio.	realnetworks.com
RealVideo	.rm	Common video format encoded using Real Network's compression algorithm. Optimized for Web delivery using a media server. MIME type: application/x-pn-realmedia.	realnetworks.com

Name	Extensions	Description	For more information
Rich Text Format	.rtf	File containing formatted text and graphics. Used for exchanging documents between word-processors. MIME type: application/rtf.	microsoft.com
Scalable Vector Graphics	.svg	XML-based format for vector graphics and text.	w3c.org
Standard Generalized Markup Language	.sgml, .sgm	International standard for defining electronic documents independent of operating system or word-processor (ISO Standard 8879:1986). MIME types: text/sgml, text/x-sgml.	www.iso.org
Synchronized Multimedia Integration Language	.smi, .smil	XML-based format for multimedia presentations. Can be viewed in some browsers and media players. MIME type: application/smil.	w3c.org
Tag Image File Format	.tif, .tiff	Common format for bitmap graphics. Widely used in desktop publishing. MIME types: image/tiff, image/x-tiff.	www.adobe.com
ToolBook	.tbk	Native format for multimedia or e-learning created using Click2learn's ToolBook program. MIME type: application/toolbook.	www.click2learn.com
Vector Markup Language	.vml	Vector format used in Microsoft Office applications and displayable in Internet Explorer.	microsoft.com
Virtual Reality Modeling Language	.vrm, .vrml, .wrl	XML-based format for three-dimensional models that users can manipulate and navigate when viewed with a special player. MIME types: application/x-vrml, model/vrml.	www.vrml.org
WAV	.wav	Standard audio format for Windows operating systems. Not optimized for Web delivery. MIME type: sound/wav.	microsoft.com
Windows Help	.hlp	Standard file format for Help files on Windows operating systems. MIME types: application/hlp, application/x-helpfile, application/x-winhelp.	microsoft.com

B

File formats for e-learning

Name	Extensions	Description	For more information
Windows Media Audio	.wma	Highly compressed audio format optimized for Web delivery using a media server.	microsoft.com
Windows Media Video	.wmv	Highly compressed video format optimized for Web delivery using a media server.	microsoft.com
Windows Metafile	.wmf	Common format for vector and bitmap graphics on Windows operating systems.	microsoft.com
XHTML	.htm, .html	A more stringent version of HyperText Modeling Language (HTML) that conforms to the rules of XML. MIME type: text/html.	w3c.org
ZIP compressed	.zip	Common format for any type of content compressed to save storage space or to reduce download time. MIME types: application/zip, application/x-zip, application/x-zip-compressed.	www.pkware.com

Index

Index

Index

Index

ABOUT THE AUTHORS

William and Katherine Horton together make up William Horton Consulting, Inc., where they design advanced e-learning and knowledge management solutions. They advise and train clients on the design, management, and technology for e-learning. On any given day you might find them speaking at a conference, prototyping a learning game, building a spreadsheet to calculate a project's ROI, or writing a book like this. Their clientele ranges from global telecoms to individual trainers.

William Horton (Bill for short) is a leading e-learning consultant. He has written numerous books including *Leading E-Learning, Evaluating E-Learning, Using E-Learning*, and *Designing Web-Based Training*. He created his first network-based course in 1971, while still an undergraduate at MIT where he earned an engineering degree. William Horton also has a degree in computer science, is a registered professional engineer, and is a fellow of the Society for Technical Communication.

Katherine Horton (Kit for short) runs the day to day business of William Horton Consulting including keeping a lot of computers working. Kit designs and builds e-learning prototypes from the initial concept through to the finished product. She also creates icons, screen layouts, publication designs, business illustrations, and technical graphics. And, she is the Web master for horton.com, designingWBT.com, and the site for this book: horton.com/tools.

William and Katherine live in downtown Boulder, Colorado, just five blocks east of the Rocky Mountains, in a hundred-year old house they are lovingly restoring. You may have caught glimpses of their kitchen and bathroom when they were featured in the April 1999 and September 2000 issues of *Better Homes and Gardens*. You can learn more about William and Katherine at horton.com.